THE CAMBRIDGE COMPANION TO PETRARCH

Petrarch (Francesco Petrarca, 1304–1374), best known for his influential collection of Italian lyric poetry dedicated to his beloved Laura, was also a remarkable classical scholar, a deeply religious thinker, and a philosopher of secular ethics. In this wide-ranging study, chapters by leading scholars view Petrarch's life through his works, from the epic *Africa* to the "Letter to Posterity," from the *Canzoniere* to the vernacular epic *Triumphi*. Petrarch is revealed as the heir to the converging influences of classical cultural and medieval Christianity, but also to his great vernacular precursor, Dante, and his friend, collaborator, and sly critic, Boccaccio. Particular attention is given to Petrach's profound influence on the Humanist movement and on the courtly cult of vernacular love poetry, while raising important questions as to the validity of the distinction between medieval and modern, and what is lost in attempting to classify this elusive figure.

ALBERT RUSSELL ASCOLI is Gladyce Arata Terrill Distinguished Professor at the University of California, Berkeley. His publications include *Ariosto's Bitter Harmony: Crisis and Evasion in the Italian Renaissance* (1987); *Making and Remaking Italy: The Cultivation of National Identity around the Risorgimento* (co-edited with Krystyna von Henneberg, 2001); *Dante and the Making of a Modern Author* (Cambridge, 2008); and *A Local Habitation and a Name: Imagining Histories in the Italian Renaissance* (2011). He is co-founder and volume editor of the electronic journal, *California Italian Studies*.

UNN FALKEID is Research Fellow at the Royal Swedish Academy of Letters, History and Antiquities, affiliated with the Department of Culture and Aesthetics, Stockholm University. She is the author of *Petrarca og det moderne selvet* (*Petrarch and the Modern Self*, 2007), the editor of *Dante: A Critical Reappraisal* (2008), and the co-editor of *Rethinking Gaspara Stampa in the Canon of Renaissance Poetry* (with Aileen A. Feng, 2015).

A complete list of books in the series is at the back of the book.

D1388517

THE CAMBRIDGE
COMPANION TO
PETRARCH

EDITED BY
ALBERT RUSSELL ASCOLI AND UNN FALKEID

CAMBRIDGE
UNIVERSITY PRESS

CAMBRIDGE
UNIVERSITY PRESS

University Printing House, Cambridge CB2 8BS, United Kingdom

Cambridge University Press is part of the University of Cambridge.

It furthers the University's mission by disseminating knowledge in the pursuit of education, learning and research at the highest international levels of excellence.

www.cambridge.org
Information on this title: www.cambridge.org/9780521185042

First published 2015

Printed in the United Kingdom by Clays, St Ives plc

A catalogue record for this publication is available from the British Library

Library of Congress Cataloguing in Publication data
The Cambridge companion to Petrarch / edited by Albert Russell Ascoli, Unn Falkeid.
pages cm. – (Cambridge companions to literature)
Includes bibliographical references.
ISBN 978-1-107-00614-0 (hardback)
1. Petrarca, Francesco, 1304–1374 – Criticism and interpretation.   I. Ascoli, Albert Russell, 1953– editor.   II. Falkeid, Unn, editor.
PQ4505.C15   2015
851'.1 – dc23   2015021715

ISBN 978-1-107-00614-0 Hardback
ISBN 978-0-521-18504-2 Paperback

For Emma, Therese, and Bernhard
and
for Mary and Sam

CONTENTS

Notes on contributors   *page* x
Acknowledgments   xiv
Chronology   xv
List of abbreviations   xix

Introduction   1
ALBERT RUSSELL ASCOLI AND UNN FALKEID

PART I   LIVES OF PETRARCH

1 Poetry in motion   13
THEODORE J. CACHEY, JR.

2 Petrarch and his friends   26
HANNAH CHAPELLE WOJCIEHOWSKI

PART II   PETRARCH'S WORKS: ITALIAN

3 *Rerum vulgarium fragmenta:* structure and narrative   39
PETER HAINSWORTH

4 Making the *Rerum vulgarium fragmenta*   51
LUCA MARCOZZI

5 Petrarch's singular love lyric   63
ULLRICH LANGER

6 The *Triumphi*   74
ZYGMUNT G. BARAŃSKI

CONTENTS

PART III PETRARCH'S WORKS: LATIN

7 The Latin hexameter works: *Epystole, Bucolicum carmen, Africa*   87
RONALD L. MARTINEZ

8 The defense of poetry in the *Secretum*   100
VICTORIA KAHN

9 *De vita solitaria* and *De otio religioso*: the perspective of the guest   111
UNN FALKEID

10 Epistolary Petrarch   120
ALBERT RUSSELL ASCOLI

PART IV PETRARCH'S INTERLOCUTORS

11 Petrarch and the ancients   141
GUR ZAK

12 Petrarch and the vernacular lyric past   154
OLIVIA HOLMES

13 Petrarch's adversaries: the *Invectives*   167
DAVID MARSH

PART V PETRARCH'S AFTERLIFE

14 Petrarch and the Humanists   179
TIMOTHY KIRCHER

15 Bembo and Italian Petrarchism   191
STEFANO JOSSA

16 Female Petrarchists   201
ANN ROSALIND JONES

17 Iberian, French, and English Petrarchisms   210
WILLIAM J. KENNEDY

CONTENTS

PART VI   CONCLUSION

18   Petrarch's confrontation with modernity   221
    GIUSEPPE MAZZOTTA

    Guide to further reading   239
    Index   252

CONTRIBUTORS

ALBERT RUSSELL ASCOLI is Terrill Distinguished Professor of Italian Studies at the University of California, Berkeley and current President of the Dante Society of America (2014–17). He is the author of *Ariosto's Bitter Harmony: Crisis and Evasion in the Italian Renaissance* (1987), *Dante and the Making of a Modern Author* (Cambridge, 2008), and *A Local Habitation and a Name* (2011), as well as of numerous essays on Petrarch and other medieval and early modern topics.

ZYGMUNT G. BARAŃSKI is Serena Professor of Italian Emeritus at the University of Cambridge and Notre Dame Chair of Dante & Italian Studies at the University of Notre Dame. He has published extensively on Dante, paying particular attention to the poet's ideas on literature and to his intellectual formation. Barański has also written on Petrarch, Boccaccio, Dante's reception, and modern Italian literature and culture. For many years he was senior editor of the interdisciplinary journal *The Italianist*: the position he now holds with *Le tre corone*.

THEODORE J. CACHEY, JR. is professor of Italian at the University of Notre Dame. He specializes in Italian medieval and Renaissance literature. He is the author and co-editor of several books, including *Petrarch's Guide to the Holy Land* and, with Zygmunt G. Barański, *Dante and Petrarch: Anti-Dantism, Metaphysics, Tradition*. His essays have appeared in such journals as *California Italian Studies*, *Intersezioni*, and *Modern Language Notes*.

UNN FALKEID is Research Fellow at the Royal Swedish Academy of Letters, History and Antiquities, affiliated with the Department of Culture and Aesthetics, Stockholm University. She has published extensively on Dante, Petrarch, and early modern literature. Among her recent publications is *Rethinking Gaspara Stampa in the Canon of Renaissance Poetry* (2015), co-edited with Aileen A. Feng. She is currently completing a monograph, *The Avignon Papacy Contested: Power and Politics in Fourteenth-Century Literature*, in which she explores how the city of Avignon became a context for textual and intellectual exchanges between different cultures of early modern Europe.

PETER HAINSWORTH is an Emeritus Fellow of Lady Margaret Hall. After lecture-
ships at Hull and Kent Universities, he taught at Oxford University from 1979 until
his retirement in 2003. As well as *Petrarch the Poet* (1986), he has written widely
on other Italian authors, including, most recently, with David Robey, a *Very Short
Introduction to Italian Literature* (2012) and a similar *Very Short Introduction
to Dante* (2015). Following on *The Essential Petrarch* (2012), his translations
of select stories from Boccaccio's *Decameron* will be published by Penguin in
2015.

OLIVIA HOLMES is Associate Professor of Medieval Studies and English at Binghamton University, and has previously taught Italian literature at Dartmouth College and Yale University. Her research is mostly devoted to medieval lyric and
the Italian Trecento. Her first book, *Assembling the Lyric Self: Authorship from
Troubadour Song to Italian Poetry Book*, won the American Association of Italian
Studies Book Award in 2001. Her second book, *Dante's Two Beloveds: Ethics
and Erotics in the "Divine Comedy,"* came out in 2008. She is working on a new
book project tentatively titled *Boccaccio and Exemplarity: Setting a Bad Example
in the "Decameron."*

ANN ROSALIND JONES is Esther Cloudman Dunn Professor of Comparative Literature Emerita, Smith College. Her work includes two books on women writers of
the Renaissance, *The Currency of Eros: Women's Love Lyric in Europe 1540–
1620* (1990) and a translation of *The Poems and Selected Letters of Veronica
Franco*, with Margaret F. Rosenthal (1998). Her most recent work has focused on
the meanings of dress in early modern Europe, including a translation with Margaret Rosenthal, *The Clothing of the Renaissance World (Europe, Asia, Africa,
America): Cesare Vecellio's Habiti Antichi et Moderni* (2008).

STEFANO JOSSA is Reader in Italian at Royal Holloway University of London.
Among his contributions on Petrarchism are: "Petrarchismo e petrarchismi. Forme,
ideologia, identità di un sistema" (with Simona Mammana), in Luigi Collarile and
Daniele Maira (eds), *Nel libro di Laura* (2004), 91–115, and two edited special
issues on *European Petrarchism* of the journal *Italique* (numbers 14, 2011 and
15, 2012). His research interests span from the Renaissance to the Italian national
identity as expressed through literature, in which field he has published *L'Italia
letteraria* (2006) and *Un paese senza eroi. L'Italia da Jacopo Ortis a Montalbano*
(2013).

VICTORIA KAHN is Hotchkis Professor of English and Professor of Comparative Literature at the University of California, Berkeley. She is the author of *Rhetoric, Pru-
dence and Skepticism in the Renaissance* (1985), *Machiavellian Rhetoric* (1994),
Wayward Contracts: The Crisis of Political Obligation in England, 1640–1674,
and *The Future of Illusion: Political Theology and Early Modern Texts* (2014).

WILLIAM J. KENNEDY is Avalon Foundation Professor in the Humanities in the Department of Comparative Literature at Cornell University. His research focuses on the history of European literature and literary criticism from antiquity to the early modern period, with particular interest in Italian, French, English, and German texts from Dante to Milton. His books include *Rhetorical Norms in Renaissance Literature* (1978), *Jacopo Sannazaro and the Uses of Pastoral* (1983), *Authorizing Petrarch* (1994), and *The Site of Petrarchism* (2003), as well as the forthcoming *Contextual Economies: Poetic Transactions from Petrarch to Shakespeare*.

TIMOTHY KIRCHER is Professor of History and Chair of Humanities at Guilford College. He researches Renaissance Humanism and is the author of numerous articles and two books: *The Poet's Wisdom: The Humanists, the Church, and the Formation of Philosophy in the Early Renaissance* (2006) and *Living Well in Renaissance Italy: The Virtues of Humanism and the Irony of Leon Battista Alberti* (2012). He also co-edited, with Luc Deitz and Jonathan Reid, *Neo-Latin and the Humanities: Essays in Honour of Charles E. Fantazzi* (2014). He currently serves as President of the American Boccaccio Association.

ULLRICH LANGER is Alfred Glauser Professor of French and Director of the Center for Early Modern Studies at the University of Wisconsin–Madison. His most recent publications include *Penser les formes du plaisir littéraire à la Renaissance* (2009) and *Lyric in the Renaissance: From Petrarch to Montaigne* (2015). He is currently interested in the concurrence between gesture, meaning, and empathy in the Orpheus–Eurydice myth and its poetic repercussions. Another project is the form of the "remonstrance" in early modern political and literary writing.

LUCA MARCOZZI is Associate Professor of Italian Literature at Roma Tre University. He studies mainly medieval and Renaissance literature, from Dante to Bembo, and its role in developing a cultural identity. His most recent books are *Petrarca platonico* (2011) and, as editor, *Nello specchio del mito* (2012), on classical mythology in Italian literature, and *Dante e il mondo animale* (2013). He has been Fulbright distinguished lecturer at the University of Notre Dame.

DAVID MARSH, PhD (1978) in Comparative Literature, Harvard, is Professor of Italian at Rutgers. He is the author of *The Quattrocento Dialogue* (1980), *Lucian and the Latins* (1998), *Studies on Alberti and Petrarch* (2012), and *Exile in Italian Writers* (2013); and the translator of Alberti's *Dinner Pieces* (1987), Vico's *New Science* (1999), Petrarch's *Invectives* (2003), and *Renaissance Fables* (2004).

RONALD L. MARTINEZ is Professor of Italian Studies at Brown University. In addition to some four dozen articles on topics from Guido Cavalcanti's lyrics to Ariosto's *Orlando furioso*, he has collaborated on several projects with Robert M. Durling, including a monograph on Dante's lyric poetry, *Time and the Crystal* (1990), and an edition, with translation, notes, and commentary, of the three cantiche of Dante's *Commedia* (1996, 2003, 2011). He is currently preparing a monograph on appropriations of medieval liturgy in Dante's works.

GIUSEPPE MAZZOTTA is Sterling Professor in the Humanities for Italian at Yale University, where he has also been serving as Chairman of the Department of Italian. He is the author of *The Worlds of Petrarch* (1993), and he intends to finish a second volume that gathers his scattered articles on Petrarch, which will be published with the title *A World of Words: The Empire of Culture*. He has recently published two unrelated volumes on Dante: *Confine quasi Orizzonte. Saggi su Dante* (2014) and *Reading Dante: Open Yale Courses* (2014). He is presently completing his Dante trilogy with the manuscript, *Dante at the Frontiers of Thought*.

HANNAH CHAPELLE WOJCIEHOWSKI is Professor of English at the University of Texas at Austin and an Affiliate of UT's Program in Comparative Literature. A cultural theorist specializing in the history of subjectivity, Wojciehowski has written on Petrarch's *Secretum* and the *Familiares*, and on his life during the post-plague years. Her recent and forthcoming publications include a study of globalization in early modernity entitled *Group Identity in the Renaissance World* (Cambridge, 2011), essays on literary and performance theory and embodied cognition, and a performance-oriented edition of Shakespeare's *Cymbeline* (2014).

GUR ZAK is a lecturer in Comparative Literature at the Hebrew University of Jerusalem. His research focuses on the inter-relations of literature and ethics in the later Middle Ages and the Renaissance. His book, *Petrarch's Humanism and the Care of the Self*, was published by Cambridge in 2010. He has also written several articles and book chapters on Petrarch, Boccaccio, Alberti, and the history of autobiography. He is currently working on his second monograph, entitled *Boccaccio and the Consolation of Literature*.

ACKNOWLEDGMENTS

When we first decided to collaborate on this volume five years ago, we had, despite past editorial experiences, no idea how long it would ultimately take. On the other hand, we expected – and our expectations were fulfilled, if often in unexpected ways – that this collaboration, in addition to filling a major scholarly lacuna, would give us each great satisfaction. Such satisfactions came abundantly, both in the dynamic of exchange that we were able to establish between ourselves (despite living on different continents!) and in our work with our distinguished authors and with Cambridge University Press, in particular Linda Bree and Anna Bond. We thank all of them for their excellent work and their (oft-tried) patience with us.

We both owe numerous debts to our home institutions and to our families for essential support at crucial moments. Unn Falkeid acknowledges the Royal Swedish Academy of Letters, History and Antiquities, which during the completion of this volume has generously funded her position as an Academy Research Fellow at Stockholm University. She also thanks the University of Oslo for her postdoctoral fellowship (2008–13) and Yale University, which hosted her during her stay as Fulbright Visiting Scholar in the academic year 2010–11. And she thanks her husband, Hans, for being who he is. Albert Ascoli thanks the University of California, Berkeley for sabbatical support and a Humanities Research Fellowship during academic year 2011, as well as the Center for Advanced Study at Ludwig Maximilians University in Munich for a month-long residential fellowship in spring 2011. And he thanks Barbara for everything.

Finally, we thank each other.

1304   Born in Arezzo, July 20, to Eletta Canigiani and Pietro di ser Parenzo (ser Petracco), a notary and White Guelf, who, like Dante Alighieri, was exiled from Florence in 1302.

1305   Moves to Incisa Valdarno with his mother.

1307   His brother, Gherardo, is born.

1311   The family gathers in Pisa with other exiles from Florence, among them probably Dante.

1312   His father gains employment at the papal court in Avignon and the family settles in Carpentras, fifteen miles from the city.

1312–16   Studies with the grammarian Convenevole da Prato, another White Guelf refugee.

1316–20   Studies law at University of Montepellier. His mother dies in 1318 or 1319, and soon after he writes a Latin elegy for her [*Epystole*, I.7].

1320–26   Studies civil law at the University of Bologna, together with his brother Gherardo and his friend Guido Sette, interrupted only by a short stay in Venice and two short returns to Avignon in 1321 and 1325. Befriends Giacomo Colonna and starts to be interested in vernacular poetry.

1326   His father dies. The brothers return to Avignon without finishing their studies.

1327   Meets Laura, April 6, in the church of St. Claire in Avignon and falls in love.

1328–29   Works on the philological restoration of Livy's *Decades*.

1330   Enters service as chaplain of Cardinal Giovanni Colonna, Gia-
        como's brother. Becomes friends with Lello Stefano de' Tosetti
        from Rome ("Laelius") and the Flemish musician Ludwig van
        Kempen ("Socrates").

1333   Travels to northern Europe. In Liège, he discovers orations
        by Cicero, among them the *Pro Archia*. On his return, he
        probably meets Dionigi da Borgo San Sepolcro, an Augus-
        tinian monk who gives him a copy of Augustine's *Confessions*.
        He buys a house in Vaucluse and begins his friendship with
        Philippe de Cabassoles, Bishop of Cavaillon.

1335   Appointed by Pope Benedict XII as canon in the cathedral of
        Lombez, where, however, he never goes to live.

1336   Undertakes the ascent of Mont Ventoux, as described in
        Fam. IV.1.

1336–37 His first trip to Rome, where he visits Giacomo Colonna.

1337–39 Back in Vaucluse, he starts to work on the *De viris illustribus*
        and the *Africa*, with hopes for future glory. His illegitimate
        son, Giovanni, is born.

1340   Invited to be crowned poet laureate by both the University of
        Paris and the Senate of Rome.

1341   Leaves Avignon for Naples, where, as a preparation for the
        coronation in Rome, he is examined by King Robert the Wise.
        Meets Barbato da Sulmona. Crowned in Rome, April 8, and
        gives his speech, the *Collatio laureationis*, or *Coronation Ora-
        tion*. Declared a Roman citizen. Visits Parma and the house in
        Selvapiana, his "Italian Helicon," offered to him by Azzo da
        Correggio, lord of the city.

1342   Returns to Vaucluse. The first version of *Rerum vulgarium
        fragmenta* (*RVF*), or *Canzoniere* as it will later come to be
        known, is collected.

1343   His daughter, Francesca, is born. Begins a friendship with
        Cola di Rienzo, who stays in Avignon for several months.
        His brother, Gherardo, becomes a Carthusian monk in Mon-
        trieux. Starts work on the *Rerum memorandarum libri*. In the
        fall, sent by Pope Clement VI on a diplomatic visit to Queen
        Joanna of Naples, where he experiences disillusion at the

difficult political situation following King Robert's death earlier the same year.

1343–45   Petrarch's second stay in Parma, cut short in February 1345, when he flees the city after it is attacked by troops of the Gonzaga and the Visconti, and returns to Avignon.

1346   Writes the first draft of *De vita solitaria* during Lent.

1347   Visits his brother in the monastery of Montrieux, and writes *De otio religioso*. Supports Cola di Rienzo's revolution and the establishment of a new Republic in Rome during Pentecost, but by the following fall is increasingly disappointed at Cola's failures.

1348   The Black Death spreads quickly in Europe. In Parma, Petrarch receives the news of the demise of both Giovanni Colonna and Laura (April 6). In this period, he probably composes *Psalmi penitentiales*, *Epystola metrica* I.14 ("Ad se ipsum"), and *Bucolicum carmen* 9–11.

1349   Obtains a canonry in Padua, which he probably holds until his death. Starts to collect the letters for the *Familiares*.

1350   Travels to Rome for the Papal Jubilee. During a stop in Florence, meets Giovanni Boccaccio, among others.

1351   Boccaccio visits him in Padua and offers him, in vain, a chaired professorship in Florence, along with the restitution of his family's property. Petrarch returns to Vaucluse for the last time (remaining there until 1353). Writes anti-papal letters for *Sine nomine*.

1352   Composes the first draft of *Invective contra medicum*, completed in 1355, and probably the first versions of the *Triumphi* (*Triumphus Cupidinis* and *Triumphus Fame*).

1353   Leaves Avignon for good and settles in Milan under the Visconti.

1354   Meets Emperor Charles IV in Mantua and expresses admiration for his learning. Starts composing *De remediis utriusque fortunae* (completed in 1360).

1355   Composes the *Invectiva contra quendam magni status hominem*.

1356   Sent as an ambassador by the Visconti to Emperor Charles IV in Prague. The hypothetical Correggio form of the *RVF* collected (1356–58).

1358   In Padua. Writes the *Itinerarium ad sepulchrum Domini*.

1359   In Milan. Supports the Visconti against Pavia. Receives a visit from Boccaccio in the spring. Composes the extant Chigi form of the *RVF* (1359–62/63).

1361   Moves to Venice because of the plague outbreak in Milan. His son, Giovanni, who has come to live with him, dies of the plague. His friend Socrates also dies. Starts to compose *Seniles*.

1363   Boccaccio visits him in Venice.

1364   Publishes the *Epystole*.

1366   Encourages Pope Urban V to transfer the papacy to Rome (*Sen.* VII.1). Concludes the *Bucolicum carmen*.

1367   In Padua. Writes *De sui ipsius et multorum ignorantia* (completed in 1370).

1370   Moves to his house in Arquà. Writes his *Testamentum* before a journey to Rome to celebrate Urban V's return. Has to return to Padua because of a sudden illness. Urban returns to Avignon, where he dies.

1371   Health problems increase, but he still works.

1373   Translates Boccaccio's story of Griselda (*Decameron* X.1) into Latin and sends it to Boccaccio (*Sen.* XVIII.3), though it never arrives. Composes *Invective contra eum qui maledixit Italie*. Sends the Malatesta form of the *RVF* to Pandolfo Malatesta. Composes the Queriniana form of the *RVF* in the same year.

1374   Completes the last version of the *RVF* and the last version of *De viris illustribus* (1371–74). Writes *Triumphus Eternitatis*. Dies in Arquà July 18 or 19.

ABBREVIATIONS

This list provides cited editions and translations of the works of Francesco Petrarca, with abbreviations.

Africa
> *Africa*. Ed. Nicola Festa. *Edizione Nazionale delle Opere di Francesco Petrarca*. Florence: Le Lettere, 2008. Reprint of *Edizione Nazionale delle Opere di Francesco Petrarca*. Vol. 1. Florence: Sansoni, 1926.
> *L'Afrique: 1338–1374*. Ed. and trans. Rebecca Lenoir. Grenoble: Jérôme Millon, 2002.
> *Petrarch's Africa*. Eds. and trans. Thomas G. Bergin and Alice S. Wilson. New Haven, CT: Yale University Press, 1977.

Buc. carm. = *Bucolicum carmen*
> *Bucolicum carmen*. Ed. Luca Canali. San Cesario di Lecce: Piero Manni, 2005.
> *Petrarch's "Bucolicum carmen."* Ed. and trans. Thomas G. Bergin. New Haven, CT: Yale University Press, 1974.

Canzoniere = see *RVF*

Coll. laur. = *Collatio laureationis*
> "Collatio laureationis." In *Opere latine di Francesco Petrarca*. 2 vols. Ed. Antonietta Bufano. Turin: Unione Tipgrafica-Editrice Torinese (UTET), 1975.
> "Petrarch's Coronation Oration." In Ernest Hatch Wilkins, *Studies in the Life and Works of Petrarch*. Cambridge, MA: Medieval Academy of America, 1955, 300–313.

De otio = *De otio religioso*
> *De otio religioso*. Ed. Giulio Goletti. Edizione Nazionale delle Opere di Francesco Petrarca. Florence: Le Lettere, 2007.
> *Petrarch on Religious Leisure*. Ed. and trans. Susan S. Schearer; intr. Ronald G. Witt. New York: Italica Press, 2002.

De remediis = *De remediis utriusque fortunae*
> [No modern critical edition of the Latin text exists.]
> *Petrarch's Remedies for Fortune Fair and Foul*. A Modern Translation of *De remediis utriusque fortune*, with a commentary by Conrad H. Rawski. 5 vols. Bloomington, IN: Indiana University Press, 1991.

De viris = De viris illustribus
De viris illustribus. Ed. Guido Martelotti. Edizione Nazionale delle Opere di Francesco Petrarca. 2 vols. Florence: Sansoni, 1964.
[There is no published English translation.]

De vita = De vita solitaria
De vita solitaria. In *Opere latine di Francesco Petrarca*. 2 vols. Vol. 1. Ed. Antonietta Bufano. Turin: Unione Tipgrafica-Editrice Torinese (UTET), 1975.
The Life of Solitude. Ed. and trans. Jacob Zeitlin, Urbana, IL: University of Illinois Press, 1924.

Disperse = Lettere disperse
Lettere disperse: Varie e miscellanee. Ed. Alessandro Pancheri. Parma: Ugo Guandi, 1994.
[There is no published English translation.]

Epystole = Epystole metriche
Epystole. In *Poemata minora quae exstant omnia/Poesie minori del Petrarca*. Ed. Domenico Rossetti, vols. 2–3. Milan: Società Tipografica dei Classici Italiani, 1831–34.
Epistulae metricae/Briefe in Versen, Latin text and German translation. Eds. and trans. Eva Schönberger and Otto Schönberger. Würzburg: Königshausen & Neumann, 2004.
[There is no complete English translation.]

Fam. = Rerum familiarum libri
Le familiari. Ed. Ugo Dotti. 3 vols. Rome: Archivio Guido Izzo, 1991.
Letters on Familiar Matters: Rerum Familiarum Libri XVII–XXIV. Ed. and trans. Aldo S. Bernardo. Baltimore, MD: Johns Hopkins University Press, 1985.
Letters on Familiar Matters: Rerum Familiarum Libri IX–XVI. Ed. and trans. Aldo S. Bernardo. Baltimore, MD: Johns Hopkins University Press, 1982.
Rerum familiarum libri, I–VIII. Ed. and trans. Aldo S. Bernardo. Albany, NY: State University of New York Press, 1975.

Invective
Invectives. Ed. and trans. David Marsh. In *The I Tatti Renaissance Library Series*. Ed. James Hankins. Cambridge, MA: Harvard University Press, 2003, revised edition, 2008.

  Contra eum = Invectiva contra eum qui maledixit Italie (*Invective against a Detractor of Italy*)
  Contra medicum = Invective contra medicum (*Invective against a Physician*)
  Contra quendam = Invectiva contra quendam magni status hominem (*Invective against a Man of High Rank with No Knowledge or Virtue*)
  De ignorantia = De sui ipsius et multorum ignorantia (*On His Own Ignorance and That of Many Others*)

Itinerarium = *Itinerarium ad sepulcrum Domini*
Itinerario al sepolcro del Signore nostro Gesù Cristo. Ed. and trans.
Franca Guelfi; intr. Francesco Surdich. Genoa: San Marco dei Giustiniani,
2006.
*Petrarch's Guide to the Holy Land: Itinerary to the Sepulcher of Our Lord Jesus
Christ.* Ed. and trans. Theodore J. Cachey, Jr. Notre Dame, IN: University of
Notre Dame Press, 2002.

Psalmi = *Psalmi penitentiales*
Psalmi penitentiales orationes. Ed. Donatella Coppini. Edizione Nazionale delle
Opere di Francesco Petrarca. Florence: Le Lettere, 2010.
[There is no published English translation.]

Rerum memorandarum = *Rerum memorandarum libri*
Rerum memorandarum libri. Ed. Giuseppe Billanovich. Edizione Nazionale delle
Opere di Francesco Petrarca. Vol. 5:1a. Florence: Sansoni, 1943.
[There is no published English translation.]

RVF = *Rerum Vulgarium Fragmenta (Canzoniere)*
Canzoniere. Ed. Marco Santagata. Milan: Arnoldo Mondadori, 1996 [2004].
Petrarch's Lyric Poems. Ed. and trans. Robert M. Durling. Cambridge, MA:
Harvard University Press, 1976.

Secretum
De secreto conflictu curarum mearum. In *Prose.* Eds. Guido Martellotti, Pier
Giorgio Ricci, Enrico Carrara, and Enrico Bianchi. Milan and Naples: Ricciardi
Editore, 1955.
The Secret. Ed. and trans. Carol E. Quillen. New York: Bedford/St. Martin's,
2003.

Sen. = *Seniles*
Le senili. 3 vols. Ed. and trans. Ugo Dotti, with Felicità Audisi and Elvira Nota.
Racconigi: Aragno, 2004–10.
Letters of Old Age: Rerum Senilium Libri I–XVIII. Eds. and trans. Aldo S.
Bernardo, Saul Levin, and Reta A. Benardo. 2 vols. Baltimore, MD: Johns
Hopkins University Press, 1992.

Sine nomine = *Liber sine nomine*
Sine nomine: Lettere polemiche e politiche. Ed. Ugo Dotti. Bari: Laterza,
1974.
Petrarch's Book Without a Name: A Translation of the 'Liber sine nomine.' Ed.
and trans. Norman P. Zacour. Toronto, ON: Pontifical Institute of Medieval
Studies, 1973.

Testamentum
Testamentum. In *Opere latine di Francesco Petrarca.* 2 vols. Vol. 2. Ed. Antonietta
Bufano. Turin: Unione Tipgrafica-Editrice Torinese, 1975.
Petrarch's Testament. Ed. and trans. Theodor E. Mommsen. Ithaca, NY: Cornell
University Press, 1957.

Triumphi

> *Trionfi, Rime estravaganti, Codice degli abbozzi*. Eds. Vincio Pacca and Laura Paolino; intr. Marco Santagata. Milan: Mondadori, 1996.
>
> *The Triumphs of Petrarch*. Ed. and trans. Ernest Hatch Wilkins. Chicago, IL: University of Chicago Press, 1962.
>
> *TC = Triumphus Cupidinis* (Triumph of Love)
>
> *TP = Triumphus Pudicititie* (Triumph of Chastity)
>
> *TM = Triumpus Mortis* (Triumph of Death)
>
> *TF = Triumphus Fame* (Triumph of Fame)
>
> *TT = Triumphus Temporis* (Triumph of Time)
>
> *TE = Triumphus Eternitatis* (Triumph of Eternity)

ALBERT RUSSELL ASCOLI AND UNN FALKEID

Introduction

No single figure has been as closely identified with the emergence of cultural modernity in Europe as Francis Petrarch. From Jacob Burckhardt and Theodor Mommsen to Paul Oskar Kristeller and Hans Blumenberg, he has been depicted as "the first modern man," a label that implies a mixture of notions, including being the discoverer of psychological interiority, the defender of natural curiosity, and the promoter of a new sense of the historical past. This bold suggestion has further been strengthened by descriptions of Petrarch the Latin author as the founder, or at least the first powerful voice, of the pervasive cultural movement known as Humanism, as well as the first person to draw a sharp distinction between the "dark ages" of medieval times and the rebirth of classical civilization in a dawning Renaissance. At the same time, we also have an abiding understanding of Petrarch the vernacular poet as the inventor of a form of the love lyric and of the lyric collection, which would soon come to dominate the Western tradition.

Gone, more or less, are the innocent days when we could speak about Petrarch in quite such confidently romanticized terms. Today we are far more aware that the notion of embodying a historical period's multitude of experiences and events in a single human being is simply untenable, no matter how well known the name or pervasive the influence. We now recognize the need to understand, as it were negatively, the many crucial aspects of the time that are effectively invisible in Petrarch's works (daily social, economic, and political realities; the lives of women and the poor), and, somewhat more "positively," those places where Petrarch's quest for solitude and autonomy, his propensity for dismissing the degraded present in favor of the classical past and a hoped-for posterity, masks profound implication in the social, political, and religious networks of his age.

The Petrarch we undertake to introduce in this volume represents neither a symbolic bridge over the chasm between historical epochs after centuries of presumed immobility, nor an autonomous agent who acted alone upon the historical stage in accordance with a new sensibility all his own that came to transform the cultural program of his time and for centuries to come. Over the last few decades, a recurring topic in Petrarch scholarship has, rather, been how deliberately he "fashioned" and refashioned himself for his contemporaries, and, even more, for the future generations by whom he confidently, and accurately, expected to be read and admired. His "self," or, perhaps better, his many and often contradictory selves, are largely the effect of skillfully deployed literary-rhetorical strategies. As many contemporary readers have argued, the inner conflicts, the self-doubts, the subjection to love, the yearning for earthly glory, and the following penance and regret are as much carefully constructed postures in dialogue with a web of other texts and voices as they are reflections of the writer's inner, psychological conditions. And we have increasingly come to recognize that our image of Petrarch standing at the boundary between historical eras, as between an old self and a new, is one that he himself initiated and fostered.

Still, despite all of the qualifications we have now introduced to the "myth" of Petrarchan modernity, there is no doubt that he remains a crucial point of reference in the history of Western culture. In our time, he is best known for his magnificent collection of vernacular Italian verse, commonly referred to as the *Canzoniere*,[1] but by Petrarch himself entitled *Rerum vulgarium fragmenta* (hereafter abbreviated as *RVF*), and its key role in the emergence and affirmation of vernacular literatures throughout Europe from the fourteenth to the seventeenth centuries, especially, though not exclusively, through the pervasive phenomenon we now call "Petrarchism." Yet, the seminal influence of Petrarch's many other works, mostly Latin, can be seen in the triumphalist pageantry and artwork of the Renaissance, so clearly indebted to his one other major Italian poem, the *Triumphi*; in the dramatic growth and evolution of the pastoral mode which his *Bucolicum carmen* helped to refound; in the resuscitation of classical epic as a leading genre, through his much-touted, if never completed, *Africa*. Petrarch is also the first post-classical figure to use the dialogue form – in *Secretum* – and the epistolary collection – notably the *Familiares* and the *Seniles* – as major cultural vehicles. His *De viris illustribus*, alongside his friend Boccaccio's *De casibus virorum illustrorum* and *De claris mulieribus*, relaunched the genre of secular biography, while his *De remediis utriusque fortunae* became an indispensable repertory of moral exempla for at least two centuries. In other words, we may still correctly claim a primary Petrarchan influence on much of Renaissance literary culture in Italy, throughout Europe, and beyond.

And though it is no longer possible to assert, given the recent work of Ronald Witt, James Hankins, and others, that Petrarch literally founded the Latin Humanist movement, nonetheless there is no doubt that he made himself its early focal point and inspiration. His antiquarianism (the collection of Roman coins), his book-hunting (the rediscovery of Ciceronian letters), his philological restoration of texts (Livy's *History of Rome*), his active celebration and circulation of the classics, his promotion of interest in Greek (including the sponsorship of a translation of Homer), his powerfully influential rearticulation of "the myth of Rome," his fusion of Christian autobiography with classical moral philosophy (Augustine with Seneca and Cicero), his attempt to reintroduce classical Latin style: all would become hallmarks of the Quattrocento and Cinquecento Humanists.

Who, then, is our Petrarch today? Contemporary scholarship is largely focused on the complexities and seeming contradictions in Petrarch's life and work. On the one hand, he is much more the prototype of the worldly courtier, advisor, and protégé of the powerful (the Colonna, King Robert, the da Correggio, the Visconti, the Carrara) than had formerly been imagined. And yet, as Charles Trinkaus already was arguing fifty years ago, he is also far more deeply engaged with problems of Christian faith than he once seemed to be, while his work at times reveals a profound investment in "medieval" theological traditions and institutions, particularly monasticism.

At the center of Petrarch's understanding of himself – and of much modern analysis of the man and his works – is his exalted conception of his special role as "poet." In 1342, at the age of thirty-eight, he was crowned in Rome as *poeta laureatus* (based largely on the unconfirmed expectations raised by the rapidly circulating news of his *Africa*), a title which he claimed had not been conferred since antiquity. Nevertheless, he was anxiously aware that he had rivals: notably, Dante and Albertino Mussato, to say nothing of Zanobi da Strada, all of whom had claims to laureation, and Giovanni Boccaccio, his younger friend and colleague, who both openly celebrated and intermittently challenged his exalted position.

"Our" Petrarch is one whose career must be read over time and in a series of transitions – both geographical and ideological – between critical political, intellectual, and spiritual contexts. Perhaps because he always took such a polemical stance in relation to the fourteenth-century papacy, we have tended to underestimate the influence of Avignon – where Petrarch spent much of the first half of his life – on his early formation. In fact, however, the papal court and the city of Avignon (where the papacy was transferred from Rome in 1309, and where it would remain, with one brief exception, until shortly after Petrarch's death), were fertile ground for the young poet-intellectual *in fieri*. They and the nearby pastoral "Vaucluse," where he sought refuge from courtly corruption and intrigue, were constant points of reference in his literary and other writings, often in dialectical relationship with a nostalgic and idealized vision of Rome, a city he would not in fact visit until he was in his late thirties.

When Petrarch's father moved the family to Carpentras, just a few miles from Avignon, the city was already turning into a kind of medieval cosmopolis. Within a few years after Pope Clement V settled in Provence in 1309, the papal curia developed into the most powerful court in Europe, and Avignon into a key political and cultural center, where intellectuals, artists, theologians, lawyers, notaries, and artisans from all over Europe (including, for instance, the painter Simone Martini, the Franciscan Ubertino da Casale, and the nominalist theologian William of Ockham) were to be found at various times. Despite the evident importance for Petrarch of the dynamic transmission of ideas and texts connected to the papal curia and to the city in general, and the nourishing patronage he received from members of that curia, notably Cardinal Colonna, Petrarch rapidly developed a strong critique of the increasing economic and secular power of the papacy, much like that in a preceding generation of Dante and the White Guelf party, to which his father had also belonged. All the popes during the seven decades of the Avignon papacy were French and closely connected to the French king: clearly a reason for resentment among the growing group of Italian immigrants, who wanted to return the papacy to Rome and to restore that city's traditional title as *caput mundi* of the Christian world.

By attending to this political context, we can shed significant light both on Petrarch's troubled relationship to the Avignon papacy and on his ambitious program of cultural renewal. Though from 1330 on he was closely linked to the curia, especially through his appointment as chaplain to Cardinal Giovanni Colonna, a recurring theme in Petrarch's work, early and late, is his diatribe against "the Babylon on the Rhône," to which he applied a dark apocalyptic rhetoric inspired by the radical Franciscans of the time (as exemplified by his polemical *Liber sine nomine*). Paradoxically, then, Avignon represented both a steady benchmark wherever else Petrarch lived in his roving life – in Bologna and Parma when younger; in Milan, Padua, and Venice when older – and a continual point of tension in his literary production. And throughout his life it formed a shadowy backdrop for his grandiose vision of Rome renewed, whether in his early support for the regime of the visionary Cola di Rienzo, his later hopes for Emperor Charles IV, or his impassioned pleas to Pope Urban V near the end of his life. For Petrarch, in comparison to Rome, Avignon was a city without memory, without past, and therefore without any future. Still, Petrarch's vision generally differed from Dante's fantasies (in the *Monarchy* and political letters, especially) of reviving the Roman Empire and his ideas about the sacred origin of power.

Despite intermittent attempts to influence great political and religious leaders of the time, Petrarch's main focus was on the cultivation of an exclusive network of friends and colleagues independent of any political or religious institution: a network that had Petrarch himself at its privileged center. The main thrust of Petrarch's cultural project increasingly became a cult of exemplary individualities from the glorious Roman past (from Scipio Africanus to the late, book-length, *Life of Caesar*; from Virgil and Cicero to Seneca), coupled with a retrieval of religious interiority modeled by St. Augustine: ideas that came to be pervasive in the following centuries. And, of course, it was at Avignon, and nearby Vaucluse, that he first created the myth of Laura and entered onto the path of collecting vernacular lyrics into a songbook, or *canzoniere*: the *RVF*, the work for which he is now best remembered. The *RVF* would go on, especially in the sixteenth century, to reshape the European poetic tradition and provide the linguistic model for Italian cultural-political identity that would endure at least through the Risorgimento or Italian unification in the mid-nineteenth century.

The effects of the "Avignon" experience would linger with Petrarch for the rest of his life. His representations of that experience, through which it is known us, would, however, be filtered and revised from the perspective of the latter half of his life, as many of the works first written in Avignon underwent considerable revision and, to some degree, ideological re-orientation. During the late 1340s and early 1350s, when Petrarch was gradually making up his mind to leave Avignon definitively for Italy, he underwent a series of traumatic and transformative experiences, which, for instance, led Hans Baron, Francisco Rico, and Hannah Wojciehowski to hypothesize a radical shift in his ideology. These included his bitter disappointment following the collapse of Cola's re-founded Roman Republic; the devastations of the Black Death, which killed both Laura and Cardinal Colonna, as well as many other friends and acquaintances; the violent deaths of two other dear friends at the hands of brigands; the offer, ultimately refused, of restitution of his confiscated patrimony by the Florentine Republic; and his budding friendship with Giovanni Boccaccio, which would become so central to him both personally and intellectually in later years.

From 1353 on, he would live primarily in Italy, under the protection of a series of powerful Northern Italian patrons – the Visconti in Milan, the da Correggio in Padua, the Venetian Republic – whom his Florentine friends, Boccaccio in particular, saw as tyrants. In reply, he would claim repeatedly, though not entirely persuasively, that (as he would say most directly in a very late letter), "I was with the princes in name, but in fact the princes were with me" (*Sen.* XVII.2). In this period, as he reached the zenith of his Europe-wide fame, he would consolidate both his humanistic scholarly project (including the joint sponsorship, with Boccaccio, of a translation of Homer into Latin) and his Augustinian-Franciscan Christianity, while ceaselessly writing new works and revising old ones. And even while continuing to write patronizingly and dismissively of vernacular poetry, he would carry out extensive revisions to and expansions of the *RVF*, and launch his new and ambitious vernacular work, the *Triumphi*.

This *Companion*, then, aims to give a wide-ranging and nuanced view of Petrarch's life, of his works, of the complex interactions between them, and of their significance in social and historical perspective, respecting the continuously evolving and dynamic pattern of his career. In this way, our book seeks to address the multiple ways in which Petrarch lends himself to the teaching and study of the periods often referred to as the later Middle Ages and early Renaissance in Europe, both as a symptom and as a transformative agent. Moreover, we seek to strike a fruitful balance between incorporating the recent and valuable tendency to bring Petrarch's long-neglected Latin works, which constitute the vast majority of his writings, back to center stage and respecting the fact that his most enduring literary legacy remains his Italian lyric collection, the *RVF*. And we take note of the fact that, for all his seeming self-absorption, Petrarch constantly positions himself in dialogue: with contemporary friends, and enemies; with peers, patrons, and, occasionally, subordinates; but also with the classical past, and, less explicitly, with more recent voices in the nascent vernacular tradition; and, of course, with the future readers whose admiration and imitation he hopes and indeed expects – not in vain, as it turned out – to win. In partial recognition of how very successful he was in reaching those future readers and evoking and provoking their response, we devote some four chapters to his reception and influence in Italy and Europe in the two centuries following his death, and a final essay to his tortuous "confrontation with modernity," as Giuseppe Mazzotta puts it.

The book is divided into six parts, each devoted to a specific aspect of Petrarch's life, works, relationships, and thought, but continually in anticipatory or retrospective dialogue with one another. Part I sets forth an intellectual and cultural biography of Petrarch organized around the crucial dates, places, and activities of his life, while simultaneously foregrounding his recurrent attempts to shape posterity's perception of him. Our knowledge of Petrarch's life is extraordinarily rich in comparison to that of virtually any of his contemporaries or precursors, even the notoriously autobiographical Dante. The reason is simple, but also creates significant complications in how we are to assess what we think we know: Petrarch writes about himself endlessly, at once documenting the events of his life, his friendships, his interests, his political values and projects, his interior conflicts and complacencies, and his style of thought. Previous biographies of Petrarch, particularly the seminal study of Ernest Hatch Wilkins, but also that of Ugo Dotti, set out to reconstruct his life based largely on Petrarch's own declarations concerning it, even as the "constructed" and even "fictive" elements of these works has long been recognized. We, instead, provide a bare-bones chronology of historically and biographically significant events in Petrarch's life, followed by two different, partial accounts of that life and the works associated with it, filtered through primary, recurrent interests and problematics that Petrarch himself makes structuring principles in telling and retelling his own story; notably, his restless penchant for travel in his life and revision in his works (Chapter 1) and his cultivation of a vast and influential network of friends (Chapter 2).

In the following two parts we introduce principal works from the two linguistic traditions in which Petrarch wrote. Part II offers four chapters on Petrarch's writings in the vernacular: three exploring the structures, themes, and compositional processes of the *Canzoniere* or *RVF* from different perspectives (Chapters 3–5) and one on the less well known, but important, *Triumphi* (Chapter 6). Part III is devoted to Petrarch's major Latin works, which in his own mind, as well as in the eyes of his contemporaries, formed his greatest and most significant accomplishments. Because of the vastness of Petrarch's Latin oeuvre, we have chosen to focus on a few key works, genres, and topics rather than attempt a comprehensive survey. This part opens with a treatment of Petrarch's most important poetic works in Latin, especially the epic *Africa* and the pastoral *Bucolicum carmen*, as well as the *Epystole metriche* or verse letters (Chapter 7). The *Africa* was Petrarch's debut as a Latin poet and constituted a deliberate effort to establish himself as the modern heir to the great classical poets. Though circulated only in fragments, and never finished, it became the basis of his international reputation and the occasion for his coronation with the laurel crown in Rome. This early, yet never fully realized success would define and haunt Petrarch throughout the rest of his career. The other two works, both complete, represent a successive and in some ways more successful realization of Petrarch's temperament and his poetic gifts. Chapter 8 offers a probing examination of Petrarch's *Secretum* or *Secret*, revealing a complex "defense of poetry" and of the imagination at the heart of a text that presents itself as the dramatization of a spiritual and vocational crisis. Chapter 9 treats Petrarch's lesser known, yet crucial, spiritual and contemplative works, especially the complementary works, *De vita solitaria* (*The Life of Solitude*) and the *De otio religioso* (*On Religious Leisure*). Chapter 10 focuses on Petrarch as letter-writer and collector of letters. Well acquainted with Seneca's moral epistles and famously the discoverer of Cicero's "lost" letters to Atticus, in his middle years Petrarch embarked on an ambitious program of collecting, editing, and rewriting (and even inventing out of the whole cloth) his own epistolary productions.

Part IV focuses attention on Petrarch's pervasive engagement with ancient, as well as late-medieval and contemporary, writers and thinkers; an engagement through which he sometimes explicitly, sometimes implicitly articulates his vision of the nature and purpose of intellectual and artistic endeavors. Chapter 11 deals with Petrarch's relationship to the ancients – the classical authors as well as the Church Fathers – and especially the ethical implications of his continuous balancing between classical and patristic Christian models of style. Chapter 12 explores the intertextual filiations that link Petrarch to the recent vernacular past: to Dante, of course, but also to lesser known precursors, as well as both the Occitan and early Italian tradition. Finally, Chapter 13 directs our attention to Petrarch's ferocious polemical invectives against intellectual, and occasionally personal, opponents of his own day: against the detractors of his beloved Italy (*Invective against a Detractor of Italy*), against the abstract speculations of Scholasticism (*On His Own Ignorance and That of Many Others*), and against those who prefer the physical sciences (especially medicine) to the moral, spiritual, and poetic disciplines (*Invective against a Physician*). The chapter carefully situates these polemical texts in the vital intellectual world of the mid-fourteenth century – emphasizing the enmity that Petrarch's fame aroused in would-be rivals – and goes on to anticipate the role of model that these texts later took on for the flourishing genre of Humanist invective.

The last two parts examine, as it were, Petrarch's "future": his vision of and importance for the nascent realm of European modernity. Part V explicitly follows Petrarch's "afterlife" in the two centuries we now call "the Renaissance." Successive chapters specify his importance for the formation of Italian and European Humanism, especially in the fifteenth century (Chapter 14), his seminal role in the courtly lyric phenomenon known, of course, as "Petrarchism" in relation to the sixteenth-century Italian context (Chapter 15), his function as privileged interlocutor for the emergent figure of the female poet (Chapter 16), and his influence on love poetry from throughout Europe (Chapter 17). Finally, Part VI is dedicated exclusively to the volume's concluding chapter, "Petrarch's Confrontation with Modernity." Chapter 18 revisits the central, vexed question of Petrarch and modernity, taking into account both the patently "modern" elements of his thought and the equally evident "reactionary" elements that seek a return to an idealized past, Christian and/or classical. The thesis, which in many ways reflects the perspective of the editors of this volume, is that "Petrarch is a modern who, paradoxically, disavows his modernity, and he does so mainly as a way of acknowledging his rootedness in the communal memories of tradition."

In conclusion, we believe that the fascination of Petrarch is as potentially alive and relevant today as it ever was – not because his works can be seen as single-handedly redefining the course of Western culture, nor because he himself can be made into a trope for the dawning of a new historical era and a new mode of consciousness, but rather because his struggles to shape and interpret his own place in the world and to negotiate a middle way between tradition and innovation, along with his evident desire to produce models that others might imitate in order to do the same, represent a singularly valuable example of the problematic intersection between individual consciousness and historical context, between personal identity and cultural constraint, between now and then.

NOTE

1 *"Canzoniere"* literally means "collection of songs."

PART I

Lives of Petrarch

I

THEODORE J. CACHEY, JR.

Poetry in motion

I have now no permanent land or sky. I am nowhere a citizen and a
wanderer everywhere.

Epystole III.19.15–16

I again returned to France, incapable of staying still, and not so much
with a yearning to see again what I had seen a thousand times, as with
an effort to cope with stiffness – as sick people do – by a shift
of position.[1]

Seniles XVIII.1

A wanderer everywhere

Given his self-proclaimed identity as "peregrinus ubique" ("a wanderer
everywhere"), it was fitting that Petrarch never completed the letter
addressed to posterity (*Sen.* XVIII.1) that was to conclude his monumental
epistolary collection, the *Seniles*, and that after many years and numerous
revisions, even near the end of his life, the last of Petrarch's *fragmenta* came
to a halt at a concluding image of the author still in movement, shuttling
back and forth between Provence and Italy, as he had so many times, before
his definitive move to Italy in 1353. A profound sense of vulnerability with
respect to his place in the world (or lack of it) had always accompanied
Petrarch on the journey of life and of writing, shadowed as both were in
his mind by the constant threat of shipwreck. Writing was, on the other
hand, the main means by which the son of the Florentine exile ser Petracco,
"begotten and born in exile" (*Fam.* I.1.22) in Arezzo in 1304, had sought
to establish and maintain his place in the world.

For Petrarch, writing truly became that place in which "the man who is
without a home finds a place to live."[2] His stateless condition inspired in
him an ongoing preoccupation with place that fundamentally shaped his life
in writing: both the general outline of the canon of his works and how those
works related to one another. In fact, the same agitated oscillations between
departure and arrival that characterized Petrarch's biography profoundly
influenced both the compositional histories of individual works and the
oeuvre as a whole. As we will see, Petrarch's twenty or so principal works

can be considered heuristically in pairs in relation to the itinerary of his life, with Petrarch moving back and forth between them, just as he did between the places we have come to associate with his biography: whether between Avignon and Vaucluse or between Padua and Arquà; whether between the *De viris* and the *Africa* or between the *RVF* and the *Triumphi*.

Scholars have recognized at least since Ernest Hatch Wilkins's classic *Life of Petrarch* that some kind of relation existed between Petrarch's frequent changes in residence and the restlessness that manifested itself in his literary activity, in his "turning from one to another of the works that he had on hand at a given time, or in the undertaking of an entirely new work."[3] But they have not, generally speaking, developed this insight as an interpretive key, nor have they attempted to understand Petrarch's spatial departures and arrivals in terms of his textual practice.[4] To start to write was tantamount to departure for Petrarch, just as to cease writing was to arrive.

At its deepest level, Petrarch's acute awareness of the fragile and fleeting hold that he had on life inspired an impulse to movement or flight. It is an awareness that he expressed throughout his writings, and most eloquently in his poetry:

> Nebbia o polvere al vento,
> fuggo per più non esser pellegrino:
> et così vada s' è 'l pur mio destino.
> (*RVF* 331, 22–24)

(A cloud or dust in the wind, I flee in order to be no longer a traveler, and so be it if that is indeed my destiny.)

The sense of dismay that accompanied this awareness is poignantly expressed in the dramatic opening sentence of the *Secretum*: "I have often wondered how I came into the world and how I would leave it." Ultimately, Petrarch found himself "between" departure and arrival in this most deeply Christian and existential sense; that is, between the birth and death that would hopefully mark the arrival of the Christian *peregrinus* at a new life, "un mondo / novo, in etate immobile ed eterna" ("a new world, immobile in time and eternal") that Petrarch aspired to and attempted to represent in the *Triumphus Eternitatis* (*TE* 20–21).

But Petrarch had other specifically biographical reasons to be preoccupied with his place in the world, and these motivated him to establish through writing his position in society as a prestigious intellectual figure. Petrarch's reputation as a living *auctor*, that is, a person possessing great intellectual and cultural *auctoritas* or authority, enabled a long series of advantageous patronage relationships through which he acquired ecclesiastical benefices (and several houses), achieving a remarkable autonomy and freedom of movement for his time. His writing was treated as a commodity of exchange within a patronage network that he deftly managed while passing from the ecclesiastical environment of the Colonna family and the papal court in Avignon, via King Robert of Naples' sponsorship of his coronation as poet laureate in Rome in 1341, to the lay patronage of the Correggio of Parma, the Visconti of Milan, the Venetian state, and the Carrara family of Padua.

That Petrarch would use writing to address both the transcendental and the more mundane challenges he faced regarding his place in the world was adumbrated when he dropped the patronymic "Petracco" and started signing himself "Petrarca" during the 1340s. Scholars have suggested that the name he gave himself, "Petr-arca," was doubly allusive: to the tomb of stone – the monument that, like writing, records an enduring identity – and to the Ark of the Covenant.[5] It thus expressed the paradoxical drive of the son of the exile Petracco both to establish his place in the world and to transcend it. Petrarch's attempt to prearrange his own burial site in his Will (*Testamentum*), which he wrote before setting out for Rome in the spring of 1370, similarly expressed the impulse both to maintain and to hold on to a place in the world and at the same time to resist and to transcend the limitations of space and time. In a proleptic postmortem "journey through Italy," Petrarch indicated an itinerary of possible sites for his eventual entombment, including the places "I have been wont to frequent in Italy," from "Padua where I am now" to Arquà, to Venice, to Milan, to Pavia, to Rome, or even to the cathedral of the city of Parma, "of which I have been a useless and almost always absent archdeacon for many years" (*Testamentum* 14–15), when, in fact, he had not been there in more than twenty years. With regard to potential burial sites in Rome, Petrarch left open two possibilities, St. Peter's or Santa Maria Maggiore, as if to squeeze out even a last bit of posthumous mobility from the dilemma his heirs faced in having to decide between the two options. In the end, within a tomb that still stands beside the parish church of Arquà, in the words of Byron, "rear'd in air/ Pillar'd in their sarcophagus, repose/ The bones of Laura's lover."[6]

Petrarch transformed vulnerability into a literary asset by making a virtue of the compulsion of his contrary impulses. At the heart of his self-fashioning as a "wanderer everywhere," the paradoxical drive both to stay and to go fundamentally characterized Petrarch's practice as a writer, his autobiographical self-portrait, and the catalog of works he left behind. In fact, since Petrarch did not so much live his life as write it, distinguishing between the empirical life spent in writing, the deliberate constructions (and often distortions) of the image of a life through writing, and the oeuvre which resulted from the life spent in writing can often prove difficult. As a self-conscious attitude toward writing, Petrarch's approach found programmatic expression in the dedicatory letter to the epistolary collection (*Fam.* I.1) that he authored around 1350. There, he compared himself to the wanderer about to depart on a journey who has to decide "what to bring with him, what to share with friends, and what to burn" (*Fam.* I.1.3). But in the very next sentence the author likened his situation instead to that of "a tired traveler [looking behind] from a vantage point after a long journey" (*Fam.* I.1.4). In other words, Petrarch located his writing according to the metaphor of his life as a journey impossibly poised between going and coming, between departing and having arrived. The project of the *Familiares*, like the *RVF* and the *Epystole*, which the dedicatory letter also announced, accordingly marked a transitional moment in terms of the author's biography between departure from Provence and arrival in Italy. But as Petrarch stated explicitly toward the end of the letter, it was the very act or "labor" of writing that for him was paradoxically located between departure and arrival; that is, it was both a journey and a place of rest: "I shall continue along the path I have been following, and shall avoid any exits as long as there is light. And the sweet labor will serve for me almost as a place of rest" (*Fam.* I.1.45).

In effect, Petrarch sought to dwell in an eternal present constituted by his practice of writing, managing by literary means thereby to experience a kind of figurative eternity. The effect on the oeuvre of this characteristic privileging of process over product in Petrarch's writing was to generate its uncanny mobility. Thus, the shipwrecked Petrarchan subject of *RVF* 189, "Passa la nave mia colma d'oblio" ("My ship laden with forgetfulness"), still asserts that "only now do I begin to despair of port" (*RVF* 189, 14); and thus the incomplete "Letter to Posterity" still speaks to us across the centuries in the present moment: "Perhaps you will have heard something about me, although this too is doubtful, whether a petty, obscure name would reach far into either space or time" (*Sen.* XVIII.1).

Between departure and arrival

Two key departure–arrivals anchored Petrarch's life: the departure from Provence and arrival in Italy in 1353, and the departure from this life and putative arrival at the hereafter in 1374. Heralded by the most famous of Petrarch's metrical epistles, "Ad Italiam" (*Epystole* III.24), the definitive move from Provence to Italy was the focal point and inspiration for several of the major works of his maturity, including the unfinished *Secretum*, in which Augustinus urges Franciscus both to stay, that is, to remain in solitude in Vaucluse, in Book II, and to go, that is, to flee to Italy, in Book III; the epistolary collections, in particular the *Sine nomine* (1350–59) (recently and aptly characterized as an account of Petrarch's "slow self-extraction from Avignon and Vaucluse");[7] the early polemical invectives, *Contra medicum* (1352–61) and *Contra quendam* (1355); the *Epystole* (1350–57; 1366); and the *RVF*.

Preparation for definitive departure from this life was well underway by the 1360s. It was marked by the "arrival," that is, the completion of the *Familiares* (1366) and the "departure" of the *Seniles* (begun in 1361); the composition of the late polemics: *De ignorantia* (1367–71) and the *Contra eum* (1373); the final manuscript copying of the *Familiares*, of the *Bucolicum carmen*, and of the *Epystole*, which were all finished in 1366; the preparation of the definitive form of the *RVF* in Vatican Latin manuscript 3195 (initiated in 1366 by the copyist Giovanni Malpaghini under Petrarch's direction and later taken up by the author, beginning in October of 1367 and continuing to the end of his life); and the assiduous contemporaneous work on the *Triumphi* that – according to manuscript annotations dating from the late 1350s – continued to the end of Petrarch's life, with the completion of the *Triumphus Eternitatis* dating from his final year (February 12, 1374).

The canon of Petrarch's works, collectively and individually, expressed the contrary and in some deeper sense competing impulses of his writing toward both departure and arrival, both movement and stasis. His works typically emerged either roughly parallel to one another in a complementary relationship tending toward stasis or equilibrium, as in the contrast between the serially ordered prose biographies that made up the *De viris* and the epic construction of the *Africa* during the early period in Provence and that between a circular series of lyric *fragmenta* in the *RVF* and the vertical trajectory of the *Triumphi* during the later Italian phase. They could also relate to one another as pairs sequentially, thereby marking points of departure and arrival, respectively. This is the case with the central pairing of the life in writing that marked the departure from Provence and successful arrival in Italy: the *Secretum* and the *De remediis*. The *Secretum* never arrived at completion, given that it was never published in Petrarch's lifetime. It was conceived and composed during Petrarch's last years in Provence, between 1347 and 1353. In the second book of the dialogue, Augustinus advises Franciscus, as a remedy for his depression ("aegritudo" or "acedia"), to write down notes of memorable passages of wisdom as he comes across them in his readings. This recommendation was the seed of the *De remediis*, the major work, also in dialogue form, that Petrarch completed during his eight years in Milan (1354–61). At the opposite pole from the fluctuations of the unfinished and only posthumously published *Secretum*, the *De remediis* would canonize Petrarch's Renaissance reputation as the Stoic Christian sage of his age. In fact, Petrarch undertook and completed the lengthy work in

Milan between 1354 and 1357 in a manner more expeditious than any other of his career. The pairing of Petrarch's only dialogues thus marks within the canon of his works, viewed retrospectively, the central biographical departure and arrival of his life.

Petrarch had already begun preparing for departure from this life when he oversaw the production of the definitive manuscript copy of the *Familiares* by his amanuensis Giovanni Malpaghini in 1366. This arrival marked the departure, on an open-ended trajectory, of a new letter collection that took its name from Petrarch's advancing old age, the *Seniles*. The polemical works, on the other hand, were located in relation to the major departure–arrivals of his life as juxtaposed pairs. Both the *Contra medicum* (1352–early 1360s), begun on the eve of the definitive leave-taking from Provence, and the *De ignorantia* (1367–71), composed toward the end of his life, were works of departure in the sense that both offered summative or valedictory discursive statements of Petrarch's intellectual, cultural, and spiritual position at crucial junctures in his life. Both works were accompanied by more expeditious and compact defenses of the poet's "arrivals," and more particularly his choice of residence: Milan in the *Contra quendam* (1355) and Italy in the *Contra eum* (1373).

Scholars have found it difficult, if not impossible, to supply a complete and adequate account of Petrarch's artistic development, largely due to philological obstacles, including uncertainties about the dating of numerous works, resulting from his method of repeatedly returning to revise his works over many years. Despite these challenges, it is clear that Petrarch's self-awareness about the competing impulses that inspired his writing informed his restless formal investigations of various genres in both prose and poetry. Ultimately, Petrarch would realize in artistic terms the resolution of these competing drives in the complementary relationship that characterized the culminating pairing of the life in writing, the *RVF* and the *Triumphi*. A development can thus be traced in the history of Petrarch's experiments with a wide variety of generic containers for his writing, both before and after the move to Italy, in both poetry and prose.

To begin with, the biographical prose of the *De viris* and the epic poetry of the *Africa* that followed shortly after it represented complementary impulses toward departure and arrival. The *De viris* constituted an open-ended work of serially reiterated biographical "departures" in the sense that each biography represented a new beginning, while the *Africa* was originally conceived in a complementary relation to the *De viris* as a destination. Perhaps the best illustration of this is found in *Epystole* II.18, where Petrarch draws a direct analogy between the renovation of the home he had purchased in Parma and the completion of the *Africa* during his second sojourn there. Petrarch would abandon his home in Parma following his last visit there in 1351, just as the poem, despite his claim in the "Letter to Posterity" (*Sen.* XVIII.1) that he had finished it while in Parma, remained unfinished.

The *De viris* never reached its destination either, though, unlike the *Africa*, Petrarch continued to return to it until the very end of his life. True to its original inspiration as a work of departure or movement, the *De viris* re-emerged on the eve of his departure for Italy, after having been set aside between 1343 and 1345 to make room on Petrarch's desk for the *Rerum memorandarum*. Sometime during the last sojourn in Provence (1351–53), the poet expanded the biographical program of the *De viris* to include the lives of illustrious men from "all-ages," including Biblical personages. The work later resurfaced in preparation for the definitive departure from this world at the end of Petrarch's life, and in response to the stimulus of his last lay patron, Francesco da Carrara, when it underwent yet another ideological overhaul and returned to its original Roman inspiration. The *De viris*, in any event, never found an autograph or even an apograph manuscript home.

The historical anecdotes that make up the *Rerum memorandarum* appear initially to have corresponded to the serial nature of the prose sections of the *De viris*, which it replaced for a time on Petrarch's writing table. On the other hand, the overarching architectural plan for the *Rerum memorandarum*, based on the four cardinal virtues, was more oriented toward arrival or stasis than the *De viris* it replaced had been. With the *Africa* reportedly completed and the *De viris* on hiatus, the *Rerum memorandarum* therefore focused within one work the impulses of departure and arrival that Petrarch had previously distributed between the other two. From this perspective, one can surmise that among other possible motivations for the abandonment of the *Rerum memorandarum* was Petrarch's realization that his artistic program had lost its equilibrium. In fact, Petrarch dropped the *Rerum memorandarum* shortly after his flight from Parma – under siege by the enemies of the Correggio family – on the night of February 23, 1345, never revising it, never publishing it, never mentioning it, never circulating any of its chapters or sections.

Work on the *De vita* in 1346 and the composition of its counterpart the *De otio* the following year signaled an abrupt turn away from the Roman historical inspiration of the earlier works in a more spiritual direction. This shift in the ideological orientation of Petrarch's project was no doubt inspired by recent events, including the death of King Robert of Naples, Petrarch's patron and the dedicatee of the *Africa*, and the entrance of Petrarch's brother Gherardo into a Carthusian monastery, both of which took place in 1343. The change in ideology corresponded to a return, in the pairing of the *De vita* and the *De otio*, to the earlier compositional equilibrium between departure and arrival that had characterized the initial combination of the *De viris* and the *Africa*.

Petrarch was evidently aware of the thematic and structural implications of this dynamic for the program of his works. He made a point of calling attention to the juxtaposition in an ostentatious or over-determined manner at the start of both the *De vita* and the *De otio*. The *De vita* opens with the celebration of the arrival of the dedicatee Philippe de Cabassoles to Vaucluse in 1346, while the *De otio* begins with a departure: that of the poet, following his visit to Gherardo's monastery in 1347. Thematically, as has been well observed, the point of the juxtaposition was to locate Petrarch's ideal of solitude between the world and the monastery; that is, "'distant' from every recognizable social construction."[8] Moreover, this dynamic alternation of theme is reversed in structural terms insofar as the *De vita* is the serially structured and more open-ended member of the pair, tending toward departure.

In fact, Petrarch returned to its composition repeatedly, and its trajectory of renewed departures is second only to that of the *De viris* in terms of the length of time for which it remained unfinished among Petrarch's Latin prose works, extending even to the last years of his life. The compact sermon-like discourses that make up the *De otio* were instead originally predisposed structurally to arrival or stasis, just as the monks in the monastery can be said to have already arrived in port. On the other hand, the *De otio* also proved to be the seedbed from which the Augustinian autobiographical project of the *Secretum* would grow, as Petrarch recounted in the last pages of the *De otio*: "Although it would take a huge volume to list my vacillations and filings, it became clear to me in that confused process that I needed to read St. Augustine's *Confessions*."[9]

The great autobiographical collections of Petrarch's maturity, in fact, were still to come. These were to issue from Franciscus's statement at the end of the *Secretum* that he would henceforward endeavor to "collect the scattered fragments of my soul, and I will diligently focus on myself alone" (*Secretum*, p. 147). Petrarch's discovery of ideal containers for the "fragments of the soul" came during the decisive period when he was preparing his definitive departure from Provence for Italy. The *Familiares, Epystole,* and *RVF* were all announced in *Fam.* I.1 (c. 1350), and each in its own way satisfied Petrarch's deepest need to strike a balance between the alternating impulses that were at the source of his writing. The composition of letters and poems corresponded to the movement of departure, while their subsequent transcription into the order of a book satisfied (at least provisionally) Petrarch's aspiration to arrival. The result was an ideal artistic compromise between the fluctuating impulses of his soul.

Between *RVF* and *Triumphus Eternitatis*

From around 1350 forward, Petrarch channeled the rhythms of his writing into the major epistolary collections, which, after the completion of the *De remediis*, became the central preoccupation of his life in writing in prose. As regards Petrarch's poetry, the story is more complicated. For Petrarch had never completely abandoned the epic ambitions of the *Africa*. He had continued to pursue them in the more congenial form of the *Bucolicum carmen*, where the epic number of twelve eclogues (rather than the Virgilian ten) signaled the persistence of the poet's epic aspirations (see Chapter 7). After his move to Italy, however, Petrarch more or less abandoned the original composition of Latin poetry.[10] The itinerary of Petrarch's poetic journey only subsequently reaches its destination in the vernacular epic *Triumphi*, which became a focus during the last fifteen years of his life, in structural and thematic counterpoint to the lyric *RVF*.

The compositional histories of the *RVF* and the *Triumphi* appear to have coincided from the time of the first redaction of the *RVF*, known as the Correggio form (named for its dedicatee Azzo da Correggio), between 1356 and 1358,[11] and of the earliest surviving dated manuscript annotations to the *Triumphi*, which date from 1357 (see Chapter 4). Completion of the two works (the composition of the *TE* and the copying out of the final form of the *RVF* in Vatican Latin manuscript 3195) took place in the last year of Petrarch's life. With few exceptions, scholars have read the final sequence of the *RVF* and the poem to the Virgin Mary that ends the book as a palinode, a recantatory repudiation of that Laura celebrated throughout the collection, and the end of the *Triumphi*, which features Laura glorified in heaven in a further palinode; that is, a retraction or correction of the *RVF*'s repudiation of her. The *RVF* and the *Triumphi* are instead complementary to one another. They represent the culmination of a life in writing that continually oscillated between contrary impulses. Petrarch concluded his poetic journey by situating himself one last time between departure and arrival; that is, poised between departure from this life in the *RVF* and arrival at the next in the *Triumphus Eternitatis*.

The *RVF* expressed the same impulse toward departure that had initially inspired the *De viris* at the beginning of his career, but formally resolved it in a manner that the *De viris* never managed to do. The ordering of the 366 poems of the *RVF* according to the liturgical calendar represented an epoch-making solution to the formal problem of how to gather the vernacular lyric fragments of the soul into a unified book. The *Triumphi* realized instead the epic impulse toward arrival that Petrarch had never entirely abandoned, even after giving up on ever completing the *Africa* following his move to

Italy, and which had not been fully satisfied by the *Bucolicum carmen*.[12] In the latter work, Petrarch had arranged twelve eclogues into a unified poem in a manner that foreshadowed the way he would later organize the twelve poems that make up the *Triumphi*, while signaling a move away from narrative as the primary characteristic of epic. The *Triumphi*, in fact, would take an unprecedented poetic form that Petrarch modeled on the traditions associated with the Roman triumph (itself a celebration of "epic" military victory). Petrarch stages in the *Triumphi* a series of increasingly climactic arrivals that culminate in the *TE*, and the poem proved to be the ultimate destination of Petrarch's restless search for a congenial epic vehicle. Together, the *RVF* and the *Triumphi* represent Petrarch's most original and culminating contributions in lyric and epic genres.

The history of the making of the *RVF* can also be understood in terms of the same alternations between departure and arrival that shaped the life and works.[13] The first redaction of the *RVF*, the Correggio form (1356–58), coincided with Petrarch's arrival and consolidation of his position in Italy at the court of the Visconti, as well as with the conclusion of the *De remediis* (1357), which was also dedicated to Azzo da Correggio. But, while the *De remediis* marked the achievement of the perspective of the Stoic Christian sage, in contrast to the ideologically unresolved ending of the *Secretum*, the Correggio form of the *RVF* still largely expressed in poetic terms the spiritual situation of the earlier *Secretum* (1347–53) in its tendency toward the repudiation of Franciscus's love for Laura, according to the programmatic proemial poem, probably written around 1350.

Thus, no sooner had Petrarch concluded the Correggio redaction than he re-opened the work. Both the Chigi (1359–63) and the Giovanni (1366–67) forms of the *RVF* variously reflect moments of renewed departure in terms of the book's compositional history. Both forms had the effect of leaving unresolved the ideological dilemma posed by the contrast between a stilno-vistic love for Laura and its Augustinian repudiation. The new departure of the Chigi *RVF* and the evident attention to the *Triumphi* that begins to be documented during the same period were, one suspects, both related to the discussions that Petrarch and Boccaccio had been having about the signifi-cance of Dante's vernacular literary legacy during the 1350s. These came to a point in 1359 when Petrarch addressed a long letter to Boccaccio in which he asserted, not very persuasively, that he did not envy Dante's reputation in the vernacular and that he was not influenced by him (*Fam.* XXI.15).

Petrarch's dissimulation regarding Dante's influence in this letter corre-sponds with his putative disregard for the vernacular as expressed through-out his writings in favor of Latin. Yet, both the massive presence of Dante's influence in Petrarch's vernacular poetry and his continuing investment in writing such poetry even to the end of his life belie the ostensibly exclusive championing of Latinity that became associated with the Humanist Petrarch. In fact, as mentioned earlier, Petrarch had more or less abandoned poetic composition in Latin after he moved to Italy, when original poetic composition in the vernacular appears to have replaced it at the center of his concerns. Boccaccio was in fact the copyist of the Chigi form of the *RVF* that has come down to us, and his exchanges with Petrarch about Dante appear to have been responsible for stimulating Petrarch to vie with Dante in the arena of vernacular poetry from the later 1350s to the end of his life, particularly as regards the poet's ambition to write an epic utilizing the *terza rima* form that Dante had invented for the *Commedia*. Petrarch clearly aimed in the *Triumphi* to supplant the *Commedia* as the modern vernacular exemplar of the epic genre.

For its part, the Chigi form of the *RVF* left still unresolved the ideological conflict between love for the creature Laura and love for the Creator, while also leaving uncertain its ending in formal terms. An important signal that the book had lost its way was the last poem of the first part of the Chigi redaction, the famous shipwreck poem *RVF* 189, "Passa la nave mia." While the relatively brief additions to both parts effected by the Giovanni form somewhat corrected the course of the Chigi, a clear turn toward the resolution of the ideological and formal challenges Petrarch faced only began to appear when the author personally took over the completion of Vatican Latin manuscript from his copyist Giovanni Malpaghini and, beginning in 1367, added poems that suggested that his port had come into sight. The resolution of the *RVF* ultimately involved a return to the original ideological setting of the Correggio form's turn away from Laura and to the book's original function of preparing for a departure, though this time not from Provence for Italy but from this world for the next.

As we saw earlier in regard to the *Testamentum*, however, Petrarch impulsively sought to remain in movement to the very end of his life, and even, as it were, post mortem. The last thirty-one poems of the *RVF* were accordingly renumbered even after Petrarch had finished copying them into Vatican Latin manuscript 3195, possibly during the last days of his life. By indicating in the margins of the manuscript another ordering of the final poems, Petrarch left posterity two different possible endings to consider, just as he left it to his heirs to decide his ultimate resting place. To locate himself between places in this way was to claim for himself a position analogous to the eternal present of his writing, the practice through which he sought to escape the limitations of time and space.

While the compositional history of the *Triumphi* is less well documented than that of the *RVF*, the work did achieve completion as regards its principal

THEODORE J. CACHEY, JR.

parts. The conclusion of the *Triumphi*, in particular of its last part, the *TE*, represented the arrival of Petrarch's project at its destination. The *TE* completed the dynamic of departure and arrival of the life in writing and crowned the artistic career with the vision of an arrival at the next life, in which the poet would be reunited with Laura. To turn to the Virgin at the end of the *RVF* was as appropriate to Petrarch on the eve of departure from this life as was the re-unification with Laura upon arrival in the next envisioned by the *TE*. The final resolution of the *RVF*, viewed from this perspective, was arguably facilitated by the parallel development of the *Triumphi* in counterpoint to it. It became possible to conclude the *RVF* in terms of a departure from this life once the arrival in the next had more clearly come into poetic view in the *Triumphi*. In the end, in the complementary movements of the *RVF* and the *Triumphi*, as along the entire course of the life in writing, we find that Petrarch sought and ultimately achieved an unstable equilibrium between departure and arrival that expressed the desire both to establish a place for the self in this world and at the same time to transcend it.

NOTES

1 The unfinished draft breaks off at this point.
2 Theodor Adorno, *Minima Moralia: Reflections from a Damaged Life*, trans. E. F. N. Jephcott (London: Verso, 1978), 33.
3 Ernest Hatch Wilkins, *Life of Petrarch* (Chicago, IL: University of Chicago Press, 1961), 19.
4 On Petrarch and the metaphorics of travel, see Thomas M. Greene, "Petrarch Viator: The Displacements of Heroism," *Yearbook of English Studies* 12 (1982): 35–57, as well as Theodore J. Cachey, Jr., "*Peregrinus (quasi) ubique*': Petrarca e la storia del viaggio," *Intersezioni: Rivista di storia delle idee* 17.3 (1997): 369–384.
5 Remo Ceserani, "'Petrarca': il nome come auto-reinvenzione poetica," *Quaderni petrarcheschi*, 4 (1987): 121–137; Corrado Bologna, "PetrArca petroso," *Critica del testo* VI. 1 (2003): 367–420.
6 George Gordon, Lord Byron, "Childe Harold's Pilgrimage," IV, xxx. 1–3, in *Lord Byron, The Major Works*, ed. Jerome J. McGann (Oxford and New York: Oxford University Press, 2000), 157.
7 Ronald L. Martinez, "The Book without a Name: Petrarch's Open Secret (*Liber sine nomine*)," in *Petrarch: A Critical Guide to the Complete Works*, eds. Victoria Kirkham and Armando Maggi (Chicago, IL: University of Chicago Press, 2009), 291–299 (293).
8 Armando Maggi, "'You Will Be My Solitude': Solitude as Prophecy," in *Petrarch: A Critical Guide*, Kirkham and Maggi, 179–195 (193).
9 Susan S. Schearer, ed. and trans., and Ronald G. Witt, intr., *Petrarch on Religious Leisure* (New York: Italica Press, 2002), 46.

10 While Petrarch continued to revise the *Bucolicum carmen* and the *Epystole*, these works were more or less complete when he arrived in Milan in 1353. Petrarch makes a point of saying that he had given up writing poetry in the "Letter to Posterity" composed around 1350: "Yet in the course of time I abandoned the latter [poetry], when I found delight in sacred letters . . ." (*Sen.* XVIII.1).

11 No manuscript survives. The existence of the form is based on annotations found in Vatican Latin manuscript 3196 and internal evidence.

12 Proposed early dates for the initiation of the *Triumphi* correspond roughly to Petrarch's abandonment of the *Africa*.

13 Editors' note: Theodore J. Cachey, Jr., "From Shipwreck to Port: *Rvf* 189 and the Making of the 'Canzoniere,'" *MLN*, Vol. 120, No. 1 (2005): 30–49. For a detailed review of the debate concerning the "making of the *RVF*," see Chapter 4.

2

HANNAH CHAPELLE WOJCIEHOWSKI

Petrarch and his friends

Petrarch was a man of many friends. Gifted with a highly social nature and a unique talent for creating and maintaining relationships, Petrarch enjoyed an active social life – a skill that helped him gain recognition as one of the premier writers and intellectuals of fourteenth-century Europe. At the same time, he was strongly inclined to the solitary pursuits of writing and study, spending months or years at a time in relative seclusion. As a consequence of these conflicting impulses, and also out of necessity, Petrarch conducted many of his friendships through letters. His carefully constructed epistolary collections provide insight into the network of friends and acquaintances, patrons and rulers whom he cultivated unremittingly throughout his life. As I consider how the writer's social network developed and furthered his career as a writer, I will also track the emergent and exceptionally influential theory of Humanist friendship articulated in his letters.

Making friends may have been a survival skill for Petrarch, who moved around frequently as a child and an adult. At the core of his social network were the friends he made as a child and a young man. Among them was Guido Sette, a boy close to Petrarch's age who had moved to Carpentras, France, near the newly established (1305) papal court at Avignon, at about the same time as Petrarch's family, in political exile from Florence. "We were immediately united in friendship," Petrarch wrote in a late-life letter to Sette, "as is normal at that age, but it was to last until the end" (*Sen.* X.2). It was Sette's uncle, Petrarch noted, who had taken the two boys on a horseback-riding trip into the mountains around Avignon, showing them the headwaters of the Sorgue river, an exquisite, isolated retreat known as the Vaucluse, where Petrarch would ultimately spend several years of his life. The two would continue their friendship during their student years at the University of Montpellier and then at the University of Bologna. Sette, who would eventually become the Archbishop of Genoa, remained a close friend of Petrarch's until the former's death in 1367.

While studying law at Bologna, Petrarch befriended several fellow students, including Matteo Longhi, Luca Cristiani, and Mainardo Accursio. There, he also made an important contact with a powerful and charismatic Roman nobleman, Giacomo Colonna, who would play a pivotal role in his life and career. When Petrarch's father died in 1326, Petrarch abandoned the legal studies imposed on him by ser Petracco and returned to Avignon, where he chose to become a cleric, taking the tonsure and perhaps minor orders.[1] At that time, Giacomo Colonna became Petrarch's first patron, providing a small stipend, after deceptive lawyers deprived Petrarch and his brother Gherardo of their inheritance, which enabled him to devote himself to the study of classical literature and moral philosophy.

In the summer of 1330, Giacomo, who had recently been named Bishop of Lombez in Gascony, hosted Petrarch at his new home in the northern foothills of the Pyrenees. He had also invited two other young guests, who would become Petrarch's life-long friends. The first was Ludwig van Kempen, who hailed from what is today the Belgian province of Limberg, and who was a chanter in the chapel of Cardinal Giovanni Colonna, older brother of Giacomo. The second was Lello di Pietro Stefano dei Tosetti, who grew up in Rome and whose family was closely associated with the Colonna clan, one of Rome's ruling families. Petrarch gave these new friends affectionate, classicizing nicknames: Ludwig became "Socrates," after the Greek philosopher, and Lello became "Laelius," an interlocutor in Cicero's dialogue *De amicitia* (*On Friendship*), and celebrated friend of Scipio Africanus.

Upon returning to Avignon that fall, Petrarch was taken into service by Cardinal Giovanni Colonna, as the chaplain of his household. Despite his repeated condemnations of the papal court in Avignon, Petrarch benefited greatly from that appointment and from living near the court, which was the hub of an international network of influential prelates, statesmen, and intellectuals. Petrarch described this network in a late-life letter: "[B]eing known for some sort of reputation, however false, as a man of genius, but much more for the favor of such eminent lords, I had formed various friendships here and there, because I was in a place where people assembled from every part of the world" (*Sen.* XVI.1).

Petrarch's contact with a wide array of individuals and social groups in Avignon reveals a late-medieval phenomenon of social mobility – a phenomenon first explained by the sociologist Georg Simmel, the father of social network theory. "As the individual leaves his established position within *one* primary group," Simmel wrote, "he comes to stand at a point at which many groups 'intersect.'"[2] Such was the case with Petrarch in Avignon, who occupied a physical and intellectual space where multiple social circles crossed and overlapped. Making friends or acquaintances with persons of high status or rank was a possibility within this network – one that Petrarch exploited to the fullest degree.

In the same letter, Petrarch spoke of having begged friends who had left Avignon to send him books from their new locales. Rare and valuable information, conveyed in the manuscripts of classical authors and by the people who exchanged them, flowed through his network from distant regions of Europe and beyond. Petrarch, in turn, circulated the information in his writings, cultivating his own fame as a man of letters. He promulgated ideas that he had gathered from these texts – those of Cicero, Seneca, Virgil, Horace, and many others. These activities – the nourishing of friendships, often at a great distance, paired with the pursuit of revitalized classical culture – would provide a model for the networks of scholars that emerged in the late Middle Ages and Renaissance.

Petrarch served Cardinal Colonna until 1337, when he acquired a house in the remote Vaucluse. He remained intermittently in the cardinal's service for another decade, on call, as it were, while living in his mountain hideaway. These were years of consolidation for Petrarch, who was able to devote large amounts of time to his poetry and other writings. Though he was isolated in the Vaucluse, he befriended the bishop of the local diocese, Philippe de Cabassoles, who would remain a life-long friend, and to whom Petrarch would dedicate his 1346 treatise *De vita solitaria*.

Petrarch's fame continued to grow, despite his relative solitude, and on September 1, 1340, he claims to have received two distinguished invitations – one from the University of Paris and the other from the Roman Senate – to be crowned as poet laureate, an honor rarely, if ever, bestowed since Roman antiquity. Opting for the Roman coronation, Petrarch sailed in February 1341 from Marseilles to Naples with his friend Azzo da Correggio. There he was examined by King Robert the Wise of Naples, his sponsor for the coronation, who hosted him in the city and conducted a formal examination on the nature and purpose of poetry, certifying him for the honor he was about to receive.[3] While in Naples, Petrarch made three new friends, Niccolò d'Alife, Giovanni Barrili, and Barbato da Sulmona, gentlemen attached to Robert's court, who would afterwards remain close to the poet.

On April 8, Petrarch received the laurel crown in Rome before a large crowd and delivered a coronation oration (*Coll. laur.*). Petrarch had become one of the most famous and sought-after private citizens of his age, a reputation that served as a testament both to his brilliance as a man of letters and to his extensive and highly effective network of well-placed friends. At this triumphant moment in his career, Petrarch found himself in a position to exert considerable influence on his own behalf and that of others, as a celebrated public intellectual and, moreover, a public friend.

A chance discovery five years later would inspire Petrarch to take his role as public friend to new heights. While visiting the Cathedral Library of Verona in 1345, Petrarch came across some little-known manuscripts of letters by Cicero and decided to compile a collection of his own letters to friends in imitation. This collection, which would ultimately be called the *Familiares* (*Letters on Familiar Matters*), consisted of letters that he had written over the years, which he had copied and would later carefully select and re-edit.

Cicero's letters also provided an image of the statesman that was full of political and psychological contradictions, an image strongly at odds with the one that had come down through the centuries. Petrarch learned that Cicero had been more involved in the political intrigues of his day than his other writings had indicated, and he was surprised by the disjunction between Cicero's theories and his practices. He later wrote Cicero a letter (as if he were a living contemporary and friend of the poet), in which he upbraided the Roman philosopher for his over-involvement in political infighting (*Fam.* XXIV.3).

Ironically, a similar fate awaited Petrarch, who would soon become involved in a failed political uprising in Rome that would permanently rupture his relations with the Colonna family. In 1347, Petrarch publically supported the rise to power of Cola di Rienzo, a charismatic but emotionally unstable leader who attempted to oust the ruling clans of medieval Rome, including the Colonna family, and re-establish the Roman republic. In that same year, Petrarch left the Vaucluse, possibly with the intention of joining Cola in Rome, though the floundering regime collapsed while he was in transit.

It was not only this conflict, however, but also a far more devastating catastrophe that shattered the world that Petrarch had previously known. In October of 1347, twelve Genoese galleys returning from the Crimea carried the Black Death to the Sicilian port of Messina. By the end of 1348 it would reduce the population of Europe by as much as one half. Many people who had been important to Petrarch died that year, including his former patron Cardinal Colonna and Laura, the woman who was the inspiration for the idealized beloved in Petrarch's *RVF*. The terrifying epidemic devastated Europe and many other parts of the world, emptying whole towns and cities of their inhabitants.

In the years immediately following the advent of the plague, Petrarch wrote poignantly about the many friends whose lives had been cut short. New and continuing friendships would serve, in part, as a compensation for these devastating losses. Friendships would also help reconstitute a social order torn apart by the plague and by the large-scale betrayals of social bonds that had resulted from it. Petrarch envisioned the possibility of creating a community of surviving friends, inviting some of them to come and live with him (*Fam.* VIII.3–5).[4] This plan disintegrated in 1349, when robbers outside of Florence attacked two of those invited, Luca Cristiani and Mainardo Accursio, old friends from the University of Bologna, and Mainardo was killed (*Fam.* VIII.10).

During the post-plague years, the project of the *Familiares* was repurposed. Petrarch began to imagine a virtual community of both the living and the dead. The ethical imperative of the collection emerged with particular force in those years, as Petrarch sought to make sense of the suffering he had witnessed and to redefine an intellectual community ravaged by the epidemic.[5] He did so, in part, by articulating for himself and for others the crucial value of friendship in civilized societies, presenting his letters as a kind of advice manual for future readers.

As it turned out, another emerging young writer had a similar idea, framing a set of one hundred short stories within a narrative about the social chaos created by the plague. That collection, the *Decameron*, would highlight the power of stories to re-establish order and civility. The writer, Giovanni Boccaccio, became Petrarch's closest friend of later life, a protégé and a support to the poet during his old age. After first exchanging letters, Petrarch met him in 1350 while passing through Florence on a Jubilee-year pilgrimage to Rome.

A great admirer and biographer of Petrarch, though not yet a friend, Boccaccio found out about the famous writer's plans and met him upon his arrival in Florence.[6] He invited Petrarch to stay with him – an invitation that the latter gladly accepted. Like the poet Dante, Petrarch's father had been exiled from Florence, and Boccaccio, along with other new friends, wanted to repatriate Petrarch and to offer him a chair at the brand-new University of Florence. The older poet, while not unappreciative, decided to return to the Vaucluse instead. Having severed ties with the Colonna, however, Petrarch ultimately moved to Milan, accepting the patronage of another powerful clan, the Visconti. Boccaccio was appalled by Petrarch's decision to receive support from Milan's despotic rulers, who were the sworn enemies of the Florentine Republic, expressing his sense of betrayal in a letter to the older writer.[7] However, despite their often intense conflicts and rivalries, their friendship, documented in more than two dozen of Petrarch's surviving letters, would continue to grow through the years. In his will, Petrarch left Boccaccio a special bequest: "fifty gold florins, for a cold-weather robe for nighttime study and meditations" (*Testamentum* 20; 4: 1352 [my trans.]) – a testament to their long and affectionate friendship.

As the preceding examples suggest, Petrarch construed the bond of friendship as founded on the shared love of knowledge, together with the disinterested pursuit of virtue. Though influenced by Christian models of spiritual friendship, Petrarch was primarily drawn to classical ideals of friendship, most notably those formulated by Cicero in his *De amicitia* and *De officiis* (*On Duties*). Composed in 44 B.C.E., the *De amicitia* presents a characteristically Roman ideal of *amicitia vera*, or true friendship. Friendship is, first of all, a form of love. "For it is love [*amor*]," Cicero writes, "from which the word 'friendship' [*amicitia*] is derived, that leads to the establishing of goodwill."[8] Friends are attracted to the virtue of the other and help each other perfect this. Selfless and self-sufficient, friends never seek friendship for their own material gain, even if there are differences in status between them (xx. 71–73). Friends give and receive advice freely, and they never compromise their virtue or honesty out of a misplaced sense of obligation or duty to the other. True friendship is rare, and its bonds unite two or at most a very few people (v. 20).

Cicero lived in a patriarchal world, and he considered friendship a masculine virtue. The *De amicitia* declares that women, though strongly inclined to friendship, are by nature more dependent than men; hence, their friendships lack the necessary self-sufficiency of true – that is, male – friendship, as do those of weak, poor, or otherwise dependent men (xiii. 46–47). Petrarch also lived in a patriarchal world, and he embraced Cicero's masculinist and elite model of friendship whole-heartedly.

Though in some sense a private bond, Ciceronian friendship simultaneously possesses a civic dimension: "[I]f you should take the bond of goodwill out of the universe no house or city could stand, nor would even the tillage of the fields abide. If that statement is not clear, then you may understand how great is the power of friendship and of concord from a consideration of the results of enmity and disagreement" (vii. 23). The survival of the republic depends on the integrity of the friendships of its citizens, and especially its leaders – a point that registered strongly with Petrarch. True friendship, exemplary in every sense, lasts beyond the absence or death of one or both members, and inspires the admiration and emulation of later generations (iv. 13–15).

In his post-plague letters, Petrarch envisioned love and loyalty for his friends that transcended separation, death, and his own loneliness. Writing to Zanobi da Strada from the Vaulcuse in 1353, he declared:

> [H]ere I gather all the friends I now have or did have, not only those who have proved themselves through intimate contact and who have lived with me, but also those who died many centuries ago, known to me only through their writings, wherein I marvel at their accomplishments and their spirits or at their customs and lives or at their eloquence and genius. I gather them from every land and every age in this narrow valley, conversing with them more willingly than with those who think they are alive because they see traces of their stale breath in the frosty air. I thus wander free and unconcerned, alone with such companions; I am where I wish to be. *(Fam. XV.3)*

Petrarch's paradoxical words call to mind those of the modern French philosopher Jacques Derrida, who identified the constitutive role of absence within friendship. "[S]urviving," he wrote, "is at once the essence, the origin and the possibility, the condition of possibility of friendship; it is the grieved act of loving."[9] To paraphrase: the love for the friend is actualized by absence, whether of that moment or a future one, and that absence must always be mourned, even from the beginning of the friendship. In the case of "friends" who had died centuries before Petrarch came into the world – friends such as Cicero – physical presence was never a possible condition of friendship, while absence was the constitutive principle.

Petrarch articulated this paradox even more clearly in a late letter to Boccaccio mourning the death of their mutual friend "Simonides" (Francesco Nelli): "Though departed, he is present, and never more so than since his departure. For before his end, I used to anticipate his absence, but since death has snatched him from me, I do not think now that he is about to return; yet he has returned, and I take comfort in his imagined presence" *(Sen. III.1)*. This letter foregrounds two themes that run through many of the letters, especially those written after 1348 and again in the *Seniles* – namely, the work of mourning and its definitive role in Petrarch's attachments to others. As Petrarch would write in *Seniles* I.3, to grow old is "to die many times with your friends' deaths."

Yet, while absent friends could be called to mind as virtual presences, Petrarch simultaneously recognized that conflicts between friends might be harder to wish away. When Socrates and Laelius had a falling out (supposedly because Socrates had spoken badly of Laelius to Petrarch in a letter), Petrarch was saddened by their conflict and begged Laelius to reconcile with their friend. Seeking to put Laelius's suspicions to rest, he wrote in the summer of 1358 the following words of admonishment:

> True friends, among whom the name of Laelius was always outstanding and illustrious, turn a deaf ear to accusations, rejecting everything that conflicts with true friendship. Yet it is not enough to reject falsehood; in this one matter

is the distinction between true and false unacceptable. Whatever is said against a friend's faithfulness (*amici fidem*) must not be believed, for when the decision has been made to be friends with someone, you must entertain no doubt about the friendship, otherwise the foundation of friendship, mutual trust (*fides*), will be forever shaky.

(*Fam.* XX.13)

For Petrarch, friendship was the deepest of all relationships, save for that between humanity and God. Friendship rivaled family ties, or indeed encompassed the strongest of those ties (as between Petrarch and his brother Gherardo), superseding even marriage, which was, in the eyes of Petrarch and of most people in his era, a qualitatively different arrangement requiring its own forms of faith. Friendship was not a bond that a person could casually reject, as Petrarch explained in that same letter to Laelius: "Friendship is a great and divine matter, but it is simple and needs careful deliberation only once; before loving, you must choose, and when the choice is made, you must love, choosing after you love is too late" (Ibid.). Like a marriage – only more so – friendship as Petrarch conceived of it entailed an irrevocable commitment to another human being, a commitment founded on mutual trust and good faith. With these arguments, Laelius came around, ultimately re-embracing his friend of twenty-eight years.

The great Petrarch biographer Ernest Hatch Wilkins identified one dominant trait in Petrarch's personality: "a constant desire to love and to be loved." This was a desire "that manifested itself not only in his love for Laura, but also in his love for members of his family and, most distinctively, in his love for his friends."[10] "Never," Wilkins wrote, "did any man form and cultivate a richer store of friendships; never did any man draw deeper devotion from his friends, or maintain a deeper devotion to them."[11] Most contemporary scholars would agree that Petrarch had an unusual capacity for friendship, even while recognizing that he could be self-aggrandizing and opportunistic, or less than honest with himself and others.

Petrarch's writings on friendship would become widely influential, particularly among later generations of Humanist scholars. Unlike Cicero, who considered perfect friendship a bond between a very few people, Petrarch represented his own network of friends, both intimate and distant, as enormous. He seemed to enjoy being "best friends" with many people and counselor to the notables of his age, like the Holy Roman Emperor Charles IV, though in certain petulant letters of later life (for example, *Sen.* VIII.2) he complained about his lack of real friends and raged against his detractors. Yet the public, high-profile aspects of his friendships existed in an uneasy balance with his need for solitude. Despite his recognition of the civic component of Ciceronian friendship, benefiting the state as well as individuals, Petrarch generally avoided public service and public life, and his attempts at civic friendship, such as his relationship with Cola di Rienzo, were often disastrous. Petrarchan friendship was bookish, reflective, and melancholic, and oriented toward the shared pursuit of knowledge.

In a world ruptured by wars, power struggles, violent conflicts, and especially the upheavals resulting from the Black Death, friendship served as a psychic oasis for Petrarch, a corrective for what was wrong with the world. Divided loyalties, conflicts, and ambivalence sometimes made friendships complicated, too, but Petrarch sought to work around such problems, in most cases maintaining his attachments to those he loved and cared about. *Fides* was paramount in those attachments, and it was their guarantor. Finally, Petrarch had an intuitive understanding of how to make friends and influence people, using his social network to advance his career and reputation, as well as those of his friends. He did not see friendship and social networking as mutually exclusive spheres, but as overlapping and interconnected domains. Petrarch sometimes fell short of his own friendship ideals, but he nevertheless articulated them clearly, and these ideals serve as one of Petrarch's principal legacies to readers today. Like the heartfelt bequest of a robe to his dear friend Boccaccio, Petrarch's friendships serve to remind us of the warmth and love provided by our friends, and by us to them.

NOTES

1 For Petrarch's biography, see Wilkins, *Life of Petrarch*, as well as Ugo Dotti, *Vita di Petrarca* (Rome: Laterza, 1987 [1991]).

2 Georg Simmel, *Conflict and The Web of Group-Affiliations*, trans. Kurt H. Wolff and Beinhard Bendix (New York: Free Press, 1955), 141. See also Hannah Wojciehowski, *Group Identity in the Renaissance World* (Cambridge: Cambridge University Press, 2011), 17–24.

3 Most of what we know of the event comes from Petrarch's own letters, esp. *Fam.* book IV.

4 Renee Neu Watkins, "Petrarch and the Black Death: From Fear to Monuments," *Studies in the Renaissance* Vol. XIX (New York: Renaissance Society of America, 1972), 196–223; Hannah Wojciehowski, "Francis Petrarch: First Modern Friend," *Texas Studies in Language and Literature* 47, No. 4 (2005): 269–298.

5 Nancy S. Struever, "Petrarchan Ethics: Inventing a Practice," in *Theory as Practice: Ethical Inquiry in the Renaissance* (Chicago, IL: University of Chicago Press, 1992), 14–32.

6 Sometime between 1341 and 1347, Boccaccio had penned a biography of Petrarch entitled *De vita et moribus domini Francisci Petracchi de Fiorentia*.

7 *Epistola* 10, in Boccaccio, *Epistole e Lettere*, ed. Ginetta Auzzas, in *Tutte le Opere di Giovanni Boccaccio*, Vol. 5, pt. 1, ed. Vittore Branca (Verona: Mondadori, 1992), 574–83; 790–93.
8 Cicero, *De Senectute. De Amicitia. De Divinatione*, trans. William Armistead Falconer (1923; Cambridge: Harvard University Press, 2001), viii. 26.
9 Jacques Derrida, *Politics of Friendship* (1994; New York: Verso, 1997), 14.
10 Wilkins, *Life of Petrarch*, 251.
11 Ibid., 252.

PART II

Petrarch's works: Italian

With some multi-lingual late-medieval and early-Renaissance writers – for example, Dante and Boccaccio – writings in "official" Latin and the upstart Italian vernacular cannot truly be read in isolation from one another, because of multiple overlaps in linguistic, thematic, and formal concerns, not to mention strong cross-referencing among works and the similar ways in which works in both languages tend to draw on the great repositories of classical and medieval culture. With Petrarch, it is easier to keep his writings in the two languages separate, because Petrarch himself did so. In his relatively few comments on the nascent vernacular, he tended to trivialize it compared to Latin, particularly because of the ignorance of the "vulgar herd" that he believed constituted its primary readership. Nonetheless, he continued revising and expanding his Italian poetic oeuvre from very early in his life to shortly before his death, although by contrast with the overwhelming quantities of work in Latin, his Italian poetic production was severely limited (and his prose virtually non-existent, in sharp contrast with the other two "Corone"). And yet, within a little more than a century after his death, his Italian works, above all the *Canzoniere*, would dramatically outstrip the Latin in both popularity and influence, especially with the rise of cosmopolitan court culture and the widespread adoption of print for the circulation of texts. And today, outside of a relatively small academic circle, he is known *only* for his role in codifying the language of love lyric, and the macro- and micro-structures that would contain it, for the Western tradition down to the present.

This part of our book treats Petrarch's two primary works in the vernacular. The first is the poetry collection popularly known as the *Canzoniere*, though titled by Petrarch himself, in Latin, *Rerum vulgarium fragmenta* (Fragments of Vernacular Things), with a probable echo of the very first line of the collection, "Voi ch'ascoltate in rime sparse il suono" ("You who listen to the sound of scattered rhymes"). The final version prepared by Petrarch shortly before his death has served as the basis of all modern critical editions.

It consists of 366 poems, including 317 sonnets, eleven short ballads and madrigals, twenty-nine multi-stanzaic canzoni of varying lengths, eight sestinas, and one double sestina. While most poems center on Petrarch's love for Laura, beginning with his "innamoramento" with her on Good Friday 1327, there are a scattering of some twenty compositions on political and other themes. The overall arrangement is ostensibly chronological, and the passage of the years since his first sight of Laura is intermittently indicated in a number of so-called "anniversary poems." Petrarch marked one definite break in the sequence, between poems 263 and 264, which almost, but not quite, coincides with Laura's death from the plague in 1348 (first reported in poem 267). Peter Hainsworth presents a richly comprehensive introduction to the forms and themes of the final version of the *RVF* (Chapter 3), while Luca Marcozzi describes the compositional process by which it came into being (Chapter 4). Ullrich Langer then offers detailed analyses of a few individual poems (Chapter 5), providing an original interpretation of what Mazzotta calls Petrarch's "language of the self."

The earliest poems in the *Canzoniere* date from the beginning of the 1330s, and the first indication that they were being gathered into a collection comes later in the same decade. The second of Petrarch's primary works in Italian, by contrast, the ascending, palinodic sequence of six long poems known as the *Triumphi*, was likely begun only around 1352 (with the "Triumph of Love" and the "Triumph of Fame"), and concluded in the last year of Petrarch's life (with the "Triumph of Eternity"). The final order of the *Triumphi*, with each successive personification triumphing over its immediate precursor, is: "Triumph of [Human] Love" (*TC*), "Triumph of Chastity" (*TP*), "Triumph of Death" (*TM*), "Triumph of Fame" (*TF*), "Triumph of Time" (*TT*), and "Triumph of Eternity" (*TE*). As Zygmunt Barański discusses in Chapter 6, the *Triumphi* were written in the *terza rima* scheme invented by Dante for the *Commedia* (a-b-a-b-c-b-c-d-c-d-e-d-e-f-e...), and earlier adapted by Boccaccio. Not treated in this volume are the so-called "rime stravaganti" ("wandering rhymes"), poems omitted from the final version of the *Canzoniere* for one reason or another. The number of such poems legitimately attributable to Petrarch remains contested, with a minimum of twenty-one securely attached to him.[1] There is also one extant letter written in Italian (as against the 638 in Latin).

NOTE

[1] For a concise overview of the editorial situation, see Justin Steinberg, "Petrarch's Damned Poetry and the Poetics of Exclusion," in *Petrarch: A Critical Guide*, Kirkham and Maggi, 85–100.

3

PETER HAINSWORTH

Rerum vulgarium fragmenta: structure and narrative

The *RVF*, popularly known as the *Canzoniere*, is unusual, if not quite unique, as a collection of lyric poems. Looked at as a whole, it seems to tell a story – the story of Petrarch's love for the woman he calls Laura – even if many narrative elements remain uncertain. At the same time, the story is not everything. Petrarch seems to encourage us also to read his poems much as we would other collections (for instance, Horace's *Odes*), treating some as going together for formal or thematic reasons, others as contrasting with the poems around them or with the tenor of the whole, and happily connecting poems that are set far apart from each other in the collection and perhaps in time. Most readers have probably managed intuitively to reconcile this piecemeal approach with a narrative one. However, once we start trying to define the narrative in any depth and asking how it relates to the arrangement of poems, we find ourselves running into difficulties, and usually disagreeing about how to solve them. On the whole, general accounts of the collection give priority to elucidating the story and the psychological and spiritual issues it raises. Here, I wish to pick out its defining features rather than explore its nuances, and to explore how these relate to the overall organization of forms and themes.

In so doing, I shall inevitably be taking up a particular critical approach. Petrarch's own manuscript of the poems amounts to an authorial edition, even if it is one that he might have gone on to tinker with had he had the chance. So we know where he positioned the poems in the collection, or, in the case of the last thirty-one, the positions he intended them to have. What is less clear is how much attention he expected his readers to pay to the arrangement, let alone whether it has an identifiable and meaningful structure. He himself provides no clear indications inside or outside the collection. The "fragments" of the title suggest disorder and lack of completeness, and the opening poem supports this, with its reference in line 1 to the "rime sparse" ("scattered rhymes") that are to follow. One approach has been to take him more or less at his word and to argue that, though groups of poems may cohere, overall there is no organization beyond chronological succession and the variety pointed to by the "vario stile" ("varied style") mentioned later in the first poem.[1] At the opposite extreme is the view that the title and the scattered rhymes are self-effacing ploys, which the serious reader is expected to go beyond.[2] I shall argue here that the collection combines order and disorder, narrative and formal patterning, without achieving or even wanting to achieve a totalizing synthesis of all its elements.[3]

We tend to forget how strange the story is. It centers around three signal events. The first two – falling in love and Laura's death – are made to parallel each other. Petrarch sees Laura for the first time on April 6, 1327, at the first hour. She dies on the same day at the same time in 1348.[4] The third event is inevitable but still to happen at the collection's end: the definitive abandonment of earthly love, either during life or at the moment of death. Apart from these crucial events, there are plenty of incidents, such as Laura leaving Avignon for a while (*RVF* 41–43), sailing along the Rhône (225), and receiving the attentions of an important visitor (238). Petrarch has her portrait painted by Simone Martini (77–78) and himself goes off on journeys such as the one through the Ardennes in 1333 (176–177; see also *Fam.* I.5), sees and talks with Laura, and gazes on her in rapture. At one point, he hangs on to a glove Laura has left with him by mistake (*RVF* 199–201). There are many other incidents, often spread over more than one poem, that we can chart in their due chronological sequence if we are so inclined. None of these changes the basic situation.

Nor does the love itself develop. Intense from the start, it continues unabated, in spite or because of not being physically consummated, over the next twenty-one years, with only a couple of moments when release seems possible (55 and 80). Moments of exhilaration and rapt contemplation alternate and merge with moments of dejection, frustration, and despair. When Laura dies in 1348, love refuses to die with her and continues for at least another ten years. From the start, Petrarch repeatedly recognizes that time is passing and marks the number of years elapsed since he fell in love in a number of "anniversary poems,"[5] but he never manages to convert into action his awareness of the risks that he is running to his immortal soul, even when Laura is dead. Either he is entrammelled in his memories of the living woman or, as happened also during her lifetime, he persuades himself that love for her is a morally and spiritually positive force in his life. In the last poems (361–366), with death coming closer, the need to turn to higher things becomes imperative. The last poem of all is a prayer to the Virgin for help and a last acknowledgment of wasted time and emotion. All in all, the story as a story is primarily one of stasis, and as such more Beckettian than

Augustinian. Only intensification of awareness and fuller articulation of the issues distinguish the later years from the earlier.

The problems the story raises have often been seen as ones of truthfulness or accuracy: Petrarch is always free with biographical facts, and in the *RVF* he adapts both these and the character of his inner life to the conventions of medieval love literature (see Chapter 12). The difficulties have not been resolved, but they seem less significant than they did for the literary interpretation of the text. Instead of focusing on biographical reality, we might think of the story as a kind of fiction, an autobiographical novel perhaps. But, however configured, terms such as "autobiography" and "novel" easily create confusion. As a collection of lyric poems, the *RVF* is constitutionally different from St. Augustine's *Confessions*, or Proust's *Recherche*, or Wordsworth's *Prelude*, even if it shares their concern with the power of memory to evoke and remake the past. Lacking the kind of linking commentary that gives narrative cohesion to the poems of Dante's *Vita nova*, it can only evoke the story in which it grounds its own authenticity, rather than tell it. Within the collection, temporal and narrative relations tend to blur or turn into formal or aesthetic patterns, the more so given the static character of the story itself.

Let us look at how the crucial matter of the story's beginning is handled. Poem 1, the introduction to the whole collection, situates itself at some undefined time after the "youthful error" (v. 3: "giovenile errore"), though implying that some form of error is still continuing. We then move closer to the actual start, though still with a degree of retrospection. Poem 2 makes falling in love the revenge Love takes on Petrarch for his previous resistance; poem 3 sets the event in church on Good Friday, the day of Jesus's death; poem 4 moves into a present, expanding the implication of the previous poem that Laura has replaced God in Petrarch's heart, while leaving at this point the obvious sacrilege implicit; poem 5 links Laura with Apollo's love for Daphne, and her transformation into the laurel tree, via her name; poem 6 allusively fills out the Daphne story with Petrarch casting himself as a frustrated Apollo; poem 7 follows through the sublimation of erotic desire implicit in the Daphne myth with an address to an unnamed friend that links the laurel with study and the love of wisdom; and another address to a friend in poem 8 takes us back to the erotic sphere.

If we rely on the poems, we will only learn the date and hour of the enamourment in poem 211. We might learn from elsewhere that the church was St. Claire in Avignon, though we might then be disconcerted by the historical fact that Good Friday fell on April 10 in 1327, not April 6. If we are attentive readers, we might also notice that various later poems which seem to refer back to the first sighting appear to situate it in the countryside, not in a church at all (for example, *RVF* 90, 127, and 196). But these disruptions of narrative consistency are still to come. Here, the striking thing is that, beyond registering the crucial event of falling in love, we are quite uncertain how to put the poems in any kind of temporal relationship to each other, and probably do not even try to do so. At most, we might think that there is a movement from passion or desire to sublimation via the laurel story, though this is quickly negated and need not be put in story terms at all. It is more accurate to say that the opening poems establish the crucial initial event, and then introduce a cluster of inter-related topics, which the rest of the collection constantly revisits, elaborating, recasting, rethinking what is summarily suggested here. Rhetorically, the fundamental maneuvers are ones of amplification, not narration.

The force of formal relationships is highlighted for the first time in the collection in a famous pair of sonnets. *RVF* 61 celebrates the positives in Petrarch's love for Laura:

> Benedetto sia 'l giorno, e 'l mese, et l'anno,
> e la stagione, e 'l tempo, et l'ora, e 'l punto,
> e 'l bel paese, e 'l loco ov'io fui giunto
> da' duo begli occhi che legato m'ànno
>
> (RVF 61, 1–4)

(Blessed be the day and the month and the year and the season and the time, and the hour and the instant and the beautiful countryside and the place where I was struck by the two lovely eyes that have bound me)

The blessings go on to cover the tribulations of Petrarch and the poems they have given rise to, continuing with the same rhapsodic intensity right to the end of the sonnet. In contrast, in *RVF* 62 Petrarch makes a plea to God for help in freeing himself from an unworthy passion:

> Padre del Ciel, dopo i perduti giorni,
> dopo le notti vaneggiando spese,
> con quel fero desio ch'al cor s'accese,
> mirando gli atti per mio mal sì adorni,
> piacciati omai col tuo lume ch'io torni
> ad altra vita et a più belle imprese
>
> (RVF 62, 1–6)

(Father of Heaven, after the lost days, after the nights spent raving with that fierce desire that was lit in my heart when I looked on those gestures so lovely to my hurt, let it please you at last that with your light I may return to a different life and to more beautiful undertakings)

No blessing on the moment of falling in love here, nor on the place where it happened, but instead regret for the wasted days and nights that have followed, leading in the concluding lines to the only place and day that should matter to the penitent Christian:

> reduci i pensier' vaghi a miglior luogo;
> rammenta lor come oggi fusti in croce.
> (*RVF* 62, 13–14)

(lead my wandering thoughts back to a better place, remind them that today you were on the Cross.)

The reader is impelled simply by the fact that one poem follows another to see the second as a corrective to the first (the effect would be quite different if the order were inverted), even if the return to love in the poems that immediately follow *RVF* 62 effectively deletes what it has fervently stated. But the suggested temporal relationship quickly becomes unclear. We can just as well read the two poems as representing conflicting states of mind, or conflicting verdicts on the same state of mind, and their juxtaposition as an aesthetic resolution through antithetical balance of what is left morally and narratively unresolved. In the larger scheme, the opposition between "good" and "bad" love will return at various points from the beginning of the collection to its end. The madness of desire was first sketched out in *RVF* 6, and the motif of blessing the moment and place of enamorment in 13. The opposition recurs in more elaborate form and achieves its most complex amplification very near the end of the collection in canzoni 359 and 360.

What I have just said raises important issues regarding the relationship between the two parts into which the collection is divided. This is by no means a straightforward matter. Older editions (up to at least Carducci and Ferrari's scholarly edition of 1899) regularly made the break fall between poems written during Laura's lifetime and those written after her death. On this story-driven schema, the break comes after poem 266, the last poem in which Laura is treated as if alive, her death being announced and lamented in 267. Petrarch himself puts the break after 263, which is followed by some blank pages. He then signals a fresh start by giving 264 an illuminated initial. Following the lead of Gianfranco Contini in the edition he first published in 1949, modern editions restore the break to where Petrarch put it. If titles are supplied, they are purely conventional ones, such as "Parte prima" and "Parte seconda."

The placement of a division between two parts after *RVF* 263 obviously creates problems, since the first three poems in Part Two either assume Laura is still alive or ignore the fact of her death, which of course is the major event in the story. One way of dealing with these problems is to argue that the division of the manuscript into two parts was a compositional convenience (see Chapter 4), which allowed Petrarch to add poems to both parts as and when he wished, and that the blank pages indicate that he might well have added more to Part One. If we follow this line, we may end up thinking that the only ordering principles in the final form of the collection are indeed chronology and variety, neither pursued with any great consistency. On the other hand, if the division corresponds to Petrarch's poetic intentions then a much greater degree of order emerges, and one that corresponds to the ambiguous interplay of narrative and formal features that I have been discussing.

Poem 264, "I' vo pensando" ("I go thinking"), is one of Petrarch's most impressive canzoni. He articulates his dilemmas and uncertainties with a depth that is unparalleled in any single poem or group of poems in Part One, though the issues have appeared fairly explicitly, especially in penitential poems (*RVF* 62, 81, 142, and 189). From a narrative point of view, we may take it that it marks a new degree of concentrated self-awareness. It also confirms the suspicions we may already have that the state of Petrarch's psyche is at least as significant within the collection as the contingent fact of Laura's imminent death, and probably more so.

More importantly, there is also an aesthetic and narrative vision at work, which has more in common with Dante's procedure in the *Vita nova* than with modern expectations. Both Dante and Petrarch prepare the ground and, while emphasizing the impact of the actual event, build bridges across the rupture they evoke. Dante lets us know that Beatrice is now in heaven at the start of his story; Laura's death is anticipated in *RVF* 33. As the deaths approach, the anticipations become more intense: the canzone "Donna pietosa e di novella etate" (*Vita nova* XXXIII, 17–28), with its dream of Beatrice's dying, interrupts the praise poems at the center of the little book, while intimations of what is about to happen recur with increasing intensity in the sonnets praising Laura that conclude Part One of the *RVF*. In both Dante and Petrarch, there follows a reversion to poems seeming to ignore the impending death. Then finally the event bursts into the text, Petrarch coming close to Dante's drama for once in the contrast between the low-key affirmations of prolonged loyal love for Laura and Giovanni Colonna in *RVF* 266 and the string of laments that unexpectedly opens 267:

> Oimè il bel viso, oimè il soave sguardo
> oimè il leggiadro portamento altero!
> oimè il parlar, ch' ogni aspro ingegno et fero
> facevi umile ed ogni uom vil, gagliardo!
>
> (*RVF* 267, 1–4)

(Alas the lovely face, alas the gentle glance, alas the proud, carefree bearing! Alas the speech that made every harsh or savage mind humble and every base man valiant!)

But the shock is quickly absorbed. A larger threat comes momentarily from elsewhere; a "pitying lady" offers specious consolation to Dante in the *Vita nova* and a similar substitute for Laura emerges in *RVF* 270, only to be immediately put aside in 271. Continuity has already been restored in canzone 268, which reverted to a more discursive mode despite continuing the laments and professions of despair of 267. It also imagined a new Laura:

> Più che mai bella et più leggiadra donna
> tornami inanzi come
> là dove più gradir sua vista sente.
>
> (*RVF* 268, 45–47)

(More beautiful than ever and more queenly she comes to my mind, as to a place where she knows the sight of her is most pleasing.)

Love now tells Petrarch that Laura is rejoicing in heaven, lacking only his company and eager for him to continue to write about her:

> "Pon freno al gran dolor che ti trasporta,
> ché per soverchie voglie
> si perde 'l Cielo ove 'l tuo core aspira,
>   "dove è viva colei ch' altrui par morta
> et di sue belle spoglie
> seco sorride et sol di te sospira,
>   "et sua fama, che spira
> in molte parti ancor per la tua lingua,
> prega che non estingua,
> anzi la voce al suo nome rischiari,
> se gli occhi suoi ti fur dolci né cari."
>
> (*RVF* 268, 67–77)

("Rein in the great sorrow that transports you; for excessive desire will lose the Heaven where your heart aspires, where she is alive who seems dead, and she smiles to herself at her beautiful remains and sighs only for you; and she begs you not to extinguish her fame, which sounds in many places still by your tongue, but rather to make bright your voice with her name, if her eyes were ever sweet or dear to you.")

The new Laura will return repeatedly in the poems of Part Two. Indeed, once dead, she acquires much more force as a literary character than she ever had during her life, largely because Petrarch now represents her as speaking directly to him and sympathizing with him, much as Dante does with Beatrice in the *Paradiso*. But unlike Beatrice, the dead Laura is not a figure for the transmission of divine realities. She makes her final appearance in *RVF* 359 to tell Petrarch that his celebrations, which have been plagued by self-doubts, are just "these sweet deceptive chatterings of yours" (v. 41) and that he persists in loving an extinct phantom, not the celestial being she now is, nor the even more beautiful – and loving – one she will become when her body is resurrected at the Last Judgment. But the poem ends with an image of awakening: "and after this she departs, as does my sleep" (v. 71). Even the unsatisfactory reassurances Laura offers may just be figures in a dream. There was no true understanding of her nature in the poems written during her lifetime. Here he acknowledges that understanding has not significantly improved since her death. The tone may be darker, the awareness more complex, but intellectually and morally that is all the progression there is.

The poems I have just now cited define the overall shape and progress (such as it is) of Part Two. They are almost all canzoni and, taken with other canzoni, they create a formal pattern, which is in strong contrast with the pattern of Part One. The opening of Part Two places three important canzoni close to each other: *RVF* 264, on Petrarch's dilemmas; 268, voicing despair at Laura's death but finding consolation in the idea of a transfigured Laura; and 270, rejecting the possibility of finding another love. The ending (in the form that Petrarch projected but did not realize) is an inverse mirroring of this arrangement: 366, the canzone to the Virgin, is preceded by 359, in which the heavenly Laura appears for the last time, and 360, in which Petrarch accuses Love of various crimes against him in the court of reason and Love defends his actions, only for judgment to be suspended.

There is a strong contrast here with Part One, which opens and closes with poems in minor forms. Poems 1–21 are sonnets interrupted by two *ballate* (11 and 14) of sonnet length. Poems 240–263 are all sonnets. The opening sequence is then brought to an end by a sestina (22), which may be a form of canzone for Petrarch as it is for Dante, followed by a "true" canzone (23). The closing sequence of this part is preceded by two sestinas close to each other (237 and 239). The two sequences are thus, as in Part Two, inverted mirror images of each other: imperfect ones, but close nonetheless.

Again there are narrative implications. In particular, the concluding sonnets of Part One are the poems which most highly celebrate Laura's and the laurel's virtues, while recognizing that they are about to be swept from this earth. The fact that these celebrations are couched in sonnet form suggests that they do not have the weight of the canzone opening Part Two, which in a sense overrules them, even if the return of the transfigured Laura in 268 and then in many subsequent poems shows that she has not been at all ousted from Petrarch's mind and poetry.

In that respect, the story has perhaps moved on, even if the situation has not progressed. We can easily go further and find various smaller patterns, which also have thematic resonances. For instance, the linking of singing and weeping in 229 and 230 is taken up more briefly and synthetically much later to emphasize the inevitability of repetition: "I wept and sang; I cannot change my style" (*RVF* 344, 12). Or, to take another instance, the fantasy of an endless night with Laura that appears in the first sestina (*RVF* 22, 31–36) recurs only in the penultimate sestina of Part One, at the same point (*RVF* 237, 31–36), creating a parallel which also suggests the long persistence of physical desire. The language and the nocturnal imagery of these poems are then echoed more painfully in poem 332 in Part Two, which, as a unique double sestina, contrasts with all the sestinas of Part One, perhaps outweighing them and simultaneously exhausting the form.

The interplay between suggested narrative and its cancellation, repetition and variation, is quite unlike the forward movement of the *Vita nova*. Nor is there anything like the poetic advance highlighted by Dante, which corresponds and contributes to the evolution of the story. Laura may be transformed into the laurel, but from the beginning the transformation is reversible, and the female figure and the tree may co-exist simultaneously (startlingly so in the conclusion to 34). There are also variations of style and form, some poems standing out in the same way that the double sestina does, such as the canzoni 30 and 205. But these are exceptions, which the collection is able to absorb. The implicit poetics remain constant throughout the fluctuations, from the first poems (whenever they were actually written) to the concluding poems of repentance.

There is, however, a moment in Part One where there is a formal shift and also a significant thematic change, perhaps the only significant thematic change in the whole collection. As with the transition into Part Two, it is carried out through overlap and interlocking. Since it lacks drama and is basically a matter of subtraction, it is easy for it to pass unobserved. Unlike Part Two, Part One contains groups of canzoni. These are all concentrated in its first half, the longest (125–129) coming at close to the half-way point. Among the poems in this group is "My Italy," the last and greatest of Petrarch's three political canzoni (28, 53, and 128). If we look back, we find that almost all of the perhaps twenty poems on subjects other than love and the laurel have already appeared.[6] So too have almost all the poems addressed to friends, whether they are also love poems or not. The last significant forays outwards are the Avignonese sonnets (*RVF* 136–138). There only remain 166, a sonnet announcing desiccation as an Apollonian poet, and 232, a tendentious sonnet on anger, which may or may not relate to Laura. The number of canzoni also diminishes in the remainder of Part One. After the isolated 135, the only examples are 206 and 207. The three sestinas (*RVF* 142, 237, and 239) provide the only other formal variety. The vast majority of poems are now sonnets, focussed overwhelmingly on love, which include some of the strongest celebrations of Laura before the concluding string. The transition is thus not immediate or abrupt, and may derive from an earlier form of the *RVF* (perhaps the so-called Correggio form: see Chapter 4). If so, Petrarch serendipitously exploits what this version offers him to create a shift from a more public poetry into the personal and private realm, from a heavy dosage of major form (the canzone) back to the minor norm (the sonnet). The result is a concealed, but by no means mysterious, tripartite structure, rather than the obvious bipartite one, even if the two halves of Part One are thoroughly locked into each other.

I have acknowledged that the patterns I have been discussing are not perfect in every way, though they seem to me to be clearly perceptible and to demand our attention. But the fact that there are patterns at all can lead to the search for an overarching structure, within which the place of every poem is significant and justified. So far, any structures of this kind that have been identified have inevitably been narrative ones.

The most radical is numerological. The argument is broadly as follows: the poems may have been written over a long period of years, but the fact that there are 366 of them points to a correspondence with the number of days either in a leap year or in a normal year, with poem 1 serving as an introductory prelude. The latter seems the more likely possibility, since the symbolic year in question will begin, following Petrarch's promptings, on Good Friday 1327, when he first saw Laura, and end with the Easter of the following year, when he turns away from Laura to the Virgin. Various poems on this reading correspond to festivals marking the progress of the Christian year. Most impressively, if we count forwards from the first poem and April 6, we find that 264, the canzone opening Part Two, corresponds to Christmas Day. The implications are plain: Petrarch represents himself as alienated from God in Part One through his love for Laura, whom he deludes himself into thinking is a beneficent force in his life, not a form of mortal temptation. With 264, God is born again in him, and Part Two as a whole points to a spiritual repentance and renewal, which is finally carried through in the concluding poem.[7]

Such an approach promises to resolve some of the evident ambiguities of the *RVF* and sets the collection firmly in the tradition of medieval moralizing literature. There are, however, serious objections, beginning with what seem to me forced readings of poem 264 and others, and much special pleading in order to get the numbers to fit. Aside from that, if Petrarch has brought off a complex structuring of short individual compositions along these lines, he has achieved something that eludes him elsewhere and that he probably never aspired to. The collections of letters, the *De remediis*, and the *De viris* show elements of patterning in terms of contrasts, repetition, and variation much like those I have identified in the *RVF*, but none has a hidden architecture with an underlying numerological basis. Within the *RVF*, the striking equation of poem 264 and Christmas Day is hard to parallel convincingly with other poems, some of which might be taken to point in other numerological directions. The first canzone in the collection (23) flaunts an ability to manipulate Ovidian metamorphoses within a complex stanza structure, and could perhaps be seen retrospectively as an empty virtuoso display. It may well appear as poem 23 in part because it was written when Petrarch was twenty-three years of age. It is hard to see how this particular principle could be extended. In other words, there may be occasional numerical patterns but they cannot be developed to account convincingly for the organization of the collection as a whole.

Petrarch himself uses the metaphor of a labyrinth for the experience of love (*RVF* 211, 14). There is no reason for thinking that he found a way through the labyrinth, other than leaving it altogether. The reader, whether fourteenth- or twenty-first-century, is invited into an analogous poetic labyrinth, perhaps with less risk to the soul than Petrarch felt he was exposed to by love of Laura and the laurel, but certainly with the same questions to answer about value and meaning in poetry and poetic pleasure.

If this is so, there is no hidden key other than ones we as readers might bring with us. At the same time, as we become more familiar with the collection, either through sequential reading or through wandering in it as our fancy takes us, the paths through the labyrinth may become clearer, the turns and high points more evident, the relationships between poems less confusing – if never completely resolved. I see no reason why we should be concerned that a definitive shaping never imposes itself. Nor need we be concerned that there might have been further relatively minor changes. Other poems could have been added to Part One and substitutions made in both parts. The last 31 poems were never re-ordered in many editions. The previous arrangement is less charged than the one we are now familiar with, but it is equally Petrarchan. There is much to be said for recognizing a degree of provisionality and openness in the collection as we have it. As Petrarch says of the pleasures of his own uncertainties, "Così nulla se 'n perde / et più certezza averne fora il peggio" (*RVF* 125, 75–76: "Thus no part is omitted

49

and to know more exactly would be a loss"). Certainly, today teleological completeness seems less and less a necessary characteristic of any work of art, ancient, medieval, or modern.

NOTES

1 See Wilkins, *The Making of the "Canzoniere,"* 154.

2 See Bartolo Martinelli, "L'ordinamento morale del *Canzoniere* del Petrarca," in *Petrarca e il Ventoso* (Bergamo: Minerva Italica, 1977), 217–300.

3 I develop here ideas already advanced in my *Petrarch the Poet* (London: Routledge, 1988), 49–77, drawing also on more recent criticism, in particular Marco Santagata, *I frammenti dell'anima. Storia e racconto nel "Canzoniere" di Petrarca* (Bologna: Il Mulino, 1993) and Teodolinda Barolini, "The Self in the Labyrinth of Time: *Rerum vulgarium fragmenta*," in *Petrarch: A Critical Guide*, Kirkham and Maggi, 33–62.

4 The dates appear in *RVF* 211 and 336 and in a note in Petrarch's copy of Virgil.

5 *RVF* 30 (1334), 50 (1336/37), 62 (1337/38), 79 (1340), 101 and 107 (1341), 118 (1343), 122 (1344), 145 (1342), 212 (1347), 221 (1346), 266 (1345), 271 (1348), 278 (1350/51), and 364 (1358 or later).

6 The definite ones are *RVF* 7, 10, 24, 27, 28, 38, 40, 53, 98, 99, 103, 104, 119, 120, 128, 136–138, 166, and 232.

7 For the positive assertion of the calendrical thesis, see Thomas P. Roche, "The Calendrical Structure of Petrarch's *Canzoniere*," *Studies in Philology* 71 (1974): 152–171; Frederic J. Jones, "Arguments in Favour of a Calendrical Structure for Petrarch's *Canzoniere*," *Modern Language Review* 79 (1984): 579–588; and Giovanni Biancardi, "L'ipotesi di un ordinamento calendariale del *Canzoniere* petrarchesco," *Giornale storico della letteratura italiana* 172 (1995): 1–55.

4

LUCA MARCOZZI

Making the *Rerum vulgarium fragmenta*

The collection of lyric poems that Petrarch worked on for nearly forty years reflects, through successive stages of composition, his evolving poetic and philosophical values. The genesis of the collection, the stratification of its many forms and stages, and its gradually emerging status as Petrarch's crowning achievement have all been studied since the sixteenth century and retraced by many modern scholars, especially after the fundamental reconstruction of the internal history of the text by Ernest Hatch Wilkins and its refinement by Marco Santagata, H. Wayne Storey, and Arnaldo Soldani.[1] In addition to drawing on information from Petrarch's biography and other works, scholars have also made use of the direct testimony of the author, including statements in his letters to Ludwig van Kempen in 1351 (*Fam.* I.1) and to Pandolfo Malatesta in 1373 (*Sen.* XIII.11), drafts and marginal notes, and erasures in the final version of the work, which is the basis of what we read today.

Petrarch's *RVF*, along with its contemporary, Boccaccio's *Decameron*, is the first classical work of Italian literature whose diffusion originates with an autograph; that is, a copy, or rather a series of copies, written in the hand of the author himself. This copy is known as the Vat. Lat. 3195 codex. It is a parchment volume measuring 27 × 20.3 cm, comprising seventy-three pages, and written in semi-gothic script, in part by Petrarch and mainly by his trusted copyist Giovanni Malpaghini, who was in his service from 1364 to April 1367. According to most authorities, the manuscript was completed by Petrarch himself shortly before his death. Besides its philological and linguistic features, it is particularly important due to its status as an "authorial book"; that is to say, Petrarch himself saw to the disposition of the single poems and to the ordering and formatting of the collection. Among the most important paratextual features are the title, "Francisci Petrarche laureati poete Rerum vulgarium fragmenta," written in Malpaghini's hand in a rubric on f. 1r; the white pages separating the first and the second parts of the collection; and the initial letters of the first sonnet and of canzone 264, "I' vo' pensando" ("I go thinking"), painted in red on a golden background with floral ornamentation.[2] However, despite the existence of a partially autographic, and wholly author-supervised, manuscript,[3] scholars have recently agreed that many textual readings should be corrected with the support of other manuscripts that seem to preserve a particular authorial intention more faithfully than Vat. Lat. 3195, which, despite its direct connection to the author, contains a number of missing, altered, or unclear passages.[4]

Still, Vat. Lat. 3195 is undoubtedly among the most precious surviving relics in the history of Italian literature, though it was some time before the importance of the manuscript and indeed of the *RVF* itself was given due recognition. The appearance of Petrarch's *RVF* and the form in which we read it today is an issue simultaneously involving interpretation, cultural paradigms, philological practices, and textual studies. The artifact itself is of small, unprepossessing dimensions. The first Humanist pupils of Petrarch in the late fourteenth and fifteenth centuries attributed little importance to the *RVF* and his other vernacular writings, following Petrarch himself, who clearly considered it a minor work. Only more than a century after the death of the author, at the end of the fifteenth and the beginning of the sixteenth centuries, did the volume become a widely venerated and closely studied object. This occurred after it became available to the most influential scholar of Italian vernacular literature of his time, Pietro Bembo. Bembo renewed the Italian language with a grammar, the *Prose della volgar lingua* (conceived in the first decade of the Cinquecento, though published only in 1525), based primarily on direct imitation of Petrarch. His theory and practice influenced the flourishing sixteenth-century phenomenon of Petrarchism.

This moment of transition played a fundamental role in the history of the text of the *RVF* and its reception. In the age before print, the work circulated in different manuscript forms, reflecting the different stages of its elaboration. The advent of the printing press, however, entailed a strong normalization of the text: first with the edition printed in Padua in 1472 by Bartolomeo di Valdezocco, based on Vat. Lat. 3195 and edited by one of Bembo's teachers, Augurello; then with the text edited by Bembo and printed by the Aldine press in 1501, based on Bembo's transcription of the manuscript in Padua (now conserved as Vat. Lat. 3197). After having for a time lost track of the autograph, Bembo finally got it back in 1544. In addition, he had acquired, perhaps as early as 1528, several pages containing the rough drafts of some poems, the so-called *Codice degli abbozzi* (Vat. Lat. 3196). As we will see, this last manuscript is an invaluable source of knowledge on how the poet wrote and revised his texts, and a key aid for reconstructing the genesis of the collection, since it clearly displays how the poems changed over time and refers to datable transcriptions of groups of poems.

When Bembo copied the text of Petrarch's *RVF* while preparing the Aldine edition, he standardized what he viewed as its rough edges and deformities. He modified it to the new reality of a printed vernacular literature, adapting the humanistic principle of imitation of unchanging examples from Latin to Italian.[5] From that moment on, and until the beginning of the twentieth century, the smooth and elusive language of Petrarch's *RVF* was considered a sort of grammar of Italian poetic discourse and the most important, if not the exclusive, point of reference for the writing of lyric poetry. In Bembo's view, Petrarch and Boccaccio were the modern Virgil and Cicero. They were to be turned into new classics, by removing variant usages from their language and monumentalizing their texts in authoritative print editions. This type of sanctification claimed to be based on the recovery of the original source text and a defense of its authority (even if, as we have seen, Bembo often disregarded the text of Vat. Lat. 3195 in his Aldine edition). Even at the time, this canonizing procedure encountered some opposition by other notables (for instance, Alessandro Vellutello). Nevertheless, the process of publication set in motion by Bembo was destined to succeed and became widely recognized as the *vulgata* of the *RVF*. In the meantime, the final manuscript version of the *RVF* (Vat. Lat. 3195), written partly in Petrarch's own hand, passed from one owner to another, eventually to be entirely forgotten.

At Bembo's death in 1549, Vat. Lat. 3195 and 3196, along with many other manuscripts and his collection of antiques, were inherited by Bembo's son, Torquato, who then sold them in 1581 to the Humanist and librarian Fulvio Orsini. Orsini later bequeathed them to the Vatican Library. In 1624, Federigo Ubaldini used the rough-draft manuscript (Vat. Lat. 3196) as the basis for a famous edition. Yet Vat. Lat. 3195 remained for almost four centuries in the comforting shadows of the Vatican armory, where Pierre de Nolhac rediscovered it in 1886.

Despite their similarity in size, these manuscripts contain quite different versions of the *RVF*. Taken together and compared in detail, they reflect the genesis and formation of the text. The erasures, the marginal notes, the *pentimenti*, and the modifications of these few pages, the subtle chiseling of each line, repeatedly rewritten and rethought: all these together demonstrate the poet's pursuit of formal perfection in a revisionary process that lasted decades. Furthermore, the *Codice degli abbozzi* offers several clues allowing us to date, at least hypothetically, the processes that led to the definitive shape of the work.

The *RVF* ostensibly narrates a story of love that took place between the years 1327 and 1351, but it contains poems certainly written after this date, and probably some from before it, and reaches its definitive 366-poem form after a series of reworkings, additions, and amplifications. Each of the successive stages of modification implies an adhesion to a new poetic model or series of moral and stylistic values that replaces the values of earlier redactions. The particular form brought to completion and transmitted by the Vat. Lat. 3195 is conceived, in both its interior and exterior shape, as a crowning of this path, reflecting the long search for internal thematic and stylistic equilibrium in relation to other balancing expedients, such as calendrical ordering, the reduction of phonic dissonance in the language, the balancing of different metrical forms, and the repetition-in-difference of key metaphors.

Petrarch's first efforts in vernacular lyric poetry can be dated with relative accuracy to the beginning of the 1330s. Among them, Petrarch specifies the demanding "canzone of the metamorphoses" (*RVF* 23) as one of his first compositions in the margins of the *abbozzi* manuscript (Vat. Lat. 3196). The poem was probably composed in its entirety at that early point, even if the poet continued to revise it until 1356.

The early "reference collection" (gathering of rough drafts) transmitted by Vat. Lat. 3196 includes twenty-five poems: twenty-two of his own sonnets, two sonnets by his friends, and part of canzone 23 (gathered in ff. 7–10, 16, and 11r of Vat. Lat. 3196). If we view the *RVF* from the teleological perspective of its final form, it is hard to recognize this cluster of poems as the true precursor of the project. In particular, it is hard to make connections with the moral strictures that dominate the further elaboration of the *RVF* beginning with the years 1349–50.

The first indication of an ordered and presumably thematized transcription comes from another annotation in Vat. Lat. 3196, on f. 9v, in conjunction with sonnet 34, of which Petrarch writes: "I started to transcribe from this place. 1342. August 21st. At noon." Wilkins hypothesized that this sonnet (composed before 1337) was the first poem in what he called the "first form" of the *RVF*,[6] but we can only say with certainty that it was the starting point for a now-lost transcription from rough draft to fair copy. In this early collection, Petrarch selected and ordered texts from between approximately 1336 and 1338, with the aim of detaching vernacular poems from the original occasions on which they were composed and of imposing a thematically determined order different from the chronological sequence of their composition.

Thus, the *RVF* first started to take shape as single poems were joined together in an order inspired by the author's aesthetics and literary interests; an order motivated by a moral project would be imposed at a later date. At least fourteen poems (*RVF* 34–36, 41–46, 49, 58, 60, 64, and 69) were transcribed from Vat. Lat. 3196 in August 1342, but it is within the realm of possibility that the first version of the *R VF* contained other texts transcribed from lost sketches and drafts. In fact, all the poems up to *R VF* 103 in the final version, as well as about twenty of those that come later, may be dated to before 1342, excepting of course *R VF* 1 (and most likely 2–5).

The hypothetical first version of the *RVF* was thematically dominated by the myth of Daphne, beginning with sonnet 34, where Apollo is apostrophized with the request of rescuing from oblivion the laurel tree into which his beloved Daphne had been transformed. Thus, the myth of Apollo and Daphne as laurel is present in the *RVF* from the very beginning, even before it is used in conjunction with Laura's *senhal*, and without many of the associations it would eventually take on. The first form of the songbook is thus rooted in the *Metamorphoses* of Ovid and in the encyclopaedic and mythographic traditions (Isidore of Seville, Fulgentius, the Vatican mythographers), displaying an uncommon learning in this field. In fact, during the 1330s and 1340s, Petrarch had devoted himself to acquiring erudition in the classics, achieving fame as the greatest expert of classical mythology in his times.

In the poems included in the "first reference collection," Petrarch's lyrics can be seen as deriving from two very different traditions, both of which he attempts to appease. On the one hand, his models are to be found in the occasional or epistolary poetry of the late *stilnovo* poets still active in his times (above all, Cino da Pistoia).[7] On the other, as just noted, we find a current that might be called humanistic, deeply connected to classical mythology and learning (for example, the episode of the weeping of Caesar in sonnet 44), that is quite atypical in comparison to contemporary lyric poets. Another example of a poem from this collection whose dominant code is the learned exhibition of scholarship is one of the first sonnets, *R VF* 35, "Solo e pensoso i più deserti campi," composed prior to 1337. This poem posits identity between the poet and a rare hero of mythology, Bellerophon, whose source is to be found in Homer, known to Petrarch through Cicero. Sonnet 35 exploits classical mythology to give poetic substance to an ancient elegiac *topos*, the solitude caused by Love, and recalls Boethius and Apuleius, as well as Fulgentius's moral interpretation of the *Aeneid*. It also makes reference to Dante's *Commedia*, which will be a constant intertext – more so than Dante's lyric poetry – in all the following developments of the *RVF*. This complex intertwining of classical references can be found throughout the entire first collection. And, in fact, the use of learned mythological periphrasis will diminish in later versions.

As we have seen, the primary myth of this group of poems is that of Daphne and Apollo, which offers a model and a structure for the expression of poetic desire. The typical themes of earlier lyric poetry, such as the discussion of the nature and origin of love and the examination of its psychological and moral effects, are given little space in the *RVF*. In this respect, more than to Dante and Guido Cavalcanti, Petrarch looks from the very beginning to Virgil, Ovid, and Cicero. His debts to the *stilnovisti* and to Dante are less immediately evident, but will be further revealed with the passing years. The classicism of this first version of the *RVF* thus corresponds to the great, unfinished epic experiment of the *Africa*, as well as to the collections of the *Rerum memorandarum*, the *De viris*, and Petrarch's editorial work with Livy's *Ab urbe condita*. At the end of the 1340s, when Petrarch shifted roles from *historicus* to *philosophus*, he transposed in his lyric poems some of the moral needs of the *Secretum* and the asceticism of the treatises on religious *otium* and the solitary life. The *RVF* embodies this intellectual metamorphosis by way of its eventual division into two parts and by other additions to later forms.

According to Petrarch, the elaboration of the collection of the *RVF* according to moral criteria happened after the plague of 1348. In a text dating from 1350–51, namely the first, prefatory, letter of the *Familiares*, Petrarch reminds his friend Ludwig van Kempen (his "Socrates") of how that fatal year left men alone, poor, sad, and hopeless. After these tragic events and subsequent reflection on the necessity of saving his works from oblivion and handing them down to posterity, Petrarch planned to collect and order them. His dual models were, on the one hand, the morality of Stoic philosophy set in opposition to the idea of emotional disorder represented by scattered poetic fragments, and, on the other, the path of repentance and recantation developed by Augustine in his *Confessions*. Like Augustine, who recalled the sins of his youth and contemplated them from the spiritually redeemed perspective of his maturity, Petrarch devoted himself to reliving his past and re-ordering its fragments in order to structure a "sizeable and varying collection of writings" that filled his desk. They could be compared with "the scattered fragments of his soul" that he aimed to put together at the end of the *Secretum* (a purpose deriving from an Augustinian matrix); at the same time, he opened the way to shaping the *RVF* in the final form that has reached us. Petrarch thus transposed various kinds of writing from an original fragmentary state into collections of prose and verse letters, as well as of lyric vernacular poems. In the works written between 1349 and 1350, mainly in the *Secretum*, Petrarch demonstrates his own changes of mind (*mutatio animi*), offering his repentant inner being as a moral *exemplum* for others. In this way, he created from different perspectives an ideal autobiography by way of literary invention, generating a multi-faceted representation of the self that would take hold among contemporaries and endure with posterity.

During this period, the *RVF* acquired what we think of as its defining structure, becoming the work that is read today. First, it was provided with an "introduction," consisting of the first sonnet (datable, like *Fam.* I.1, to the period immediately following the plague year), in which one of the fundamental dynamics of the work is disclosed, namely, the inconclusive and contradictory dialectic between error and regret, past and present, revelation of one's own moral weakness and concurrent request of empathy from readers, justified by the common and sinful human condition.

In addition to this introductory poem, Petrarch composed sonnets 2–3 (and probably the two that follow), in which he begins the story with recourse to the traditional rhetorical categories of cause, time, place, character, origin, and name. This compositional stage is documented by a later form of the *RVF* carried out fifteen years later. We know this form, as in other cases, from Vat. Lat. 3196, which indicates Azzo da Correggio (the dedicatee of *De remediis*) as the addressee of a collection of vernacular poems that Petrarch was preparing between 1356 and 1358. This form, the so-called "Correggio form," of which we do not possess a copy, is also referred to as the "Pre-Chigi form," because it precedes the Chigi form of 1359–63, the next extant form of the *RVF*.

Concerning the Correggio form, we have no additional manuscript evidence aside from a reference in Vat. Lat. 3196 dating to November 29, 1357, which was transcribed by a copyist named Gerolamo and is said to have come, hyperbolically, "a thousand years" after the author had last engaged with his vernacular poems. Gerolamo copied sonnets 67 and 68 in their final versions (both dedicated to the portrait of Laura) for Lord Azzo. The *abbozzi* manuscript also documents Petrarch's feverish work on the vernacular poems during his years in Milan. It records that on November 10, 1356, canzone 23 (of which other annotations document an intense reworking between 1350 and 1351) was "transcribed in order." From the evidence we possess, it is possible to assert that the Correggio form consisted of 171 poems, divided in two sequences, 1–142 and 264–292, most likely interrupted by blank pages.

In the Correggio form, the first sequence of poems probably ended with sestina 142 of the final form, dated variously by scholars to between 1345 and 1350. In a Roman setting contrasting with the landscape of Provence, which is the scene of Petrarch's love for Laura, the poem develops a palinode condemning sensual love and the longing for glory, and addressing the poet's desires to follow "altro lume, / altro salir al ciel per altri poggi" (*RVF* 142, 37–38: "another light, / another climbing to Heaven by other hills") and "altri rami" (v. 39: "other branches"), instead of those of the laurel tree. It also introduces the repentance of the following canzone, "I' vo' pensando"

("I go thinking"), which came just after the sestina and would be numbered 264 in the final form. That canzone, charged with Boethian resonance, constitutes a second introduction dating back to the same years as sonnet 1 and has dense intertextual connections both with the opening sonnet and with the previously mentioned sestina (142).

"I' vo' pensando" (*RVF* 264) is the first in the section that later critics would call *in morte*, that is, after the death of Laura, even though Laura is clearly still referred to as alive in it, and even though it is not the first poem to represent the experience of mourning. Its function, rather, is to separate the penitential process from the external event of Laura's death, a separation implying that the author's repentance is in fact the result of an internal transformation. The first canzone actually *in morte*, whose composition is almost contemporary with "I' vo' pensando" is *RVF* 268, "Che debb' io far? che mi consigli, Amore?" ("What shall I do? What do you counsel me, Love?"). This poem is related to the Occitan poetic genre of the *planctus* mourning the death or the absence of the beloved. Vat. Lat. 3196 preserves its complex and layered genesis, including an opening deemed "not sufficiently sad" that was later discarded and a double transcription dating back to November 1349. The composition of the entire poem may be dated to the summer of the previous year (1348), and the canzone continued to undergo significant elaborations until 1351. The poet carried out further revisions until at least 1356, when it was transcribed.

Whether or not the division was clearly marked by a break in the text, the Correggio form certainly had a two-part structure that juxtaposed sin and recantation, passion and reason, which would carry over to the final form. From this point on, many poems would be added to the *RVF*, but only relatively minor adjustments were made to its basic organization and thematic focus. The most important from the latter point of view was the substitution of madrigal 121, "Or vedi, Amor, che giovenetta donna" ("Now see, Love, how a young woman"), for the ballad "Donna mi vene spesso ne la mente" ("A lady comes often to my mind"). The ballad was excluded from later forms of the *RVF*, probably because it revealed a new love object and emphasized the non-exclusivity of the love for Laura. From approximately 1356–58 on, then, the *RVF* reflects a stable thematic and narrative core based on the author-narrator's idealized moral–spiritual autobiography.

From the Correggio form of the *RVF* derive the various succeeding forms, to which other poems from the *abbozzi* manuscript would be added. The form established between 1359 and 1363 is named "Chigi" after the manuscript designated as Vaticano Chigiano L.V.176, an autograph copy by Boccaccio made in 1363. It is the first tangibly attested form of the collection handed down to us. Compared with the hypothetical Correggio form, it has thirty-two poems added to the first part and twelve to the second, for a total of 163 poems *in vita* and forty-one *in morte*. The first part of the Chigi form ends with a triptych of sonnets dedicated to the allegory of life as journey and navigation (176, 177, and 189 of the final form). Page 71, placed between these sonnets and canzone 264, is blank.

The material process of the making of the *RVF* passed through another important stage three years later. In October 1366, Petrarch charged Giovanni Malpaghini, his scribe and secretary, with copying the texts connected with his lyric vernacular production into a wide and spacious manuscript, following the sequencing of the two previous forms. On April 21, 1367, Malpaghini quit mid-endeavor, having copied poems 1–120, the later-excluded "Donna mi vene spesso ne la mente," 122–178, and 180–190 (leaving a blank space between 178 and 180) for the first part, and 264–318 for the second. The only significant changes to affect this order from that point on were the addition of a series of poems at the end of the first and the second parts, and a few variations in the ordering of the texts. Several blank pages were interposed between the two parts, enough to eventually be filled up with the additional poems. This happened between October 1367 and approximately 1372, when Petrarch, scribe and archaeologist of himself, successively added twelve, then another twelve, then a further thirty-one poems, and then, finally, the last seven of the first part and nine of the second, including the last song (*RVF* 366), "Vergine bella" ("Beautiful Virgin"). In particular, Petrarch's additions to the "Giovanni form" (that is, the part of Vat. Lat. 3195 transcribed by Malpaghini) were made in four separate periods: between October 1367 and May 1368, he added 179 and 191–198 for the first part and 319–321 for the second; then, after having given the manuscript to a rubricator in order to put in the decorations for the initial poems of the two parts (1 and 264), he resumed work between September and October 1368, adding the sequences 200–207 and 322–326; between May and December 1369, he added the series 208–227 and 229–231 for the first part and 328–334 for the second; finally, after 1369, he added the series 232–238 to the first part and 335, 336, and 350–354 to the second, completing the composition of the work and the perfection of his moral project with canzone 366. In so doing, most critics have argued, Petrarch took definitive control of what had to that point been an "open text," arriving at a final draft through various stages that allowed him to polish and refine any remaining structural unevenness.

On January 4, 1373, Petrarch, then in Padua, wrote a letter to Pandolfo Malatesta, lord of Fano (*Sen.* XIII.11), attaching a copy of the *RVF* as a gift. This copy sent to Malatesta contained 244 poems in the first part and 88 in the second. Its order varied in some places from those of the previous forms.

In Petrarch's letter to Malatesta, these "vernacular trifles" are described as bearers of unstable emotions and of a rough style, most of them being poems from his youth. The hesitation concerning their defective style allows Petrarch to open a window onto the difficult material conditions of writing. He complains of how hard it is to find a good copyist even in the famous university town of Padua, of the incompetence and indolence of those who have previously worked for him, and of the disorder and small number of the poems, though he does not deny that he revised the work before sending it to Pandolfo (mainly by switching the positions of sonnets 2 and 3). Finally, he declares in a *post scriptum* transmitted only in the first version of the letter that his endeavor is not finished, because he still has "many of these vernacular things, in old folders, so wasted from time that they are barely readable; and if I have a free day, I apply myself to gathering them, if only for my amusement."[8] He also says that he left ample space at the end of each of the two parts so that he could pull some poems from the old files and insert them when the time is ripe.

Another manuscript held in the Queriniana Library of Brescia (known as D.II.21; other manuscripts were subsequently copied from this one) documents an intermediate form between the one sent to Malatesta and the final draft, thus demonstrating Petrarch's continuous engagement with the text, beyond mere gathering on a "free day." The ballad "Donna mi vene spesso ne la mente" is finally expunged and many changes are made in the sequence of the single poems, in order to achieve a uniformity in tone and register that would prove definitive. The last form is documented by the final interventions in Vat. Lat. 3195; that is to say, the addition of some poems in the blank pages in the first part, the definitive replacement of "Donna mi vene spesso" with madrigal 121, the erasure and replacement of some poems by others in the second part, and the addition of twenty-three poems (337–349 and 356–365) in the pages previously left blank. The author's last intervention is the renumbering of the final thirty-one poems. In the margins of each poem, in a fine, steady hand, he adds a new numbering with the aim of partly changing the order from that in which they were transcribed. In particular, the sonnets now numbered 363–365 are moved forward from their original position and put closer to the final canzone, with the effect of emphasizing at the opposite end of the book the regret for the "youthful error" that the lover recounts in the first sonnet. Having accomplished these revisions, so the legend goes, he lay his head down on the manuscript and passed away.

This last series of interventions was read by Wilkins as a supreme effort to perfect the work and deliver it to its readers and posterity in a finished state.[9] Recently, Wayne H. Storey has asserted that the form of the *RVF* in Vat.

Lat. 3195 represents neither the "last will" of its author nor his wishes for the final version (as if a "last will" could really be found in any of Petrarch's ceaselessly revised works).[10] According to Storey, the rearrangement of the last poems in a copy that served in its later *folia* as more of a work space than a definitive transcription suggests that, *pace* Wilkins, Petrarch's final renumbering and other modifications should be interpreted as a "layer of editorial signs and devices," a means of communication with other, later copyists. If this is so, the making of the *RVF* had not yet come to an end. Another hypothesis concerning this last sequence and its mutations is that of Arnaldo Soldani, who argues that the last two pages in which these modifications appear were inserted in the only available space before the last canzone, so that the Arabic numbering of the last sequence was not the product of a *pentimento*, but was simultaneous with the moment in which the new poems were inserted into the last form of the *RVF*.[11]

In any event, it is now possible to argue that modern readers confront a project never truly completed. At the time of Petrarch's death, Vat. Lat. 3195 was unbound, composed of a collection of thirty-six *bifolia*, and still, at least in principle, open to inclusions and exclusions, insertions, erasures, experiments, selections, and new organizational possibilities. Despite the many structural and thematic elements that bind the "scattered rhymes" of the *RVF* together in its final form, it may still be considered a working rather than a completed copy, an *opera aperta* (open work), with no final authorial conclusion. The idea of perfection it offers to posthumous readers may seem to derive as much from the contingent historical circumstances of the author's death as from his final and definitive will concerning the work, which can never now be known.

NOTES

1 Santagata, *I frammenti dell'anima*; H. Wayne Storey, "Doubting Petrarch's Last Words: Erasure in Ms Vaticano Latino 3195," in *Petrarch and the Textual Origins of Interpretation*, eds. Teodolinda Barolini and H. Wayne Storey (Leiden and Boston, MA: Brill, 2007), 67–91; Arnaldo Soldani, "Un'ipotesi sull'ordinamento finale del *Canzoniere*," *Studi petrarcheschi*, 19 (2006): 209–247.

2 "Paratexts" are features of a manuscript or book – titles, illustrations, pagination, and so on – that frame, enhance, or explicate the primary text (i.e., the poems themselves). Some features of the text, added by later annotators, can be easily distinguished from those originating with Malpaghini and Petrarch.

3 Of seventy-three *folia*, forty-seven are in Malpaghini's hand, and only twenty-two in Petrarch's (three sheets are left blank and one is a later addition)

4 In other words, some passages in Vat. Lat. 3195 have been deemed by philologists to reflect errors or lapses on the parts of the copyists (both Malapaghini and Petrarch), while other, earlier copies seem to have been made more correctly,

and thus in some cases are used to supplement Vat. Lat. 3195 as the basis for modern printed editions.

5 He took the position defended by Paolo Cortesi in his exchange with Poliziano, who instead argued for creative imitation of multiple models. Bembo would elaborate this position in the treatise *De imitatione* of 1510, addressed in letter form to Giovan Francesco Pico, nephew of the more famous Pico della Mirandola.

6 Wilkins, *The Making of the "Canzoniere,"* 7.

7 Editors' note: The term *stilnovo* was coined originally by Dante (*Purgatorio* XXIV.57) to refer to his own love poetry of praise for Beatrice and has been adopted to refer a group of late thirteenth- and early fourteenth-century poets, including Guido Guinizelli, Guido Cavalcanti, Dante himself, and Cino da Pistoia, who wrote of the transformative psychological and spiritual effects of love.

8 This version of the letter is included in the *Disperse* as an appendix, 532–539. The translation is the author's.

9 Wilkins, *The Making of the "Canzoniere,"* 76.

10 Storey, "Doubting Petrarch's Last Words," 71.

11 Soldani, "Un'ipotesi sull'ordinamento finale del *Canzoniere*," 240.

5

ULLRICH LANGER

Petrarch's singular love lyric

Petrarch's love poetry conveys an existential intensity that marked the European lyric tradition for many centuries. It exhibits a radical, conscious focus on a human being living here and now, whether it be the "beloved" or the "lover," and which is apparent to readers today and to poets succeeding him. His poetry does so without resorting to copious, varied language or the other resources that contemporary rhetoric provided any poet; it does so without presenting much detail about his own life or the life and death of his beloved; it does so without, on the other hand, inserting the individual into grand historical or cultural narratives and without resorting, except occasionally, to the universally attractive meanings of mythological fables; and it does so, finally, without presuming to disclose truths in the recording of his own feelings that can be, or should be, applied to general categories of human beings. To be sure, there is at the very beginning of the *RVF* and at its end a wiser and older persona of the poet, who has in some sense sublimated the love whose suffering and intermittent joy he represented, but his voice does not disqualify those sufferings and intermittent joys: every poem transmits an intensity that points to a particular human being here and now.[1] Indeed, the poetry can be read as defining the very conditions by which language and affect can designate another person as radically singular.

The *RVF* repeatedly marks the moment when everything changed. It recalls the first moment, it celebrates further moments, it imagines or hypothesizes others, and it deplores another, final one. The formulation "una rivolta d'occhi" (*RVF* 72, 34–35) – one turning, turning-around of the eyes (to look at me) – concentrates many of the meanings of the moment that makes everything change. Its context is less important than the expression itself, though the context is telling enough: the poet would not exchange "una rivolta d'occhi," one glance of Laura's eyes, for the happiness that Love or Fortune can give to their favorites. The ecstatic moment is then evoked famously in terms of "angelic sparks" descending as sweetness into the lover's heart, filling it and driving out all else (37–45). This expression of pleasure is less important for me, though, than the gesture setting it off: Laura *turns* to look at the poet. The glance is sudden – it is not an observing, or a comprehensive viewing, or, more brutally, a staring. Laura's glance represents a break in time both in relation to the past and, perhaps, implicitly, in relation to the future. As the term "rivolta" suggests today (and then), there is something of a violent rupture, a transgression of static, continuous, or progressive time.

There are other representations of change, of movement in time, in the *RVF*.[2] Poems occasionally record the passing of years: twenty-one years go by between the poet's first meeting of Laura and her death, ten more between her death and the end of the collection. Petrarch evokes the seasons, the passing of days and nights, and even the gradual shaping of storm clouds. He mentions his aging. But this particular change is produced by the encounter of two individuals; it is not subsumed into a natural cycle, it does not participate in a general, universal progression of life. Laura turns to look, which also means that she turns to the poet, in a gestural equivalent of specific intention. The glance is directed at him and at no other (anticipating the exclusive reign of sweetness in his heart). Petrarch indicates "one" turn: one turn of the eyes to look at me will suffice to unleash this sweetness. But also: this one turn of the eyes is directed to one person. Only one glance suffices because it concerns me as only me.

This gesture condenses in a very few words the existential impact that lies at the heart of Petrarch's love lyric; it displays how an instant of specific encounter can constitute an event that disrupts everything, that infiltrates all other states or movements, and that, concurrently, radicalizes the singular appeal of poetic language. The event that is the *rivolta d'occhi* signifies the "being out there" of a particular person, a place, a time, and Petrarch's poetry, then, *optionally*, provides information by which this person or place or time can be understood by resorting to meaning. It is this beginning that counts, the prelude to the semantic.

The early poems in the *RVF* evoke the first impact of Laura's eyes, but I will discuss to begin with a later sonnet in the collection, to show how Petrarch represents its repercussions in time. The poet-lover occasionally marks the anniversary of his first meeting of Laura, and its memory is delineated with an extreme precision, as if precision were the only way that language could convey its significance.[3] Sixteen years have passed since Laura's turning glance made everything change:

> Rimansi a dietro il sestodecimo anno
> de' miei sospiri, et io trapasso inanzi
> verso l'estremo; et parmi che pur dianzi
> fosse 'l principio di cotanto affanno.

> L'amar m'è dolce, et util il mio danno,
> e 'l viver grave; et prego che gli avanzi
> l'empia fortuna; et temo no chiuda anzi
> Morte i begli occhi che parlar mi fanno.
>   Or qui son, lasso, et voglio esser altrove;
> et vorrei più volere, et più non voglio,
> et per più non poter fo quant'io posso;
>   et d'antichi desir lagrime nove
> provan com' io son pur quel ch' i' mi soglio,
> né per mille rivolte anchor son mosso.
>
> (*RVF* 118)

(Now remains behind the sixteenth year of my sighs, and I move forward toward the last; yet it seems to me that all this suffering began only recently. The bitter is sweet to me, and my losses useful, and living heavy; and I pray that my life may outlast my cruel fortune; and I fear that before then Death may close the lovely eyes that make me speak. Now here I am, alas, and wish I were elsewhere, and wish I wished more, but wish no more, and, by being unable to do more, do all I can: and new tears for old desires show me to be still what I used to be, nor for a thousand turnings about have I yet moved)

The narrative component of this sonnet is slight: the poet confirms his unchanged love for Laura, expresses his wish not to be suffering, and fears that death will overtake Laura before his fortune changes (and he can see her again). The tradition emerging from Petrarch will highlight the antitheses: bitter is sweet for me, what is useful is damaging, and life is painful, crushing (an important meaning of "gravis" in Latin). Indeed, the self-destructive paradoxes of love, as exacerbated in many poems of the *RVF*, were profoundly fascinating and unsettling to a culture for which the inherent desirability of life was given by nature and God, and for which ethical behavior assumed a reasoned, enduring choice of what is good for the human being itself. But the poem also, and most importantly, showcases several features of Petrarchan lyric language: the primacy of the instant over development in time, a certain use of the deictic,[4] a willed redundancy of vocabulary, and the delineation of a singular gesture on the background of the indefinite.

The meeting with Laura is so incisive because it is "as if it were just now" (v. 3: "dianzi") and yet sixteen years have passed. Over the duration of the past, Petrarch projects a simultaneity: such an instant is always absolutely present. Absolute not only because the instant can be "relived" after sixteen years, but also because, in the same quatrain, Petrarch evokes the ultimate end (v. 3: "l'estremo"), the beginning (v. 4: "'l principio"), and the feeling of a gradual passage of life's stages (v. 2: "io trapasso..."); *whatever* the measure of temporal duration, however, this event is always stronger than the progression from one stage to another, and it collapses the end into the beginning, into this instant.

What do sixteen years mean? They are not represented in terms of aging, work, development of a person praiseworthy in his achievements; instead, they are sixteen years of "sighs" (v. 2: "de' miei sospiri"), recalling the sonnet that inaugurates the collection: you, reader, are listening to "quei sospiri ond'io nudriva 'l core" (*RVF* 1, 2: "those sighs with which I nourished my heart"). The sigh is not what one says or writes, but the primary connection between voice and affect that will then give rise to speech. And it has not changed since that event. The poet's sighs, in their faithful identity and imperviousness to time, are contrary to "empia fortuna" (v. 7: "cruel" Fortune, but also "impious," in the Latin sense of lacking "pietas": reverence and faithfulness in one's duties), which threatens to close Laura's eyes.

The first tercet voices the poet's sigh itself ("lasso," "alas") in the middle of a line that poses the poet's condition as sparsely and yet as effectively as no other: "Now here I am, alas, and wish I were elsewhere" (v. 9). The sentence contrasts what we are and what we wish to be in spatial terms: it can mean literally that the lover wishes to be with Laura, but the deictic "qui" is insistent, and seems to encompass all the experience that this encounter has entailed: temporal, spatial, and "psychological." Petrarch does not say, "I am in Italy and I wish to be in Provence," but, "I am *here*." In another sense, it says nothing at all: if Petrarch had only said, "alas, and wish I were elsewhere," the same meaning would have been conveyed. "Now here I am" is unnecessary. But the simple gesture of designating a "here" has the effect of concentrating all of the suffering and weight (another sense of "'l viver grave," "living heavy") of his life and making it available to the reader, even though the words are semantically evanescent.

The two following lines are replete with forms of "to wish" and "to be able to," reflecting no doubt Augustinian reflections on the will, as Petrarch laid them out in his *Secretum*, but more importantly, for our purposes, crowding out other semantic material. The words' redundancy is frustrating, just as are the endless paradoxes of individual will and action. Hence the inefficacy of these reflections faced with the persistence of the event of Laura's *rivolta d'occhi*. And that is what we end with: the final line contrasts the "mille rivolte" (v. 14: "a thousand turnings") – meaning here literally the thousand, innumerable (other) events, vicissitudes – with the poet's own singular faithfulness in turning back to the single and singular glance of Laura.

Both the frequent theme of the beloved's eyes and the similarly frequent contrast between an indefinite "mille" ("thousand") and the definite "uno" ("one") allow me to move to a further illustration of Petrarch's language of existential intention. The praise of Laura's eyes or glance constitutes one of the main rhetorical elements of the poetry; that is, evoking the beauty, but especially the force, of her glance enables the poet to justify, to render plausible, his implausibly persistent love and suffering. A stanza from the canzone "Ben mi credea" instantiates this rhetorical orientation, but rather than ostentatiously record the failure of epideictic rhetoric[5] to capture the object of praise, which itself can be used to rhetorical purposes, Petrarch seems to dispense with the need to render his behavior plausible, and concentrates instead on something like an essence of human contact:

> Ch'i' ò cercate già vie più di mille
> per provar senza lor se mortal cosa
> mi potesse tener in vita un giorno.
> L'anima, poi ch'altrove non à posa,
> corre pur a l'angeliche faville,
> et io che son di cera al foco torno;
>   et pongo mente intorno
> ove si fa men guardia a quel ch'i' bramo,
> et come augel in ramo
> ove men teme, ivi più tosto è colto,
> così dal suo bel volto
> l'involo or uno et or un altro sguardo,
> et di ciò inseme mi nutrico et ardo.
>
> (*RVF* 207, 27–39)

(For I have sought more than a thousand ways to find out if any mortal thing could keep me alive one day without them. My soul, since it finds rest nowhere else, still runs to those angelic sparks, and I, who am of wax, return to the fire; and I consider where what I desire is least guarded, and as a bird on the branch is soonest taken where he is least afraid, so from her lovely face I steal now one, now another glance, and by them I am both nourished and set on fire)

The poet amplifies the notion, taken from previous stanzas of the poem, that he is incapable of not seeking the glances of Laura, despite his age, and despite the fact that he is reduced to becoming a thief (v. 8: "ladro") to obtain them. His efforts have taken the form of a thousand "vie," that is, paths or means, in order to "provar," to find out, experience or to prove whether any mortal thing (as opposed to God, presumably) could keep him alive one single day without the "occhi soavi" (v. 14: "gentle eyes"). The contrast between the thousand paths and the one day deprived of the eyes of Laura speaks negatively, first of all, to the determined path the Christian wayfarer takes on his way to salvation. Instead of choosing the one path and confronting endless contingencies, the lover has tried an endless number of paths and always returns to the one (self-destructive) contingency. The indefiniteness of all the recourses to "mortal things" recalls as well the metaphor of the lover's "wandering" in the first sonnet (*R VF* 1, 3: "giovenile errore") and shows what is lacking: a rectilinear moral orientation, instead of the lover circling around fire and the thief's thoughts circling around the bird. But the terms "via" and "provare" also derive from rhetorical discourse: the first can have the sense of "method" or "instrument," and in Latin can be found coupled with "ratio" ("reason"); the second connects to rhetorical or dialectical proof. In other words, the poet's attempts to free himself from the effects of love have taken the form of endless reasoning and yet left him with persistence in behavior that is impervious to reason. Instead of following one Christian path or being persuaded by a proof, the soul (the "anima") and the mind (the "mente"), those parts of the human being susceptible, respectively, to moral–religious reflection and to rational discourse, go running about or devise furtive plans inspired by desire.

However, and this is where one steps outside of the rhetorical–didactic frame, something else becomes more important; indeed, *exclusively* important. It is conveyed through two analogies, the first with the wax figure drawn to fire and the second involving the thief waiting to ensnare the bird. The analogies do not seem compatible with each other, since in the first the poet will destroy himself by approaching the fire, whereas in the second it is the bird who seems to be the victim of the poet-lover. One possibility is that the two comparisons concern the soul and the mind: what is a clever pastime for the mind is destructive to the soul. The soul only finds "posa" (v. 30), rest or peace, or simply (and paradoxically) stable support, in the "angeliche faville" (v. 31), the angelic sparks of Laura's eyes, as the poet, made of wax, is drawn to fire. This gesture of the soul is a move away from moral direction and reasoning: "[l]'anima...corre pur" (v. 30–31: "my soul...still runs"); it *nevertheless* runs to the sparks of love, like the wax figure that invites its own destruction in the flame. The mind, on the other hand ("mind" I take to be contained within the expression "pongo mente," "I consider"), unbothered by the consequences for the soul, circles around its prey and succeeds in stealing glances from the unwary bird. But whatever the scenario of conflicting interior faculties, vaguely recalling the medieval tradition of the *psychomachia*, it all comes down to an "io" ("I") who acts, desires, and suffers: "torno," "pongo mente," "bramo," "involo," "nutrico," and "ardo" (the inevitable consequence of approaching fire). It is this that counts. The "io" exhibits an insistence and an existential density corresponding to the "ciò inseme" (v. 39: "this together") of the conclusion.

The two comparisons, set one after the other, hint at a possibility of reciprocity. The lover is drawn to a deadly fire, but he also sets his mind to ensnaring the bird and succeeds in stealing glances from his lady. The lover's desire leads not to a retreat into utter solitude and separation, but projects into the beloved a guardedness, and also moments of unguardedness, so effectively that the occasionally captured glances of Laura nourish him. This reciprocity – you trap me and I trap you – is inherent in the glance itself; that is, "catching" a glance means that when I look at you, you look at me, and it is only you and only me. The scenario is very different from the "gaze" of the voyeuristic subject, whose desire does not require a return, and who never projects the desired object as a subject in her own right. Laura is not interchangeable with any beautiful woman who can be looked at and enjoyed without her knowledge.

Petrarch's choice of the verb "cogliere" ("take" or "catch") in its past participle form "colto" (v. 36: "taken") to indicate the ensnaring of the bird is telling. In sonnet 181, the poet speaks of himself being caught in a snare laid by Love: "Così caddi a la rete, et qui m'àn colto / gli atti vaghi et l'angeliche parole" (*RVF* 181, 12–13: "Thus I fell into the net; and I have been captured here by her sweet bearing, and her angelic words"). The same past participle expresses capture of the lover and capture of the beloved. What is more, the verb "cogliere" suggests not just capture of an animal, but perhaps foremost the collecting of flowers, with all the attendant sensual (and poetic) implications, some of which will be developed in the ecstatic and erotic vision of Laura with which I will conclude.

Before doing so, we need to return to features of Petrarch's singular language in the stanza I quoted from *RVF* 207. The first feature could be called spatialization of affect: the soul "*altrove* non à posa" (v. 30), cannot find rest *anywhere* else: love, the obsessive thoughts of Laura, attempts to find her glance, are a *place* that is unlike anything else. Similarly, when the lover sets out to steal her glances, he turns, literally, "*ove* si fa men guardia a quel ch'i' bramo" (v. 34: "to where there is less watchfulness against what I desire"). And the maxim-like "ove men teme, ivi più tosto è colto" (v. 36: "is soonest taken where he is least afraid") makes the branch on which the bird alights an extension of its lack of guardedness. It is as if the soul had prepared a space of intimacy, enabling the exchange of glances, the mutual capturing that is the exclusive hope of the lover.

Within this space, then, the thief can steal here one, here another glance (v. 38: "or uno et or un altro sguardo"). Petrarch does not say "I stole charming glances" and leave it at that; instead, he spaces out the instances of visual and amorous contact, as if to fill out that intimate space with moments of time, and extend the pleasure that they provide. The deictics here, from "altrove" (v. 30: "nowhere") to "ove" (v. 34: "where") to "quel che" (v. 34: "what") to "ivi" (v. 36: "where") to "or" (v. 38: "now") accumulate and are summarized in one final deictic, "ciò inseme" (v. 39): all *this together* is my nourishment. The deictics are immensely significant and simultaneously semantically poor. The fact of being able to point to *this*, to indicate, to designate contacts with Laura is the basic manifestation of language's ability to convey a singular existence, and only convey it, that is, not describe it, not fit it into a traditional, rhetorically crafted discourse of praise. And furthermore, the constructions involving these deictics are not "elegant" but rough and awkward, and lexically uninteresting. But perhaps those are the conditions of lyric singularity that Petrarch is setting out in his *RVF*.

Many of the features of Petrarch's lyric language and existential intention that we find illustrated in *RVF* 118 and 207 are developed in a justly celebrated ecstatic vision of the beloved in the famous "Chiare, fresche et dolci acque" (*RVF* 126). The canzone contains a stanza constituting a euphoric pendant to the melancholy "Now here I am" of 118 and to the "My soul, since it finds rest nowhere else" of 207 as spaces of intense affect. As the poem is traditionally understood, it describes first, apparently, a bath taken by (a possibly nude) Laura in the Sorgue river in the Vaucluse, and then the nature surrounding her when she is sitting on its shores, all of which was witnessed by the poet, whose memory of it is manifestly rapturous.

> Da' be' rami scendea
> (dolce ne la memoria)
> una pioggia di fior' sovra 'l suo grembo;
>   et ella si sedea
> umile in tanta gloria,
> coverta già de l'amoroso nembo;
>   qual fior cadea sul limbo,
> qual su le treccie bionde,
> ch'oro forbito et perle
> eran quel dì a vederle,
> qual si posava in terra et qual su l'onde,
> qual, con un vago errore
> girando parea dir: "Qui regna Amore. "
>   (*RVF* 126, 40–52)

(From the lovely branches was descending (sweet in memory) a rain of flowers over her bosom, and she was sitting humble in such a glory, already covered with the loving cloud; this flower was falling on her skirt, this one on her blond braids, which were burnished gold and pearls to see that day; this one was coming to rest on the ground, this one on the water, this one, with a lovely wandering, turning about seemed to say: "Here reigns Love.")

Petrarch's knowing, but more chaste, almost religious version of Danaë's seduction by Jupiter,[6] seems semantically fuller than many of his other visions of a beatific Laura, and even resembles a portion of a narrative. The erotic charge of the description derives not from an evocation of Laura's body itself, but from the contact with her body, or merely the proximity to her body, that the falling flowers enjoy.[7] The flowers softly descending onto Laura all seem to caress her, or mark and embellish a space of intimacy surrounding her. This cascading effect, similar to the series of effects set off by one turn of her eyes, "una rivolta d'occhi," in the earlier quoted *RVF* 72, culminates in the simple declarative "Qui regna Amore" (v. 52: "Here reigns Love.") The final deictic "qui" ("here") is preceded by a series of demonstrative adjectives detailing the path, or, rather, the destination, of each falling flower. *This one* here, *this one* there: the process of singling out each individual in a "rain" of flowers could be endless, a drawing-out of the instant of pleasure into a duration without end. The "loving cloud" covering her is not sufficient, but the poet traces the intention, as it were, of each caress: her bosom, her dress (or lap), her hair . . . The deictic instantiates that caress: I indicate that flower which is touching your hair. Which seems equivalent to "I (want to) touch your hair," through the act of indicating itself. The demonstrative adjectives create a proximity, both as an erotic intention and as, explicitly, a re-calling (v. 41: "dolce ne la memoria"):[8] a calling back or a drawing close to oneself of past ecstatic experience.

The deictics represent "variety" by indicating various, apparently random, single elements in a "cloud." They give a depth and a "texture" to the more indistinct and rapid expression of multiplicity in "amoroso nembo" (v. 45: "loving cloud"). However, as we have seen, the path of each flower is not random, but is given a spatial intention by the poet, and an erotic intention.[9] Variety is less a fullness of language and of the world than a reiteration of the poet's desire, its intensification. These are the ways in which I caress you again and again.

The final flower seems to land nowhere in particular, but is only movement, combining the "errore," the "wandering" of the *RVF*'s opening sonnet (yet a wandering innocent of moral reprobation), and the winding, turning that is opposite to the directed path of the virtuous. It becomes the symbol of desire itself, the letting-go that Laura seems to accept, in this vision, and that makes this memory so irresistibly sweet to the poet. The concluding demonstrative adjective "qual" ("this") incarnates a choice by the poet, and also calls for a response that summarizes all of what he has seen. "Qui regna Amore" is both a response and an expression of the poet's thought, literalizing the dialogic nature of the deictic and literalizing the identification of poet and natural elements touching Laura that his presentation of the scene had suggested all along. But "Qui regna Amore" is also not "I love you." Petrarch has preferred to establish a space, a proximity, an intimacy through the various demonstratives that envelope Laura in flowers, in caresses, and has prepared a "seggio" ("seat") within this poem, within this memory, and in the "real" past that only Laura can occupy. Love is triumphant, in general ("regna Amore"), but the "qui," as well as the demonstratives, singularize the space: love is triumphant *here* only for *you* and *me*.

NOTES

1 The formula "here and now" is loaded with theoretical freight, to which this essay cannot do justice. The notion that lyric poetry transmits the "singular" and emanates from an empirically located single subject is essentially a modern notion, analyzed in Käte Hamburger, *The Logic of Literature*, trans. Marilynn J. Rose, 2nd edn. (Bloomington, IN: Indiana University Press, 2003), 272–287. Early modern lyric is assumed to de-personalize the subject addressing and the addressee: "As a speaker shifts the role of target away from even (let us say) a real, hearing addressee, the effect is to abstract or 'fictionalize' that speaker's use of the pronoun 'you' until it only weakly means the interlocutor who is genuinely present and the reversibility of I and you is frozen. This is the communicative situation of the vast body of European poetry in the courtly love and Petrarchan traditions..." (William Waters, *Poetry's Touch: On Lyric Address* (Ithaca, NY: Cornell University Press, 2003), 28). My reading of Petrarch marks features of his language that allow for a singularity, despite the poetic and rhetorical conventions of his time that militate against subjectivity of lyric, and without assuming an empirical density of Laura or a strictly biographical presence of the poet.

2 On the role of time in the *RVF*, see Teodolinda Barolini, "The Self in the Labyrinth of Time," in *Petrarch: A Critical Guide*, Kirkham and Maggi, 33–62.

3 See *RVF* 61, 1–4: "Blessed be the day and the month and the year and the season and the time and the hour and the instant [punto] and the beautiful countryside and the place where I was struck [giunto] by the two lovely eyes that have bound me." These gradations of time point to the rhyme "punto"/"giunto": the point (in Latin, "punctum") is both the wound and the moment, the instant. Time is measured by what it *does*.

4 By "deictic" I mean those elements of language that "point to" or show directly something about the situation in which the speaker finds himself or herself; examples are "here," "this," "that," and "now."

5 Following classical models, in Petrarch's time rhetoric was divided into three types: deliberative (speech concerning actions to be accomplished), judicial (speech judging past action), and epideictic (speech praising or blaming a person, a city, etc.). Poetry was thought to be informed mainly by the latter.

6 On the surface, the motif of the "rain of flowers" lends this scene a sense of "divine consecration," which is its meaning in Dante (*Purg*, XXX.28–32) and in the Latin classical tradition (see Marco Santagata, "Note," in Francesco Petrarca, *Canzoniere*, ed. Marco Santagata, 2nd edn. (Milan: Mondadori, 2004), 597–598). Similarly, Laura seated "umile in tanta gloria" cannot but evoke praises of the Virgin Mary. One does not exclude the other.

7 This eroticizing of contiguity or contact with natural elements – branches that she touches, grass that her naked feet walk on or that she sits on – constitutes a discreet and distinct sexual tone of the collection. See especially *RVF* 121, 4–5: "and she in a mere robe with loose hair is sitting barefoot amid the flowers and the grass," *RVF* 125, 53–54: "You know well that so beautiful a foot never touched the earth," and *RVF* 125, 72–74: "to walk through the meadows beside the river, and sometimes to make herself a seat, fresh, flowering, and green."

8 For the function of detail, memory and imitation in this canzone, see Nancy J. Vickers, "Remembering Dante: Petrarch's 'Chiare, fresche et dolci acque,'" *MLN* 96 (1981): 1–11.

9 The anaphoric deictic "qual" ("this") in Petrarch recalls a similar "place" of love ("Est qui nequitiam locus exigat": "There is a place that requires wantonness") in Ovid's *Amores* (trans. Grant Showerman, 2nd edn. (Cambridge, MA: Harvard University Press 1977), III.14, 17): the deictic "illic" ("there") punctuates a series of erotic actions or movements that emphasize the pleasures of sex (III.14, 17–26). The Ovidian source reinforces the erotic intention that designates the falling flowers caressing Laura; Petrarch, as always, is immeasurably more discreet than his Latin predecessor.

6

ZYGMUNT G. BARAŃSKI

The *Triumphi*

The *Triumphi* is a poem of considerable artistic and intellectual ambition. In the Petrarchan canon, it is the work which more than any other, if not actually exclusively, bears the responsibility of offering a broad-based, integrated, and overarching assessment of its author's complex cultural, historical, ethical, and ideological preoccupations – preoccupations which are made more intricate by being closely entwined with matters of a more strictly personal nature, most notably his relationship with Laura. The poem constitutes Petrarch's great attempt to harmonize and resolve his intellectual and spiritual conflicts, thereby overcoming the dichotomies of his life and artistic career. At the same time, like Dante's *Commedia*, its primary source and interlocutor, the *Triumphi* focuses on universalizing moral–didactic and cultural questions. Consequently, the choice of the vernacular for such a definitive and demanding project might seem problematic in light of the poet's repeated claims as to its subordinate status in relation to Latin. Yet, Petrarch never downplayed the significance of the *Triumphi*, as he did that of the *RVF*. Instead of *nugae* (trifles) and *fragmenta* (fragments), he confidently spoke of the *Triumphi* as his "magnum opus" (*Sen.* V.2: "great work").

At every level of the poem, beginning with its title, now definitively established on the basis of manuscript evidence as the Latin *Triumphi*, Petrarch made clear its classicizing character, and hence its imposing cultural substance. The poem is a synthesis of classical and vernacular elements – a text to inspire the renewal of a degraded present, the "secol noioso" (*TC* I, 17: "wearisome century"), which draws on the lessons both of the past and of more recent times. On the one hand, the *Triumphi*'s division into twelve *capitula* (chapters) mirrors the canonical number of books of the *Aeneid*, while, on the other, its recourse to *terza rima*, the rhyme scheme invented by Dante for the *Commedia*, and its use of the eleven-beat hendecasyllable, the quintessential line of Italian verse, underscore its vernacular affiliations. Furthermore, Petrarch unevenly distributed the twelve "chapters" between six discrete yet narratively interlocking units, each with its own Latin designation and dedicated to a particular triumph: Love (four "chapters"), Chastity (one), Death (two), Fame (three), Time (one), and Eternity (one). Though the organization of the *capitula* into the further textual component of "Questi triumphi" (*TE* 121: "These triumphs") recalls Dante's ordering of the *Commedia*'s "cantos" into "canticles," Petrarch's irregular allocation, in sharp contrast to his predecessor's regular patterning, is an obvious pointer to the personal and original nature of his poem.

The *Triumphi*'s rich array of sources – which embrace the Latin historians, rhetoricians, encyclopaedists, moralists, and, most notably, epic and elegiac poets, as well as the Bible, the Church Fathers, medieval Latin allegorical poetry, and Romance vernacular narrative and lyric verse – not only reaffirms its synthesizing imperative, but also draws attention to Petrarch's unique reworking of and mastery over most of the main areas of his culture. To this already exhilarating mix, Petrarch added personal ingredients, engaging in a constant dialogue with his own works, most especially the *RVF*, the *Secretum*, the *Africa*, and the *De remediis*, placing himself at the center of the *Triumphi*'s general account of the attainments and limitations of human existence, and highlighting the poem's contemporary relevance. From this latter perspective, the *Triumphi* appears to address and attenuate major concerns regarding the compatibility of classical and vernacular, of pagan and Christian, and of literature and other intellectual disciplines. Indeed, in its form and in the syncretic view of history that dominates its diegesis, the *Triumphi* provides concrete exemplary evidence that different civilizations, systems of belief, and epistemologies can co-exist harmoniously, not least because they are all subject to the same emotional, intellectual, and existential pressures and realities – the six "triumphs" which form the poem's narrative and ideological core.

Despite its seeming structural, intellectual, and cultural consistency, the *Triumphi*, like so much of Petrarch's oeuvre, is unfinished. Indeed, its manuscript transmission is especially complicated, bedevilled by corrections, variants, a major rewriting of the opening of *TM* I, and an alternative treatment of the *TF* in two "chapters." At present, no satisfactory critical edition of the text exists, though it is likely that this would not differ considerably from the vulgate, that is, traditionally adopted, version. Equally problematic is the question of the *Triumphi*'s dating. Some critics have assigned its beginnings to the early 1340s; however, most present-day scholars, admittedly on the basis of fairly weak evidence, believe that Petrarch began to compose the poem in 1352, and that he only penned the final "triumph" in 1373–74, a matter of months before his death. The evidence for this last dating is strong.

The *Triumphi* is the first-person account of a dream-vision experienced at dawn in early spring by the poet-protagonist, who had fallen asleep while considering the ambiguous and complex nature of his "dolce" (*TC* I, 2: "sweet") yet anguished love for Laura, whom he had first espied at the same time of year. By closely mirroring the lover's mood, the dream, a mix of "assai dolor con breve gioco" (*TC* I, 12: "much pain with little pleasure"), is presented as psychologically realistic, thus enhancing its reliability, which is strengthened by its occurring at dawn, when dreams were considered to be true. Unlike in the *Commedia*, there is no suggestion that the vision has a supernatural provenance.

The dream's origins and substance are to be sought in the central character's reflections, and hence in Petrarch himself, since the poem leaves no doubt as regards the identity of the nameless protagonist, openly alluding to the poet's friends, to Laura, to his poetry, and to his poetic crowning in 1341. The dream is thus a testament to Petrarch's unique spiritual and intellectual accomplishments, as well as to his moral and cultural authority, both of which are established during the course of the poem. The sight that immediately greets the visionary is alien to the present (*TC* I, 16–18): standing on a "triumphal carro" (v. 15: "triumphal chariot") drawn by "quattro destrier, vie più che neve bianchi" (v. 22: "four horses, much whiter than snow") is a "victorïoso...duce" (v. 13: "victorious...leader"). Petrarch wastes no time in fixing the poem's fundamental triumphal paradigm, and thus its affinity to ancient Roman culture. Equally, and repeatedly, he underscores the "marvellous," frequently inexpressible character of what he saw, thereby affirming his vision's, and, by extension, the *Triumphi*'s, exceptionality. The victor is he "colui che 'l mondo chiama Amore" (v. 76: "whom the world calls Love"), the embodiment of the destructive emotion. Like a Roman conqueror celebrating his military *triumphus* on the Capitoline Hill (v. 14) – the evident model for Amore's parade – Love is followed by a long procession of those whom he has vanquished (vv. 28–30).

Much of the remainder of the first "chapter" (vv. 88–159) is taken up with a lengthy catalog of Love's victims, all of whom belong to the ancient world (further figures from antiquity, as well as Scriptural and Arthurian personages, and one contemporary couple, Paolo and Francesca, made famous by Dante in *Inferno* V, are listed in *TC* III, while the first part of the fourth *capitulum* is dedicated to an inventory of lovestruck Greek, Latin, Italian, and Occitan writers). Enumeration is a key element of the *Triumphi*'s organization, and catalogs of varying length reappear in the *TP* and in all three "chapters" of the *TF*.

These lists, a combination of proper names and scholarly circumlocutions, are the primary means by which Petrarch signals his idea that the past and the present are closely enmeshed, and that the past is of lasting and crucial relevance for the present. The processing figures, despite coming from different epochs, have been subject to the same experiences and make obvious, by their spatial and physical proximity in the triumphal parades, the poet's sense of history as being less chronologically evolutionary than exemplary, syncretic, and providential. More importantly, the lists confirm the breadth, coherence, and rigor of his learning, which is not deployed as an end in itself but with a firm moral purpose.

Though Petrarch's learning is predominantly classical and secular, recent research has demonstrated that the final "triumph," as befits its metaphysical concerns, reveals through its subject matter and intertexts a profound and sophisticated engagement with Scriptural and Christian sources, in particular Paul, Augustine, and Bonaventure. Equally, the poem's key principles and beliefs are largely Christian – focused on renunciation, charity, and salvation – but at the same time allow room for classical values of heroism and fame. Petrarch's Humanism is thus religiously inflected, and the *Triumphi* substantiates the claim, which the poet often repeated in later life (*Fam.* X.4, XXII.10; *Sen.* XVIII.1, or the so-called "Letter to Posterity"), that his new literary and ideological ideal had become the fusion of his religious and secular models. The erudite reference is not in fact restricted to the catalogs but is a constant feature at every level of the poem, from similes to authorial asides and from characters' speeches to descriptions of settings and events. Petrarch thus leaves little doubt as to his fitness as an intellectual and moral "authority" for his contemporaries, namely, someone "worthy of faith and obedience," the highest accolade that the medieval world could grant an individual or an institution.

Though Petrarch's recourse to the catalog has illustrious precedents in the classical and vernacular epic, no earlier narrative poem is as dependent on the device as the *Triumphi*. Indeed, readers have complained that the enumerations severely compromise the poem's aesthetic success, making it "lifeless" and mechanistic; and there is no doubt that the narrative efficacy of the list is at best limited. At the same time, to equate the *Triumphi* primarily with the catalog is reductive. Equally reductive are those definitions of the poem which term it "allegorical," that is, made up of symbolic events and figures enacting a moral drama, and hence conforming to the conventions of the most popular form of medieval story-telling. Though Petrarch does make recourse to such figurative writing, for instance, to make concrete some of the six abstractions around which the *Triumphi* revolves (a personified Sun as a symbol of Time in the *TT*), the overwhelming historical and intellectual force of his catalogs places a severe curb on the poem's allegorical character.

In fact, the narrative of the *Triumphi* is quite varied. The poem is marked throughout by shifts between distinct narrative modes: between events narrated from the point of view of the protagonist and events depicted from the narrator's perspective, and between personal "lyric" moments and "epic" universalizing ones (nowhere is this more apparent than in the transition from *TM* II to *TF* I, from the intimate and loving conversation between Laura and the protagonist to the solemn parade of Roman heroes). Indeed, even the controlling triumphal motif is treated differently in each "triumph," ranging from the reproduction of the Roman procession in the *TC* to the allegorical representation of the rapidly moving chariot of the Sun in the *TT*, a symbol of the victory of time over human fame and memory.

The opening "chapter" of the *TC* establishes the poem's narrative ambition. After describing Amore (Love) in largely allegorizing terms (*TC* I, 13–30), and before composing his pageant of defeated lovers (vv. 88–159), Petrarch pens a wide-ranging interlude (vv. 31–87) in which he begins to flesh out his protagonist. The dreamer meets a Tuscan acquaintance, whose identity is never revealed, but with whom he converses, and who, as the role of guide demands, helps the bewildered visionary find his bearings. This episode is obviously different in structure and tone from the chapter's two other principal segments and is narratively more sophisticated, touching on matters of psychology, biography, and character interaction. Overall, the first "chapter," as befits its status as "prologue" to the poem (according to medieval poetics, the *proem* was meant to offer an introduction to the form and content of the work as a whole), efficiently displays Petrarch's principal compositional practices throughout the *Triumphi*. *TC* I furthermore establishes the poem's main literary sources and its thematic and ideological concerns – "tempo" (v. 1: "time"), "memoria" (v. 2: "memory"), love, existential anguish, glory (v. 15), the discrepancies between an illustrious past and a mediocre present, death (obsessively), friendship, learning, the relationship between the human and the divine, Laura, and, of course, the self – concerns which, while they define and organize the poem, are also, not surprisingly, the great constants of Petrarch's oeuvre in general.

The *TC* ends with the inexplicable arrival of Amore and his victims on Cyprus, the island "sacred" (*TC* IV, 107) to Venus, where the triumphant lord imprisons his countless victims in a "tenebrosa e stretta gabbia" (v. 157: "dark and narrow prison"). Amore's victory, however, is short-lived. After a violent conflict – a lengthy piece of bravura writing rich in imagery, learned reference, and shifts in perspective and register (vv. 19–126) – Amore is "legato" ("bound") to a "D'un bel diaspro ... colonna" (*TP* 124 and 120: "column of beautiful jasper") by the protagonist's "donna ... [che] avea in dosso ... candida gonna" (vv. 116 and 118: "lady ... clothed in ... a

snow-white dress"), the embodiment of Chastity, who frees the god's pris-
oners. Laura thus "triumpha...di colui che pria / ...avea del mondo tri-
umphare" (vv. 146–47: "triumphs over him who previously / ...had triumphed over the world"), and, like a Roman general, leads her cortege to "la
città sovrana" (v. 178: "the supreme city"). This journey, like that to Cyprus,
is confusedly handled by Petrarch, who not infrequently is careless with the
workings and verisimilitude of his story. The celebrations of Laura and her
"brigata allegra" (*TM* 29: "happy company") are also quickly brought to a
halt when a "donna involta in veste negra" (v. 31: "woman swathed in black
clothing") fiercely intervenes. Death inexorably "triumpha" (*TF* I, 1: "triumphs") over Laura, who in the past had "triumphato" (v. 2: "triumphed")
over her lover; and just as inexorably, Fame triumphs over Death, before
itself being defeated by Time, which, in turn, is conquered by Eternity.

The classical Roman triumph is indisputably the key structuring mechanism and ideological motif that controls the narrative and intellectual logic
of the *Triumphi*; and, significantly, Petrarch was the first to appreciate its
potential as a literary device – a powerfully distinctive mark of the originality of his "great work." In the fourteenth century, of course, the triumph
was more than just a handy textual expedient. As the narrator remarks on
first seeing Love triumphant, he was quite unused to such a grandiose sight.
For Petrarch (and his world), the triumph was no longer a real event, but
a quintessential cultural symbol, a potent memory of Rome's achievements,
a telling trope with which to evoke all that was best and most typically
Roman (see especially *TC* I and IV and *TF* I and III). Thus, Scipio Africanus,
in the *Triumphi* (*TF* I, 23–25) and throughout the poet's oeuvre the supreme
representative of Roman virtue thanks to his victory over Hannibal in the
Second Punic War, is "lui che...sol per triumphi...nacque" (*TP* 176–77:
"he who...was born solely for triumphs").

The triumph was already a key feature of classical Latin literature, appearing in the works of authors as different as Virgil, Cicero, and Livy. Like the
other sights experienced by the dreamer – "giungea la vista con l'antiche
carte / ove son gli alti nomi e' sommi pregi" (*TF* II, 4–5: "I conjoined what
I saw with the ancient pages / in which are the lofty names and the supreme
merits") – it was a textual construct. Through his personal reworking of
the Roman triumph, both the pageant and its literary treatment, Petrarch
indicated his admiration for and his debts to a whole culture. At the same
time, it is highly significant that no precise and exclusive reference to a particular classical text is to be found in the poet's treatment. Even as Petrarch
acknowledged imitative dependence, he asserted an authoritative originality.

In keeping with his own theory of "imitation" (*Fam.* XXIII.19), Petrarch
refused to follow automatically any single source, fashioning instead a new

personal invention out of his readings in the Latin classics, as well as in other writers. Though the poet was acutely sensitive to the triumph's literary power and remit, he was equally aware of the astonishing breadth of its artistic, ideological, and biographical connotation. In fact, the motif of the triumph also introduces a Christian dimension into the poem, since, as early as the reign of Constantine (first decades of the fourth century), Roman triumphal symbolism was appropriated to represent the victory of Christianity over paganism and that of Jesus over death. Indeed, in the *TE*, Petrarch stressed his ties to this tradition by openly citing John's Apocalypse (see *TE* 20–23 and Rev. 21, 1), whose closing chapters depict Christ's victory. In other words, the triumph pointed to the possibility of a harmonious co-existence between the two basic yet conflicting sides of Petrarch's intellectual, spiritual, and cultural experience.

In his poem's richly informative "prologue," Petrarch underscored the syncretist character both of the triumph in general and of his treatment of it in particular. The initial description of "victorïoso" (*TC* I, 13: "victorious") Amore is a hybrid (vv. 13–15, 22–30), a mix of elements loosely taken from historical accounts of the Roman triumph, from Ovid's application of triumphal imagery to portray the power of Love in the *Amores* (I, 2, 19–52; I, 9, 1–46; II, 9, 1–24; II, 18, 11–40) and from subsequent appropriations of *Amor triumphans*, such as that in the *Roman de la Rose*, a leading vernacular moral–didactic allegorical narrative poem, whose imprint is discernible at various junctures of the *Triumphi*. As with his recourse to the classics, Petrarch's formal dependence on later Latin and vernacular authors who can be said to have exerted an influence on his idea of the triumph is little more than fleeting. Parallels noted between the *Triumphi* and Lactantius's and Boccaccio's presentations of the triumph, in the *Divine Institutes* and the *Amorosa visione* (*The Amorous Vision*) respectively, are in most cases commonplaces. Even Dante's memorable depiction of the triumph in the Earthly Paradise (*Purgatorio* XXIX, 106–154; but see also *Purgatorio* X, 73–81) is barely apparent in the weave of Petrarch's poem. Manifestly, the poet's aim was to guarantee that the *Triumphi* was considered in the light of the literary tradition of the triumph as a whole, and not of any single part of it.

Petrarch's "imitative" skills offer a brief glimpse of his sources before drawing attention to the novelty of his synthesis – a synthesis which uniquely combines the martial, religious, ethical, erotic, historical, and celebratory features of the triumph, as well as its personal reverberations: like the victors of old, the poet too had "triumphed" and been rewarded with the laurel crown (*TC* IV, 79–81). Other writers had only dealt with particular aspects of the triumph. Petrarch, on the other hand, the new "authoritative" author, who, crucially, himself embodied the triumphal, had succeeded in fusing all its possible cultural associations, just as the *TE*, the defining emblem of the *Triumphi*'s summative ambitions, brings to an end the repeated alternation of defeat and victory, and embraces all the vanquished and the victors and the whole of Creation.

Despite efforts to see precedents and models in the visual arts, there is no doubt that the poem's primary inspiration is in the literary tradition. Petrarch's treatment of the triumph incorporates the three canonical subjects – love, arms, and virtue – of the "tragic" style – the "highest" and thematically and linguistically most refined of the three arch-genres into which classical and medieval poetics divided literature. In fact, Petrarch expressly defines the *Triumphi* as a "tragedy" when he declares that it presents "materia di coturni, e non di socchi" (*TC* IV, 88: "subject matter of buskins,[1] and not of slippers"), namely, of tragedy and not of comedy (the arch-genre in antithesis to the "tragic": Horace, *Ars Poetica* 80). And the poem's dominant rhetorical register, its dependence on tropes, ambitious imagery, classical motifs and reminiscences, proper nouns, elaborate wordplay, and accumulative techniques, conventionally confirms its "tragic" character. Petrarch's language, too, generally satisfies "high" sensibilities of elegance and coherence, even though, especially as a result of the *Triumphi*'s persistent reliance on Dante's linguistically eclectic and transgressive *Commedia*, the lexis is somewhat more varied than that of the *RVF*. Still, Petrarch's lyric verse provides the bulk of the vocabulary, while the majority of the remaining words have clear origins in classical Latin, in the Romance lyric tradition, and in the less extreme linguistic choices of the *Commedia*.

Indeed, a principal aim of the *Triumphi* is to refute the *Commedia*'s standing, and hence that of its author, whose authority was widely acknowledged in fourteenth-century Italy. As a consequence, Petrarch and his poem would "triumph" as the new authorities of the "modern" world. The poet's borrowing from the *Commedia*, in stark contrast to that from the classics, is largely "destructive," intent upon showing up Dante's supposed artistic and intellectual deficiencies. For instance, the repeated mention that Dido had committed suicide out of love for Sichaeus and not for Aeneas – "Dido / ch'amor pio del suo sposo a morte spinse, / non quel d'Enea, com'è 'l publico grido" (*TP* 10–12: "Dido / whom pious love for her husband drove to death, / and not that for Aeneas, as common opinion would have it"; see also *TP* 155–159) – is a barely concealed attack on Dante, who, most notably in *Inferno* V, 61–62, had claimed the opposite. Petrarch charges his great predecessor with ignorance and with wishing to appeal to the untutored – accusations that he reiterates elsewhere in his oeuvre (for example, *Fam.* XXI.15). As far as Petrarch was concerned, Dante lacked intellectual and poetic sophistication. Thus, the protagonist's meeting with Sophonisba and Massinissa (*TC* II, 5–87), which presents doomed lovers of established consequence, is meant to serve as a "tragic" corrective to Dante's parochial "comic" lovers, Paolo and Francesca.

Another example is to be found in *TM* II, the formal center of the poem, which describes a highly unusual occurrence, a dream within a dream in which the dead Laura appears to her lover. Unusually, when compared to her customary behavior in the *RVF*, "Laura" speaks eloquently and at length; and, even more unexpectedly, and uniquely, admits to having always loved Petrarch,[2] but of not having returned his love so as not to endanger his immortal soul. The *Triumphi* thus goes beyond and corrects the lyric collection, thereby indicating its own intellectual and literary superiority.[3] More significantly, the dream of Laura stands in explicit contrast to Dante's encounter with the dead Beatrice in the Earthly Paradise. Petrarch casts doubt that such a meeting between the living and the dead can in effect occur, thereby undermining Beatrice's status as an otherworldly guide, the *Commedia*'s metaphysical claims, and Dante's honesty. In their place stand the "glorïosa" (*TM* I, 1: "glorious") "alma . . . diva" (*TM* II, 19: "life-giving . . . goddess") Laura and, by extension, the visionary text that records her celestial triumph.

In line with this overall diminishing approach to Dante, despite the many allusions to it, Petrarch never mentions the *Commedia*, and only once curtly alludes to its poet: "ecco Dante e Beatrice, ecco Selvaggia, / ecco Cin da Pistoia, Guitton d'Arezzo" (*TC* IV, 31–32: "here are Dante and Beatrice, here is Selvaggia, / here are Cino da Pistoia, Guittone d'Arezzo"). As far as Petrarch is concerned, Dante is one among a group of Italian love poets (vv. 28–38), a secondary tradition, in fact, when compared to the poets of antiquity (vv. 13–27) and even the Occitan lyricists (vv. 38–57), and one which will only achieve proper prestige thanks to his *RVF* (see Chapter 12). At best, Dante is a relatively minor vernacular lyric poet, his epic efforts undeserving of mention. His only real rival thus despatched, Petrarch is free to present the *Triumphi* as a vernacular epic that, for the first time in the post-classical world, can match the refinement of the ancient poets by following their example in a rhetorically and ideologically sensitive manner (see Chapter 11), thereby revealing the true potential of the vernacular as a medium of culture and literature, a refined language that will no longer be automatically associated with the "common" people, among whom Dante has inappropriately abandoned it (*Fam.* XXI.15).

From this perspective, Petrarch's choice of the vernacular for the *Triumphi* is quite understandable. Earlier poets, including the authors of the two best-known Romance epics, the *Roman de la Rose* and the *Commedia*, had distinctly lacked a proper familiarity with the classics. Unlike the tight-knit (the poem is full of internal reminiscences) yet wide-ranging *Triumphi*, their poems, according to Petrarch, were overlong, poorly structured, and insensitive to classical ideals of literary and linguistic decorum. The *Commedia*'s disregard of established, classically legitimated literary convention was especially deplorable. Indeed, Petrarch's formal borrowings from the *Commedia* can be read as an attempt to restore propriety to Dante's linguistic choices. By restoring and "imitating" the values of the ancients, the poem would become the great "modern" epic in absolute terms.[4]

The *Triumphi* is a substantial and ambitious, if also a prickly and self-satisfied, work, which – especially during the Renaissance – exerted significant literary, iconographic, and pedagogic influence. Yet, since the turn of the twentieth century, readers have been dismissive of the poem, often terming it a "failure." The principal and best-grounded criticisms arise from the *Triumphi*'s tense relationship with the *Commedia*. Though Petrarch clearly wished his readers to compare his epic to Dante's masterpiece, its frequent recourse to the *Commedia* means that, in practice, the comparison does it few favors. In particular, in genre terms, the *Triumphi* marks a substantial step back from the *Commedia*'s exhilarating literary inventiveness. Equally, unlike the *Commedia*, it fails both to regularly integrate its sources, including its borrowings from Dante, into a coherent, self-sufficient personal register, and to resolve fully, in the *TE*, its ideas on the inter-relationship between the earthly and the divine, placing too much emphasis on the here and now. It is possible that, in keeping with Petrarch's customary preference for irresolution, the *Triumphi*'s ultimate lack of closure is deliberate, though, given its general harmonizing aims, this seems doubtful.

Other criticisms are less well founded. Too much has been made of the poem's incompleteness, not least because there is extensive evidence to suggest that the *Triumphi* was relatively close to being concluded. Petrarch confirms its definitive overall organization in the *TE*: "Questi triumphi, i cinque in terra giuso / avem veduto, ed a la fine il sexto, / Dio permettente, vederem lassuso" (*TE* 121–23: "These triumphs, the five down on earth / that we have seen, and in the end the sixth, / which, God willing, we will see up there"); and, as I hope to have demonstrated, it is possible to establish with reasonable precision its stylistic, generic, literary, narrative, ideological, and cultural parameters. At the same time, it is nonetheless the case that, on account of its breadth of reference and its deliberate shifts in tone and focus, the *Triumphi* is not easy to pin down, at times betraying an apparent lack of coherence. As a consequence, starkly contrasting interpretations of the poem have been proposed. Thus, the poem has been defined as both subjective and objective, allegorical and anti-allegorical, epic and lyric, secular and religious, historical and ahistorical. The truth of the matter is that all these elements are present. The fact that, elsewhere in his oeuvre, Petrarch almost never refers to his "great work," and thereby offers no interpretive guidance to its readers, has obviously not helped its critical reception. Equally, the fact that it is impossible to fix precisely the dates of its composition has made it difficult to use external evidence to aid in its exegesis.

Nevertheless, there is also much to admire in the *Triumphi*. Petrarch largely succeeds in developing a new model of vernacular Humanism, in creating a new lyrically inflected epic, and in establishing a cogent and independent textual and cultural space within which to define himself and his career. If he and his poem fail to "triumph" over Dante and the *Commedia*, they are undoubtedly superior to the efforts of other fourteenth-century authors, including Boccaccio and his *Amorosa visione*,[5] to imitate Dante's great narrative-didactic poem. More specifically, in the *Triumphi*, Petrarch accomplished what he had suggestively and calculatedly avoided doing elsewhere, namely, bringing a degree of closure to his intellectual and spiritual conflicts. The poet revealed his profound rapport with the classical tradition, while at the same time highlighting that he had been able to modify and revive his relationship to antiquity thanks to his Christianity, his use of the vernacular, and his love of Laura. In personal terms, as far as Petrarch was likely concerned, this was undoubtedly a triumph.

NOTES

1 Editors' note: A buskin is an open-toed boot, which was the traditional footwear of tragic actors in the classical Athenian theater.
2 "Laura" hints at her feelings in *RVF* 302.
3 It does the same as regards Petrarch's other works. For instance, the *TE* resolves the ideological conflict left suspended at the close of the *Secretum*.
4 From this perspective, the *Africa* appears as a work that, formally, linguistically, historically, and ideologically (in its failure to engage with Christianity), is overly constrained by its classicism, thereby compromising its relevance for the present.
5 The precise nature of the relationship between the *Triumphi* and the *Amorosa visione* is a matter of significant disagreement. Indeed, some scholars actually claim that Boccaccio's poem exerts greater influence on Petrarch than the *Commedia*. This is almost certainly an exaggeration. Until the dating of both epics, and until the *Triumphi*'s links to the *Amorosa visione*'s different versions are properly established, it is best to approach the question of their ties with considerable caution.

PART III

Petrarch's works: Latin

As already noted, the vast majority of Petrarch's writing, in a wide variety of forms and genres, was in Latin. It was on this work that he primarily rested his claims to fame as a poet, scholar, moral philosopher, and religious thinker. It was on this work that he would first gain widespread reknown among his contemporaries throughout Europe. And it was through much of this work that he would first exert a powerful influence on European intellectual culture, particularly that scholarly-pedagogical-philosophical movement known as Humanism, which would promote a revival of classical culture and come to be virtually synonymous with the period we now (with increasing trepidation and qualification) call the Renaissance. His first major endeavor, never properly finished, and hauntingly present throughout the rest of his oeuvre, is the neo-classical epic *Africa*. In Chapter 7, Ronald Martinez treats that poem together with Petrarch's other Latin verse productions, his verse letters (the *Epystole*), and his twelve-composition pastoral collection, the *Bucolicum carmen*. In Chapter 8, Victoria Kahn discusses what is perhaps Petrarch's best-known Latin work today, the dialogic debate between "Franciscus" (Petrarch) and "Augustinus" (St. Augustine) known as the *Secretum*, over the former's inability to renounce his worldly passions (Laura and fame) for higher moral–spiritual values and pursuits. In Chapter 9, Unn Falkeid introduces the paired, and yet in some ways opposed, treatises *De vita solitaria* and *De otio religioso*, which celebrate, respectively, the *otium* of the Humanist philosopher-poet and the value of monastic retreat as practiced by his brother Gherardo. Finally, in Chapter 10, Albert Ascoli offers a selective analysis of Petrarch's two major letter collections (made in imitation of the classical Ciceronian and Senecan models), the *Letters on Familiar Matters* and the *Letters of [and about] Old Age*. Later chapters treat other of the Latin works to a greater or lesser extent. In particular, in Chapter 13, David Marsh reviews the four great polemical works of Petrarch's later years: *Invective against a Physician*, *On His own Ignorance and That of Many Others*, *Invective against a Man of High*

Rank with No Knowledge or Virtue, and *Invective against a Detractor of Italy*.

Because of Petrarch's vast Latin production, it has not been possible to treat, extensively or at all, some major and highly influential works, including the collection of exemplary classical lives, *De viris illustribus* (*On Illustrious Men*), which would help launch a new Renaissance genre of biography; the dialogue *De remediis utriusque fortunae* (*On the Two Kinds of Fortune*), which became another repertory of examples of the ways in which human life is constantly subjected to virtually random changes from prosperity to abject deprivations and vice versa, and a vehicle for the neo-Stoic exhortation to resist making one's emotions and one's life subject to either form of "Fortuna"; and the anonymous *Liber sine nomine* (*Book Without a Name*), a collection of embittered letters on the failure of Cola Rienzo and others to restore Rome to its proper glory as political *caput mundi* and the depravity of the "Babylonian" papacy which has abandoned Rome for Avignon, in the process giving itself over to corruption of all kinds. Other less well known works given cursory or no treatment include *Collatio laureationis* (*The Coronation Oration*), delivered at the time Petrarch was awarded the laurel crown in Rome based on the reputation of the unfinished and largely unread *Africa*; the *Rerum memorandarum libri* (*Book of the Things to be Remembered*), an unfinished collection or *florilegium* of memorable sayings and observations; the *Itinerarium* (*Guide to the Holy Land*), an influential travelogue compiled without having ever visited the titular destination; and his *Testament* or Will. Omitted, finally, are also his *Psalmi penitentiales*, religious poems probably composed at the height of the Black Death in 1348, as well as a handful of occasional diplomatic orations. Many of these works left indelible and pervasive marks on later fifteenth- and sixteenth-century Humanist and vernacular culture, and others merit attention that cannot be offered here.[1]

NOTE

1 The full range of Petrarch Latin production is surveyed in the essays collected in *Petrarch: A Critical Guide*, Kirkham and Maggi.

7

RONALD L. MARTINEZ

The Latin hexameter works:
Epystole, Bucolicum carmen, Africa

Petrarch's three major works in Latin hexameter verse – the epic *Africa*, the pastoral *Bucolicum carmen*, and the verse-letter collection *Epystole* – are closely related through their origin, development, and association with Petrarch's claim to fame.[1] While each took years to approach completion – with the *Africa* remaining unfinished – Petrarch thought of all three as conceived in Vaucluse (*Fam.* VIII.3.11; *Africa* IX.278–280). More important, all three works – two inspired by Virgil (the epic *Aeneid* and the bucolic *Eclogues*, both in hexameter), the third by Horace's *Epistulae* (also in hexameter) – sprang from Petrarch's conception of the status and responsibilities he assumed when crowned with the laurel in Rome in 1341. The crown was, in fact, conferred largely because of the early promise of the *Africa*, which became the implicit focus for the other hexameter works as they progressed, to the extent that Petrarch presents both the *Bucolicum carmen (Fam.* X.4.10–11) and the verse letters (*Epystole* I.1.70–82, III.10.1–17) as simultaneously distractions from and satellites of his persistently stalled epic. Work on the *Africa* also probably coincided with preparations for publishing the *Bucolicum carmen* in 1357–58 and the *Epystole* in 1364.

Indeed, Petrarch had early envisioned his poetic career as the attempt to equal, if not surpass, the achievement of Virgil. In 1338, the year he began work on the *Africa*, Petrarch had Simone Martini paint in the flyleaf of his copy of Virgil's works, accompanied by the late-classical commentary of Servius on the *Aeneid*, an image showing a warrior or captain holding a spear, a farmer pruning vines, and a shepherd milking a ewe, which represented in personified form Virgil's three hexameter poems: the *Aeneid*, the *Georgics*, and the *Bucolics* (this image, in fact, graces the cover of the present volume). In medieval rhetorical treatises, for instance John of Garland's *Poetria*, the three figures represented the so-called *rota Vergilii*, respectively the high, middle, and humble styles of poetry. Behind a curtain (signifying Virgil's obscurity, which Servius's commentary elucidates), in a grove of laurel trees, a semi-recumbent figure holds a pen over a large codex and gazes upward for inspiration. This figure is undoubtedly Virgil, but the image should also be taken as an aspirational portrait of Petrarch himself in his laurel-shaded retreat of Vaucluse, preparing to compose the works that he hoped would rival Virgil's achievement: chiefly, of course, the epic *Africa*; eventually also the *Bucolicum carmen*.[2]

Dante had arranged to surpass his Virgil in the *Commedia* in large part because the Roman poet had not known Christianity, an event registered in the poem by Virgil's departure at the arrival of the sainted Beatrice in *Purgatorio* XXX. But as a crowned poet laureate who would almost single-handedly launch a new Humanist standard of historicism and philological acuity, Petrarch felt the need to compete on Virgil's own terms in established classical genres of epic and bucolic. In the *Africa* itself (III.424–427), for example, Petrarch makes a point of correcting Virgil's anachronistic rendering of Dido as unfaithful to her dead husband Sichaeus through a love affair with Aeneas, an injustice that had not escaped notice in the tradition of commentary on the Roman epic, for example, Servius's note on *Aeneid* IV.36.

As concerns the larger question of patterning a poetic career on that of the great Roman poet, however, Petrarch faced a thornier problem, for which he was himself in part responsible. The premature consecration of an unfinished *Africa* with the Capitoline laurel in 1341 inverted the prescribed sequence of humble *Bucolic*, mixed-style *Georgic*, and high-style epic, and placed him in the difficult position of striving to fill out the Virgilian program after already having won the prize for achieving it: playing catch-up, so to speak, with himself.

Epystole

Petrarch first assembled his three-book collection of hexameter poems on various subjects, *Epystole*,[3] by 1350, when he likely wrote the dedicatory poem to Barbato da Sulmona. Like Horace's *Epistulae*, Petrarch's classical models, Petrarch's verse letters are all addressed to named recipients, with the exceptions of I.14, to himself, and III.24, to Italy.[4] Along with regret for the passage of time, the most conspicuous elements of Horatian imitation of manner and theme include a preference for country leisure over city bustle (*Epystole* II.3.43 cites *Epistulae* 2.2.77; *Epystole* III.23.1 cites *Epistulae* 1.1.76–77). The epistles in which Horace appraises fellow poets and proclaims the need for rigorous poetic craft also struck responsive chords in Petrarch,[5] who was familiar as well with Horace's role as a preceptor of poetic art in the *Ars Poetica*, couched as an epistle to the Piso family, and widely commented on in the Middle Ages. Statements by Boccaccio make it clear that Petrarch was responsible for the arrangement and publication of all three books of verse letters. Books of fourteen, eighteen, and thirty-four poems distribute the sixty-six-poem total. The number six, and by extension sixty-six, was especially resonant for Petrarch: because the Genesis story has Adam created (and fallen) on the sixth day, the poet emphasized the number six in the formal organization of some of his works,[6] as in the sixty-six-line sestina stanzas of the *RVF* and the six planned *Triumphi*.

The *Epystole* have the greatest temporal range of Petrarch's four epistolary collections,[7] including the *epicedium* for his mother (I.7), putatively written in 1318, when he was fourteen, and two from the 1330s (I.2–3). The last poems, chronologically speaking, are from 1353 (III.24, 29) and 1355 (III.8). Taken together, the three books reflect the autobiographical chronology discernible in the other letter collections and in the *Bucolicum carmen*. Petrarch is envisioned turning away, not without repeated backsliding, both from his obsession with Laura and from Avignon and Vaucluse, to a more penitential posture and to engagement with Italy both as place and as idea. The turn is most elaborate in the last book: Poem III.19.19 sounds the note of Petrarch's status as "peregrinus ubique" ("a pilgrim everywhere"), while several poems (III.21–23) that treat Avignon as "the Hell of the living" prepare the poem with which the poet hails Italy at his return, "Salve chara Deo tellus" (III.24: "Hail, land dear to God"). Though Petrarch left Vaucluse for good in 1353, his departure is symbolically announced only in the last letter of the collection, discussing his pilgrimage to Rome's 1350 Jubilee (III.34), which concludes with a signature and a farewell: "to the world, to what pleased me when young, and to the nearly subdued flesh" (34.38–40).

A more fundamental narrative organizing the *Epystole* concerns Petrarch's long career as poet laureate: how (and if) he came to deserve the laurel and what status and responsibilities the laurel conferred on him. All but two of the fourteen poems in Book I – the prologue and I.8 – have been dated as written and circulated to Petrarch's friends by the time of the 1341 coronation, making the book an anthology of the poems for which he first became famous. Along with early versions of individual poems known to Boccaccio, such as I.4, 12, 13, and 14, there is manuscript evidence of early and separate circulation of Petrarch's "political poems"; from a recently discovered exchange of verse letters with Rinaldo da Villafranca of Verona, we know that the future *Epystole* I.2 and 3 had been read and commented on in public in Verona in about 1336, when Petrarch was still "Francis of Florence."[8]

If Book I registers Petrarch's preparation for the coronation, Book II records his post-1341 status as the laureate poet of Rome and Italy and the subsequent progress – and checks – on his composition of the *Africa*. Notably, Petrarch describes the laureation in detail to Giovanni Barrili in *Epystole* II.1. But joyful reminiscence is qualified by the emphasis in Book II on the memory of Robert of Anjou, the king whose examination of Petrarch on the subject of poetry and whose audition of portions of the *Africa*, prior to the coronation, had justified Petrarch's reputation, but who died shortly after the great event, in 1343. The king's epitaph is poem II.8, near the book's center, and he is mentioned sorrowfully in seven other poems, focusing the theme of poetic mourning, which haunts the collection from the outset (for example, I.1.70–74). Closely related to Robert's absence are numerous references to the *Africa* and to the laurel, reflecting the fact that the king's death had put completion of the epic at risk (II.10 paralleled in *Africa* IX.422–426).

Through his coronation, Petrarch became an authoritative teacher, a *magister*, and according to the *privilegium* granted at his coronation, possessed of the right to confer the laurel himself.[9] Books II and III thus include numerous instances of Petrarch writing to and about poets and giving advice on the art of poetry. In Book II (poems 2–4), for example, he advises Cardinal Bertrand d'Albi on the poetic art, and later chastises him for being guilty of both prosodic errors and monstrous prolixity.

In the two last books, Petrarch also expresses, with some candor, his misgivings about his early Capitoline triumph. The topic was, again, first encountered in the prologue letter to Barbato: I.1.34–35: "a precipitous glory expelled me, still unfledged, from the warm nest"; and in Book II Petrarch twice responds to Brizio Visconti with a rebuttal of the latter's accusation that the Capitoline laurel was undeserved (II.10, II.17), though he concedes that his laureation had been premature (esp. II.10.124–131). In the same vein, Book III reflects Petrarch's anxiety about the *Africa* (III.10.10–17), in language taken from Virgil's *Georgics*. Petrarch describes the poem figuratively as terrain that has become unresponsive to cultivation, and in another place he defends himself at length regarding a supposedly incorrect metrical scansion in the text of the epic (III.26.19–30).

Bucolicum carmen

Petrarch claimed that he had conceived and written the *Bucolicum carmen* in 1346–47, in Vaucluse. Eclogues II, III, and IV, and most of XII, were ready in 1346, and in 1347 he wrote I, V, VI, and VII; poems reflecting the Black Death (IX and XI) were clearly written after 1348 (also VII.19–26). Though the work was essentially complete by 1350, Petrarch added a few lines to VII in 1351–52 and in 1357 wrote the last eleven verses of XII, and over eighty lines' worth of names were added in 1364 to the vast catalog of poets in X. In 1357, Petrarch himself copied all twelve eclogues in a manuscript that bears his signature (now known as Vat. Lat. 3358); individual eclogues had, however, circulated earlier. Emendation continued as late as 1367, driven by Petrarch's desire to mask imitations of Virgil (*Fam.* XXIII.19).

The title of the work given in Vat. Lat. 3358 is *Bucolicum carmen meum* (*My Bucolic Song*). Petrarch's models for the collection are Virgil's ten bucolic eclogues, a filiation announced with the title to Petrarch's first, "Parthenias," a Virgilian sobriquet. In the preface to the *Sine nomine*, Petrarch describes his *Bucolicum carmen* as a "double-meaning kind of poem" that will reward readers able to penetrate its difficult allegory. As noted earlier, Petrarch was following Servius in thinking that pastoral poetry shrouded hidden meanings: Servius had glossed Tityrus in Virgil's first eclogue as representing Virgil himself, but "not always" – thus Petrarch, a solitary dweller in the woods, portrays himself as Silvius in *Bucolicum carmen* I, and as Silvanus in *Bucolicum carmen* X. Virgil's eclogues also include allusions to historical events and personalities such as Julius Caesar; thus, in the *Bucolicum carmen*, Petrarch tackles papal Avignon (VI and VII) and the Hundred Years' War between France and England (XII). Recognizing that understanding such poetry requires a key, Petrarch wrote brief explanations of *Bucolicum carmen* I (*Fam.* X.4.10–34), II (*Disperse* 7), and V (*Disperse* 11).

Summaries of three individual eclogues, two concerning the poet's life and one contemporary politics, illustrate some of the allegorical translations of the pastoral code, as well as the oblique relationship of *Bucolicum carmen* to the epic *Africa*, still underway:

I. *Monicus*. A dialogue between Silvius and Monicus, representing Petrarch and his brother Gherardo, a Carthusian monk, which dramatizes Silvius's choice of writing *Africa* and pursuing secular glory over the religious vocation of his brother and the biblical poetry of the Psalms (see also *Secretum* III.182–214 and *Fam.* IV.1).

III. *Amor pastorius* (Pastoral Love). Stupeus (Petrarch, so named because "stupa" ("tow") is easily set on fire; that is, he is in love) pursues Dane (Laura). When he shows her a laurel given him by Calliope, she recognizes his devotion to the Muses and crowns him with laurel on a hill evoking the Capitoline.

V. *Pietas pastoralis* (pastoral filial piety). Martius (the Colonna family) and Apicius (the Orsini family, rivals of the Colonna) discuss how to restore their aged mother, the city of Rome. Volucer (winged rumor) reports that a younger shepherd (Cola da Rienzo) has already begun Rome's return to prominence.

Unlike Virgil's ten eclogues, a true anthology, the *Bucolicum carmen* is conceived as a single work "divided" into twelve eclogues (*Fam.* X.4.10), announcing a link to Virgil's twelve-book *Aeneid* and thus betraying a generic ambition to exceed traditional limits of the pastoral (*Sen.* II.1, dated 1363). Despite the intrusion of historical contingencies in several eclogues (for example, V, VI, and XII), there is a high degree of formal and thematic coherence to the *Bucolicum carmen* as it finally left Petrarch's hand. The eclogues are spatially arranged: the eulogy of Robert in II is balanced by the eulogy of Laura in IX, while the meeting with the Muses and receipt of the laurel in III is balanced by the allegory of the cultivation of the laurel and the catalog of poets in X.

Readers have also discerned in the twelve poems a continuous narrative that follows Petrarch's struggle (as in the *Secretum*, composed 1348–53) with the urges of poetic ambition and political engagement, set against the vanity of human striving and the claims of divine law. This narrative is articulated in three sections: I–IV concern Petrarch's poetic vocation; V–VIII draw from Petrarch's investment in Cola da Rienzo's reform of Rome, the seat of secular power, and from his dismay over the Avignon papacy, seen as wholly corrupt; and IX–XII confront the apocalyptic topics of death, pestilence, and war, already anticipated in VII. Eclogue XI unfolds at Laura's tomb; her death is narrated in allegorical terms in X. Eclogue XII concerns the great war between England and France.

The penitential tendency is frequently but subtly emphasized. References to Christ are detectable in at least six eclogues.[10] In XI, Petrarch rewrites the scene of the three Marys at the tomb of Christ in Mark 16.8. Poem XII conserves the religious context with reference to Jerusalem, the "unhappy old woman" (XII.73; see also I.72–74) neglected by contemporary monarchs and popes. Allusions to Christ and Jerusalem extend throughout the collection the dilemma dramatized in the first eclogue, between following the Carthusian Gherardo to God's holy mountain and aspiring, through the writing of *Africa*, to the secular glory of the Capitoline laurel (a conflict repeatedly staged in Petrarch's oeuvre).

If Petrarch emulates Virgil in checking off the pastoral box, so to speak, with the *Bucolicum carmen*, he also competes with Dante, whose epistolary exchange in 1320–21 with the Bologna rhetoric professor Giovanni del Virgilio sparked the great Florentine's single-handed resurrection of the Virgilian pastoral – including the fashion for allegorical riddling.[11] Petrarch fine-tunes his attempt to usurp Dante's precedence by taking Horace's description of Ennius as a second Homer ("alter Homerus," *Epistulae* 2.1.51) and applying it to himself in the *Africa* as a second Ennius ("Ennius alter," II.444), supplanting del Virgilio's heralding in his *Egloga* of Dante as a second ("alter") Virgil (lines 33–34). Such games of primacy are even more earnestly played within the arena of epic.

Africa

Near the end of his life, in the unfinished "Letter to Posterity" (*Sen.* XVIII.1), Petrarch recalls beginning the *Africa* in 1338–39, in Vaucluse. Enough of the poem, possibly much of Books I–IV, was written by the time of the 1341 laureation for King Robert to ask that the poem be dedicated to him (*Epystole* II.10.98–112). In the next two years, Petrarch made sufficient progress (likely Books V–VIII) to persuade himself the work would soon be completed. It was not, either then or later, even if further periods of composition have been detected.[12] Though Petrarch never published the work (the first edition appeared twenty-two years after his death), he made available to Pierre Bersuire the ekphrasis of Syphax's palace decoration (III.88–264) and released to Francesco Nelli and other friends the first verse and half of the next; in 1343, Petrarch also sent Barbato da Sulmona part of the description of the death of Hannibal's brother Mago (VI.885–918), which then circulated independently of the full epic. Because of these anticipations, and because Petrarch's coronation had been based on the early promise of the poem, the *Africa* has long suffered the dubious distinction of having been more celebrated before it was read than after publication.

The name of the epic, explicit only at IX.235–236, is implicit in its first lines because Scipio took the agnomen Africanus as conqueror of the African continent. The poem as we have it is in nine books, though more may have been intended, in conformity with real or supposed forerunners. As epic models (and rivals), Petrarch mentions the *Aeneid*, as well as Statius's *Thebaid* and *Achilleid* (I.50–52). The first two lines of the poem, "And also to me, Muse, will you tell of a man outstanding for great deeds and redoubtable in war," echoes Virgil's famous opening to the *Aeneid*, as well as the beginning of Homer's *Odyssey*, which Petrarch knew through Horace (*Epistulae* 1.2; *Ars Poetica* 141–142). By beginning *in medias res* with the final phase of the Second Punic War, the poem follows both its classical predecessors and Horatian prescription (*Ars Poetica* 148–150). The action commences as Scipio, having wrested Spain from the Carthaginian yoke, deliberates his next moves at the Pillars of Hercules, a geographical pivot for the narrative which Petrarch conceived of as a *bivium*, a crossroads of moral choice (I.127–138 et passim). The war culminates with the battle of Zama, narrated in Book VII. Echoing Lucan (*De bello civili* VII.131), Petrarch declares the battle decisive for the fate of the world (II.60–61): because of Scipio's victory at Zama, medieval Europe wrote not in Punic, but in Latin.

Near the end of the poem, Petrarch's theory of epic emerges in the speech of the poet Quintus Ennius, the self-styled Latin successor to Homer (IX.93).

It is the poet's job, Ennius proclaims, to build upon historical facts, but to clothe them with fictional veils, so that readers will be agreeably challenged to discover the underlying truth. The required historical basis of the *Africa* is Livy's history of the Second Punic War, included in Books 25–30 of the *History of Rome*, edited by Petrarch himself in Avignon as a young man, and which he drew upon to compose the life of Scipio for inclusion in *De viris*. Only three historical episodes in the epic are invented out of whole cloth: the meeting of Laelius – Scipio's close friend – and Syphax (all of Book III); the Carthaginian legation to Rome (VIII.682–832); and the conversation between Scipio and Ennius (Book IX). Among the fictional veils are dreams and waking visions and the debate before Jupiter/God of Carthage and Rome personified.[13]

The epic action unfolds as follows: in the exordium, the author appeals to the Muses, to Christ, and to King Robert, who will shield the poem from envy and ensure Petrarch's fame; the poem's subject will be Rome's defeat of Carthage. The first two books narrate the dream of Scipio,[14] in which he meets his father and uncle in the stars of the Milky Way, where civic virtue and martial valor are rewarded. More specifically, Book I narrates the heroic deaths of father and uncle, recalls other Roman worthies, and emphasizes the fragility of earthly glory even as Rome's triumphant destiny is unfolded. Book II predicts Scipio's fate: though he will be exiled, his victory over Carthage means his fame will endure and his praises will be sung by a future poet (Petrarch). Laelius's embassy to Syphax, King of Numidia in Book III, includes a description of his palace and the banquet held there, plus poetic retellings of the stories of Hercules and of Dido's founding of Carthage. Laelius then narrates the founding of Rome and recalls illustrious Romans up to the founding of the Republic.

In Book IV, Laelius tells Syphax of Scipio's virtues and recounts Scipio's siege of New Carthage in Spain. This book breaks off at line 388 with a truncated line. In Book V, the liaison of Scipio's erstwhile ally Massinissa, ruler of the Massyli, with Sophonisba, the daughter of Hasdrubal, whose marriage to Syphax had been designed to bring him into the Carthaginian camp, is checked by the Roman general, who insists that the queen be turned over for display as a captive in Rome.[15] The result is the suicide of the queen, who descends to Hades to begin Book VI, in which the defeated Syphax is sent in chains to Rome and the threat of Scipio forces the recall from Italy of the Carthaginian generals Hannibal and Mago (in an ominous gesture, Hannibal massacres the citizens of Croton as he departs).

Book VII relates the generals' parley: Scipio refuses Hannibal's peace proposals, while Carthage and Rome, personified, appeal to Jupiter. The two armies clash, and though Hannibal's army of mixed nations is routed, he eludes capture. After the victory, in Book VIII, Scipio, his commanders, and Laelius debate whether Hannibal or Alexander is the greatest general – or perhaps Scipio himself. Hannibal flees Carthage to seek employ in the East against the Romans. A Carthaginian embassy to Rome led by Hasdrubal is granted both a peace and the release of captives. On Scipio's order, the Carthaginian fleet is burned. In Book IX, the last, Scipio and Ennius discuss the theory of epic and the meaning of the laurel crown (IX.1–123), while returning to Rome by sea. Ennius recounts his dream of Homer, which concludes with a vision of the future encomiast of Scipio, Petrarch (IX.158–289); Scipio and Ennius are given a triumph and crowned on the Capitol in Rome (IX.322–397); and Petrarch bids farewell to his book (IX.421–83), asking that it find a receptive audience in a more enlightened posterity.

The *Africa* is dedicated to the praise of Rome and of Scipio: Petrarch will "collect" the scattered evidence (IX.234–38) of the hero who first achieved supremacy for Rome (II.117–118), and for himself enduring fame (I.1–2, II.100–101, and so on). Scipio's role in saving Rome is providential, as if he had descended from heaven (III.446, recalling Virgil's *Eclogue* IV.1–3); several details suggest he is a forerunner of Christ (III.21, 43). If Scipio is providential, so is Rome; the destinies and praise of the hero and his nation are closely associated (IV.94–98, IX.255–63). As much is proclaimed by Jupiter, a thinly veiled Judeo-Christian God, who announces his imminent incarnation in a passage that also hints at Rome's future as the seat of Christendom (VII.656–58, 710–714). Indeed, for Petrarch, it was Rome's destiny to dominate the world from its Capitol (IV.94–98), and historiography itself was nothing if not the praise of Rome. As Scipio's father Publius foresees in Book II, though Pompey, Caesar, and Augustus will conquer the world for Rome, the Empire will thereafter decline. But though led by barbarian emperors (non-Italians), it will never see defeat in battle, and will survive until the world's end (II.285–300). Romans are especially praised for their fidelity, and for the valor that, as Syphax observes, makes every Roman, from the greatest to the least, willing to endure unto death (IV.13–16).

Rome's destiny is to destroy Carthage, which it opposes not only politically but also geographically, across the Mediterranean (I.102–108 et passim, recalling Virgil's *Aeneid* IV.628–629). The cause of the war is Carthaginian envy of Rome's expansion, and envy also disfigures the personified figure of Carthage in Book VII. If Rome's "art" is fidelity, Carthage is persistently treacherous in her dealings (for example, IX.355–356). Envy and discord corrode Carthage from within as well, especially through the rivalry between Hanno, who favors peace with Rome, and Hannibal, the brilliant Punic commander implacable in his hatred of Rome (V.554–555, VII.8). Stereotyped as reptilian (II.82, VI.415) and characterized as spurning divine law like the mythical Titans (VI.485, VII.164–167), Hannibal is vainly exhorted to piety by Scipio during their parley. But despite a largely negative portrayal, Rome's fiercest antagonist demonstrates, especially in defeat, a psychological depth that the wholly immaculate Scipio lacks, and it is to the Carthaginian that the most stirring speeches in the poem belong, such as those at VII.864–915 and VIII.276–287.

The traits that lead Carthage to threaten Rome are also those that threaten Petrarch's poem. Petrarch, adapting a commonplace of classical epic, identifies the envy of readers and writers as a menace to his poem (I.33–37, IX.483; see also *Sen.* II, 1). The epic has subtler, or rather subtextual and meta-textual, antagonists, as well. The famous account of Alexander's regret, when visiting Homer's tomb, that his victories would inspire no comparable poet (*RVF* 187; *Africa* IX.51–54), which Petrarch encountered in Cicero's *Pro Archia* (X.24) and included in the *Collatio laureationis*, informed Petrarch's decision to praise the otherwise unsung Scipio.[16] But the choice was also part of a life-long argument favoring Latin and Italian culture over French, and Latin over Greek. After Scipio's victory (VII.1072–1073), Petrarch envisions his poem and its hero outstripping panegyrics of generals like Alexander, notably those found in the twelfth-century *Alexandreis* by the Gallic Walter of Châtillon.

The correlation of Scipio's epic deeds with the poet's epic undertaking derives in part from the *topos*, dear to Petrarch's heart, that the laurel was suited both to successful generals (or rulers) and to poets. Petrarch accordingly magnifies the role of Quintus Ennius, who had reportedly accompanied Scipio on campaign. Petrarch knew from Cicero (*Pro Archia* 22; *De re publica* VI.10.10), among others, that Ennius, Rome's first major epic poet, claimed to have been visited in dreams by Homer himself, and to have received Homer's soul by metempsychosis. Petrarch's Ennius thus funnels Homeric authority directly to Petrarch himself: as Ennius wrote the first "Italian" epic (II.444), it falls to Petrarch to restore the Muses of poetry to Italy (II.447, IX.404–409). The final event of the epic narrative is thus the crowning of both Ennius and Scipio with laurel on the Capitol after a triumphant entry to Rome (IX.236–253).

Victories require a contest, and it is the competition or *certamen* for the glory of poetic first place that chiefly guides Petrarch's autobiographical appropriation of epic. The agonistic emulation of poet-rivals pervades the last book: Petrarch's fiction of Scipio's sea-journey back to Rome imitates the journey of Ulysses and Achilles to Troy in Statius's *Achilleid*, so that, just as Scipio excels Alexander, he also displaces the young Achilles; Petrarch in turn replaces his antique competitors, including Ennius himself.

But in having his Ennius bow to Petrarch's future superiority in praising Scipio, Petrarch also draws a bead on a more recent and formidable rival:

> In the course of years one shall perhaps be born who will raise to heaven in worthy song your condign praises and brave deeds, and whom Calliope will lend a voice more sonorous and endow with a lyre whose strings will better respond under the sweet and fluid plectrum. (IX.60–64)

These hexameters assigned by Petrarch to Ennius embroider Dante's concession just after beginning the *Paradiso* (I.35–36): "perhaps, following after me, with better voices, others will pray so that Cyrrha will reply."[17] With this allusion, Petrarch tacitly equates Dante with the notoriously primitive Ennius. Indeed, the line that Petrarch establishes leading from Homer, through Ennius, to himself is designed to supplant the poetic succession that Dante – with scarcely less chutzpah, if more justification – establishes in making himself sixth in a school of poets led by, of course, Homer, "the lord of highest song" (*Inferno* IV, 102; 94–96).

More specifically, if the Massinissa episode channels Petrarch's attempt to surpass in historical accuracy Virgil's anachronistic treatment of Aeneas and Dido, Massinissa's crisis regarding Sophonisba also calls forth Petrarch's most direct challenge to Dante's supremacy among the modern vernacular writers (V.545–556). Seeking to evade Scipio's prohibition of marriage to Sophonisba, Massinissa imagines a reunion with Sophonisba in Hades, analogous to that of Virgil's Dido and Sichaeus in the myrtle grove assigned to "those whom harsh love wasted with bitter languishing" (*Aeneid* VI.442).

Elaborating Massinissa's fantasy, Petrarch's poetry enciphers a challenge to the Paolo and Francesca episode in the *Inferno*, in which Dante's Francesca strikingly uses "Amor" anaphorically at the beginning of three consecutive tercets (*Inferno* V, 100–108). Petrarch, for his part, places the word for Massinissa and Sophonisba's love, "amores," at the end of a hexameter four times in ten lines – thus, at three-line intervals – a simulacrum of Dante's *terza rima*. The subtle variation and repetition of terms within Petrarch's Latin hexameters is meant to overshadow with a magisterial display Dante's merely vernacular rhyming. And given the multiple echoes linking the poem's central erotic figure, Sophonisba, with the Laura of Petrarch's vernacular lyrics, the carefully contrived overgoing of Dante can also be viewed as a palinode of Petrarch's own vernacular lyrics, the "rime sparse," and of the transgression (*RVF* 1, 3: "... il mio primo giovenile errore," "... my first youthful error") that he claimed they represented, so that this episode, too, records an autobiographical moment central to Petrarch's mythology of himself.

But the poem's real goal, its first and final cause, is not so much the Capitoline crowning of a general and his poet as it is Ennius's prophetic vision, related to Scipio during their shipboard conversation in Book IX, of the future author who will sing the Roman's praises and be celebrated on the Campidoglio fourteen centuries later. With Ennius's report that "sitting in an enclosed vale / I descried a young man" (IX.217–218), Petrarch is depicting himself as the thirty-four-, possibly thirty-five-year-old poet beginning the *Africa* in 1338–39 and envisioning the success he attained very shortly after (IX.218–219). Ennius's vision is sufficiently reminiscent of the image on the flyleaf of Petrarch's Virgil manuscript – both Simone Martini's Virgil and the Ennian Petrarch are recumbent among laurels, caught at the threshold of inspiration with pens suspended (IX.275–276) – to conclude that what Ennius sees is not only the moment of the poem's inception, a *mise-en-abîme* of the epic's origin, but the genesis of Petrarch's entire ambitious poetic project of emulating Virgil (IX.279–280): a project of which the indisputed protagonist is Petrarch the author, for whom the epic *Africa* was destined to be the enduring monument, "the effigy of my mind and simulacrum of my genius," as he announced in the first letter of the *Familiares* (I.1) – though one which was never finished.

NOTES

1 No complete critical edition exists of any of these works. A critical edition of *Bucolicum carmen*, by Nicholas Mann, is in preparation; usable editions include *Petrarch's Bucolicum carmen*, trans. and annot. Thomas G. Bergin (New Haven, CT and London: Yale University Press, 1974), the translation adapted here, which includes facing-page Latin. A critical edition of the *Epystole* is being prepared by Michele Feo. The only convenient complete Latin *Africa* is Pétrarque, *L'Afrique*, ed. Rebecca Lenoir (Grenoble: Jerome Millon, 2002). I have also consulted *Petrarch's Africa*, trans. and annot. Thomas G. Bergin and Alice S. Wilson (New Haven, CT: Yale University Press, 1977). Translations of the *Epystole* and *Africa* are my own.

2 Admittedly, Petrarch's hexameter *Epystole* do not overtly emulate the *Georgics*, though his borrowings from the *Georgics* do warrant further study.

3 On the *Epystole*, see Giuseppe Velli, "A Poetic Journal: *Epystole*," in *Petrarch: A Critical Guide*, Kirkham and Maggi, 277–290.

4 Petrarch had a copy of Horace's works by about 1325.

5 For instance, compare Horace, *Epistulae* 1.3.12–20, 1.19.23–34, 2.1.50–85, 2.2 with Petrarch, *Epystole* II.2–4, 10, 17, III.26.

6 On the symbolic value of six and sixty-six in the *RVF*, see Robert M. Durling, "Introduction," in Francesco Petrarca, *Petrarch's Lyric Poems*, ed. and trans. Robert M. Durling (Cambridge, MA: Harvard University Press, 1976).

7 On the epistolary collections, esp. *Seniles* and *Familiares*, see also Chapter 10.

8 See Michele Feo, "La prima corrispondenza poetica fra Rinaldo da Villafranca e Francesco Petrarca," *Quaderni Petrarcheschi* 4 (1987): 13–33.

9 The *Privilegium* is printed in Wilkins, *The Making of the "Canzoniere,"* 53–61.

10 I.65–69, II.29–30, III.150, VI.180, IX.88–89, and X.320–321.

11 On this rivalry, see Albert R. Ascoli, "Blinding the Cyclops: Petrarch after Dante," in *Petrarch and Dante: Anti-Dantism, Metaphysics, Tradition*, eds. Zygmunt G. Barański and Theodore J. Cachey, Jr. (Notre Dame, IN: Notre Dame University Press, 2009), 114–173.

12 The long gestation of *Africa* is detailed in Pétrarque, *L'Afrique/Affrica*, ed. and trans. Pierre Laurens (Paris: Les Belles Lettres, 2006), i–cxviii.

13 For the dreams and visions, see all of Books I and II, V.260–272, V.605–611, and IX.158–289; for the debate, see VII.506–724.

14 The text of Scipio's dream, part of the sixth and last book of Cicero's dialogue *De re publica*, which survives only in fragments, was the object of an extensive fifth-century C.E. Middle Platonic commentary by Macrobius, and it was in this guise (one of the most influential books of the Middle Ages) that Petrarch knew Cicero's work.

15 Sophonisba's fate had also interested Giovanni Boccaccio, who related her story in his *De mulieribus claris* (Chapter 70) of about 1362, and subsequently stimulated Renaissance playwrights: a *Sofonisba* by Galeotto del Carretto dedicated to Isabella d'Este (1502) survives, and Giangiorgio Trissino's tragedy *Sophonisba* (c. 1515, published 1524) is the first Italian tragedy to follow Aristotle's rules for the genre as derived from the *Poetics*.

16 Petrarch was evidently unaware of Silius Italicus's first-century C.E. treatment of Scipio's campaign against Carthage, the *Punica*.

17 A partial list of echoes of Dante in *Africa* is given in Marco Baglio, "Presenze dantesche nel Petrarca latino," *Studi petrarcheschi* n.s. 9 (992): 77–136.

8

VICTORIA KAHN

The defense of poetry in the *Secretum*

Petrarch's *Secretum* is a Latin dialogue, occurring over three days, between two fictional characters, one named "Franciscus" and the other "Augustinus." Franciscus is, like Petrarch, a poet struggling with his desire for worldly fame, while Augustinus, a version of St. Augustine, combines the roles of father confessor and Stoic philosopher. According to Francisco Rico's now widely accepted account, the dialogue was first written in 1347, then revised on and off through 1353. Though Petrarch circulated practically everything he wrote in the hopes of achieving literary fame, the *Secretum* was deliberately withheld from publication during his lifetime. In the prologue, Petrarch tells us he wanted to have a private record of his struggles and "secret cares," one that he could re-read at leisure and in contemplation. Yet, it is hard to understand the desire for secrecy, since, in many ways, the work conforms to Petrarch's public persona. It imitates and revises a classical genre (the Ciceronian dialogue); it stages a complicated debate between Christianity and classical culture; it combines an intimate, autobiographical idiom with a pyrotechnic display of literary allusion; it meditates self-consciously on its own practices of interpretation; it speaks to us of conflicts that seem, even after almost 700 years, recognizably modern.

Chief among the dilemmas staged by the *Secretum* is the problem of how to read classical literature and how to reconcile this literature with the teachings of Christianity. Writing decades before the flowering of Italian Humanism in the work of Coluccio Salutati, Leonardo Bruni, and Lorenzo Valla, Petrarch helped shape the Humanist ideal of imitation, even as he also anticipated the critique of Humanist learning. The Humanist defense of classical learning in Petrarch's own letters and in fifteenth-century Italy was that it inculcated moral virtue and, in this respect, was not at odds with Christian doctrine.[1] And yet, in the *Secretum*, Augustinus points out that Petrarch has not become a better person by reading Virgil; to the contrary, his love of antiquity has distracted him from the serious business of moral and spiritual reform. It's hard to know whether this amounts to a defense of classical literature, read correctly, or an attack on its uselessness. When Augustinus encourages Franciscus to read allegorically, ascending from the text to a world of pre-established spiritual meanings, he implies there is a role for classical literature as a handmaiden to Christian conversion. But in granting a role to fiction and illusions (the word translated here and throughout is "fantasmata") that he elsewhere denies, he also opens the way for a different use and appreciation of classical texts. In response, Franciscus repeatedly proposes alternative readings of literary texts, appropriating them to justify his own behavior. Where Augustinus focuses on the spiritual meaning of texts, Franciscus focuses on beauty and eloquence, and the pleasure these afford.

Equally vexed in the *Secretum* is the relationship between Stoic and Christian accounts of the will: a relationship that is encapsulated in the title of the work, which suggests that it is, among other things, a reading of Augustine's *Confessions*. As David Marsh has noted, Augustine uses the word "secretum" in Book 8 of the *Confessions* to refer to his retreat into the garden where his conversion occurs with the help of divine grace.[2] In the *Secretum*, however, Augustinus suggests that Petrarch has only to will more fully in order to change his ways and devote himself completely to the spiritual life of a Christian. This optimistic view of the will is more reminiscent of Stoicism than of what we usually think of as Augustinian Christianity. At the very least, it conflicts with Augustine's notorious depiction in the *Confessions* of his divided will, his will both to convert and not to convert, summed up in the younger Augustine's "Give me chastity, O Lord, but not yet." In the *Secretum*, Augustinus uses this line to describe Franciscus's deferral of the moment of conversion, but in emphasizing the will he sometimes implies that Franciscus can bring about this conversion on his own.[3]

Clearly, Petrarch is revising Augustine for his own purposes, but what are they? Before we can address this question, it's important to note that Petrarch modeled both Augustinus and Franciscus on different aspects of St. Augustine. Petrarch modeled Augustinus in part on the Augustine who wrote *De vera religione*, a text that Petrarch had annotated and that he explicitly mentions in the *Secretum*. *De vera religione* stages a dialogue between Augustine and Reason, in which Reason shows that Plato anticipated some of the doctrines of Christianity, but that the existence of God cannot be proved by pagan reason. Instead, it is necessary to ascend from the world of images and illusions (again, "fantasmata") by faith to divine truth. By contrast, Petrarch models Franciscus on the young, preconversion Augustine of the *Confessions*, who struggles to overcome his divided will. But neither version of Augustine in the *Secretum* conforms fully to the Augustinian text on which it is modeled. Augustinus departs from the Augustine of *De vera religione* in stressing the Stoic ideal of autonomy to the exclusion of faith, and Franciscus departs from the Augustine of the *Confessions* in his endless deferral of the moment of conversion.

What does Petrarch intend with these revisions? Carol Quillen has argued that the *Secretum*'s Augustinus authorizes Petrarch's reading of classical literature, even as he also exposes the limitations of the Humanist project of imitation for the Christian reader desiring to convert. But Franciscus, I suggest, amounts to a far more radical revision of Augustine. Whereas Augustine saw phantasms as an object of sinful idolatry, Petrarch turns Augustine's analysis of phantasms into a new poetic, one that emphasizes the autonomy of the aesthetic artifact and the powerful pleasure to which it gives rise. In this way, Petrarch "re-occupies" the Augustinian problematic of sin, turning it from a condemnation of his desire for poetic fame to its surreptitious justification. The *Secretum*, we could then say, is Petrarch's defense of poetry, conceived of as both this-worldly aesthetic pleasure and posthumous reputation.[4]

I take the notion of "re-occupation" from Hans Blumenberg's *Legitimacy of the Modern Age*. In that work, Blumenberg takes issue with the secularization thesis, which argues that modern notions of progress or sovereignty are secularized versions of Christian concepts. According to Blumenberg, the secularization thesis cannot account for what was distinctively new in the early modern period: the will to break with medieval theology. This break was particularly apparent in the emergence of the new science, which presupposed the legitimacy of curiosity about the natural world.[5] Whereas "vain curiosity" had been condemned as a vice in the Christian Middle Ages, in the early modern period curiosity was no longer seen as a product of the Fall; rather, it was a way of exploring human nature and the natural world. This in turn meant that curiosity became a virtue rather than a vice. Curiosity, one might say, had been re-occupied.

Petrarch has a cameo role to play in Blumenberg's account of the gradual rehabilitation of curiosity. "As one of the great moments that oscillate indecisively between epochs," he writes, "I would like to mark April 26, 1336, when Petrarch ascended Mont Ventoux – 'purely out of the desire,' as he writes, 'to see the unusual altitude of the place.'"[6] Though Blumenberg describes Petrarch's record of this experience as "an amazing transposition of the category of conversion onto the beginnings of a new consciousness of nature and the world, which was ostensibly put on paper on the evening of the same day and turned into a humanistically stylized communication, into conscious literature," he concludes that Petrarch ultimately remained confined by the assumptions of Catholic theology, "retracting his aesthetic curiosity about the world before it had scarcely begun."[7]

In fact, Petrarch did not "retract" his aesthetic interest in his account of his ascent of Mont Ventoux (*Fam.* IV.1). Though he stages his failure to imitate Augustine's conversion in the *Confessions* as a consequence of his desire for literary success, the very existence of the letter and its inclusion in the collection of familiar letters that was one of Petrarch's crowning literary achievements testifies to Petrarch's enduring interest in his literary reputation. But if Blumenberg underestimates Petrarch's desire for literary fame, he is right that the question of salvation is re-occupied in aesthetic terms. Aesthetics, here, needs to be seen in terms of not only the natural world of Mont Ventoux and its surroundings, but also the literary world of Petrarch's own making.

The relation of this aesthetic realm of illusion to the very real problem of salvation is one of the central preoccupations of the *Secretum*, where the question of the afterlife is posed, insistently, if at times indirectly, by Augustinus. The saint's chief preoccupation is to get Franciscus to meditate on his mortality and cast off earthly attachments. In response to Augustinus's urging, Franciscus is quite willing to mediate on death. In fact, he gives the impression that he is already obsessed with it, but not in the way Augustinus recommends. Instead, what wins Franciscus's attention, as a mortal creature, is *mortalia* – mortal or perishable things, including his own works of literature. Rather than casting off earthly attachments, Petrarch focuses on a pagan version of the afterlife, the reputation one achieves for this-worldly deeds.

In defending the work of literature, Petrarch re-occupies the Augustinian problematics of illusions. Augustine's *Soliloquia* and *De vera religione* are both obsessed with the problem of distinguishing truth from falsehood, and, as a subset of this, the problem of interpreting images, phantasms, or illusions. In the *Soliloquia*, Reason argues that truth and falsehood are intertwined in all sense perception, but then goes on to distinguish between deception and mere falsehood. "The difference between the fallacious and the mendacious is that the former all wish to deceive while the latter do not at all wish to do so. Mimes and comedies and many poems are full of lies, but the aim is to delight rather than deceive."[8] In *De vera religione*, however, Augustine is considerably more critical of the realm of literary illusion. Instead of exempting it from the charge of deception, Augustine includes it in the larger category of fantasmata, which are responsible for leading us away from God: "There could have been no error in religion had not the soul worshipped in place of God either soul or body or its own phantasms."[9] While acknowledging, with Plato, that we come to knowledge of incorporeal things through carnal sense and carnal or corporeal forms, Augustine condemns those who "love the works of the artificer more than the artificer or his art, and are punished by falling into the error of expecting to find the artificer and his art in his works." Augustine then concludes that "God is not offered to the corporeal senses, and transcends even the mind."[10]

In a marginal note in his copy of De vera religione, Petrarch writes that readers of Augustine's text might appreciate Cicero's criticism of his contemporaries in the Tusculan Disputations: "For they could see nothing with the mind, they understood all things in terms of their eyes. It belongs to a great intellect to recall his mind from the sensible things and to lead thought away from the bonds of the customary."[11]

The Augustinian problem of interpreting images is an issue from the very outset of the Secretum. In the prologue, Petrarch recounts the sudden appearance of "a woman, radiant with an indescribable light surrounding her," who addresses him with the following words: "Don't be afraid. Do not let my sudden and strange appearance [species nova] alarm you in any way" (p. 45). In response, Petrarch addresses the figure with the words Aeneas addresses to Venus in Book 1 of the Aeneid (I.327–28): "By what name should I call you, maiden? For your face is hardly mortal, and your voice is not that of a human being" (p. 45). The maiden then gently reminds Petrarch of her identity: "I am she... whom you have depicted with deliberate elegance [curiosa quadam elegantia] in your poem Africa, and for whom you, with the energy of Amphion of Thebes, have built with stunning art and (so to speak) poetic hands a brilliant, beautiful palace in the far west on Atlas's highest peak" (p. 46).

Prompted by reference to his own earlier work, Petrarch finally remembers "that this could be none other than Truth herself" (p. 46). In this complicated exchange, Petrarch first addresses Truth as Venus, and then learns that the warrant for Truth is Petrarch's own representation of her in his epic poem about Scipio Africanus. What, we are prompted to wonder, is the relationship between truth and Virgil's epic, or between truth and the species nova of Petrarch's own elegant writing? And what are we to make of the fact that Petrarch says he has recorded his conversation with Augustinus so "that through reading it, I may be able to renew as often as I wish the pleasure I took in the conversation?" (p. 47), especially when Augustinus goes on, in the first dialogue, to chastise Franciscus for his devotion to the pleasures of this world?

The question of the relationship between truth and classical literature is further complicated by the fact that Augustinus regularly cites the ancients rather than the Bible. In the first dialogue, when he urges Franciscus to seek virtue, Augustinus does not say that such virtue will receive its reward in heaven. Instead, he remarks that it will "merit hearing the poet's praise: 'On, my son, with strength and virtue; thus is the path to the stars'" (*Aen.* IX.641, 52). But Augustinus doesn't just quote the ancients for their moral exemplarity. Instead, like Franciscus, he seems to enjoy quoting out of context for literary effect. In one striking example, Augustinus quotes Virgil's "the mind remains unmoved, fruitless tears pour down" to describe Franciscus's very un-Stoic recalcitrance in the face of Augustinus's instruction (*Aen.* IV.449, 56). Whereas in Virgil the phrase movingly conveys the emotional costs of Aeneas's Stoic resolution to leave Dido and found Rome, Augustinus uses it to describe how Franciscus remains unmoved by the appeal of virtue. Elsewhere in the *Secretum*, it almost seems as if Augustinus is colluding with Franciscus to make the point that our rewards for virtuous behavior are worldly and literary, rather than heavenly and spiritual, as when he tells Franciscus that earthly glory will follow up virtuous deeds. At other times, it seems that Petrarch is suggesting through Franciscus's recalcitrance that literature – both the ancients' and his own – captures more vividly and accurately the divided will of fallen Christian experience than do the theological treatises of St. Augustine.

The relationship between truth and the imagination, truth and illusions, is vividly dramatized in the first dialogue when Augustinus urges Franciscus to meditate on death, to call up its effects on the body and the terrors of the afterlife, "not as fiction but as truth, not as remote possibilities but as necessary and inevitable and imminent future events" (p. 64). Franciscus replies, "I imagine [confingo] this so intently, that feeling myself in the grips of death, I seem to discern Tartarus and all the evil things you speak of" (p. 58). But precisely at this moment – the only moment in the text when the name of Jesus is invoked – Franciscus asks for mercy in the words not of the New Testament but of Palinurus in the *Aeneid*: "'Take me, unconquered one, from these evils . . . Give your right hand to this miserable creature, and carry me with you through the waves, so that at least in death I may rest in a peaceful place'" (*Aen.* VI.365, 370–371).

In these exchanges, Petrarch enacts the encounter between Christianity and classical learning.[12] On the one hand, the quotations from classical texts dramatize Petrarch's Humanist conviction that the works of the ancients are exemplary for Christian readers. On the other, at least some of the quotations seem to occupy the place where one might reasonably expect biblical quotations to be found. What is seamless continuity from one perspective is usurpation and re-occupation from another. The tension between Christianity and classical culture is evident in the fact that Franciscus obediently imagines his own death, but doing so brings him no closer to God: "I say these things and many others to myself just like a delirious person whose wandering and fearful mind is moved by every impulse. And I speak also to my friends, in whom my crying sometimes induces tears, although after the tears we all return to the way we were before" (p. 65). Is Franciscus's imagination of death then *ut ficta* (as though it were fictional) or *ut vera* (as though it were true)? And isn't *ut vera* a version of *ut ficta* anyway, just as the figure of Truth is a fiction or representation in Petrarch's *Secretum*? Is Petrarch showing the inefficacy of the imagination to persuade to Christian truth? Or is he suggesting that the truth or falsehood of the imagination can only be judged by its moral and spiritual effects?

A little later on, despite having urged Franciscus to conjure up images of death, Augustinus seems to condemn the whole earthly realm of the senses as an obstacle to conversion:

> For innumerable shapes and images of visible things, which entered through the bodily senses one at a time, come together and crowd into the innermost parts of the soul. And the soul, not made for this and not able to take in so many different images, gets weighed down and confused. And so that plague of apparitions [pestis illa fantasmatum] rips and mangles your thinking, and with its fatal multiplicity obstructs the way to illuminating meditation, through which we are raised up to the one and only highest light. (p. 68)

Characteristically, Franciscus's reply suggests that he has missed Augustinus's point. Noting that Augustinus had written about this plague in *De vera religione*, Franciscus describes how he read this text "like a traveler, far from his homeland [peregrinatur a patria] and eager to see the world, who, crossing the unfamiliar border of some famous city, is captivated by the sweetness of the sights [captus locorum dulcedine] and stops frequently here and there to study everything he sees" (p. 68). Franciscus's use of the term "peregrinatur" (see Chapter 1), as well as "captus locorum dulcedine," suggests that his reading of *De vera religione*, like his reading of the *Confessions* and, as we will see, his own *Secretum*, is an aesthetic experience but not necessarily a spiritual one.

The problem of *fantasmata* – how to judge them, how to transcend them – continues to occupy Augustinus and Franciscus at the beginning of the second dialogue. Augustinus worries that Franciscus fails to see that what appears harmless at a distance is really evil at close hand (p. 70). Chief among these evils – or what Augustinus calls "empty cares" – is Petrarch's boasting about his extensive reading and his own eloquence (p. 71). Such eloquence is a distraction at best, and sinful at worst. Like a stern Humanist schoolmaster, Augustinus asks, "What good has all of your reading done you? Of all the things you have read, how much has really stayed in your soul?" And he proceeds to allude to the passage from the *Confessions* that Petrarch himself read as a rebuke to his curiosity about the natural world in the "Ascent of Mont Ventoux": "What does it matter if you have learned about the orbits of the planets... if you do not know yourself?" (p. 72).[13]

Augustinus's solution is to encourage Franciscus to read allegorically, that is, to allegorize from the material surface of a text to its spiritual meaning. He cautions with Plato that "nothing presents a greater obstacle to recognition of the divine than carnal appetites and burning desire" (p. 89), including the desire simply to rest in the surface of the text, or what he earlier calls its "illusions" (p. 86). Franciscus says he knows this well from Virgil's *Aeneid*: just as Venus obstructs Aeneas's vision after the fall of Troy (*Aen.* II.361–369), so is delighting in the surface of the text a distraction from truth. Augustinus then praises Franciscus for allegorizing away the surface of poetry: "For this is how truth dwells in poetic creation [poeticis inest veritas figmentis]: It must be brought out into the light from the dark corners" (p. 90). In this exchange, Augustinus sees poetry ideally as a self-consuming artifact, useful as a point of departure but dangerous if one merely succumbs to its aesthetic lure. But this is precisely what Franciscus is inclined to do, even when the spectacle at hand is disturbing.

The problem of the correct interpretation of *fantasmata* reappears in the beginning of the third dialogue, where Augustinus accuses Franciscus of confusing the chains of his earthly love and glory with "great jewels" (p. 103). Franciscus replies that Augustinus is trying to deprive him of "speciossimas michi curas" ("his most glorious occupations") (p. 103), to which Augustinus counters that Franciscus has confused "false opinions" with "the only truth" (p. 104). The phrase "speciossimas curas" sums up the dilemma of the *Secretum*, whose full title is *De secreto conflictu curarum mearum* (*On the Secret Conflict of My Cares*). Chief among these cares are the love of Laura and the desire for glory or literary fame. Both cares illustrate the problem of imaginative illusions insofar as these cares are not only *for* beauty and glory but themselves *appear* most beautiful and glorious to Franciscus's eyes. In charging Franciscus with the sins of love and glory, however, Augustinus doesn't just call our attention to the parallels between physical desire and poetic ambition, Laura and the laurel; he also accuses Franciscus of being "captivated as much by the beauty of Laura's name as of her person" (p. 117). Though love and glory are equally distracting passions, Augustinus suggests that Laura's person is less important to Franciscus than the polysemic linguistic potential of her name. And this in turn means that Laura is both the object of desire and the means to poetic glory, but poetic glory is also for Franciscus an object of desire in its own right. Thus, in Augustinus's account, Franciscus's love for Laura is displaced by his desire for literary reputation.

That literary fame is more important than Laura is illustrated by the rest of Book 3. When Augustinus urges Franciscus not to postpone thoughts of his salvation, Franciscus replies, "I persuade myself that the glory that it is permitted to hope for here must be sought for while I am here. The greater glory is to be enjoyed in heaven... Among mortals, the first care is for mortal things" (p. 140). When Augustinus cites Petrarch's own epic, the *Africa*, to convince Franciscus of the transience of human glory and books (p. 142), Franciscus parries with a defense of his literary efforts (p. 144). And when Augustinus cites Virgil's description of the beauty of a night that can be used for doing evil or good in order to encourage Franciscus to use mortal life in the right way (p. 144), Franciscus likewise turns this argument to his own advantage. He tells Augustinus that the saint's "place is in heaven, whereas my time on earth is not yet finished"; and, in case Augustinus missed the point, he adds "I will attend to myself as far as I am able. I will collect the scattered fragments of my soul, and I will diligently focus on myself alone. But now, even as we speak, many other obligations, though admittedly mortal ones [mortalia], still await me" (pp. 147, 212). In these exchanges, what Augustinus describes as spectacle and illusion, Franciscus equates with *mortalia*: the realm of mortal things, which, as a mortal, he is not ready to abandon. It's not surprising, then, that Franciscus's phrase "scattered fragments" echoes the "rime sparse" ("scattered rhymes") and fragments of the *RVF*, the literary text that has done more than any other to secure Petrarch's posthumous fame.

By the end of Book 3, Augustinus's instruction in allegorical reading of aesthetic surfaces has unraveled. At the same time that he urges Franciscus to read with attention to his salvation, Augustinus also makes it clear that unless one already knows the truth toward which one is aiming, and already has the right disposition of the will, correct reading will be all but impossible. Franciscus confesses his own confusion:

> Now I am really confused. You offer me the prescription of flight for a recuperating and healing soul, yet you simultaneously proclaim that my soul must be cured and healthy before it can flee. But this does not resolve the problem of how one gets cured. For if a person is already cured, what more is sought? And if not cured, and if a change of scene... will not help, then tell me more explicitly what remedies should be used. (pp. 121–122)

If, however, reading and writing cannot produce salvation, perhaps they have another future as instruments of aesthetic pleasure.

If we now return to the preface to the *Secretum*, we can see that the entire dialogue is framed by the secret of aesthetic pleasure:

That this conversation, so intimate and deep, should not be lost, I have written it down and made this book, I would not, however, classify it with my other works, nor do I desire any credit for it. My thoughts aim higher. What I desire is that through reading it, I may be able to renew as often as I wish the pleasure [dulcedinem] I took in the conversation itself. (p. 47)

It may be for this reason that Franciscus addresses the figure of Truth with the same words Aeneas addresses to the goddess of pleasure, Venus. In Petrarch's hands, his own text has become an enjoyable *spectaculum* and the reader has become a spectator who takes pleasure in the dialogue and conflict represented within it. It is fitting, then, that Franciscus's final apostrophe in the preface is not to Truth or Augustinus, but to his own book: "So little book [libellus], I bid you to flee from public places. Be content to stay with me, true to the title that I have given you. For you are my secret [secretum enim meum], and thus you are titled. And when I think about profound subjects, speak to me in secret [in abdito] about what has been in secret [in abdito] spoken to you" (p. 47).[14]

If we now return to Blumenberg, we can say that Petrarch re-occupied what the Middle Ages condemned as vain curiosity, transforming it into a celebration of this-worldly activity, including above all the activity of poetry. In the *Secretum*, Petrarch pitted the stern Augustine of *De vera religione* against the unconverted Augustine of the *Confessions*, taking the latter as the model for Franciscus, and thus as his alter ego. In the process, Petrarch also appropriated and transformed the literary and spiritual model of the *Confessions*: the secret Franciscus confesses is the open secret of his love of literature, both of the ancients and his own. But, even without the *Secretum*, it would be no mystery that Petrarch could not abandon his interest in – and desire to represent – the cares and spectacles of this world (p. 148). More than any other poet of the later Middle Ages or Renaissance, Petrarch made a forceful case for the power of poetry, conceived of as both aesthetic illusion and aesthetic pleasure.

NOTES

1 See *Fam.* X.4 on the first theologians being poets (also XXI.10 on the compatibility of Cicero and Christianity).
2 David Marsh, *The Quattrocento Dialogue. Classical Tradition and Humanist Innovation* (Cambridge, MA: Harvard University Press, 1980), 17.
3 Petrarch, *The Secret*, 88.
4 See John Freccero, "The Fig Tree and the Laurel: Petrarch's Poetics," in *Petrarch: Modern Critical Views*, ed. Harold Bloom (New York: Chelsea House, 1989), on how Petrarch turns the thematic of the sin of idolatry into a "poetics of presence" (54).

5 Hans Blumenberg, *The Legitimacy of the Modern Age*, trans. Robert M. Wallace (orig. 1966; trans. Cambridge, MA: MIT Press, 1983).

6 Ibid., 341.

7 Ibid., 342, 343. A full legitimation of curiosity required the absent God of nominalist theology, who vacates the world and thus makes room for human activity, including aesthetic activity. With the legitimation of curiosity, the question of salvation did not disappear but was instead reoccupied by an interest in what one could expect from the secular world (346).

8 St. Augustine, *The Soliloquies (Soliloquia)*, in *Augustine: Earlier Writings*, trans. John H. S. Burleigh, The Library of Christian Classics, vol. VI (Philadelphia, PA: Westminster Press, 1953), 2.9.16–17, 50.

9 Augustine, *Of True Religion (De vera religione)*, in *Augustine*, Burleigh, 10.18, 234.

10 Ibid., 36.67, 259.

11 Cited in Carol Everhart Quillen, *Rereading the Renaissance: Petrarch, Augustine, and the Language of Humanism* (Ann Arbor, MI: University of Michigan Press, 1998), 83.

12 See Victoria Kahn, "The Figure of the Reader in Petrarch's *Secretum*," *PMLA* 100 (1985): 154–166, and Quillen, *Rereading the Renaissance*, on how the *Secretum* both illustrates Humanist practices of reading and questions their efficacy.

13 See Augustine, *Confessions*, 10.8. For a discussion of the imagination and images in Augustine and Petrarch's "Ascent," see Albert Russell Ascoli, "Petrarch's Middle Age: Memory, Imagination, History, and the 'Ascent of Mount Ventoux,'" in *"A Local Habitation and a Name": Imagining Histories in the Italian Renaissance* (New York: Fordham University Press, 2011), 21–58.

14 On this point, see also Brian Stock, "Reading, Writing, and the Self: Petrarch and His Forerunners," *New Literary History* 26 (1995): 717–730.

9

UNN FALKEID

De vita solitaria and *De otio religioso*: the perspective of the guest

Petrarch's two contemplative works, *De vita solitaria* and *De otio religioso*, are often regarded as different, and even opposed visions of life that reveal the different existential choices of the sons of ser Petracco: Francesco's withdrawal to the pastoral scenery of Vaucluse and Gherardo's retreat to the Carthusian monastery of Montrieux. As in many other texts by Petrarch, the two books restage the fork in the road at which the brothers went their separate ways. Nevertheless, the two paths share the same terrain. In both cases, the human being is figured as a guest (*hospis*) on earth. With reference to Prosper of Aquitaine, the Late Antique poet who, not unlike Petrarch himself, ardently took part in the theological and political controversies of his time, Petrarch writes in the second book of *De otio*: "I live my life as a guest for a limited period of time." The image is a both a warning and an encouragement. The many appearances entice the guest during his journey, but his status as stranger may also fortify him in confronting the secret plays of power that continuously surround him. Against a background of solitude, the guest may turn his mind toward the cacophony of life, while raising his voice against the many dangers he discovers. We must bear in mind that the Avignon papacy, which Petrarch so profoundly despised, was the historical context that nourished the two treatises. In other words, by celebrating *otium* – an active leisure, or a life spent on studies, writing, contemplation, and friendship – *De vita* and *De otio* offer strong critiques of the contemporary political situation in Europe.

Both texts were first composed during Lent, a period particularly suitable for contemplative activities (*Sen.* VI.5 and X.1). *De vita* was written in 1346, and *De otio* the year after, in 1347. But according to Petrarch's usual habit, the texts were subsequently edited and elaborated; hence, Gherardo and the monks in Montrieux did not receive *De otio* until 1357, and *De vita* reached its recipient even later.[1] It was not until 1366 that Philippe de Cabassoles, the bishop of Cavaillon and one of Petrarch's closest friends, could read the invitation to come and stay with him in Vaucluse, which by that point Petrarch had already left for good.[2] However, Petrarch and Philippe de Cabassoles had previously spent much time together in the serene valley some miles from Avignon, where the bishop's castle towered atop the steep cliff behind Petrarch's more modest house by the Sorgue river. And the pleasures of solitude weren't all the two friends shared: their political ideas also overlapped, as evidenced by two letters addressed to the bishop in Petrarch's *Sine nomine* (1 and 12), which are present in *De vita* as well.

As we immediately understand, friendship plays a pivotal role in Petrarch's idea of solitude. Many readers have noticed the profoundly dialogical character of most of his works, and he always had a distant friend in mind when he wrote, thereby establishing, as Giuseppe Mazzotta has argued, the viewpoint of an "otherness" that transcends the narrow limits of a subjective vision.[3] *De vita* and *De otio* are written within the Christian tradition of *Soliloquium*, which goes back to St. Augustine and his rejection of the classical Ciceronian dialogue. The way to freedom for Augustine went inward through a contemplative method of memory and a conversation with God within the self. Nevertheless, Petrarch's soliloquies are essentially dialogic, and he presents self-knowledge as a journey and exchange of thoughts with other human beings, for, as we read in the foreword to *De vita*, our life will be judged by our conversations with others. When the proof of our actions is gone, only the evidence of our speech will remain. Equally important is that, through a web of friends, the poet attempted, in an oblique way, to create a counter empire of culture that offered new and critical perspectives on the political and intellectual debates of his time.

In Petrarch's vision of solitude, the classical celebration of *otium* and the religious ideal of contemplation converge in a harmonic balance. In the opening of *De vita*, the poet recalls Cato's statement in Cicero's *Pro Plancio* (XXVII.66): "Men of great and unusual gifts must look with as careful an eye to their leisure as to their business" (p. 99). Throughout the first book, leisure and business – the Stoic opposites of *otium* and *negotium* – are then exposed as contradictory ways of life. In the city, the life of the busy man (and for Petrarch, this person is indeed normatively male) is burdened by grievous worry, as he is caught in his own web of deception and power, which creates nothing but shame and misery around him. And what is worse, as a slave to his senses and his belly's demands, his mind is frozen in laziness. Petrarch writes that he attempts to create an imaginary solitude within the turmoil of cities, and to master himself through an effort of the mind. In other words, the mind's triumph over the lower senses to which busy humans are usually subjected requires some form of solitude, a privacy of thought, which it may be possible to create even in the midst of the vulgar populace. However, this gift is reserved for the few: according to Petrarch, it is better to leave the city and conduct a life in simplicity far away from the crowd. Both in the monastery and in the secular world, active leisure, or *otium* connected to intellectual work, leads to the highest desirable state for a human being, namely freedom of the mind.

The author most frequently quoted in *De vita* is Seneca, who, along with Cicero, Horace, Livy, and Ovid, celebrated a life dedicated to leisure, which recalled the Greek ideals of both *skolé* and *theoria*: the cultivation of the mind within the liberal arts in order to contemplate the truth. It was also this form of leisure that was adopted by the Church Fathers and practiced by the monastic tradition during the Middle Ages. Thus, *otium* was not to be understood as laziness, though lazy idleness is always lurking in the shadows of solitude, according to Petrarch. By referring to Seneca (*Ad Lucilium* 82), he connects leisure to work: "Leisure without study is death; it is a tomb for the living man." Petrarch adds that "isolation without literature, is exile, prison, torture; supply literature, and it becomes your country, freedom, and delight" (p. 131). Solitude is therefore associated with liberty and a life of letters.

As many scholars have argued, by reintroducing classical *otium* into contemporary secular life, Petrarch articulates the conditions for intellectual freedom, which became such an important subject for Humanists in the centuries to come, from Valla to Montaigne, and from Rousseau to Sartre. However, Petrarch's praise of solitude also involves theological and political concerns, as solitude is a necessary step both for the individual mind's ascent to God and for the freedom of humanity as a whole. By referring to Plotinus's chain or ladder of virtues – the political virtues, the purgatorial virtues, the virtues of the purified mind, and the exemplary virtues – explained in the *First Ennead* (Book II), Petrarch brings the material and the spiritual, or the contingent and the infinite, together in such a way that the lower steps are just as important as the higher ones in man's return to God (pp. 139–140).

In order to reach the heavenly freedom from which he was once expelled, a human being must cultivate the entire range of virtues, including those connected to the earthly city and political life. As Petrarch explains, Christ is present in all places and at all times. This creates a possible intimacy between humanity and divinity that not only transforms a human being's status as a guest and stranger into that of a member of God's household in a world to come but also incorporates human activities into the economy of history, and gives authority to both the layman and the priest, to the poor as well as to the rich. Thus, according to Petrarch, to partake in the world is essential because the freedom, or redemption, of the world and the redemption of the individual soul are inextricably linked to each other. In this way, freedom becomes a political question in Petrarch's work, and not only an inner, ethical pursuit as it mostly had been for the Christian thinkers of the Middle Ages, such as Augustine and Boethius, whose philosophies moved within the confines of the Stoic-Platonic tradition.

According to Petrarch, contemplation, which etymologically conveys the act of marking out a space for observation, may give the spectator a glimpse of the invisible correlations between the finite world and the universal order, as the Neo-Platonic image of the chain suggests. More importantly, by excavating leisure from one's daily labors through contemplation, human beings may achieve the necessary corrections that give them the strength and power to return to the battlefields of their times. As Petrarch explains, the fruit of the solitary life is:

> To know that this life is but the shadow of life, that it is not home, but an inn, not the fatherland but a road, not a chamber of rest but an arena; . . . sometimes to rise, with thoughts that are lifted above yourself, to the ethereal region, to meditate on what goes on there and by meditation to inflame your desire, and in turn to encourage and admonish yourself with a fervent spirit as though with the power of burning words. (p. 150)

It will soon appear that the "burning words" are addressed by Petrarch not only to himself, but also to those with whom he is in conversation. Thus, the quotation discretely shows that Petrarch's vision of the solitary life has both a theological and a political foundation. The glimpse of the eternal attained by contemplation may offer a new perspective on the actual life and inspire the guest to work for his own and his fellow man's happiness – and of course, the Humanist's work is the words that endure longer than his actions.

In addition to the previously mentioned foreword, *De vita* is divided into two books. The first is a mapping of solitude from both a theoretical and an ethical point of view, while the second consists of examples from the vast history of human beings who have chosen a solitary life. The list of names begins with Adam, followed by Biblical persons such as Abraham, Isaac, Jacob, Moses, Elijah, and Jeremiah. Next come the Church Fathers, Pope Sylvester, St. Ambrose, St. Augustine, and St. Jerome, then the founders of the monastic orders, St. Benedict and St. Francis, and lastly contemporary figures such as Pope Celestine V.

As some readers have suggested, it may well be that through this lineage Petrarch charts a historical geography of solitude which finds its center in Italy. More important, however, are the political conflicts that rumble at the fringes of solitude, and which become louder as we approach the poet's own time: the presentation of Pope Celestine V is a prelude to Petrarch's bitter attack in subsequent paragraphs, in which the hidden aims of the book unfold. With the intensity of a prophetic voice, Petrarch criticizes the current situation in Europe, from east to west, and from north to south. The pious pope, who abdicated in order to live a simple life in solitude, was captured by his successor, Pope Boniface VIII, and died shortly thereafter in the infected air of prison. Whereas Dante regarded Celestine as a coward in *Inferno* III (59–60) precisely for having paved the way for a figure such as Boniface VIII, Petrarch celebrates him as a saint. This does not mean that he judges his successors more gently than Dante did. In Petrarch's opinion, the piety of Celestine strongly contrasts with the contemporary degeneration of the Avignon papacy – this latest Babylon, as he calls it.

In a few pages, but highly important ones, the author turns his burning words against popes and monarchs. "If you are loth to put your faith in words," he rhetorically writes, "you will at least believe the facts, which, as it is said, are not in the habit of lying. Look about you, I pray, and survey the countries and ask what is happening among us" (pp. 240–241). The greed of the leaders of the Church, as well as the negligence of the European kings, has led to the loss of the Holy Land. The French and Britons are quarreling, while Spain is rife with religious conflicts. The Italian city states, Venice and Genoa, share a thirst for gold and power, and thus are bitter enemies. Rome has not only been deserted by the Pontiff, but also betrayed by the Roman emperor (Charles IV), who fled the city immediately after his coronation and returned to Germany, where he now arms mercenary brigands for the destruction of Italy. According to Petrarch, even Greece, "turned away by her own errors or our pride, despises the ancient fold and our pastures" (p. 242). Worst of all, the empire of the Catholic faith, whose boundaries once were larger than those of the Roman Empire, is nothing more than an image and shadow of its former self. With a quotation from Augustine's *De vera religione* – "In every part of the earth inhabited by man, the holy Christian practices are handed down" – Petrarch argues that one may easily measure the vastness of the loss, not only in Europe, but in Africa and Persia, Syria, Egypt, and Asia as well (p. 245).

Against this loss, and against the wars and many threats facing the Catholic faith, Petrarch tries to create a counter-power, a cultural territory that transgresses the ordinary limits of time and space. It is articulated in solitude, remote from the city and powerful institutions, and cultivated in a dialogue within a network of friends. Throughout *De vita*, the reader is repeatedly confronted with various metaphors of cultivation. In the beginning of the first book, Petrarch writes that "the human mind teems with errors like a fat field overrun with brambles, and if these are not diligently uprooted and with studious toil cleared away, the fruit in both cases will equally perish with the flower" (p. 105). However, the mind may be cultivated by studies in solitude, and as we have seen, the fruits will come in abundance. The fruits of the solitary life are a freedom of the mind and a resistance to worldly power. Moreover, the fruits are to be shared with friends, just as farmers offer their first fruit of the field in gratefulness. And they are to be shared with posterity, thus indirectly fulfilling the debt that one cannot pay to the dead for the gift of their writing. In other words, the pleasure of reading one's forerunners' work may result in writing things that later generations might wish to read. As such, the Humanist's empire, as cultivated in active leisure (*otium*), involves present and distant friends, as well as past and future generations, both without borders and without any institutional intrusion.

While the discussions in *De vita* take place within the horizon of how to return to the social life of *polis* against the background of the changes of perspectives that solitude may give, *De otio* is best characterized as a vertical movement. Here, the central question is how to avoid losing sight of the world in a monastic life. However, as we understand from *Seniles* VI.2, the letter addressed to Philippe de Cabassoles that accompanied *De vita*, Petrarch regarded the two books as being closely related to one another, both in material and in style. *De vita* is also mentioned in *De otio*, in which Petrarch writes that the former precedes the latter in time and order of consideration, but that all the points in both aim toward one conclusion (p. 10). In both cases, the classical idea of active leisure is connected to the medieval tradition of contemplation, equating the different paths of the two brothers. Just as the retreat of the lay Humanist requires a Christian perspective in order to achieve its fulfillment, *otium*, or the study of secular literature, may enrich the contemplations of the monk. The title of the volume makes this clear, as does Petrarch's explanation to Gherardo in the second book: "By this study, just as in writing prose I sometimes season my pen for a secular audience with religious citations, so I am delighted by secular references (which were my first and for some time my only reading) when my audience consists of clerics and monks" (p. 101).

De otio is commonly considered somewhat atypical and old-fashioned, belonging more to the medieval celebration of the monastic life than to Petrarch's future-oriented project. However, rarely is Petrarch more articulate and bold in his Christian Humanism than in this text, which touches on some discussions that will be of great importance in the centuries to come. Written out of gratitude for the monks' hospitality after the poet's visit to the monastery in Montrieux, it rethinks ethics through the lens of the guest. The metaphor evokes Dante's story about Brother Alberigo in the lower *Inferno* (XXXIII) and the severe punishment for those who violate the sanctity of the hospitality owed to the guest. However, Petrarch not only exposes the traveler's vulnerability but also grounds it as a universal human experience.

The Latin word *hospis* refers equally to "guest" and "host." According to Petrarch, then, every human being is both a guest on earth and a host to future generations. This insight, which involves nothing less than the ability to discern Christ in the other, depends above all on our capacity to take time and to see. Indeed, the entire text is built around this quotation: "vacate et videte," taken from Psalm 45, verse 11: "Take time and see that I am God" (p. 5). The words may be understood as a reminder of the holy purpose of the brothers' contemplation. By marking out an empty space through contemplative studies in silence, the monks would free their minds from worldly occupations and prepare themselves for the coming beatitude. The Biblical quotation was usually interpreted in this way in the patristic and mystical traditions of the Middle Ages, yet Petrarch reverses this.[4] In its original Biblical context, the reader is exhorted to admire Creation, and through this admiration to discover the traces of God within. Consequently, the first book of *De otio*, which like *De vita* is divided into two, may be read as an invitation not to forget the outer world even in the silence of the cell. In this way, Petrarch refutes the Augustinian notion of *contemptus mundi*, the necessary scorn of the world required to liberate the soul. According to Petrarch, the dualism that such contempt conveys may result in the idea of an endless distance between God and man, and in a deep distrust of human actions. As he ironically writes in *De otio*, "As a matter of fact, that thought disturbs people's minds: certainly God is the best, but I am the worst. Is there any proportion to such a discrepancy?" (p. 37).

Against this distrust and its inherent nihilism, Petrarch emphasizes the incarnation of Christ. By humbling himself, by becoming a mortal man who can be heard, touched, and seen, Petrarch says, the physical world of humanity is elevated. This is not only a celebration of human dignity, which will become such an important theme for later Renaissance Humanists. The mystical union between humanity and God, which the incarnation affirms, includes human actions and historical events in the economy of salvation. In *De otio*, Petrarch retrieves the Neo-Platonic idea from *De vita* about the chain between the material and the spiritual world, subsequently complicating the dualism of the Stoic-Platonic tradition:

To be sure, I confess that the distance between heaven and earth is really huge, but it is finite, whereas between God and humanity the distance is infinite. Indeed, humanity is the earth, from which he has received his name. Humanity has risen from earth, lives on the earth, and is destined to return to the earth. God, however, is not heaven, but the Creator of heaven, as high from heaven as from earth, as much present and as much distant in both places. (p. 59)

The complexity brought forth by this passage is that the dangers continually surrounding humans are as much spiritual as they are material in nature. Thus, no place is safe from danger, not even the monks' seclusion from the world, because the real battle is not between a sinful body and a divine soul. As Petrarch explains, with a quotation from Paul (Eph. 6:12), "You are not contending against flesh and blood, but against princes and powers, against the rulers of the shadow of this world, against spiritual forces of evil in the heavens" (p. 27). Again, we see the political ground of Petrarch's theology. The *otium* of the monks is as ambiguous as the solitude of the Humanist; both require attention to the noises of life and to the wide circle of other human beings in order not to end in selfish solipsism and scorn of the world.

While admiration for the world is the subject of the first book, the illusions, the many appearances of the secular world, which tempt humans to forget the perspective of the eternity, are the subject of the second. As Petrarch writes at the end of the first book, "Limits of place offer us something to love; limits of time take away what we love and leave in our minds crowds of illusions by which our desire is aroused to one thing or another" (p. 65). Creation is worth being lauded and loved, but within the classical tradition of *memento mori*, Petrarch admonishes the monks to always remember that life is a journey, and that the abundance of all earthly things belongs to exiles.

According to Petrarch, no one understood this mobile perspective of the guest better than St. Francis, who, by humbling himself, by both love and suffering for the world, became Christ-like. Both in *De vita* and in *De otio*, Francis is described as the most outstanding of all human beings. With this celebration, we may also assume an underlying sympathy with the contemporary Franciscans' critique of the Avignon papacy, so clearly expressed elsewhere in Petrarch's work, such as in the letters of the *Sine nomine*. What is striking in *De otio*, however, is that the two perspectives – discovery of the beauty of the world and simultaneous preparation of the soul for eternal bliss – depend on each other. In both cases, it is a question of the capacity of man to take time and to see. As Petrarch explains in another allusion to Psalm 45, verse 11, by managing leisure, "You will realize that I am God" and "You will see that I am God" (p. 65).

In the first explanation of the Biblical verse "take time and see," Petrarch stressed the carnal eye's gift to see and know the mysteries of God. The second book dwells on the other perspective, the all-seeing eyes of the eternal Spectator, which in a Neo-Platonic sense is at the origin of the human capacity of seeing. The eternal Spectator is the true source of the pleasures of the world. Without the perspective of God, the human being would not be able to admire the spectacle of the Creation at all. According to Petrarch, this is the hidden wisdom of *vacate et videte*, which connects the paths of the two brothers together: the eternal viewpoint facilitates the guest's journey and makes him able to love, to act, and to leave the world behind.

NOTES

1 Wilkins, *Life of Petrarch*, 17–18.
2 Dotti, *Vita di Petrarca*, 151–154.
3 Giuseppe Mazzotta, *The Worlds of Petrarch* (Durham, NC: Duke University Press, 1993), 148.
4 Susanna Barsella,"A Humanistic Approach to Religious Solitude (*De otio religioso*)," in *Petrarch: A Critical Guide*, Kirkham and Maggi, 202–203.

10

ALBERT RUSSELL ASCOLI

Epistolary Petrarch

Petrarch's letters are no secret. Or, perhaps, as collections, as complex "macro-textual" wholes, they are. My allusion to the *Secretum* is deliberate. Among Petrarch's Latin works, the *Secretum* has been by far the best known, supporting a number of key assumptions that drove nineteenth- and especially twentieth-century scholarship: in particular, on the one hand, the idea of Petrarch as "first modern man," the model of self-conscious, autonomous and yet divided, selfhood, and, on the other, the complex engagement with St. Augustine's theology of the will. The *Secretum* has a more obviously polished structure than the letter collections do, but at the same time it presents itself as a private text, never intended for circulation. The collected epistles are, instead, individually addressed to others, and, even when they never arrived at their destinations, or when they were in fact never intended to do so, they predicate interpersonal communication, in a way that the dialogic *Secretum* does not, since Petrarch alone is its intended audience. Of the four principal collections – the *Familiares*, the *Seniles*, the verse *Epystole*, and the *Liber sine nomine* – all but the *Sine nomine* (which assumes anonymity) is dedicated to one of Petrarch's dearest friends, and all frequently describe his interactions with others. They also range over a far wider set of topics, and far more specific historical, geographical, and social circumstances, than does the dialogue. In other words, though the *Secretum* and the epistles are unmistakably products of the same self-obsessed author, the latter give a far more dynamic, historicized, multi-faceted, and socially situated picture of Petrarch. It will, then, be a founding assumption of this chapter that the letter collections, especially the *Familiares* and the sequel the *Seniles*, represent the pinnacle of Petrarch's achievement in the Latin language.

Over the quarter-century between the beginning of the *Familiares* in 1350 and his death in 1374, Petrarch would create four distinct collections, each of which, atypically for his oeuvre, would achieve "completed" shape. These were:

1) The 350 letters of the *Familiares*, composed between 1325 and 1366, organized into a collection between 1345 and 1366, and dedicated to "Socrates" (Ludwig Van Kempen).[1]

2) The sixty-six verse *Epystole* in three books, conceived in parallel with the *Familiares*, composed between c. 1318 and 1355, circulated as of 1364, and dedicated to Barbato of Sulmona (see esp. *Epystole* I.1; *Fam.* XXII.3; *Sen.* III.3–4).[2]

3) The nineteen "letters" plus preface of the anti-papal, anti-Avignon, pro-Roman *Sine nomine*, composed between 1342 and 1359 and organized c. 1351–61).

4) The eighteen books and 128 letters of the *Seniles* – composed between 1358 and 1374, organized 1361–74 – which pick up, chronologically, approximately where the *Familiares* leaves off, and which are dedicated to Francesco Nelli, the most frequent recipient of letters in the *Familiares* (twenty-nine missives), whom Petrarch belatedly dubbed "Simonides," after the Greek poet-priest (*Sen.* I.1–3, III.1).[3]

A certain number of letters, currently estimated at seventy-six, have survived that were not collected at all,[4] testimony to the value assigned to Petrarch's letters during his own lifetime, a point which he himself makes (*Fam.* XVIII.7). For comparison, one may look at the thirteen letters usually attributed to Dante and the twenty-four to Boccaccio, neither of whom created letter collections.

Until relatively recently, the 638 extant Latin letters were assigned three distinct functions.[5] First, they symbolized Petrarch's commitment to the "Humanist" project of recovering and reproducing the classical past. Though the first letters date from Petrarch's youth (the 1320s and 1330s), the idea of producing collections of letters was conceived after his "discovery" of Cicero's collected letters to Atticus, Brutus, and Quintus in the Cathedral library of Verona in 1345. Within a year he had formed the idea of a series of letters directed to the great *auctores* of classical times – first of all Cicero, but then Seneca, Horace, Virgil, and other Latin authors, and finally Homer – which would be subsumed at decade's end into the larger project of his *Familiares*, ultimately constituting the bulk of the twenty-fourth and final book. Though Petrarch had, naturally, been trained in the late-medieval *ars dictaminis* or art of letter writing, his epistolary oeuvre would inaugurate a newer, or, rather, a very old style, based on Ciceronian and Senecan models, in tacit polemic with the decadent Latin culture of his own times.

In the second place, the letters were treated as the privileged locus of historical, social, and especially biographical information, notably by Petrarch's biographers, Ernest Hatch Wilkins, and, subsequently, Ugo Dotti. Many are addressed to leading ecclesiastical, political, and intellectual figures of the fourteenth century – for instance, King Robert the Wise of Naples, Cola di Rienzo, Emperor Charles IV, Francesco da Carrara, Cardinal Colonna, and Pope Urban V – and refer to the great events of the period – the Avignon residency of the papacy, the Black Death of 1348–49, and so on. Others are directed to lesser known or unknown figures (with one exception – an empress – all male (*Fam.* XXI.8)). They generally recount local and domestic incidents, and are virtually all, even those directed to the high and mighty, couched in terms of familiarity, friendship, and/or candor. Ordered explicitly, if roughly, according to chronology and covering virtually the entirety of Petrarch's adulthood until shortly before his death in 1374, the letters seemingly give unprecedented access to and knowledge of an individual late-medieval life (the self-documentation of Dante's life pales in comparison). And there is no doubt about the value and credibility of much of the information furnished, despite the fact that the collected letters were extensively revised for rhetorical, literary, and propagandistic purposes, and that many others were repressed entirely.[6] It is one of the curious features of the collections, however, that on one hand they often do provide relatively reliable historical and autobiographical information, and on the other they frequently – beginning with the first, "proemial" letter of the *Familiares* – open a deliberately revelatory window onto the filtering, at times distorting, process by which Petrarch selected and revised the texts to be included.

Finally, the third traditional treatment of the letters has been to isolate and celebrate individual texts, or in a few cases thematically linked groupings of texts, extracting them from the larger structures in which Petrarch so carefully placed them. Among the most famous examples of these are: the "Letter from Mont Ventoux" (*Fam.* IV.1), dramatizing the tension between outwardly directed "naturalist" and historicist curiosity and inwardly directed pursuit of spiritual change; the letters to Boccaccio denying and yet displaying an envious attitude toward Dante (*Fam.* XXI.15; *Sen.* V.2); a series of letters on literary imitation (*Fam.* I.8–9, XXII.2, XXIII.19); the letters to classical authors (*Fam.* XXIV.3–12); the letter conducting a "tour" through the ruins of Rome (*Fam.* VI.2); the influential translation of Boccaccio's Griselda story (*Dec.* X.10) into Latin (*Sen.* XVII.3); and, of course, the "Letter to Posterity," the last letter of the *Seniles* (XVIII.1).

These uses of the letters continue to be central to Petrarch scholarship; indeed, they have become even more prevalent, because access to the texts has become far easier with the production of complete Italian, French, and English translations, the arrival of new critical editions of the *Familiares*, *Seniles*, *Sine nomine*, and *Disperse*, and the introduction of some exciting new scholarly tools.[7] But this accessibility, together with the work of a few pioneering interpreters (especially Bernardo, T. Greene, Mazzotta, and Struever), has also added new dimensions to our understanding of the Petrarchan epistolary oeuvre. Of particular value is the theoretical–methodological distinction between individual micro-texts (in this case, letters) and the macro-textual superstructures within which they are contained,[8] which invite interpretation of the relations between individual micro-texts, as well as an understanding of the signifying dynamics within substructures (the single books of the *Familiares* and *Seniles*; individual thematic threads which link letters in different books over the course of the collections) and in the collections considered as coherent wholes.

It is a striking feature of many of Petrarch's works, and of other key texts of the emergent literary-intellectual tradition in Italy, that they are more easily characterized as macro-texts than as continuously narrated and/or argued works. The most obvious examples are, of course, Boccaccio's *Decameron* and Petrarch's own *RVF*. The same, however, is true of much of Petrarch's Latin oeuvre: the series of lives of famous men (*De viris*), of memorable things (*Rerum memorandarum*), of pastoral eclogues (*Buc. carm.*), and so on. This is not true in every instance: the *Secretum* and the *Africa* standing as counter-examples. But the *Africa*, Petrarch's most ambitious narrative project, in its incompletion and, most would say, aesthetic failure, rather suggests why the poet sought out a looser structure for future expressive projects.

In the balance of this chapter, then, I will focus on the relative novelty, complexity, and, be it said, fascination of the "macro-textual" dimension of the Petrarchan epistles, especially in the two longest collections (*Familiares* and *Seniles*). I will argue that these two are constructed so as to constitute a kind of "mega-macro-text" between them. The other collected and uncollected letters certainly deserve attention, but limitations of space preclude them from receiving it here. The *Epystole* as verse letters belong in a sense to another subgenre of the epistolary, with other classical models (notably, Horace).[9] As Martinez has pointed out, the *Sine nomine* is as easily understood as a form of invective as it is a letter collection,[10] and it has other features (anonymity; a non-epistolary preface; topical and polemical focus; the subordination of the epistolary genre per se to a distinct socio-political purpose (the restoration of Rome as political and ecclesiastical capital of the world)) that clearly set it apart.

Both the *Familiares* and the *Seniles*, according to the internal and external evidence adduced by scholars,[11] were conceived of and executed as carefully selected, ordered, and revised collections that represent only a fraction of Petrarch's total epistolary production. The letters are on the whole, though not in every instance, tokens of friendships conducted at a distance, and can thus be seen as *sermo absentium* – the period designation recently revived to describe the generally epistolary character of Italian literature at the *origini*.[12] Both are cast by the author as macro-epistles to their dedicatees: explicitly to Socrates at the beginning and the end of the *Familiares*; explicitly to Simonides at the beginning of the *Seniles*, but then implicitly, but clearly, to Boccaccio, as we shall see. Both are also addressed to imaginary audiences that extend the "speech of the absent" backward and forward in historical time (*Fam.* XXIV.3–12; *Sen.* XVIII.1).

The oft-noted symmetry between the return to the classics in the former collection and the positing of Petrarch himself as a classic-to-be in the latter is one of the many ways in which Petrarch cultivates the impression of the mega-macro-textual nature of the combined collections. Both begin, of course, in the shadow of death. In *Fam.* I, he speaks of the deaths of Laura, of Cardinal Colonna (the patron of both Petrarch and his addressee, Socrates), and of "many other friends" during the plague of 1348. In the *Seniles*, we learn at the outset of the deaths of Socrates himself, Zanobi da Strada, and Petrarch's young son, Giovanni, all adduced in the three opening letters to Nelli (I.1–3), and then, shortly after, of the death of Nelli himself, revealed by the letter (probably I.3) "returned to sender" – a pattern repeated when the two letters sent to "Laelius" (II.4, 5) are similarly returned (III.1, addressed to Boccaccio).

The collection is then left without its privileged interlocutor (though he remains its dedicatee; *sermo absentium*, indeed) and under the shadow that repeatedly and increasingly falls on Petrarch's own decaying body and impending death, also anticipated at the outset, when Petrarch insists that his epistolary project will end only when he dies. Significantly, Petrarch reveals to Boccaccio in III.2 that the immediately preceding letter announcing the deaths of these friends was never in fact sent, because of the fear that it too would be returned unopened – and this in many ways signals Boccaccio's role as "sole survivor" and as the measuring stick of Petrarch's mortality, which he takes on over the course of the *Seniles* (on this point, more anon).

Needless to say, notable devices also signal the coherence of each of the collections taken singly. In the case of the *Familiares*, critics have justly called attention to generic markers that align the work with other types of writing. The "fragmentary" nature of the text itself, which is nonetheless marked by subcategories, makes a parallel with the lyrics of the *RVF* obligatory, despite the fact that Laura, love, and women are excluded from the text, with a very few exceptions (I.4, II.9, V.4, XXI.8). One might well argue that the *Familiares* represents the masculine, Latin, homosocial flip-side of the feminine, vernacular, heterosexual *RVF*'s poems,[13] with Petrarch, and especially the quest for glory (Laura/laurel),[14] bridging the gap. At the same time, as the criticism has now made plain, there are a series of allusions to (Homeric) epic that ratify the ambitious scope of the enterprise. First of all, there are the twenty-four books of the final version, paralleling both the *Iliad* and, especially, the *Odyssey*. Then there is the comparison of Petrarch's own biographical wanderings to those of Ulysses in the first letter, which is matched by the penultimate letter of the collection, ostensibly replying to a missive sent to him (by Boccaccio?) in the name of "Homer." That Ulysses-Petrarch is presented in the guise of a wanderer, and Homer himself as, in effect, a wanderer in a strange language, a strange country, a strange era, suggests that, perhaps more than "epic," one might wish to see the generic affiliation as open-ended "romance."

The "epic" association is complicated by repeated references to the long-deferred completion of the *Africa*, the work that would haunt Petrarch throughout his later years (see, for example, *Fam.* I.1, VII.18, X.4): from this perspective, the *Familiares* stands as both a sign of Petrarch's failure to achieve the status of epic poet and a substitute and/or place holder for that achievement. In other words, for the greater part of Petrarch's career, the *Africa* is not so much being written as it is the subject of other writings, including, of course, the *Bucolicum carmen*, the *Epystole*, and the *Secretum*, in addition to the *Familiares*. And it is critical to remember that Petrarch's primary models are classical letter collections, particularly those of Cicero and Seneca. Petrarch avers that he has followed the Ciceronian model of occasional reflections more closely in the *Familiares* (I.1), but Seneca's philosophical didacticism is anything but absent, and the Senecan, neo-Stoic strain becomes more pronounced in the *Seniles*.

A similar variety of modalities characterizes the *Seniles*, though the organizational principles seem quite different. While the division into eighteen books suggests a formal model has been followed, it is not so clear as in the *Familiares* what the generic precedent for that model might be. Not that the *Seniles* fails to incorporate other genres: a recurrent elegiac note for the departed; invective (particularly against medicine); hortatory rhetoric (especially exhorting Urban V to take the papacy back to Rome; see VII.1); a political treatise in the *De regimine principium* tradition (see XIV.1); (auto-)biography (XVIII.1); the novella (XVII.3); and so on. But its most prominent orienting features are internal. Where separating thematic/problematic coherence from quasi-chronological ordering in interpreting individual books in the *Familiares* can be challenging, in the *Seniles* it is far easier. Book I, for instance, focuses intently on death and old age: the death of life-long friends (1–3); the refusal of onerous appointments because of the infirmity of old age (4); the inevitability of death and the futility of prophecies that claim to pierce its veil (5, 7). Partly this stems from the more restricted range of themes in the collection, and even more from the regular appearance of short books containing very few, very long letters directed to one person and/or focused on one theme: Book VII, the single hortatory letter to Pope Urban; Book IX, two long letters celebrating the (short-lived) return of the papacy to Rome (1367–70); Book XII, two letters to a famous physician denigrating the healing powers claimed by doctors; Book XIV, two very long letters of advice to Francesco da Carrara (XIV.1–2); Book XVII, four letters to Boccaccio; and Book XVIII, the "Letter to Posterity," set in splendid isolation. Alternations between books with one or two longer letters and books with more, and generally much shorter, letters reinforces the strong sense of a structural design internal to the text and independent of chronology (or rather, since that design generally highlights the inevitable march to mortality, thematizing the chronologies it deploys), and also suggests a careful plotting of the sequence of books, as will be seen in the sequences of *Sen.* VII–VIII–IX and XVII–XVIII.[15]

Let me turn now to some detailed illustrations of the "macro"-structures that bind the two collections internally and between themselves. Out of many possible thematic configurations, I focus on two aspects of materiality Petrarch repeatedly foregrounds, and at crucial moments links: the material, corruptible body and the materiality of texts, an excellent, egregious, first example of that linkage being the extraordinary letter in which Petrarch describes the wounding of his leg by his massive volume of Cicero's writings (*Fam.* XXI.10).[16] And out of many interlocutors with whom Petrarch constructs ongoing conversations, I will focus on the one who best bridges the project of the *Familiares* to that of the *Seniles*, namely Boccaccio.

I have just said that the thematic coherence of individual books of the *Familiares* is far less obvious than that in the *Seniles*. But that does not mean it is non-existent. The most thoroughly explored examples of such coherence are to be found in Books IV, VIII, X, and XIX of the *Familiares*. Of these, three are organized around varieties of a fundamental tension in Petrarch's thought and practice, which manifests itself in the related but not identical oppositions between active and contemplative, secular and religious (or classical and Christian), public and private lives. In Book IV, the first letter, the "Letter from Mont Ventoux," stages an incomplete Augustinian conversion from worldly concerns to faith (contrasted with his brother Gherardo's monastic vocation) and is then set off against the next seven letters,[17] concerning Petrarch's coronation with the laurel and his symbiotic relationship with King Robert the Wise. Book X, at six letters the shortest in the collection, is framed by letters to Emperor Charles IV and his chancellor, linked to Petrarch's activist pursuit of a restoration of the Empire to Rome, but then elaborates a series of reflections on the tensions just described, culminating in the face-off between literary and religious vocations, Petrarch and Gherardo (and Dante) in X.4. Book XIX is in some sense a sequel to the appeal to Charles in X.1, as it charts the arrival (several years later) of the Emperor designate for coronation in Rome, the disappointment generated by his hasty departure, and Petrarch's attempts to negotiate between his all-too-public relationship with the powerful and his assertion of an autonomous, contemplative, privacy.[18]

Book VIII is one of those for which we have the most extensive documentation of a deliberate process of revision of previously written letters.[19] It is most famous as Petrarch's primary representation of the plague, but in fact it constitutes an even more complex meditation on presence and absence, friendship and solitude, life and sudden death, in narrating a failed encounter at his home with two close friends, one of whom was then murdered on his return journey. The book, in fact, explicitly charts the harshest spatio-temporal realities of *sermo absentium* in an age when letters were often the only means of contact with friends, and a conspicuously faulty one at that.

The more extended example I now offer, *Familiares* XVIII, has not received much attention, though it is arguably *the* meta-epistolary book of the collection. The letters date from 1354 to 1355; that is, early in the period when Petrarch had left Vaucluse and Avignon for the hospitality of the Visconti rulers of Milan, having entertained and rejected an offer to come to Florence, with restitution of family property, brought to him by Boccaccio (XI.5). That move resulted in a fierce attack by Boccaccio, in an allegorical letter (*Epistola* X) accusing Petrarch of consorting with tyrants, against his own previously declared principles. As is well known, Petrarch responded to these accusations more or less directly in letters to Nelli (*Fam.* XVI.11–12), even more extensively in Book XIX, in one of his *Invectives* (from 1355), and in several other places – though not until the *Seniles*, where he is still worrying over the question, does he address a response directly to Boccaccio in one of his collected letters.[20]

It might at first seem that Book XVIII, too, is principally concerned with politics – like its immediately sequel, Book XIX – since it opens with Petrarch's third epistolary appeal to Charles to come into Italy (the earlier appeals are X.1 and XII.1) and closes with one of several letters, *Familiares* XVIII.16,[21] in which Petrarch engages in the role of private mediator in the conflict between Venice and Genoa (a satellite of Milan). But the book takes another tack: virtually all of the other fourteen letters are concerned with the circulation, reproduction, and production of manuscript texts, with scrupulous attention to the basic material details thereof. In many ways, then, this is the book that seeks to define and describe the nascent Humanist project of the recovery and diffusion of classical Greek and Latin texts, as well as the lay appropriation of early patristic Christianity, especially Augustine; it moves on to connect this project to the production and circulation of new texts by this elite community of learned scholars and poets, illustrated, principally, by these letters themselves.

Letters 2–5, as well as 11–12 and 14, concern the exchange of unknown or difficult-to-obtain texts across the arduous and dangerous terrain of late-medieval Italy, Europe, and the Mediterranean basin. The first of these is paradigmatic, a letter of thanks to the Byzantine court official who has sent him a copy of the Homeric epics, noting that he has also received a Plato in Greek, and now asking for Hesiod and Euripides, all texts known only indirectly in the Middle Ages, and even now linguistically inaccessible to Petrarch notwithstanding an abortive attempt to learn Greek. The letter "materializes" the structuring references to Homer, especially anticipating the production of a Latin translation thereof previewed in the concluding letter to Homer, a production co-sponsored by Petrarch and Boccaccio (*Sen.* III.6, V.1, VI.1–2). It is no coincidence that the next two letters are directed to that same Boccaccio, thanking him first for the gift of Augustine's commentary on the Psalms, and then for sending a manuscript containing works by the classical Latin authors Cicero and Varro. The fifth letter, then, is addressed to Gherardo, accompanying a gift of Augustine's *Confessions*, Petrarch's favorite patristic text. The alternation of Christian and classical texts seems deliberate, and reinforces, again in "materialized" form, the struggle between Scripture and poetry, Gherardo and Francesco, dramatized in Book X (see also XVIII.12).

XVIII.5 takes us deeper still into material aspects of the reproduction of manuscripts for circulation, listing the several occupations that go into book-making:

> [A]mong us, some scrape parchment, some write [that is, copy out] books, others . . . illuminate them [that is, create decorative visual ornaments, rubrics etc.], others bind them, others adorn the covers; the noble intellect aspires to higher things, foregoing the humbler ones.

Petrarch's final point is that those who actually author books and read them seriously for content are in fact unreliable copyists, with the result that manuscripts in circulation are often themselves unreliable. In subsequent letters, additional aspects of this book culture are brought forth. In *Fam.* XVIII.7, to Nelli, Petrarch notes his "excessive attachment" to his collection of manuscript books – and makes the connection between his collectionism and that of which Cicero speaks in his letters. In XVIII.11, he writes to Nelli, asking him to see to the delivery of a Cicero manuscript that risks being lost in the perilous journey through war-torn Italy. In XVIII.12, addressed to the probable recipient of that manuscript, he apologizes for having kept a borrowed Cicero for several years because he was unable to find a competent scribe to copy it (a phenomenon which, generalized, is made to account for the loss and/or corruption of the great classical works in the present age). He then gives a fascinating account of the physical process by which he himself at once read and copied out the text, returning us to the problems of XVIII.5, and delineating a sharp tension between interpretation and material textuality.

In these letters, Cicero's are among the books that are collected, but they are also presented as the model for collecting books, and, of course, for writing letters about that activity.[22] After the four letters on the circulation of books, Petrarch turns to praise the style of letters he has received from one Forese (XVIII.6) and from Nelli (XVIII.7), before launching into the most comprehensive account of his own "poetics" of letter-writing besides I.1, in XVIII.8:

> I speak...to my friends [in letters] as I would with myself...with myself I often deal with matters not only weighed and approved but more often ambiguous and uncertain, and I strive for the truth by hesitating, pondering, and deliberating...at times I accept one opinion, at times another...I shall offer my friends not only my deliberations but the thoughts and movements of my mind, which are called spontaneous, nor will I write merely summaries and conclusions, but the particulars of their beginnings and their progress.

Not only are the matter and the style made to reflect the contingencies of language and of thought, but he also stresses the contingency of the material transmission of his words:

> I know that several of my letters addressed to you have not reached you. This is caused by the insolent and insatiable thirst for my letters, similar to that felt by persons who covet harmful drinks when burning with fever. Thus whatever slips from my fingers they thirstily intercept, and do not abstain from doing harm to scholars while passionately drinking what they cannot digest. (XVIII.7)

The presumptuousness of those who intercept his letters remains a recurring theme to the end of his life, as in *Sen.* XVII.4.

Finally, let us look briefly at the third and last letter to Boccaccio (XVIII.15), the next to last of the book, which brings us back to the apparently discarded question of politics, and anticipates the key role of Boccaccio in the *Seniles*. In the *Familiares*, Boccaccio first appears in Book XI, in three letters (1, 2, 6) closely connected to the younger man's role in attempting, unsuccessfully, to bring Petrarch back to his ancestral home of Florence (see again XI.5). He is the addressee of only ten letters total in the *Familiares*, compared to twenty-nine to Nelli, twenty-two to Socrates, and so on, though three of these are among the most famous (XXI.15, XXII.2, and XXIII.19). Three, however, are concentrated in Book XVIII, and they come near the very beginning and the very end. Moreover, as already suggested, Boccaccio is the oblique target of political letters in Books XVI and, especially, XIX. The letters explicitly directed to him, however, apparently avoid the political for the fantasy of a "Republic of Letters" centered around the circulation of manuscripts and epistles among a group of learned friends. In *Fam*. XVIII.15, Petrarch chides Boccaccio for his intemperance, and in particular insists that his friend is not merely a "transmitter" of ancient books (he refers again to their exchange of manuscripts) but, like Petrarch himself, worthy of the name of poet, and thus can anticipate the day when his own works will be avidly sought after and circulated. And yet there is a subtext that acknowledges a friendship traversed by political antagonism: "I have read and understood your allusions to Syracuse and Dionysius. But what of it?" As will become plain only in *Fam*. XIX.3, Syracusan Dionysius is evoked as the tyrant par excellence, and thus a coded reference to Petrarch's deplorable connection to the Visconti.

Already in the *Familiares*, then, around Petrarch's new disciple and friend, and sometime critic, Boccaccio, are clustered key questions that will become even more prominent in the *Seniles*: humanistic scholarship (in the *Seniles* embodied in the shared project of translating Homer), and other references to the circulation and collection of books (for example, I.5); Petrarch's association with tyrants; and a range of issues concerning the role and status of poetry and poets, including vernacular poets – above all, Dante.[23]

In the *Seniles*, and especially after the news of Simonides's and Laelius's deaths, Boccaccio emerges as Petrarch's key epistolary interlocutor, with far more letters – eighteen – addressed to him than to any other correspondent, on what are clearly *the* central topics of the book. This also includes the extraordinarily rich cluster of letters on the sorrows and concerns of old age: the loom of death (I.5, VII.1 et passim), loss of friends (III.1–2, VI.2), physical ailments and diminished capacity (III.5, XV.8), and the ignorance and incompetence of doctors (III.1, 5, V.3).[24] Four of eighteen books, indeed, can be said to be partially or entirely structured around the figure of Boccaccio: Book III, with the first two letters, and four of nine total, addressed to him; Book V, balanced between three letters to Boccaccio (1–3) and three to Donato Appenninigena (4–6); Book VII, which begins and ends with Boccaccio; and, of course, Book XVII – in many ways the conclusion not only of the *Seniles*, but also of Petrarch's career as a letter writer and, emblematically, of his life – with all four letters addressed to the closest friend and collaborator of his old age.

By looking briefly at two of these books, VIII and XVII, and with a final glance at the concluding "Letter to Posterity," we can see not only the internal "macro-textual" patterns of the *Seniles* – the through-lines of topics and correspondents; the careful ordering of individual books – but also the "mega-macro-textual" features that link the *Seniles* to the *Familiares*. Book VIII is marked off in the collection, as we have seen, by being flanked by books with only one and two letters, respectively, both concerned with the "public matter" of the return of the papacy to Rome, while it itself has eight letters. More importantly, it begins and ends with letters to Boccaccio, which explicitly mark the beginning and the end of the year during which his age will be sixty-three. In VIII.1, on his sixty-third birthday, Petrarch considers a venerable (astrological, numerological) belief that "the sixty-third year is dangerous to the human race." He quotes the classical author Maternus to the effect that "for a certain natural but hidden reason the seventh and ninth years of life are dangers and bring destruction, crisis, a sort of plague to mortals [*Astrology* 4.14]. This is why [Maternus] says [that] since seven times nine" equals sixty-three, the danger at that age, the so-called "grand climacteric," is multiplied. But, even as he raises this specter of disaster, he denies believing in it, following earlier letters, including one to Boccaccio, in which he attacked astrology and other forms of prophesying imminent death (I.5, III.1; see also I.7). He does, however, take the occasion to recall his birth in Arezzo and a notable military action of the Florentine exiles against their native city. In VIII.8, a year to the day after the date assigned to VIII.1, he confesses to Boccaccio that he was in fact half-persuaded by the old belief, confessing to a fault that he had earlier criticized in his friend. Now, however, on his sixty-fourth birthday, he looks back serenely on the year gone by, which saw the signal event of Pope Urban restoring the papacy to Rome, which is, in effect, narrated by the passage from Book VII to Book IX.[25]

The structuring principles of the book, then, are quite clear, and its thematic burden of confronting one's mortality and reflecting back over one's life is reinforced by a number of other letters in Book VIII, especially 3, 4, and 5. Particularly notable, though not previously noticed, is the way in which Petrarch appropriates the astrologer's numerology to his own purposes: the numbers seven and nine, which are the constituent multipliers of sixty-three, are also the numbers of the flanking books. In the mirroring of the number of this book by the number of letters it contains (eight and eight, which, multiplied, make sixty-four), Petrarch builds in the symbolic overcoming of the prophetic number, while at the same time acknowledging the inevitability of passing time and of approaching death. Boccaccio, as already anticipated in III.1–2, thus becomes the privileged witness and accomplice to Petrarch's struggle with mortality.

In closing, we now come to Books XVII and XVIII, which contain the most famous individual letters in the *Seniles*: Petrarch's translation/adaptation of *Decameron* X.10 and the "Letter to Posterity," the fragmentary letter to his future readers – both dated from the last year of his life. And while these two texts have repaid, with interest, the critical attention that has been given them individually, they have not been duly considered according to their "macro-textual" significance – in relation to each other, to their immediate context, to the *Seniles* as a whole, to the *Seniles* and the *Familiares* seen together as part of a greater epistolary project, or, in fact, to Petrarch's writing career in its entirety, to which they stand as a grudging, reluctant, but also carefully plotted, valediction.

Book XVII consists of four letters to Boccaccio. The first is a short preface to the next two, explaining that after having decided not to respond to a letter from his friend – which, it would seem, lamented its author's poverty (contrasted with Petrarch's relative wealth), expressed concern about Petrarch's many ailments, and urged Petrarch to cease his constant writing in order to preserve his health – he has written instead two long letters, one of which is a point-by-point response, and the other a text of a different sort, namely the Latin translation of Boccaccio's Griselda story. The fourth letter then comments on his decision to make the translation, reports on the contrasting responses of two friends who heard the tale, says he has just learned that the first three letters never reached Boccaccio, and finally renounces all further letter-writing, in the name of devoting himself to more important works. Book XVIII is made up of one letter, in which he recounts "his background, conduct, and the development of his character and studies" for a posterity that might possibly have heard his name. The letter goes no further in this account than his first stay in Padua (1350–51) at the invitation of Jacopo da Carrara, whose sudden death, by assassination, led Petrarch to set off again for Avignon. The letter does not cover the remaining 20-plus years of his life, ending more or less at the point when he first met Boccaccio in person. Among other things, it makes the assertion that the *Africa* was completed in the early 1340s, a claim that modern scholars do not accept, and which Petrarch himself seems in other works, for example the *Secretum* and *Familiares* X.4 (1349), to deny. Even more to the present point, Mazzotta has argued that the "Letter to Posterity" stands in polemical relation to Boccaccio's *Life of Petrarch*, written prior to 1348.[26]

In fact, Book XVII deliberately presents itself as the culmination of most of the principal themes and problems of the *Seniles* and even the *Familiares*, of Petrarch's complex relationship with Boccaccio, of his life-long dedication to cultivating friendships through letters, and of epistolarity itself as a mode of writing. This drive to summary and to closure appears in many ways, including overt recalls of earlier letters.[27] Letters 1 and 4 evoke the material problematics of letter-writing explored so extensively in *Familiares* XVIII (the author–scribe relationship, the difficulty in ensuring that letters arrive at their destination, and so on). Letters 2–4 foreground the condition of old-age, ill-health, and impending death in which Petrarch finds himself. They filter his constant return to the question of the vocation of poetry by once again debating the relative merits of Latin and vernacular as literary languages. They also offer yet another variant of his obsessive attempts to cope with Boccaccio's accusation that he has consorted with tyrants: this appears not only in the tyrannical figure of Gualtiero in the Griselda story, but more directly in XVII.2, when he baldly, and unconvincingly, asserts that "I was with the princes in name, but in fact the princes were with me."

Most telling of all, of course, Book XVII offers the most extensive dramatization of Petrarch's intense and complex relationship with Boccaccio, juxtaposing a dismissive account of the *Decameron* ("I leafed through it . . . like a hurried traveler who looks around from side to side without halting") with high praise for how his friend "perfectly described . . . that plague-ridden time" in the introduction and for the Griselda story, which "nearly made me forget myself." Readers have mostly emphasized the ways in which Petrarch's "translation" is actually a transformation and appropriation, implying the superiority of Latin to the original and of the translator to the author. At the same time, by setting Boccaccio, as writer, in a place of honor at the end of the *Seniles*, and by putting his Latin in the service of Boccaccio's Italian, he also acknowledges the supreme importance of their friendship to him. Moreover, Petrarch gives Boccaccio a key role in his decision to bring an end to the *Seniles* and to letter-writing in general. In XVII.2, he rejects at length his friend's advice to preserve his health by giving over his writerly vocation. But in XVII.4, he in fact takes that advice, with an ironic twist: putting an end both to the writing of letters and to the friendships that those letters were intended, in part, to foster:

> I have not only had my fill of writing, I am sick of it. All this together leads me to say to you, dear friend, and to all to whom I used to write, insofar as it concerns my epistolary pen – a last farewell, in order that flimsier scribblings may not to the end hinder me . . . Farewell, dear friends. Farewell, dear letters.

Petrarch died little more than a year later, and, ironically, the *Seniles*, along with the *RVF* and the *Triumphi*, written in the vernacular he so frequently made light of, were, with the *De viris*, the principal works he completed in that time.

A further irony is that, having just presented his readers with a rigorously constructed conclusion to his book and his epistolary career, Petrarch then tacks on an autobiography that is clearly unfinished. One explanation, though not a popular one, is that Petrarch did not intend to include the "Letter to Posterity" in the *Seniles*, since it made its first appearance as part of the work in the sixteenth-century *editio princeps*.[28] An alternative version of this hypothesis is that he intended to bring it up to the present time, but died before he could do so. More typically, however, scholars accept that XVIII.1 belongs in the *Seniles*, pointing, among other things, to the symmetrical relation with Book XXIV of the *Familiares*. Such a reading posits the letter as leaving behind the contemporary audience saluted in XVII.4 and turning toward Petrarch's textual future, when he will have "become a name."

Nonetheless, I believe it possible to point out interesting significant continuities with Book XVII. We have already seen that Boccaccio, in the form of his *Life of Petrarch*, may well be an implicit audience and target of the "Letter to Posterity." Moreover, XVII.2 rehearses a number of key biographical facts from Petrarch's later life, proleptically supplementing the restriction of the extant "Letter to Posterity" to the earlier years. More interesting still, the retrospective orientation of the "Letter to Posterity" is systematically anticipated in Book XVII. Petrarch, having just defined himself as "almost continuously sick" and in need of the help of an amanuensis, introduces the two principal letters as follows: "When you come to the end [of the Griselda translation] you will be worn out and will say: 'Is this my sick friend, that busy old man? Or someone else with the same name, a healthy young man with time to spare?'" By contrast, XVII.2 is spent largely in considering the condition of old age, and in refusing Boccaccio's advice of "retirement" from writing, all in the name of making up for the idleness of youth. The following letter, however, reinforces the conceit of XVII.1 by claiming that the *Decameron* was the product of Boccaccio's youth (which, strictly speaking, it was not), and then proceeding to appropriate one part of that youthful work as his own.

This undercurrent of nostalgia for his own youthful self fits very well indeed with the restriction of the "Letter to Posterity" to his younger years, and with making its focus the fantasy of a completed *Africa* (whose continued incompletion, presumably, is one of the reasons Petrarch renounces letter-writing in XVII.4). This speculative hypothesis is supported by a curious detail in which Petrarch seemingly misremembers the facts of his own life: claiming to have finished the *Africa* in Parma at the age of thirty-three or thirty-four (thirty-five traditionally marks the end of youth: see Dante, *Convivio* IV.xxiii), when in historical fact he would have been thirty-seven or thirty-eight (1341–42). Posterity, it would seem, is meant to guarantee Petrarch not only fame, but also a kind of eternal youth, one in which, in fantasy, he becomes the man – the author of a new classical epic – that the ceremony of the laurel crown predicted he should be.

As ever with Petrarch, however, that is not the end of the story: instead, the text breaks off with a remarkable final sentence, as he describes his departure from Padua for Avignon in 1351, in the process rejecting the Florentine offer of repatriation. He left, he says, because he is "incapable of staying still, and not so much with a yearning to see again what I had seen a thousand times, as with an effort to cope with stiffness – as sick people do – by a shift of position." He thus invokes the restless wandering without resolution that we know to have characterized much of his life. We have seen that in the *Seniles*, materiality, particularly the materiality of an aging body, encroaches on the attempts to live a purely spiritual, intellectual, literary life – and I cannot resist the temptation to see that sick body as a displaced image of Petrarch's own in the final years of his life. In this sense, then, the "Letter to Posterity" is doubly appropriate as a conclusion to the "Letters of Old Age": in its incompletion it reproduces Petrarch's life-long commitment to the "perspective of the middle," the refusal to claim a final and certain metaphysical perspective, like the one Dante arrogates to himself the *Commedia*; at the same time, obliquely, it offers us fitting closure to one of the greatest literary lives of the Western tradition.

NOTES

1 On the *Familiares* as collection, see Aldo Bernardo's introductions to each of the three volumes of his translation, as well as Giuseppe Mazzotta, "Petrarch's Epistolary Epic," *Petrarch: A Critical Guide*, Kirkham and Maggi, 309–319.

2 On the *Epystole*, see Chapter 7.

3 On the *Seniles*, begin with Bernardo's introduction to volume I of the English translation, as well as David Wallace, "*Letters of Old Age*: Love between Men, Griselda, and Farewell to Letters (*Rerum Senilium Libri*)," in *Petrarch: A Critical Guide*, Kirkham and Maggi, 321–330.

4 These letters, in the past separated into *Variae* and *Miscellanee*, are now all in Francesco Petrarca, *Lettere disperse*, ed. Alessandro Pancheri (Parma: Guanda, 1994).

5 There is only one surviving, though uncollected, letter in Italian (*Disperse* 49).

6 Giuseppe Billanovich, *Petrarca letterato. I. Lo scrittoio del Petrarca* (Rome: Edizioni di Storia e Letteratura, 1947); Vittorio Rossi, "Sulla formazione delle

raccolte epistolari petrarchesche," *Annali della Cattedra Petrarchesca* 3 (1932): 53–73; Aldo S. Bernardo, "The Selection of Letters in Petrarch's *Familiares*," *Speculum* 35 (1960): 280–288.

7 These tools include a massive two-volume concordance to the *Familiares* prepared by Bernardo; analytical tables dividing the *Familiares* by date, placement in the collection, and recipient (in Roberta Antognini, *Il progretto autobiografico delle "Familiares" di Petrarca* (Milan: LED, 2008)); and a complete edition with translation of all known letters written to Petrarch (Ugo Dotti, ed., *Lettere a Petrarca* (Turin: Aragno, 2012)).

8 Antognini, *Il progetto autobiografico*, offers a good example of how the distinction can profitably be applied to Petrarch's letter collections.

9 See Chapter 7. In *Fam.* I.1, Petrarch does cast the *Epystole* as a companion collection.

10 Martinez, "The Book without a Name," in *Petrarch: A Critical Guide*, Kirkham and Maggi, 295. On Petrarchan invective in general, see Chapter 13.

11 See *Fam.* I.1, XXIII.19, XXIV.13; *Sen.* I.1.

12 Scott Millspaugh, "Sermo absentium: Rhetoric, Epistolarity, and the Emergence of Italian Literary Culture." Dissertation, University of California, Berkeley, CA, ProQuest, UMI Dissertations Publishing, 2013, #3616495.

13 Wallace, "*Letters of Old Age*," makes a similar point regarding the *Seniles*.

14 On the Laura/laurel equation (deriving from the Apollo and Daphne myth), see the *Secretum* and *RVF* (esp. poem 5).

15 Petrarch calls attention to this pattern, for instance, by making and then immediately breaking a promise to write only short letters from Book XI on (*Sen.* XI.4; see also XVII.4).

16 See Ronald L. Martinez, "Petrarch's Lame Leg and the Corpus of Cicero: An Early Crisis of Humanism?" in *The Body in Early Modern Italy*, eds. Julia Hairston and Walter Stephens (Baltimore, MD: Johns Hopkins University Press, 2010), 42–58, 289–299.

17 The remaining eleven letters are less obviously connected, though two iterated topics – the deaths of friends (10–13) and the specificity of the literary vocation (15–17) – are certainly pertinent.

18 Albert Russell Ascoli, "Petrarch's Private Politics," in Ascoli, *"A Local Habitation and a Name,"* 118–158.

19 Aldo S. Bernardo, "Letter Splitting in Petrarch's *Familiares*," *Speculum* 33 (1958): 236–241.

20 *Sen.* VI.2, XVII.2. The issue is addressed, however, in *Disperse* 19 and 40

21 Other references to the war and Petrarch's unofficial diplomatic role in it are in XI.8, XIV.5, XVII.3–4, 6, XIX.9; *Sen.* IV.3.

22 Also pertinent are XVIII. 4, 7, 8, 11–14, and 16.

23 On this latter topic, see *Fam.* XIII.6, XVIII.15, XXI.15, XXII.2, XXIII.19; *Sen.* I.5, II.1, V.2, XVII.3, 4.

24 See also III.8, V.4, VIII.3, XI.15–17, XII.1, 2 (i.e. the entire book), XIII.15, XV.14, XVI.2, 3, as well as *Fam.* V.9 and, again, the *Contra medicum*.

25 For the pivotal role of Book VIII in the *Seniles*, see Ronald L. Martinez, "Places and Times of the Liturgy from Dante to Petrarch," in *Petrarch and Dante*, Barański and Cachey, 320–370, esp. 348 and 349.

26 Giuseppe Mazzotta, "A Life in Progress (*De vita et moribus Francisci Petrarchi de Florentia*)," in *Boccaccio: A Critical Guide to the Complete Works*, eds. Victoria Kirkham, Janet Smarr, and Michael Sherberg (Chicago, IL: University of Chicago Press, 2013), 207–212.

27 *Sen.* I.1 and VIII.1–2 are recalled in XVII.2 and V.2, and XI.4 is recalled in XVII.4.

28 Silvia Rizzo, "Introduzione," in Francesco Petrarca, *Res Seniles, Libri I–IV*, ed. Silvia Rizzo, with Monica Berté (Florence: Le Lettere, 2006), 10.

PART IV

Petrarch's interlocutors

11

GUR ZAK

Petrarch and the ancients

On August 1, 1348, Petrarch addressed a letter to one of his favorite ancient authors, the Roman philosopher Seneca, in which he declared: "I enjoy speaking with you, O illustrious man ... about whom our age has permitted ignorance and total oblivion. For my part, I daily listen to your words with more attention than one would believe, and perhaps I shall not be thought impertinent in wishing to be heard by you" (*Fam.* XXIV.5). This personal address to an ancient author, long dead, reveals much about Petrarch's passion for classical antiquity and for its central figures; it conveys his belief in the value of the lost habits and teachings of this culture for his own society. In addition, though addressing a deceased ancient author, the letter does not reveal an ahistorical mentality, but rather paradoxically points to the author's often-celebrated historical consciousness. By carefully documenting the date of writing at the end of his letter, and stating that he writes from the "land of the living," Petrarch discloses his awareness of the gap that separates him from his addressee, a gulf which he hopes to bridge – as the very writing of the letter shows – by means of new practices of reading and writing.

Petrarch's idea of writing letters to ancient authors began three years before this letter to Seneca with a letter he addressed to Cicero, inspired in turn by his rediscovery of Cicero's *Letters to Atticus*. For such writings and discoveries, among other reasons, Petrarch has often been given the title the "father of Humanism," the initiator of the age of revival of classical antiquity. Recent scholarship has done much to challenge this hyperbolic title, pointing both to important precursors in this effort and to the ongoing "medieval" features of his intellectual and artistic practices.[1] Still, despite such qualifications, Petrarch's importance for the humanistic Renaissance is undeniable.

We should begin by highlighting the unparalleled scope and systematic nature of his scholarly efforts.[2] Petrarch began to amass his extensive library of ancient books in his teens, and in the early 1320s he presided in Avignon over the preparation of his celebrated manuscript, known to posterity as the "Ambrosian Virgil," which contains the three major works of Virgil, as well as poems by Statius and Horace. This manuscript is filled with Petrarch's marginal notes – which range from comments on the texts to inscriptions commemorating events in his life, such as the death of his beloved Laura. It was also in Avignon in the late 1320s that Petrarch compiled and corrected manuscripts of three of the first four decades of Livy's *History of Rome*, creating the most complete version of the text known in the period and laying foundations for Humanist philology. In addition, Petrarch stressed the crucial importance of ancient Greek culture, acquiring texts by authors such as Plato and Homer, and arranging, with Boccaccio, for the first Latin translation of the Homeric epics, carried out by the eccentric Calabrian scholar Leontius Pilatus.

Petrarch's classicism took a more active political form as well, leading him to support the mid-1340s revolutionary Cola di Rienzo, who sought to restore the ancient Roman republic – an attempt which ended in failure. Above all, Petrarch's unprecedented investment in antiquity was ethical in character. As is well known, Petrarch repeatedly asserted that the return to ancient culture – particularly to ancient precepts of living and the classical literary genres and styles through which they were expressed – would bring about a moral renewal in his society.

It is on this last aspect of Petrarch's relationship with the ancients – the pairing of ethics and style – that the present chapter focuses. Petrarch's ethical program, I assert, was based on a return to the ancient identification of philosophy with the care of the soul, *animi cura* (*Fam.* I.9). In the *Tusculan Disputations*, Cicero defines philosophy as the "medicine of the soul" (*Tusc.* 3.3.6), and in his *Moral Letters to Lucilius*, Seneca describes his own task as a philosopher as "curing the disease" of the soul (*Ad Lucilium* 75.7). Petrarch revived in his works this ancient notion and also followed Seneca in asserting that the central means of attaining this goal of philosophy is by engaging in moralized techniques of reading and writing. Throughout his works, Petrarch advances the notion that the attentive reading of ancient works, and the imitation of the ancient style and moral vocabulary, is the most effective means of cultivating and shaping the self. Petrarch at once describes his own self-care and claims for himself the role of a philosopher caring for his readers – inciting them to engage in a similar process and providing them with the texts through which they might do so.

This ethical project took multiple forms in the Petrarchan oeuvre: his works are divided among several ancient traditions of writing, each characterized according to Petrarch by a distinct style, genre, and ethical goal. The dominant model to which he returns is associated with the prose works of

Cicero, Livy, and Seneca and the poetic compositions of Virgil and Horace, which he consistently describes as "strong" and "manly." In his works, this tradition stands in constant tension with two central alternatives: the first identified mainly with the Roman poet Ovid and described as "weak" and "effeminate"; the second associated with the sacred humble style, the *sermo humilis*, of the Bible and the Church Fathers.[3] Whereas the ethical goal of the first, "strong" writing tradition is the cultivation of virtuous self-mastery, the second, "weak" one serves Petrarch as an emotional outlet, and the third, "humble" style is aimed at the attainment of both virtuous constancy in this life and eternal salvation in the next. In what follows, I explore in greater depths Petrarch's appropriation of these three ancient writing traditions and the conflicts that emerge between them in his works. I conclude with some reflections on Petrarch's synthesis of these diverse traditions later in life and its significance for understanding the nature of his revival of antiquity.

Reading, writing, and self-care

The crucial role that Petrarch attributes to the practice of reading, and especially the reading of ancient texts, in the process of caring for the self comes to the fore in Book II of the *Secretum*, Petrarch's imaginary dialogue with St. Augustine, written and revised in 1347–53. Discussing Franciscus's disease of melancholy, Augustinus advises him to cure his condition by "inscribing upon his soul" the salutary precepts of living contained in his readings of Cicero and Seneca: "work them [these precepts] deep into your memory and make them most familiar to you through diligent study, so that just like experienced doctors, no matter when or where some urgent illness strikes, you have the cure, as it were, written in your soul" (*Secretum* 98–99). The "diligent study" to which Augustinus refers here includes, as he describes a little beforehand, the literal taking of notes on the texts in question. The mixture of reading and note-taking allows Franciscus to make the ancient texts an inherent part of who he is, arming himself against the blows of fortune and curing himself of melancholy.

Augustinus's exhortation concerning the need to "absconde" ("hide deep") such precepts in one's memory is a direct echo of letter 84 of Seneca's *Moral Letters to Lucilius*, in which the Roman philosopher refers to the need to shape the self through reading: "This is what our mind should do: it should hide away [abscondat] all the materials by which it has been aided" (*Ad Lucilium* 84.7). The ancient works of Seneca, therefore, both inspire Petrarch's chosen technique of reading as a means to cultivate the self and provide the textual material through which he strives to effect that cultivation.

In Petrarch's view, the aesthetic and persuasive qualities of a text are crucial in enabling it to mold the reader's inner being. In his later work *De ignorantia*, written in 1367, Petrarch praises Aristotle's statement that the aim of ethics is not to lead us to know the good intellectually, but rather to make us virtuous. However, he criticizes Aristotle's writings precisely for failing to achieve this goal. Reading Aristotle, he is left unmoved: "my mind is the same as it was; my will is the same; I am the same" (*De ignorantia* 107). Aristotle's words, according to Petrarch, do not have the power to remain in his memory and shape him inwardly (*De ignorantia* 105). When he reads his favorite ancient authors – Cicero, Seneca, and Horace – the situation is different: "Everyone who has read our Latin authors knows that they touch and pierce our vitals with the sharp, burning barbs of their eloquence" (*De ignorantia* 108–109). The true philosopher must therefore be able to speak eloquently in order to care for souls; philosophy and rhetoric, as well as philosophy and poetry, are intrinsically intertwined.

In his efforts to promote a "philosophy of care," Petrarch imputes crucial importance not only to the meticulous reading of eloquent ancient works, but also to the writing of new works based on their model. In letter I.9 of the *Familiares*, Petrarch stresses the value of his own compositions – modeled on the "Ciceronian springs" of eloquence (*Fam.* I.9) – for the moral edification of both himself and his readers, emphasizing in particular the curative value he attains from re-reading his own works.

Petrarch's writing style in *Fam.* I.9 itself exemplifies some of the stylistic features of a "salutary composition." Though he speaks specifically of Cicero as his model, Petrarch takes care not to follow him exclusively. True to the Horatian and Senecan admonition that a writer should not imitate only one model but rather draw upon several sources and blend them into one in the manner of the bees producing honey, Petrarch constructs the letter as a mosaic of echoes and allusions to a variety of ancient sources, including Seneca, Virgil, Juvenal, and Cicero. Thus, while Petrarch echoes Cicero's *De oratore* (1.15.68) at the beginning of the letter when he states that the correction of "life and conduct" (*Fam.* I.9) is the primary concern of virtue, later he bases his definition of the wise man (*sapiens*) – the one who is in full control of his desires – on a Senecan definition of wisdom (*Ad Lucilium* 20.5). Through this appropriation of the vocabulary of a variety of ancient sources, Petrarch aims to secure both the aesthetic and the moral effectiveness of his writings.

In addition to alluding to a variety of ancient sources, Petrarch purposefully revives classical stylistic features of syntax, word order, and sentence structure, believing that he thereby intensifies the moral efficacy of his texts. Among the classicizing aspects of Petrarch's style, we might mention his relatively limited use of rhetorical colors and figures of speech, his rare employment of the medieval *cursus* (rules for using meter in prose compositions), and his efforts to follow classical syntactical rules, such as the use of the infinitive in indirect speech. When one of his correspondents, Cardinal Talleyrand, accused his classicizing style of being too difficult, Petrarch answered that such a style is the most suitable for discussing moral matters pertaining to all, describing it as one of "moral eloquence" (*Fam.* XIV.1).

Among his own writings, Petrarch attributed special ethical importance to two works, both begun early in his career: his collection of biographies of ancient men, *De viris*, which he likely began in 1338–39, and his epic poem *Africa*, upon which he embarked shortly thereafter. Both works were much revised in the course of Petrarch's life, and were ultimately left unfinished. Modeled on the writings of ancient historians such as Livy and Suetonius, and composed in highly classicized Latin, Petrarch's initial plan was to portray in *De viris* the lives of ancient figures from Romulus to Titus. His stated aim in composing these lives follows the basic formula of epideictic rhetoric; that is, pointing to readers "those things that are to be followed and those to be avoided" (*De viris* pref. 6).

The first biography Petrarch composed, as Martellotti has demonstrated, was that of Scipio Africanus, the hero of the Second Punic War.[4] The goal of this early biography was probably to aid in the composition of his *Africa*. Petrarch envisioned his poetic portrayal of Scipio – written in Latin hexameters in emulation of the "high style" of the Virgilian epic – as another means of shaping his readers' characters. As he writes in his discourse on poetry in Book IX, the poet's task is to deliver under the guise of a "light [allegorical] veil" (*Africa* IX.101) lessons pertaining to the "cultivation of the virtues" (*Africa* IX.98). These lessons, as he insists, should be firmly rooted in history; those who invent their subject matter should be considered "liars" rather than poets. The ethical merits of his epic poetry thus depend for Petrarch on its faithful adherence to classical historical content and form – an approach to epic which is quite different from that of his immediate poetic predecessor and fellow admirer of Virgil, Dante, whose own *epos* concentrated on theological themes and was filled with stylistic innovations.

In sum, through his emphasis on the value of the careful reading of ancient orators, poets, and historians, as well as the imitation of their style and subject matter in his own works, Petrarch establishes himself as a "doctor of souls," directing both himself and his readers on the path to virtuous self-mastery. The notion of "care of souls" was usually used in the later Middle Ages to describe the work of priests caring for their flock. By returning to the ancient assertion that the "care of souls" is the proper task of philosophy, and emphasizing the value of ancient writings and moral techniques for this purpose, Petrarch established his humanistic project as an intellectual and spiritual alternative to the dominant intellectual movements of his day, especially monasticism and Scholasticism.

Petrarch between "strong" and "weak" styles

Petrarch's approbation of the eloquent writings of Cicero, Seneca, Virgil, and others for the purpose of cultivating the self is established in his works in opposition not only to the arid style of Aristotle but also to the emotionally charged type of writing he tends to associate with the Roman poet Ovid. As anticipated at the start of this chapter, Petrarch critiques this latter style as "weak" and "effeminate," yet often reluctantly yields to it himself.

The conflict between these two types of writing – the "strong" style of Cicero and company versus the "weak" style of Ovid – emerges in Petrarch's masterful introductory letter to the *Familiares*, written to his friend Ludwig Van Kempen (his "Socrates") in the early 1350s, in which he describes the circumstances that led him to gather together the many letters he wrote over the years and discusses the collection's stylistic features. Toward the end of this introduction, he mentions a stylistic aspect that causes him deep concern: "Another matter which I would gladly remain silent about must be mentioned...I am ashamed of a life fallen into excessive softness. The very order of my letters will testify to this. My style was strong and sober in the early years, an indicator of a truly strong mind, of the type which was a source of comfort not only to myself but often to others. With the passage of time it became weaker and more humble, full of laments and lacking in virility" (*Fam.* I.1). Petrarch here creates a clear dichotomy between two distinct types of writing dominating his letters, a distinction which carries with it explicitly gendered overtones: one type is "strong" and "manly," able to both reveal and fashion virtuous minds (serving as a "source of comfort"); the other is "fragile" and "full of laments," manifesting its author's inability to withstand the blows of fortune and control both his emotions and the language of his texts.

The letters written in the "weak" style were probably composed mainly following the Black Death of 1348, in which he lost many of his close friends, as well as his beloved Laura. In *Fam.* VIII.7, for example, Petrarch laments the horrors of the plague, opening with an outcry that echoes Cicero's *Ad Quintus* 1.3.1: "Oh brother, brother, brother...what shall I say?" He then turns within the same letter to imagine the reaction of his readers to this mournful cry, again distinguishing between the two styles:

You who seem to offer comfort and aid to others, who had promised us things that were superior... see how weakly you bear your burdens, see how often you direct your frequent wailings to us. Where is that loftiness of soul which now especially should mark your profession?... We expected from you a heroic poem, we get elegiac verses; we hoped for biographies of illustrious heroes, we are getting the story of your sorrow. What we considered letters are laments.

Identifying here again the goal of his writings with the care of the soul – providing aid for himself and his readers in the face of the blows of fortune – Petrarch at the same time confesses his failure to live up to his ideal, in producing writing that exhibits his lack of self-control. What is especially striking about this is the association Petrarch creates between the two types of writing and specific ancient genres: the "weak" and "mournful" writing is associated with elegiac poetry and the "story of one's sorrow," while the "strong" writing is linked with epic poetry, historical biographies, and letters of consolation (referring, we might assume, to his epic *Africa* and his book of biographies *De viris*, as well as the letters of consolation that fill his collection, modeled mainly upon Seneca).

The central model that Petrarch associates with the "weak" and mournful style of writing is Ovid. For example, in the previous quotation, the line "we expected from you a heroic poem, we get elegiac verses" echoes the opening of Ovid's *Amores*, in which the Roman poet contrasts the heroic hexameter with the elegiac meter of his love poetry. Further, the statement "we hoped for biographies of illustrious heroes, we are getting the story of your sorrow" might be an allusion to Ovid's own story of his sorrows in *Tristia* 4.10. In a work from the mid-1340s, *De vita*, Petrarch directly contrasts Ovid's "effeminate character" with the "firmer intellect" of Virgil, Horace, and Seneca, and harshly criticizes Ovid for his "weak" attitude toward his exile as revealed in his poetry (*De vita* 273). Finally, in *Fam.* XXIV.1, Petrarch specifically refers to Ovid as the main inspiration behind his passionate writings.

Though repeatedly stressing his shame at writing in such a mournful, elegiac style, Petrarch claims it has therapeutic value for him. As he tells his addressee in *Fam.* VIII.7, "I realize that a man must either drive away grief or destroy it, or control it, or finally conceal it. But what can I do? I shall die if I cannot pour out my grief in tears and words." This style, therefore, serves Petrarch as an emotional outlet, a means to alleviate his grief. This same conception in turn dominates Petrarch's collection of vernacular poems, the *RVF*, which repeatedly portrays his experience of unrequited desire, and which Petrarch often considers among his "weak" writings.

In canzone 23, for example, he describes his motivation for writing thus: "perché cantando il duol si disacerba, / canterò com' io vissi in libertade" (*RVF* 23, 4–5: "because, singing, pain becomes less bitter – I shall sing how then I lived in liberty").

The claim that mournful writing has therapeutic value and allows the writer to forget his grief is a dominant theme in Ovid's elegiac poetry of exile. For example, in *Ex Ponto* 1.5.53–6, he writes: "Ponder my options well, you'll find nothing more useful / than this art of mine that has no use – / from it I win oblivion to my misfortunes: / harvest enough if my soil yield only this!"[5] As a result, in addition to the Ovidian tone and subject matter, Petrarch's mournful writings also echo Ovid's emphasis on the emotional value of such writing. This therapeutic use clearly contradicts the "manly" Ciceronian–Virgilian mode, with its focus on the need to eradicate the passions. And while Petrarch no doubt considered the "manly" style superior, and attempted to lead himself to renounce the "weak," he was never fully able to detach himself from the latter and give up on its emotional merits.

Petrarch between "Christian" and "pagan" styles

Despite Petrarch's recurring stress on the value of imitating the "strong" eloquent style of his favorite ancient authors, at times these efforts emerge in themselves as a detriment to the pursuit of virtue. In several of his works, mainly in the period from the late 1340s to the late 1350s, Petrarch reflects on the problematic nature of his engagement with classical style, especially as it emerges as an end unto itself: a source of pleasure or a means of satisfying his desire for literary glory and authority. In Book III of the *Secretum*, for example, the figure of Augustinus pinpoints Franciscus's hope to win glory through his eloquent Latin compositions – especially his *Africa* and *De viris* – as the main source of his restlessness, ensnaring him in an experience of desire and longing that cannot be put to rest (*Secretum* 135–137).

Petrarch's realization of the moral dangers involved in the pursuit of eloquence and glory fuels the second major stylistic conflict in his works: that between the eloquent pagan style and the humble Christian style of the Bible and the Church Fathers, known as *sermo humilis*. There is no doubt that at times Petrarch explicitly looked down upon the Biblical style, associating it with the "weak" elegiac one. In the first eclogue of his *Bucolicum carmen*, for example, the figure of Silvius, Petrarch's alter ego, describes the Biblical poet David as "always tearful, pouring forth hoarse sounds from his breast" (*Buc. carm.* I.74; see also *Fam.* X.4) and asserts his commitment to his epic predecessors Virgil and Homer (though he had not read the latter!). However, in a series of other works beginning from the late 1340s, Petrarch advances the notion that the path to true care in fact resides in rejecting the false and misleading charms of pagan eloquence altogether and following instead the humble style of the Bible.

This assertion comes most explicitly to the fore in a letter Petrarch wrote to his friend Francesco Nelli in 1358, in which he contrasts what he describes as aesthetically pleasing, yet vain, eloquent pagan writings with salutary sacred texts. He pledges that henceforth he intends to dedicate his time only to reading works that are "good for him": "Now my orators shall be Ambrose, Augustine, Jerome, and Gregory, my philosopher shall be Paul, and my poet David" (*Fam.* XXII.10). It is striking to what extent Petrarch's religious crisis revolves around writing style and the question of what type of writing might allow him to best care for himself and his readers.

Petrarch's turn to sacred literature in this period is reflected also in a writing style he himself occasionally adopts. In a letter written in 1348–49 (*Fam.* X.3), Petrarch exhorts his brother, the Carthusian monk Gherardo, to persevere in his monastic calling. To attain his goal, Petrarch steeps his exhortation in allusions to Christian rather than classical works, and uses short, concise, and colloquial sentences reminiscent of the Bible or the sermons of the Church Fathers: "In the meantime, rejoice and hope and sigh, serving the Lord in fear, exalting Him with trembling, and rendering Him gratitude because He gave you the wings of a dove that you might fly away and find rest" (*Fam.* X.3). The reference to the "wings of a dove" in this sentence is based upon Psalms 54.7, a passage upon which Augustine expatiated in his *Commentaries on the Psalms* 121.1 – a book that, as Billanovich has shown, Petrarch owned and read carefully.[6] Furthermore, the lack of subordinate clauses in the sentence, the repetitive use of the indicative ("gaude spera suspire"), and the predilection for rhyming and alliteration ("timore"/"tremore"; "gratias"/"agens") all point to Petrarch's conscious adoption of a sermon-like sacred style. At the end of the letter, Petrarch explicitly describes such style as "monastic" and declares that writing in this way has been especially beneficial for him personally:

> I have written these things to you, dear and only brother of mine, not in my customary style but in a strange one that is almost monastic, in consideration of you rather than myself. You will read them as time allows, and if nothing of this contributes to your improvement, know that at least I gained considerable benefit in writing them.
> (*Fam.* X.3)

This letter to Gherardo is placed right before *Fam.* X.4, in which Petrarch provides an interpretation of the first eclogue of the *Bucolicum carmen*, where he had declared his unwavering commitment to the pagan poetic style. The juxtaposition of these two letters thus serves to underscore the conflict between the sacred and pagan styles in Petrarch's mind.

Petrarch's belief in the benefits of following the Biblical *sermo humilis* is also evident in other works from roughly the same period, such as *De otio* and his *Psalmi*. It was in the early 1350s that Petrarch reworked his two major classicized projects – the *Africa* and *De viris* – in accordance with his new adherence to the sacred style and the ethical values associated with it. As Enrico Fenzi has pointed out, in this period Petrarch added twelve new biographies to *De viris*, most of them of Biblical figures, and revised the first two books of the *Africa*, adding to Scipio's father's speech in Book II an invective against the pursuit of earthly glory, which closely recalls Augustinus's position in Book III of the *Secretum*.[7] The way to true care and virtue, Petrarch thus suggests, is through following the sacred style and ideals, and not by imitating the "strong" style of Cicero and Virgil. Yet, this rejection of the "strong" style in this period, even in his works that openly condemn it, should not be exaggerated. For even while the figure of Augustinus urges Franciscus in the *Secretum* to renounce his adherence to ancient eloquence and his own classicized works, he often quotes from these very same works – especially the *Africa* – to persuade Franciscus to do so (*Secretum* 141). Thus, Petrarch in fact continues to assert the moral value of pagan eloquence even as he critiques it.

The synthesis of styles in Petrarch's later years

The conflicted role played by Augustine in the *Secretum* – at once praising and repudiating the value of pagan eloquence – points to Petrarch's commitment to his humanistic project even in periods of acute self-doubt. In later works, such as the invective *De ignorantia*, his adherence to the "strong" style is particularly emphasized, and the entire work in fact provides us with a remarkable example of Petrarch's efforts as he got older to combine the two styles – the sacred and the pagan – for the purpose of caring for the self.

Written as a fierce response to four of his presumed friends, all devoted Aristotelian philosophers, who declared that Petrarch was "a good man but alas ignorant," *De ignorantia* defends Petrarch's position by claiming that his detractors ridicule him due to his Christian faith and devotion (see Chapter 13). Responding to their accusation, Petrarch states that he would prefer to be ignorant than to share in the arrogance of his critics: "I must and shall prefer You [God] to Aristotle, to all philosophers and poets, to all who 'talk loudly and speak arrogance'" (*De ignorantia* 26). This devotional statement is based on Hannah's prayer in *Samuel* 1.2–3, and thus provides us with an example of Petrarch's appropriation of the Biblical humble style. Nonetheless, later in the work, as we have seen, Petrarch asserts that the eloquence of Cicero, Seneca, and Horace is not in opposition to this devotional style, and that it is in fact necessary to lead us to both virtue and salvation (*De ignorantia* 110–111). By stressing in this fashion the moral value of the two, apparently opposed, styles, and masterfully combining the virulent rhetoric of the ancient invective with humble devotional statements, *De ignorantia* offers an example of how these styles might go hand in hand to bring about a moral renewal.

The strong defense of the moral value of ancient pagan eloquence in Petrarch's *De ignorantia* is also reflected in many of the letters he wrote in his later years, which are gathered together in the second collection of his Latin letters, the *Seniles*. As he states in a letter to Boccaccio from 1362, "[Literature] advances the journey of life, it does not delay it" (*Sen.* I.5). Care for self and care for texts, he suggests, in fact go together. His central focus in his writings in old age is thus not the conflict between the pagan and sacred styles – this, as we have seen, he seems to have resolved quite satisfactorily – but rather the one between the "strong" Ciceronian-Virgilian type of writing and the "weak" and "effeminate" Ovidian style.

This conflict is made evident in the introductory letter of the *Seniles*, in which Petrarch recalls the opening letter of his previous collection, the *Familiares*, and stresses the changes between the styles of the two. Both letters were written after the ravages of the plague – the first following that of 1348 and the second following the outbreak of 1361. Yet, while in the previous letter, as Petrarch writes, he "gave vent to uncontrollable laments and tears," he now has no intention of giving in to the same emotions:

> I have no wish to weary my pen describing the loss of other friends, lest the sad memories make me weep anew, and lest this plague-ridden year force me once again to do what I would rather not – burst into plaints unworthy of my years, of my studies, unworthy of me altogether ... Earlier I allowed myself much that I now reject.
>
> (*Sen.* I.1)

The brevity and restraint with which Petrarch ends this introductory letter serve to demonstrate this new steadfastness.

This new-found resilience, reflecting and in turn fashioning a virtuous mind, is a recurring motif in Petrarch's *Seniles*. Writing to Boccaccio in 1363 after the deaths of two of his close friends, Petrarch asserts his resolution once again: "Regardless of where my old habit has pushed my tongue or pen, I have recently made a resolution and fixed it in my mind ... to disdain hope and fear, joys and griefs" (*Sen.* III.1). And yet, despite these assertions, the disavowal of the "weak" and mournful Ovidian style in his later years is not complete, as is made evident by the ironies governing the penultimate book of the *Seniles*, which includes Petrarch's translation into classicized Latin of the closing part of Boccaccio's *Decameron*, the story of Griselda.

In his translation, Petrarch turns Griselda into the ultimate *exemplum* of his humanistic ideal, a figure worthy of inclusion in his *De viris* – one who is able to withstand with complete constancy the vicissitudes of fortune, both good and bad (see Chapter 18). At the end of his tale, Petrarch directly declares that his aim in retelling it was to provide his readers with a model of constancy to be imitated (*Sen.* XVII.3). In the following letter, immediately after he has described this ideal of constancy in his elevated classicized Latin, Petrarch goes on to detail the fate of the translation he sent to Boccaccio. As we learn, the letter that contained it was stolen by border guards and never reached its destination. Upon hearing the news, Petrarch was filled with grief and anger. Unable to control his emotions, he writes: "Nobody is more galled than I by such insolence, no one more impatient, so that often it has turned me aside from writing and often driven me to grief for what I have written" (*Sen.* XVII.4). In dramatic contrast to Griselda's "manly" constancy, Petrarch ironically ends the book with a description of his inability to withstand a relatively minor misfortune, thus highlighting his failure to live up to his own humanistic ideal and attain complete control over both his emotions and his texts.

This ironic portrayal of Petrarch's own weakness at the very end of the *Seniles* takes us back to the opening letter of the *Familiares*, in which he established the opposition between the two types of writing: the "manly" – virtuous and the "feminine" – mournful. Significantly, immediately after professing his shame for his weak writings, Petrarch describes his indignation with the softness revealed in the letters of none other than Cicero himself: "In [his] adversities Cicero revealed himself so weak that while I take pleasure in his style I often feel offended by his attitude" (*Fam.* I.1). It is precisely this weakness that leads Petrarch, as he tells us in the letter, to address to Cicero in a "fit of anger" a letter reproaching him for his softness, "forgetting," as it were, "the gap of time" that separates them (Ibid.). The incentive for Petrarch's writing of letters to ancient authors, with which we began this discussion, was thus Cicero's disclosure of his own weakness. No less than his strong writings, it is therefore the documentation of his all-too-human weaknesses that allowed Cicero, according to Petrarch's account, to transcend the boundaries of space and time and intimately speak to those who are absent. By ironically revealing his own shortcomings at the very end of his correspondence, in the passage cited from *Sen.* XVII.4, Petrarch thus not only makes manifest his inability to forego laments but also expresses hope that his own revelation of his frailty will allow him, like Cicero, to speak "beyond the grave" with future readers, creating in this fashion a timeless community of readers and writers, a point reinforced by the final letter of the collection, the unfinished "Letter to Posterity" (*Sen.* XVIII.1).

In the same way in which Petrarch managed to combine the sacred and pagan styles in *De ignorantia*, so too does the ending of Book XVII of the *Seniles* demonstrate an apparent compromise between the "strong" and "weak" types of writing, asserting the superiority of the former without fully giving up on the latter. It is this synthesis of a broad range of ancient styles and ethical perspectives – pagan and biblical, heroic and elegiac – that ultimately defines the ethical and stylistic nature of Petrarch's revival of antiquity, and it is perhaps the stubborn persistence of his all-too-human "weak" writing that has proved to be his most enduring legacy, allowing him to continue to speak so intimately to us more than seven centuries later.

NOTES

1 Marco Santagata, *Per moderne carte: La biblioteca volgare di Petrarca* (Bologna: Il Mulino, 1990); Ronald G. Witt, *"In The Footsteps of the Ancients": The Origins of Humanism from Lovato to Bruni* (Leiden: Brill, 2000).

2 Nicholas Mann, *Petrarch* (Oxford: Oxford University Press, 1984), 29–38; Mazzotta, *The Worlds of Petrarch*, 18.

3 See Erich Auerbach, "Sermo Humilis," in *Literary Language and Its Public*, trans. Ralph Manheim (Princeton, NJ: Princeton University Press, 1965), 25–81.

4 Guido Martellotti, *Scritti petrarcheschi*, eds. Michele Feo and Silvia Rizzo (Padua: Antenore, 1983), 9.

5 Ovid, *The Poems of Exile*, trans. Peter Green (London: Penguin, 1994), 121.

6 Giuseppe Billanovich, "Nella biblioteca del Petrarca: Il Petrarca, il Boccaccio, e le *Enarrationes in psalmos* di S. Agostino," *Italia medioevale e umanistica* 3 (1960): 1–58.

7 Enrico Fenzi, *Saggi Petrarcheschi* (Fiesole: Cadmo, 2003), 345–357.

12

OLIVIA HOLMES

Petrarch and the vernacular lyric past

As a Tuscan who spent much of his life residing near Avignon, in what is today the south of France, Francesco Petrarca was heir to three centuries of written vernacular poetry in both Old Occitan (or Provençal) and Italian, as well as to untold ages of unwritten, orally transmitted songs. The lyrics of about 2500 troubadour songs have come down to us from the twelfth and thirteenth centuries, bearing witness not only to one of the earliest secular literary movements in a European vernacular, but also to an immensely popular mode of musical expression. The Italian lyric tradition, which largely derived in form and content from the Occitan troubadours, began somewhat later, with the poets of the Sicilian School gathered in the *Magna Curia* of the Holy Roman Emperor Frederick II (reigned 1220–50). From there, it traveled to Tuscany and northern Italy in the second half of the thirteenth century and flowered in the works of Dante Alighieri and the poets of the *Dolce stil novo*. Italian poetry appears from the beginning to have been composed independently of music and transmitted in writing – though, as Petrarch's madrigals especially demonstrate, it has frequently been set to music at a subsequent stage by someone other than the author. Critics have considered Petrarch's youthful sojourn in Bologna in the 1320s to study law as the probable period of his initial formation as an Italian lyric poet, but Petrarch is usually careful to erase or camouflage the traces of his vernacular poetic influences, especially where Dante is concerned. His poems (with one significant exception) seem to admit no precedents, presenting themselves as the spontaneous product of a historical individual who experienced their contents in his own person.

The 366 vernacular pieces collected in the *RVF* generally adhere closely to the conventions of medieval lyric poetry. They are mostly composed in the two principle genres of contemporary Italian lyric: the canzone, a strophaic form inherited from the troubadours, with a repeated rhyme scheme and a fixed number of syllables per line; and the sonnet, an invention of the Sicilian School that, with Petrarch's help, was soon to dominate European poetry. Petrarch alternates and intermingles various metrical forms in the *RVF*, unlike the scribal anthologies of the previous century, which strictly separated the different forms into distinct sections – for *cansos*, *sirventes*, and *tensos* in Occitan songbooks; for canzoni, *sonetti*, and *tenzoni* in Italian ones. Petrarch radically transformed the format of the contemporary poetry-manuscript by including only his own poems and arranging them – at least ostensibly – chronologically, rather than by genre, interspersing his love lyrics with political or moralizing poems and poetic exchanges. His intermingling of metrical forms had already been anticipated, however, by Dante's organization of his own early lyrics into an autobiographical sequence with prose connectives in the *Vita nova*.

Petrarch's vernacular poems are, for the most part, conventional in content as well as form, adopting the psychology and language of troubadour *fin' amors* (often called "courtly love" by modern critics), which strives for a reward that only the lady can bestow, leads the first-person speaker to become a better person or poet, and is impossible to attain because unreciprocated and/or unequal (the beloved is typically of higher social status than the lover). In Petrarch's lyrics, as in the troubadours and Italian Duecento generally – and often in classical literature – this impossible love is usually experienced as something negative: a physical blow, a wound or disease, a war between the component parts of a divided self (see, for instance, *RVF* 2). Love frequently leads to death; indeed, the pairing of "amor" and "mort[e]" is among the oldest and most widespread puns in Romance lyric. One of the earliest troubadours, Marcabru (flourished 1130–50), says of Amors (Love), for instance, "it has killed [a mortz] a thousand men with a sword," and, in the following century, the Italian poet Guittone d'Arezzo (flourished 1250–90) proclaims, "Love [Amor] can be called painful death [dogliosa morte]" (or "painful to death [doglios'a morte]") because "it's a word that can be divided / into 'a' and 'mor,' which are its two parts, / and 'mor' means death."[1] Another century later, Petrarch puns similarly: "questo è 'l colpo di che Amor m'à morto" (*RVF* 73, 90: "this is the blow with which Love has killed me").

Petrarch appears to have taken directly from the troubadours his taste for wordplay and cult of technical refinement, of difficult verse forms involving the repetition of rhyme-sounds or rhyme-words, which return with a different meaning each time. Early Occitan poetry is generally more formally experimental than its Italian counterpart, each love song proposing a combination of rhyme and meter never employed before, and tending to repeat rhyme-sounds (or words) from stanza to stanza. Petrarch maintains the Italian preference for *coblas singulars* (every stanza of a poem having a new set of rhymes), but he does devise a different metrical scheme for each canzone in his book. He further picks up one particularly difficult Occitan verse-form, the sestina, used apparently only once by its inventor, Arnaut Daniel (flourished 1180–1200), and closely imitated by Dante in his poem "Al poco giorno" ("To the short day"), and he deploys it repeatedly in the *RVF* as a marker. Petrarch also returns over and over to a few key puns, especially those based on his beloved's name: Laura is a "lauro" ("laurel tree" or "wreath"), "l'auro" ("gold" or "blonde"), and "l'aura" ("the breeze").

Petrarch also seems to have adopted the motif of the beloved-as-wind from his favored troubadour, Arnaut Daniel, who famously ends one *canson*, "I am Arnaut, who hoards the breeze [q'amas l'aura], / and chases the rabbit with the ox, / and swims against the swelling tide."[2] Petrarch clearly elaborates on Arnaut's *congedo* or poetic envoy in the opening verses of sonnet 212:

> Beato in sogno et di languir contento,
> d'abbracciar l'ombre et seguir l'aura estiva,
> nuoto per mar che non à fondo o riva;
> solco onde, e 'n rena fondo, et scrivo in vento;
>
> (*RVF* 212, 1–4)

(Blessed in sleep and satisfied to languish, to embrace shadows, and to pursue the summer breeze, I swim through a sea that has no floor or shore, I plow the waves, and found my house on sand and write on the wind.)

He echoes Arnaut's signature again in poem 239, a sestina with the rhyme-word "Laura" (also a rhyme-sound in the earlier *canson*) beginning its *congedo*: "In rete accolgo l'aura..." (v. 37: "I catch the breeze in a net..."). Once more, however, Petrarch is using a motif that goes back to the earliest Occitan lyric. Marcabru's contemporary Cercamon begins a poem, for instance, "When the sweet air [la douch'aura] grows bitter [s'amarcis] /.../ and the birds change their chatter, / I also sigh and sing here / of love which holds me tied and bound."[3] It is arguable, however, that whereas in the early troubadours the warm breeze merely functions as objective correlative for the lady's sweet breath; and in Arnaut, gathering or reaping the wind means not only loving an unresponsive woman, but also composing difficult poetry; in Petrarch, embracing the breeze (along with the other Arnaut-derived *impossibiliae*) has come to stand for more metaphysical struggles as well, for the desire to stop time and vanquish death, and for the search for a transcendent truth or faith that always escapes him. Petrarch takes courtly commonplaces and twists them into new shapes, but the changing and twisting of *topoi* is itself part of the poetic tradition.

The *RVF* contains undeniably conventional poems, crammed with what were familiar clichés (the butterfly, the salamander, the lover as a fish on a hook or a limed bird, the lady as angel, etc.), and makes them richer and stranger. Occitan lyric makes abundant use of seasonal motifs, for instance, and the seasons are generally polarized. In the typical *Natureingang*, spring and its various accouterments – flowers, new leaves, birdsong, warm breezes, babbling brooks, green meadows – correspond to the burgeoning of the speaker's love. On the other hand, the coming of winter – accompanied by cold wind, rain, ice, falling leaves, and so on – usually corresponds to the frustration of love, or is set in contrast to the flowering of love (that is, the troubadour loves *despite* the season). See, for example, the opening of the Cercamon *canson* just quoted, which employs the customary opposition of sweet and bitter as well. (The pairing of "amar[e]" ("to love") and "amar[o]" ("bitter") is another widespread pun in Romance lyric). The Cercamon stanza also contains the image of being bound by love, much utilized by Petrarch (in sonnets 196–197, for instance, the golden ringlets of Laura's hair become metaphoric chains that bind the speaker).

Petrarch tends to favor winter *topoi*, with their sad associations, over spring *topoi*, with their joyous ones – see his sonnet 17, "Piovonmi amare lagrime" ("Bitter tears rain from me") – but he does not entirely eschew positive evocations of nature, perhaps using them to most brilliant effect in canzone 126, "Chiare fresche et dolci acque" ("Clear, fresh, sweet waters"). He also likes to mix up the seasons, declaring, for example, "tremo a mezza state, ardendo il verno" (*RVF* 132, 14: "I shiver in midsummer, burn in winter"). Even defying seasonal expectations is conventional, however: compare the Duecento poet Paolo Lanfranchi's similar declaration: "I do everything by contrary . . . : / in summer I'm colder than ice, / in winter I burn [ardo] with great heat."[4]

Polarized seasonal motifs are a subset of Romance literature's ubiquitous use of antitheses, paradoxes, oxymorons, and so forth to express the lover's contradictory feelings and/or the impossible nature of the love situation. We have seen that Petrarch particularly echoes Arnaut Daniel's use of the *adynaton*, or impossibility *topos*; see also, for example, *RVF* 66, a sestina, in which the speaker declares that before he encounters Laura without her usual ice and fog (or emotional coldness toward him), he will see "secco il mare e' laghi, e i fiumi" (v. 24: "the sea dry, and the lakes and the rivers") – that is, hell will freeze over. But the taste for poems consisting of lists of antitheses goes back to the first troubadour on record, Guilhem de Peitieu, and can be found throughout the tradition. Giraut de Borneil (flourished 1165–1200; Dante cites him in *De vulgari eloquentia* 2.2.8) complains in one *canson*, for instance, "I am sick, yet never was there a fitter man, / and

I call a wicked man good, / and give much when I have nothing, / and curse the man who blesses me."[5] Petrarch writes, to similar effect:

> Pace non trovo et non ò da far guerra,
> e temo et spero, et ardo et son un ghiaccio,
> et volo sopra 'l cielo et giaccio in terra,
> et nulla stringo et tutto 'l mondo abbraccio.
>
> (*RVF* 134, 1–4)

(Peace I do not find, and have no wish to make war; and I fear and hope, and burn and am of ice; and I fly above the heavens and lie on the ground; and I grasp nothing and embrace all the world.)

Giraut's poem concludes, "She can bring me to my senses again if only she deigned to show me some regard," and Petrarch's concludes, "In this state am I, Lady, on account of you" (v. 14). I do not mean to say that Petrarch necessarily knew Giraut's poem – indeed, there are Italian sonnets along the same lines by Lanfranchi and Cecco d'Ascoli, among others – just that Petrarch adheres to common schemes.

Another binary opposition that Petrarch frequently alludes to is that of day and night. In his first sestina, *RVF* 22 – as also in other poems of his on the theme of insomnia – all the creatures of earth are granted rest from their labors after the day, except the poet: "I never have any truce from my sighs with the sun; and then when I see the stars flaming I go weeping and longing for the day" (vv. 10–12). This is a variant of the version of the winter *topos* in which the lover goes on "ardendo il verno," sighing and singing of love even after the leaves have fallen, and clearly contrasts with more conventional poems, such as, for instance, the *canson* by the troubadour Arnaut de Mareuilh that begins, "It is beautiful to me when the wind blows on me / in April, before May comes, / and all through the calm night, / the nightingale and the jay sing."[6] In the earlier song, the birds rejoice "as each approaches its companion"; Petrarch laments, however, with another pair of *adynata*, that in his case, "But I will be under the earth in dried wood, and the day will be lit by the tiny stars, before the sun arrives at so sweet a dawn" (vv. 37–39).

We find an even closer model for the impossibility figures from poem 22's envoy in the last full stanza of Dante's sestina "Al poco giorno": "But the rivers will return quite back to the hills / before this wet, green wood / catches fire – as a beautiful woman is wont to do – / for me, who would consent to sleep on stone [petra] / all the time, and to subsist on grass, / only to see the shadow made by her clothes" (vv. 31–36).[7] Petrarch takes from Dante not only the structure of the trope ("ritorneranno i fiumi a' colli / prima che..."

becomes in *RVF* 22, 38 "'l giorno andrà pien di minute stelle / prima ch[e]" ("and the day will be lit by the tiny stars")), but also its content: for both speakers, the impossible will have to happen before their ladies requite their loves. He also echoes Dante's promise to subsist on grass in the poem's earlier verses: "I do not believe that there ever grazed in any wood so cruel a beast" (*RVF* 22, 19–20).

Petrarch clearly knows Arnaut Daniel's original sestina "Lo ferm voler" ("The firm desire"), from which he repeats one of the rhyme-words, "arma" (Italian "alma" or "soul"), in sestina 239, "Là ver l'aurora" ("At the time near dawn"), which also uses in rhyme-word position the "Arnautian" term "l'aura." But he just as clearly knows Dante's imitation of Arnaut, and begins each stanza of his own sestinas with an *endecasillabo*, or eleven-syllable verse, as Dante does, in contrast with Arnaut's practice of beginning each stanza with an eight-syllable verse (though all the other verses have eleven). Petrarch also picks up from Dante's sestina the rhyme-word "petra," which he does not use as a rhyme in any of his own sestinas, but which does appear (not in rhyme position) in the sixth, *RVF* 214, 17 – and he comes close to "petra" in meaning with the rhyme-word "scogli" in the fourth, *RVF* 80. He also uses the word to pun on his own name in his first canzone (which immediately follows the first sestina): "tremar mi fea dentro a quella petra" (*RVF* 23, 82: "she made me tremble within that stone"). Indeed, the absence from his sestinas of the rhyme-word "petra" – which Dante places in rhyme position in all four of the so-called *rime petrose* (or "stoney poems") – is striking; it almost seems as if Petrarch interposes echoes of the troubadours where his poetry is actually closest to Dante's, ending the first stanza of *RVF* 22, for instance, with the very Occitan rhyme-word "alba" (concluding every stanza with the word "alba" is a genre-marker of the troubadour dawn poem). Petrarch diminishes Dante as a source here by making him appear to be just one influence among a number of others – a technique for delimiting his greatest Italian predecessor's importance that Petrarch also effectively employs in his lists of vernacular poets in the *Triumphi*.

Dante's sestina "Al poco giorno" and the other *rime petrose* represent the moment in his lyric production when it is most technically driven, when the coldness of the lady and the impenetrability of her defenses correspond to the poet's taking on of exceptionally "hard" and repetitive verse patterns.[8] Dante's sestina – like all sestinas – uses only six rhyme-words in thirty-six verses (plus an even more densely packed *congedo*), and its companion canzoni "Io son venuto al punto" and "Amor, tu vedi ben" also both repeat a few key rhyme-words over and over, many of them – "petra," "donna," "tempo," "erba" – the same from poem to poem. Dante learned this *trobar clus* technique from Arnaut in particular. Dante's poems "Al poco giorno" and "Io son venuto al punto" can also be seen as conveying extended, and particularly exasperated, versions of the winter *topos*, in which the heat of the speaker's passion defies the starkness of the winter setting. In "Così nel mio parlar" – clearly related to the other poems of Dante's *petrose* series, though not grouped with them in the textual tradition – the equation between form and content is made explicit: the poet says that he makes his words harsh because he has been treated harshly, and goes on to relate an act of sexual violence as an allegory of poetic mastery. Petrarch cites this poem in particular as an influence at the end of stanza 3 of "Lasso me, ch'i' non so" (*RVF* 70: "Alas, I do not know"), but clearly all the *petrose*, with their difficult meters and stony ladies in frozen landscapes, influenced his presentation of Laura as hardening into ice, "whiter and colder than snow not touched by the sun many and many years," or into a tree, "my idol carved in living laurel," like Daphne escaping from Apollo (*RVF* 30, 2–3 and 27).

Poem 70 is the exception to the general rule that Petrarch's poems tend to disguise their sources and admit no precedents. He establishes an ideal list of his major vernacular poetic influences up to that point in the *RVF*, concluding each stanza with the first verse of a predecessor's canzone, except the final one, which concludes with the *incipit* of his own early canzone (the first in the book), "Nel dolce tempo de la prima etade" (*RVF* 23, 1). The opening stanza of "Lasso me" ends with the first verse of a poem that Petrarch apparently thought was by Arnaut Daniel, "Drez et rayson es qu'ieu ciant em demori" (*RVF* 70, 10), though modern commentators mostly accept its attribution to the minor troubadour Guilhem de Saint Gregori.

The poem does sound very much like Arnaut, with its sensual celebration of the lady's body as "whiter than any piece of ivory" and its paradoxical declarations that "sweet is the branch with which she beats me" and that he finds it "sweet and beautiful to die of longing for her."[9] In the context of *RVF* 70, however, the verse might also be taken as representative of Occitan poetry in general. The Italian poems that Petrarch goes on to quote in the final verses of the following stanzas are Guido Cavalcanti's "Donna mi priegha, per ch'io voglio dire" – another poem which famously equates love and death – Dante's aforementioned "Così nel mio parlar voglio esser aspro," and Cino da Pistoia's "La dolce vista e 'l bel guardo soave" (vv. 20, 30, 40). In each case, the quotation is integrated into the logic of the stanza as if it were Petrarch's own words; indeed, the italics or quotation marks with which these verses are set apart in modern editions are editorial interventions.

The first stanza of "Lasso me" (*RVF* 70) ends with the assertion that it is right and just that the speaker sing and enjoy himself (considering what he has been through), but he goes on in the second to complain that his laughter

will never be equal to his tears, and that the most he can hope for is to be able to say someday that his lady bids him to write (v. 20: "Donna mi priega...").
He then reveals in the third stanza, however, that she does not care for him or his poetry, and he therefore wishes for his words to be as harsh as the bitterness he feels (v. 30: "Così nel mio parlar..."). He begins the fourth stanza by asking "Che parlo?" (v. 31: "What am I saying?"), and now denies that any responsibility for his pain can be attributed to "the sweet sight" of his lady – shifting to a poetics of pure praise, in other words. But this stance also turns out to be inadequate, since, as he points out in the final stanza, the eye with which he observes her is weakened by his own sin (vv. 44–48).

Each quote from a previous poet is contradicted in the stanza that follows; Petrarch does not so much celebrate poems that he admires and imitates here as condemn them as bad influences to be overcome. Even so, the list is obviously skewed in favor of poets in whose context he wants his vernacular poetry to be read. It does not include, for instance, any Italians who predated the *stilnovisti*, such as the Tuscans Guittone d'Arezzo, Chiaro Davanzati, and Monte Andrea, echoes of whom his most recent editor, Marco Santagata, detects repeatedly in the *RVF*. And Petrarch cites Dante only as author of the *rime petrose*, though his poems more frequently echo the *Commedia*.[10] Nor do any of the poets whom Petrarch cites in *RVF* 70 seem to have collected or organized their own lyrics except Dante – but, again, he cites the Dante of the *rime petrose*, not of the *Vita nova* or the *Commedia*. There are other author-ordered collections of poems that predate Petrarch's, not only by Dante, but also by the troubadour Guiraut Riquier and the Italians Guittone d'Arezzo and Nicolò de' Rossi (the latter resided in Avignon in the 1330s), and though he may never have admired these authors as much as he apparently admired Guido Cavalcanti and Cino da Pistoia – most readers don't – his avoidance of any association with poets whose practice was actually quite close to his own suggests a concern for shaping the terms of his own legacy.

As already mentioned, Petrarch rehearses his debts to previous vernacular lyric also in his allegorical narrative *poema* in Dantean *terza rima*, the *Triumphi*. In the first section, *TC*, the brief procession of Italian love poets with their beloveds (*TC* IV, 28–38) starts with Dante and Beatrice and includes the same writers as those alluded to in canzone 70, with the additions of "I Ciciliani" (the poets of the Sicilian School), Guittone d'Arezzo, a second Guido (presumably Guinizzelli), and a few minor figures: Onesto da Bologna; Sennuccio del Bene, with whom Petrarch corresponded; and Franceschino degli Abizzi, a relative of Petrarch's. The procession of troubadours that follows (in *TC* IV, 38–57) has almost twice the number of verses devoted to it as the Italian section, and mentions almost twice the number of poets – fifteen, as opposed to eight – starting with Arnaut Daniel, "great master of love, who still honors his land with his difficult, beautiful verses" (vv. 41–42), and including Folquet de Marseille and probably Gaucelm Faidit (simply listed as "Gauselmo"), both authors of anniversary poems. Petrarch seems generally to treat the Occitan love poets with greater respect than the Italian ones, and I see no reason to doubt that this reflects a real preference on his part, stemming perhaps from his youth in Provence.

In his more "official" Latin writings, however, Petrarch generally makes little of his vernacular influences, favoring classical ones, and seems reluctant to speak of his Italian poetry at all, implicitly negating not only his debts to other medieval writers, but also his own creative investment in vernacular lyric. He refers to these poems with affected modesty as "fragmenta" ("fragments") and "nugae" or "ineptiae" ("trifles"), that is, as mere youthful experiments, belittling their importance and making a show of being ashamed of such compositions now.[11] In a famous letter to Giovanni Boccaccio (*Familiares* XXI.15), he denies envying Dante's popularity as a vernacular poet, asking how he could envy a man "who devoted his entire life to those things that were only the flower and first fruits of [Petrarch's] youth?" Here, as in *RVF* 70 and 287, Petrarch recognizes his great predecessor only as a lyric love poet, not as the author of a vernacular epic, which book he says he never possessed. He claims to have abandoned Dante's style of composition for fear of what he saw happening to his verses, which were constantly mangled and befouled by the ignorant multitude's recitation. Petrarch specifically associates Dante with the inexact and unreliable diffusion of vernacular texts.[12] Ironically, Italian poetry, with its mixture of oral and written transmission, represented for Petrarch the past – or at least the corrupt present – whereas Latin literature, which circulated almost exclusively in a more stable written form, represented for him the future.

In the opening sonnet of the *RVF*, Petrarch refers to the poems it contains as "rime sparse" (v. 1: "scattered rhymes") from the period of his "primo giovenile errore" (v. 3: "first youthful error"). Material evidence suggests, however, that he never actually stopped composing vernacular poetry, but went on writing and revising his verses for Laura until the last years of his life (see Chapter 4). And the poems are not, in fact, mere fragments or miscellaneous rhymes, but rather carefully integrated components of a large, complex mechanism. In both form and thematic content, Petrarch struggled to make his individual texts hold together in a vernacular context that tended toward dispersion: oral transmission through musical performance and collection in scribal anthologies, which were themselves interpretive performances. Petrarch endeavored to prevent, and arguably succeeded in preventing, this sort of transience – related to and embodied in Laura's (and his own) mortality – by assembling his micro-texts into a macro-text, into a monument, thus naturalizing them and making them seem not conventional and interchangeable, but unique, chronologically ordered expressions of historical experience.

If we still read the *RVF* today, and indeed consider it Petrarch's greatest work, this is – at least in part – because Petrarch has convinced us that the poems are in some sense sincere and unprecedented, though the feelings relayed may nonetheless be universal. Teodolinda Barolini, among others, has suggested that a major element in achieving the effect of authenticity is the representation of time.[13] Petrarch depicts the passage of time by periodically including poems marking the anniversary of his falling in love and, in the final part of the collection, of Laura's death, and by mentioning specific dates. Anniversary poems were already a minor genre in Occitan lyric. Various troubadours mention the number of years for which they have celebrated their ladies, but usually only once; an exception is Raimon de Miraval, who refers in different poems to having been in love for two and for five years. Another is Guiraut Riquier, who compiled and dated his own poems in the second half of the thirteenth century and who commemorates both the twentieth and the twenty-fifth anniversaries of his suffering for love.

Italians who composed anniversary poems – just one each – are Guittone d'Arezzo and the Sicilians Mazzeo di Ricco da Messina and Cielo d'Alcamo. Dante also includes an anniversary in his lyric collection the *Vita nova*, and anticipates Petrarch significantly inasmuch as it marks the anniversary of Beatrice's death, rather than of his *innamoramento*. But the author who most closely anticipates Petrarch's system of anniversary poems is the early Trecento poet Nicolò de' Rossi, who organized 100 sonnets into an ostensibly chronological sequence, marking the first four anniversaries of the speaker's falling in love in sonnets 24, 63, 75, and 94, and culminating with the lady's death in sonnets 97–99. Nicolò's second anniversary sonnet, "La tençone ch'è fra li cortesani," is structurally similar to Petrarch's anniversary poem 145, "Ponmi ove 'l sole occide i fiori," which also consists of an extended list of things that do not affect the speaker, or that are nothing compared to what he has suffered for love.

As the work of the critic Marco Santagata has extensively demonstrated, another way in which Petrarch naturalizes the poems in the *RVF* and makes them seem unique expressions of real experiences is by fixing the order in which they occur and employing intertextual connections to ensure that their order remains unchanged when they are copied or performed. Many of the troubadours composed highly complex verse-forms with stanza-linking devices such as *coblas capcaudadas* and *capfinidas* – in which the last rhyme or rhyme-word of each stanza becomes the first rhyme or rhyme-word of the next – to bind their poems into a fixed sequence to which nothing can be added and from which nothing can be removed.

Arnaut Daniel's sestina-form is one instance of this technique, but some later troubadours, such as Guiraut Riquier, also show an affinity for elaborate metrical schemes with multiple concatenating devices. Connective mechanisms are used by the poets of the Sicilian School as well, who link the two parts of a sonnet by repeating a word from the octave in the sestet, for instance. Composers of sonnet cycles such as Guittone d'Arezzo, Folgore da San Gimignano, and the author of the so-called "Corona of Love Casuistry" (an anonymous Duecento collection) use what were traditionally stanza-linking devices to enchain entire sequences of poems together. Petrarch likewise employs lexical connectives to solder his individual poems into a seamless succession. For example, poem 22, the first sestina, ends with the verse "prima ch'a sì dolce alba arrivi il sole," and poem 23, the first canzone, begins, "Nel dolce tempo de la prima etade," creating a chiasmus with the reversed repetition of the words "prima" and "dolce" (poems 79 and 80 are enchained similarly). See also the final verse of poem 24, a sonnet, "except for that which weeping [lagrimando] I let fall," and the opening verse of poem 25, another sonnet, "Love... used to weep [piangeva], and I with him at times," which repeats not a word, but a concept.[14]

There are numerous instances of this sort of concatenation in the *RVF*. Sometimes the word acting as lexical unifier is only etymologically related, or is even antithetical, to a word in the previous poem. Adjacent poems are also linked at times by having the same first word or by repeating a word or concept in their final verses (unlike the *capfinidas* linkage, this technique contributes nothing to preserving the poems' specific order, however).

In the manuscript of the *RVF* that Petrarch personally supervised, the poems are arranged for the eye according to aesthetic and geometric criteria, as well as in terms of content. Different poetic genres are interspersed throughout the book, but the poems are formatted visually in such a way that textual confines tend to coincide with those of the page, and related pieces are likely to be grouped together on a single page or on facing pages.[15] Thus, Petrarch also used layout to promote the perception of intertextual connections and to organize meaning in a way not found in contemporary, scribally – composed anthologies. For earlier vernacular poets and composers whose medium is sound, the organization of the written text is secondary – just a way of transmitting in space an object that primarily exists *in time*. Petrarch self-consciously conceived of his poetry collection as a book, however, and thus as a physical object in space, though the *referent* of this complex material signifier is time, indeed, the timespan of the author's amorous autobiography.

The *RVF* distances itself from the contemporary lyric tradition by assembling its lyrical fragments into something bigger and less evanescent, something more like what ancient writers – or, as Armando Petrucci points out, contemporary notaries – produced,[16] but even in this, Petrarch's work can be seen as the culmination of tendencies already present in later Occitan and Italian lyric. Both Riquier and de' Rossi assembled collections celebrating their love for one lady over a number of years and then lamenting her death (and Riquier – like Petrarch – addresses his poetry to the Virgin Mary after his lady's death). Dante especially led the way, not only in the *Vita nova*, but also in his efforts to organize his allegorical canzoni into an encyclopedic macro-text in the *Convivio*, and in his further sublimation of courtly love in the *Commedia*.

The *RVF* is thus very much a product of its time, but Petrarch's general strategy was to exclude evidence of contemporary conversations from his vernacular work, and to project these poetic endeavors onto the idealized screens of ancient letters and literary posterity. Analogously, manuscript research into the poet's *abbozzi* or drafts reveals a tendency to exclude from his authorized self-anthology verses written for specific occasions and love poems for women other than Laura (see Chapter 4).[17] The pattern is not wholly predictable, however: the lady who dies is not immediately reincarnated as the Virgin Mary or entirely sublimated into something higher (this failure is, indeed, part of the book's thematic content), and the two major divisions, contained in two distinct fascicles in the autograph manuscript, do not precisely coincide with later editors' division of the poems into those *in vita* and those *in morte*.

Petrarch has contrived that we read his somewhat conventional poems as "authentic" and "original" by gathering together what were indeed fragmentary utterances and assembling them into a masterwork of complex formal and expressive interconnectivity. He juxtaposes static moments to create the illusion of movement, as in a film, but simultaneously undermines their narrative linearity by setting up expectations for a straightforward conversion story that does not entirely take place. Part of Petrarch's artistic genius was in understanding where the wind was blowing in his time and riding the evolution of vernacular lyric from oral to written transmission and from a popular form to high art, composing a richer and more accomplished, but also less predictable, author collection than those that preceded it.

NOTES

1 *Marcabru: A Critical Edition*, eds. Simon Gaunt, Ruth Harvey, and Linda Patterson (Cambridge: Brewer, 2000), 242–243; Guittone d'Arezzo, *Le rime*, ed.

Francesco Egidi (Bari: Laterza, 1940), 270. The Guittone translation – and all translations from non-English-language editions – is my own. It should be borne in mind that the use of an apostrophe to indicate where a word has been truncated (as in "doglios'a") and the use of capitalization in personifications (such as "Amor") are modern editorial conventions; the only punctuation in Petrarch's partially autograph manuscript of the *RVF* (Vat. Lat. 3195) indicates poetic meter rather than syntax; sonnets are written on seven lines, for instance, with the rhymes at the ends of odd-numbered verses treated as internal rhymes, and marked by dots.

2 James Wilhelm, ed., *The Poetry of Arnaut Daniel* (New York: Garland, 1981), 42. See also Arnaut's poem "L'aura amara" ("The Bitter Breeze"), 34–39.

3 Roy Rosenstein and George Wolf, eds., *The Poetry of Cercamon and Jaufre Rudel* (New York: Garland, 1983), 41.

4 Gianfranco Contini, ed., *Poeti del Duecento*, vol. 1 (Milan: Ricciardi, 1960), 356.

5 Ruth Sharman, ed., *The Cansos and Sirventes of the Troubadour Giraut de Borneil* (Cambridge: Cambridge University Press, 1989), 371–372.

6 Ronald Carlyle Johnston, ed., *Les poésies lyriques du troubadour Arnaut de Mareuil* [1935] (Geneva: Slatkine Reprints, 1973), 100–101.

7 Dante Alighieri, *Rime*, ed. Domenico De Robertis (Florence: Le Lettere, 2002), 115.

8 The complex structural patterns of Dante's *rime petrose* and their micro-cosmic relation to the human body and the larger cosmos are elucidated in Robert M. Durling and Ronald L. Martinez, *Time and the Crystal: Studies in Dante's "Rime Petrose,"* (Berkeley, CA: University of California Press, 1990).

9 The poem "Drez et rayson" is edited in Maurizio Perugi, *Trovatori a Valchiusa: Un frammento della cultura provenzale del Petrarca* (Padua: Antenore, 1985), 10–17.

10 Paolo Trovato, *Dante in Petrarca* (Florence: Olschki, 1979), 19.

11 The modesty *topos* is a stock formula of classical rhetoric and poetry (see, for instance, Catullus 1.4).

12 Justin Steinberg, "Dante *Estravagante*, Petrarca *Disperso*, and the Spectre of the Other Woman," in *Petrarch and Dante*, Barański and Cachey, 265.

13 See Teodolinda Barolini, "The Making of a Lyric Sequence: Time and Narrative in Petrarch's *Rerum vulgarium fragmenta*," *MLN* 104 (1989): 1–38.

14 Marco Santagata distinguishes between two types of intertextual connection in the *RVF*: those involving a transformation, such as here, and those of equivalency, which usually involve the identical repetition of a single word; Marco Santagata, *Dal sonetto al canzoniere: ricerche della preistoria e la costituzione di un genere* (Padua: Liviana, 1979), 37.

15 Furio Brugnolo, "Libro d'autore e forma-canzoniere: Implicazioni petrarch-esche," *Atti e memorie dell'Accademia patavina di scienze lettere ed arti* 103.3 (1990–91): 259–290.

16 Armando Petrucci, "Minuta, autografo, libro d'autore," in *Il libro e il testo*, eds. Cesare Questa and Renato Raffaelli (Urbino: Università degli studi di Urbino, 1984), 399–414.

17 Steinberg, "Petrarch's Damned Poetry and the Poetics of Exclusion," in *Petrarch: A Critical Guide*, Kirkham and Maggi, 85–100.

13

DAVID MARSH

Petrarch's adversaries: the *Invectives*

As he invented his career as a Humanist, Petrarch sought and won the friendship and patronage of many eminent contemporaries. He celebrated his success by publishing his correspondence with princes and prelates: indeed, he called his most important epistolary collection *Letters on Familiar Matters* (*Familiares*). Many of Petrarch's letters draw moral lessons for his distinguished correspondents and ambitiously cast the Humanist as a mentor of the mighty, as do his prose treatises and historical works, which are also often dedicated to men of prominence. Petrarch even offers future generations a self-portrait in his epistle *Seniles* XVIII.1, the so-called "Letter to Posterity," in which he recounts with a heavy dose of false modesty how he was courted by potentates like Cardinal Giovanni Colonna and King Robert of Anjou.

Petrarch's social ascent inevitably aroused the suspicion and enmity of figures who regarded themselves as superior to this verbose upstart. If his "Letter to Posterity" remained incomplete, this was not the case with his *Invectives*, which he composed and published with dispatch and determination, keen as he was to silence his fiercest critics with virulent reprisals. In the *Invectives*, he replied to his critics and cultural adversaries by assailing four bastions of Trecento culture: (1) medicine in the *Invective against a Physician* (*Contra medicum*); (2) the aristocracy in his *Invective against a Man of High Rank but No Knowledge or Virtue* (*Contra quondam*); (3) the Aristotelian basis of Scholasticism in *On His Own Ignorance and That of Many Others* (*De ignorantia*); and (4) French nationalism in the *Invective against a Detractor of Italy* (*Contra eum*).

Classical invective had been developed by ancient orators, who established a rhetorical framework for expressing praise and blame in public speaking. The topics of epideictic praise were to become favorites of Renaissance Humanists, who often celebrated men and cities both ancient and modern in biographies, encomia, and treatises. But the rhetoric of vituperation also had its uses, especially in the factious cultural and political climate of early

Humanism. In this respect, Petrarch follows the important model of Jerome, whose own invectives spare no opprobrium in assailing his adversaries. If Augustine was Petrarch's spiritual mentor in introspection and confession, Jerome was the epistolary and polemical model for the Humanist's more public compositions.[1]

Nevertheless, it is Petrarch's particular achievement that he balances his negative censures with a positive vision of his own values, thus offsetting outbursts of Juvenalian indignation with passages of Horatian idealism. Despite the negative tone of these works, they also contain some of the most passionate formulations of Petrarch's new cultural ideals of eloquence, poetry, and moral reflection.

Invective against a Physician

In December 1351, Pope Clement VI fell seriously ill at the papal court in Avignon. After a relapse in February 1352, Petrarch sent a message by a common friend urging the pope to rely on a single physician, rather than on several. (Some twenty years later, Petrarch related this first stage of the drama in an epistle – *Seniles* XVI.3, May 1, 1374 – that he sent to Francesco Casini, a Sienese professor of medicine who was physician to Pope Gregory XI.) Soon thereafter, Clement VI asked Petrarch to write him a letter that would make his advice more explicit. The Humanist eagerly did so in *Fam.* V.19, dated March 12, 1352, in which he inveighed against the medical profession. This epistle offers a stinging condemnation of medicine that soon provoked an angry response (not extant) written by one of the pope's personal physicians. Petrarch replied in a quickly drafted composition, which later became his first invective. The angered physician wrote a second attack, to which Petrarch again responded from Vaucluse between January and May of 1353. His response took the form of three additional invectives, which he soon revised together with the first at Milan as the four *Contra medicum*. In the event, the pope and his maladies were now history: Clement VI died on December 6, 1352, and was succeeded by Innocent VI, as Petrarch notes in his fourth invective.

Petrarch articulates the argument of his invectives through a series of antitheses contrasting the arrogant beliefs of the hostile physician to his own more modest philosophy. From the outset, Petrarch claims that he is not attacking medicine in general, but only certain doctors. But his general view of the medical profession owes much to medieval discussions of the status of medicine as an art. For example, when he calls medicine a "mechanical" art, he echoes the *Didascalicon* of Hugh of St. Victor (c. 1091–1141).

And he adapted some observations found in the *Conciliator of Differences between Philosophers and Physicians* by Pietro d'Abano of Padua (c. 1246–1315). Building on such foundations, Petrarch's adversarial relations with the medical profession were perforce heightened by the infirmities of his later years; and his continued animosity is expressed in several of his *Seniles*, especially in Book XII, which includes two epistles (1–2) addressed to the noted Paduan physician and scientist Giovanni Dondi (1330–89).[2]

Petrarch's accusations center on two themes. First, there is the alleged venality of physicians, who kill with impunity while amassing fortunes – a charge already leveled by Pliny the Elder in Book 29 of his *Natural History*. Second, he decries the papal physician's pretensions to eloquence, an art which is superfluous to the medical profession. Indeed, the physician's writings reveal a shocking ignorance of poetry and rhetoric, liberal arts which, according to Petrarch, are in fact far superior to the mechanical art practiced by doctors.

After impugning the physician's ignorance of Latin literature in Book 1, Petrarch mocks the little book that his adversary has scribbled. In Book 2, Petrarch describes how he is filled with anger when he reads the doctor's boast: "I am a physician . . . Consequently, I am a philosopher" (*Contra medicum* II.52). Not content with trespassing into philosophy, the physician further claims that he can cure men's souls as well as their bodies – as if he had mastered rhetoric as well as medicine! Petrarch berates him for this ignorant pretension, while making no such claims for himself: he is neither a physician, a philosopher, nor a dialectician. Does his foe fancy himself a philosopher because he has the pallor of one closeted in his contemplative studies? Petrarch attributes this unhealthy complexion instead to the filthy urine and excrement the physician examines daily. In the virulent conclusion of Book 2 (99–100), Petrarch "explains" the reasons for his adversary's habitual pallor:

> You move in dark, livid, fetid, and pallid places. You rummage around in sloshing chamber-pots. You examine the urine of the sick. You think about gold. Is it any wonder if in the midst of pallid, dark, and sallow places you yourself become pallid, dark, and sallow? If the wisest patriarch's flock changed color when it was exposed to mottled branches [Genesis 30: 32–39], is it strange that the same thing happens to you? You're waiting for me to say that your color comes from gold. No, it comes from what you are exposed to. I have spoken at great length, and would rather have been silent. But the subject demands its true name which may be tolerated here a single time – a name which is often found in the Holy Scriptures. I say that your color, smell and taste come from the stuff to which you are exposed – shit.

After the *ad hominem* opprobrium that concludes Book 2, Petrarch turns in Book 3 to the world of his beloved poets, whom the physician has assailed. The defense of poetry that follows is one of the most powerful statements of Petrarchan Humanism, and it derives its power in part from its rhetorical vehemence. But it also invokes the Church Father whom Petrarch revered above all others, Augustine, who in his *City of God* (18.14) countenances "theological poets" like Orpheus. In his peroration, Petrarch demolishes the physician's conceited subordination of all the arts to medicine, which he condemns as the ludicrous apotheosis of a mechanical art.

In Book 4, Petrarch turns to the sphere of personal ethics by replying to attacks on his solitary way of life. Balancing praise and blame, the Humanist celebrates the freedom and integrity of his rural studies, and vilifies the sordid and venal lifestyle of this urban quack. Since antiquity, philosophers and holy men have chosen the salubrious tranquility of solitude, whereas cities – like Avignon, he implies – are cesspools of foul and filthy matter. In his peroration, Petrarch begs the reader's indulgence for the violence of his prose, but protests that he is justified in responding to an unmerited attack; and he invokes the literary tradition of invective as the self-defense already employed by great men like Demosthenes, Cicero, and Jerome. For Petrarch, this was only the beginning of a series of invectives that he would compose over the next twenty years.

Invective against a Man of High Rank but No Knowledge or Virtue

While residing in Milan in 1355, Petrarch composed a shorter work with a longer title: *Invectiva contra quendam magni status hominem*. Directed against Cardinal Jean de Caraman, the invective both assails the sanctimonious arrogance of this powerful prelate and defends the Humanist's residence in Milan (1353–61), a city governed by the supposedly "tyrannical" Visconti.[3] Adopting themes common in classical satire, Petrarch argues that the wealthy cardinal is a slave to his position, while he himself retains his freedom at the Milanese court.

Who was this man of high rank? Jean de Caraman d'Euse was born in Cahors in southwest France, like his great-uncle, Pope John XXII (1316–44), the second pontiff of the Avignon papacy. He was created cardinal by Pope Clement VI in the consistory of December 17, 1350, and later became cardinal-deacon of the minor Roman basilica San Giorgio in Velabro. Two years later, he participated in the conclave of 1352, which elected Innocent VI. He died of the plague on August 1, 1361.

Earlier, while Caraman was still a protonotary in Avignon, Petrarch had been on friendly terms with him. But after wealth and family connections had raised him to the cardinalate, the haughty prelate took to defaming Petrarch, accusing him of ignorance and servility. Petrarch laments that Caraman's elevation a decade earlier has now undermined their friendship. Still, let me be ignorant, the Humanist writes, as long as I am virtuous. But the cardinal censures him for consorting with evil men at the court of Milan. Petrarch's residence at the "tyrannical" Visconti court, which was often the target of censure, now occasions an impassioned defense of his personal virtue and independence. As in his other invectives, he contrasts his modest freedom to the slavish venality of his opponent. Whereas Caraman greedily defrauded his Visconti patrons, Petrarch staunchly defended himself against the slurs of the duke's son, Brizio. Power and politics are not his sphere. "While others at dawn seek great palaces," he writes in a Horatian spirit, "I seek my familiar woods and solitude" (*Contra quendam* 35). Confident in his virtue, Petrarch is not afraid of the vain and vainglorious cardinal: "So find someone else to fear you and revere your petty insignia. Nothing can ever induce me, I confess, to worship your great dearth of virtue amid all that gold" (*Contra quendam* 42).

On His Own Ignorance and That of Many Others

From late 1362 to 1367, Petrarch was living in Venice, where he eventually found himself under attack from an unexpected quarter. In 1365, a conversation with four friends turned into an ambush, in which he was mocked for decrying Aristotelianism. All four of his interlocutors enjoyed powerful social standing in Venice: indeed, they represented a sort of cross-section of the Venetian patriciate. Petrarch characteristically omits their names, but they are identified in the marginalia found in two manuscripts. The patrician Leonardo Dandolo (c. 1326–1406) was a son of the doge Andrea Dandolo (1343–54), and played an important role in the Serenissima's military and diplomatic elite. In his invective, Petrarch calls him a soldier, and the least educated of the four. Of Tuscan descent, Tommaso Talenti was a wealthy silk merchant and notable book collector. Zaccaria Contarini (c. 1320–96), who was descended from a noted patrician family with several doges in its history, studied law in Paris for seven years. On his return, he played a prominent part in the Venetian republic – as legal expert, senator, ambassador, and military commander. Born in Reggio Emilia, Guido da Bagnolo (c. 1320–70) studied medicine in Bologna, and became the personal physician and advisor to King Peter I of Cyprus. In this service, Guido took part in diplomatic missions to northern Italy, Rome, Avignon, and Venice.

In response to the attack of these "friends," Petrarch composed what is not strictly an invective, but rather an ironic "apology" for his own ignorance, albeit an apology that includes lengthy polemical passages. He wrote the first draft in 1367, revised it over the next two years, and dedicated it to Donato Albanzani in a letter of January 13, 1371.[4] The work pits the pagan learning of Aristotelianism against Petrarch's Humanism, which countenances the reading of classical authors as long as they are morally edifying. The Humanist grants that both Aristotle and his beloved Cicero were great men, but with Pauline severity he denounces them as pagan authors incapable of knowing Christ. Despite its elements of invective, Petrarch's *De ignorantia* offers an intellectual autobiography and a cultural manifesto that shaped the course of Italian Renaissance Humanism.

The historical context of the debate nevertheless remains unclear. Why did four Venetians, with successful secular careers, take up the cudgel for Aristotle and the sciences? Though none of them was strictly an academic, the physician Guido da Bagnolo may have resented the object of Petrarch's invectives *Contra medicum*; and in his will, Tommaso Talenti funded the first Venetian school of philosophy in logic (1408).

From the outset, Petrarch portrays himself as an innocent victim of envy, too old and poor to merit attention. All the same, his literary fame and the favor shown him by popes and potentates have provoked the attack of his wealthier friends, who decry his "ignorance." At this point, Petrarch offers the reader a summary autobiography not unlike the one composed in his unfinished "Letter to Posterity" (*Sen.* XVIII.1).

The immediate provocation for the attack lay in Petrarch's dismissal of their constant appeals to the authority of Aristotle. He is forced to defend himself against "these scribes, who consider themselves most learned, not in the law of Moses and Christ, but in that of Aristotle" (*De ignorantia* 19). From this opening sally, the embattled scholar gradually develops a program of Christian Humanism, endorsing the example of Augustine and Jerome. For Petrarch, the natural sciences and rigorous dialectics of the universities are useless disciplines; and he finds intolerable their indiscriminate exaltation of Aristotle. Yet for all his love of the ethical writings of Cicero, after lauding the providential cosmology expressed in *On the Nature of the Gods*, he erupts with indignation, and condemns the great Roman orator for espousing polytheism. In the discussion of the universe that follows, Petrarch condemns the Aristotelian assertion of the world's eternity, which openly contradicts the biblical account of the Creation.

Turning now to the human sphere, Petrarch denounces the ethical writings of Aristotle (so beloved in Paris, he sneers) as incapable of moving the reader to moral betterment. Far preferable are the writings of the Romans, whose eloquence moves us to embrace virtue: witness Cicero's dialogue *Hortensius* (now lost), which encouraged Augustine in his search for truth.

And among the Greeks, Plato is superior to Aristotle, as the judgment of many philosophers and Church Fathers confirms. But envy has inspired carping criticism since antiquity: Caligula sought to banish Virgil and Livy from Roman libraries, and men as learned as Cicero and Sallust, or Seneca and Quintilian, exchanged invectives. In the end, Petrarch can only appeal to posterity to judge him, and beg his friends for greater tolerance and compassion.

Invective against a Detractor of Italy

The "Babylonian captivity" of the Avignonese papacy (1305–78) – a crisis contemporary with the Humanist's life – had long troubled Petrarch: witness the denunciations of his epistles in *Sine nomine*. To this end, he wrote a letter – his *Seniles* VII.1, dated June 29, 1366 – to Urban V (Guillaume de Grimoard, 1310–70), urging him to return to Rome. Petrarch's letter provoked staunch opposition in France and the Curia. The French king, Charles V, sent the eminent jurist Ancel Choquart to dissuade the pope; but nevertheless Urban V left Avignon on April 30, 1367 and took ship at Marseilles. (The pope's decision to return to Rome in 1366, largely to stabilize the situation in Italy, was probably reinforced by Petrarch's letter.) After spending three months in Viterbo, while repairs were being made to the papal palace in Rome, he arrived in the Eternal City in October. During the journey, French members of the papal court continued to pressure Urban to change his mind. Hearing this in Venice, Petrarch wrote another missive to the pope, his *Seniles* IX.1, which he probably sent in the spring of 1368. (Significantly, Petrarch placed his two letters to Urban at the beginnings of Books VII and IX of his *Seniles*.) Evidently, this letter soon circulated and aroused a further reaction: on January 2, 1369 Coluccio Salutati – the future chancellor of Florence, then in the papal service – warned Petrarch of the mounting anti-Italian slanders of the French cardinals.

Around this time, the Paris-trained cleric and theologian Jean de Hesdin (c. 1320–1400) composed a tract denouncing Rome as a corrupt city and vaunting the superiority of France as the ideal seat of the papacy. At first he hesitated in publishing it, perhaps because in 1370 the pope announced his decision to return to Avignon. (In the event, Urban reached the city in September of that year, but died a month later.) It was only in January 1373 that the papal nuncio Uguccione da Thiene brought Petrarch a copy of Hesdin's tract. The response was swift and violent: Petrarch's invective was completed by March of the same year.

Jean de Hesdin was born in the French Artois, and became a friar in the Order of Hospitalers of St. John of Jerusalem. After finishing his studies, he moved to Paris, where he was appointed professor of theology, and eventually dean of the faculty of theology at the Sorbonne. Troubled by the plans of Pope Urban V to return to Rome, Hesdin wrote a passionate denunciation of the former Holy City, using the form of a thematic sermon – a set of rhetorical variations on a Scriptural text. For his treatise, Hesdin chose the verse that introduces the story of the Good Samaritan: "A certain man went down from Jerusalem to Jericho and fell among thieves" (Luke 10:30). The provocation of this citation is immediately clear, since it suggests that the pope had left the holy city of Avignon for the treacherous society of Rome, which threatened to despoil him.

As an Italian and a passionate student of Roman history, Petrarch could not resist confuting the friar's treatise. The systematic refutation of Hesdin's tract in Petrarch's last invective (*Contra eum*) points the way toward the polemical exchanges of the Quattrocento, in which Humanists confuted the texts of their opponents passage by passage, as in Lorenzo Valla's declamation on the Donation of Constantine. Against the public denunciations of Rome, Petrarch offers a lively defense of the city's ancient glory and of learned Romans like Cicero and Varro. Indeed, in describing the Roman consulship of Cola di Rienzo, Petrarch employs the impassioned tones of a patriot and prophet:

> If only omnipotent God would grant peace and brotherly harmony to her sons – her oldest sons, I mean – how quickly and easily Rome would reduce the rebellious barbarians to their ancient yoke, aided as of old by Italian forces! If this was unclear before, it recently took shape when one man – a person of obscure origin, without wealth, and possessing (as events showed) more courage than constancy – dared to support the state on his weak shoulders and to proclaim the defense of the tottering empire. How suddenly all of Italy was aroused! What great terror and rumors, inspired by the name of Rome, spread to the ends of the earth! (22–23)

In this work, Petrarch adopts some of the same strategies that characterize his earlier invectives. He never names his adversary, but ridicules his writing as inept and unfair. And he rails against the French, calling them Gauls, as if to invoke their barbarity and hostility to Rome. Latin *gallus* also means "rooster," and Petrarch repeatedly complains of his adversary's "squawking": "Now let us hear our Gallic rooster, or more truly, our raven, who has blackened his white feathers with dark lies and learned to hail Caesar and Antony. Let us hear him croaking, I say, and repeating his madness in hoarse squawks" (40).

Petrarch now begins a point-by-point refutation of Hesdin's tract, each argument of which he finds wrongheaded and offensive. As in the other invectives, Petrarch here balances his sharp critique with assertions of more positive values, insisting on the nobility and importance of Rome in antiquity: by contrast to Roman virtues, the "Gauls" abound in vices such as gluttony and drunkenness. Stressing the central role of Rome in the growth of the Church, Petrarch notes with pride that Pope Urban V praised his letters on the return of the papacy to Rome; and he compares Hesdin to the Pharisees who doubted Christ. What's more, Hesdin borrows disparaging remarks about Rome from Bernard of Clairvaux's treatise *On Consideration*, and in a powerful digression Petrarch attacks the famous twelfth-century mystic, later made a saint, for his errors. As Petrarch notes, Bernard wrote his treatise early in life, apparently motivated by hatred of the Curia; but his youthful views are clearly contradicted by the praise of Rome expressed by Ambrose and Jerome, two Doctors of the Church. To Bernard's charges that the Romans were shameless in asking favors and ungrateful in accepting them, Petrarch counters with examples of Roman magnanimity recorded by Latin historians. After refuting Bernard, Petrarch mounts another attack against "Gallia" (Gaul), noting that it was a place of exile for disgraced Romans and that one prominent Gaul was Pontius Pilate!

At length, Petrarch turns to Hesdin's beloved citadel of Scholastic culture, Paris, which he denigrates with particular vehemence. If the Sorbonne had any luster, it was due to Italians like Peter Lombard, Thomas Aquinas, Bonaventure of Bagnoregio, and Giles of Rome! Far from being the "rose of the world and balsam of the globe" – to quote Hesdin – Paris for Petrarch is a "fetid balsam, and malodorous rose," second only to Avignon. Next, in a further assertion of his intellectual values, Petrarch dismisses Hesdin's preference for Greek philosophy over Roman ethics. As in *De ignorantia*, he berates the Scholastic's fascination with Greek texts that he scarcely understands, and ridicules him for dismissing the great writers of Rome: Cicero, Varro, and Seneca. And finally, in his peroration Petrarch returns to Roman history, the fertile field of culture that he has so thoroughly mastered, in order to rebut the vain and vapid claims of his adversary. It is hardly surprising that Petrarch could respond so richly and eloquently when he was challenged on territory that he had carefully surveyed for so many years.

After his death, Petrarch's invectives enjoyed considerable fortune, especially *Contra medicum*, which was translated into Italian by Domenico Silvestri in the 1380s, and included in Petrarchan manuscripts and early printed editions from 1496. Taken as a group, the four invectives formulate the Humanist's personal response to attacks from various quarters, offering a coherent program of cultural values that would shape the course of Italian Humanism. At the same time, their polemics furnished a valuable model for combative Quattrocento Humanists like Poggio Bracciolini and Lorenzo Valla, who soon brandished many of the rhetorical weapons forged by Petrarch.

NOTES

1 On the use of Jerome and his contemporaries, see David Marsh, "Petrarch and Jerome," *Memoirs of the American Academy in Rome* 49 (2004): 85–98.

2 Bartolo Martinelli, "Il Petrarca e la medicina," in Francesco Petrarca, *Invective contra medicum*, ed. Pier Giorgio Ricci (Rome: Edizioni di Storia e Letteratura, 1978), 205–249; Nancy Struever, "Petrarch's *Invective Contra Medicum*: An Early Confrontation of Rhetoric and Medicine," *MLN* 108 (1993): 659–679.

3 When Petrarch's move was criticized by Boccaccio and other Tuscan friends, he replied in a pair of letters addressed to Francesco Nelli (*Fam.* XVI.11–12).

4 Petrarch's revisions are described by James Hankins in Francesco Petrarca, *Invectives*, ed. and trans. David Marsh (Cambridge, MA: Harvard University Press, 2003), 476–478.

PART V

Petrarch's afterlife

14

TIMOTHY KIRCHER

Petrarch and the Humanists

Petrarch's influence on Renaissance Humanism seems undeniable. If the research of Ronald Witt has questioned his title as the "father of Humanism," his import remains enormous. Yet it is also, we shall see, elusive and unpredictable. In defining the scope of Petrarch's legacy for later Humanists, we first examine the moments when those Humanists cited his life and works. On this basis, we can chart the changes in the way they articulated his importance. Subsequently, we explore how various aspects of Petrarch's work, both formal and conceptual, influenced their studies, even when he goes unmentioned. These avenues of inquiry will allow us to review assessments by Humanists and modern scholars, and to trace out, in conclusion, more general patterns in these judgments.

Throughout this inquiry, we face certain ineluctable challenges. First of all, Renaissance Humanists, at any given time, were no more monolithic in their writings than Petrarch himself in his own oeuvre. It would be in the spirit of his paradoxical way of thinking to call Humanists members of a splintered movement, a *res publica* of writers and thinkers, of which contrariety was a salient characteristic. Furthermore, Petrarch actively shaped his own legacy through shifting self-proclamations, from the *Collatio laureationis* of 1341 to the incomplete "Letter to Posterity" (*Sen.* XVIII.1). Contributing to the challenges are the linguistic and disciplinary categories imposed by the Humanists themselves, and by modern scholarship. Petrarch contributed to these categories, for example in rigid distinctions between Latin and vernacular expression, or between prose and verse, even as the themes of his Humanism traversed these boundaries. The setting of various boundaries and two-fold binaries affected the subsequent appreciation of his life and work. In the modern era, historians have tended to investigate his Latin prose as his "Humanist" compositions, yielding to Italianists the field of Tuscan verse. His Latin verse, the basis for his laurel coronation in 1341, has received less attention.

While bearing these challenges in mind, we may divide the overt recognition of Petrarch's Humanism into three phases. The first period lasted till about 1400, through the generation after Petrarch; the second phase through the mid-Quattrocento; and the third phase, which helped shape Bembo's linguistic program, into the sixteenth century. While my remarks pertain primarily to Humanism on the Italian peninsula, there are also noteworthy developments of Petrarch's *fortuna* beyond the Alps, illustrating the pan-Latinity of the period.

For the first period, Boccaccio (1313–75), Filippo Villani (c. 1330–c. 1405), and Coluccio Salutati (1331–1406) offer the richest biographical testimony. Boccaccio began composing his *Life of Petrarch* most likely in the 1340s, while Petrarch was still very much alive.[1] As the coronation in Rome is the apex of his treatment, it appears to respond to the literary precedents that Petrarch himself set forth in the *Collatio laureationis*. Commenting briefly on Petrarch's vernacular verse, Boccaccio emphasizes the power of the Muses on his subject's writing and study. He mentions Petrarch's friends and patrons, but focuses on the classical poets and writers with whom he, by this account, found the strongest kinship. Thus, the *Africa* elicits comparison to Homer's epics, the *Secretum* to Cicero's dialogues, the pastoral poetry to the eclogues of Virgil, and even Petrarch's lost comedy, the *Filostrato's Philology*, to the plays of Terence. In Boccaccio's later works, the *Genealogy of the Pagan Gods* and the *Expositions on Dante's Comedy*, he praises time and again Petrarch's Latin writings and his poetics.

Villani's late-Trecento biography of Petrarch is found in *The Origins of the City of Florence and Its Famous Citizens*, a work edited by Salutati. The biography includes more titles than Boccaccio's *Life*, elaborating various eulogies for Petrarch, especially that of Pietro da Castelletto. Almost all the Latin works are cited, except his comedy. As for the Tuscan verses, Villani is more expansive: "they flow with such sweetness that even the gravest elders cannot refrain from reciting them."[2] Despite their differences, Boccaccio and Villani both value Petrarch as a teacher and poet. He is an exemplary Florentine, a model of erudition as well as moral conduct. For Boccaccio, Petrarch's coronation sealed the return of the "fortunate era and rule of Saturn that had lapsed long ago."[3] For Villani, Petrarch equaled or exceeded the ancients with his eloquence. The work of Salutati not only sums up this appreciation, but also confronts the new, more reserved evaluations of the next generation of Humanists.

In the months following Petrarch's death in 1374, Salutati praised the life and work of "that divine man."[4] His eloquence, both in prose and in meter, surpasses that of Cicero and Virgil. Salutati strove to collect and edit Petrarch's manuscripts, and his ranking of Petrarch's writings above Cicero's prose and Virgil's poetry trumps Petrarch's more modest self-assessment in his last letter to Boccaccio (*Sen.* XVII.2, dated April 1373). Thirty years later, however, Salutati found it necessary to defend Petrarch's importance to the Humanist avant-garde. This younger generation was more devoted to the stylistic models of Cicero and Quintilian, and was also engaged in the learning of classical Greek, a revival anticipated by Petrarch and established by Salutati himself, who in 1396 invited the Byzantine Manuel Chrysoloras to Florence.

Among this generation, it appears that Poggio Bracciolini (1380–1459) first challenged Petrarch's role as exemplary Humanist, though his letters to Salutati on this topic are now lost. In 1405, Salutati initially responded to Poggio's charges that Petrarch committed errors in Latin style (*vetustas*). True oratory, the elderly chancellor asserts, depends on wisdom (*sapientia*); and as Petrarch possessed higher, Christian wisdom, so too did his oratory outshine that of the pagan ancients. These ancients may have been more expert in the traditional liberal arts, including rhetoric, but they erred in the fields of advanced learning: natural science, moral philosophy, metaphysics, and theology. Petrarch, whatever his stylistic shortcomings, was superior to both Virgil and Cicero "in the learning and knowledge of the truth."[5]

Salutati thus reassessed Petrarch's abilities, admitting that pagan authors were, as a rule, more eloquent than contemporary writers, Petrarch included. He states in a second letter to Poggio, written shortly before his death, that he would now hesitate to compare Petrarch with Cicero "in oratorical skill, not to mention written prose eloquence."[6] Salutati's defense of Petrarch was situational, on the grounds that standards of language inevitably change with the times. But since Salutati valued prose eloquence as superior to metrical skill, the way was open for the avant-garde to re-evaluate Petrarch's primacy.[7] To these Humanists, he no longer ranked first in ability, but rather chronologically as the *praeceptor* of the classical revival. In advocating this reassessment, the Humanist avant-garde had to contend not only with Salutati, but also with other parties that viewed these Humanists' pursuit of *vetustas* either as overly fussy or as overly secular. Yet Salutati himself had reinforced genre distinctions that the younger Humanists employed for their own mission: prose versus poetry; secular versus Christian; and Latin classicism versus scholastic or vernacular language. As did many other Humanists, Salutati largely overlooked Petrarch's Tuscan lyrics, except to set them in passing beside Dante's verse.[8]

Pier Paolo Vergerio (1370–c. 1445), another student of Salutati, composed a brief biography of Petrarch around 1400, which adapts these categories to diminish Petrarch's accomplishment. Petrarch's main talents were in moral philosophy and poetry, he writes, consciously echoing the "Letter to Posterity" (*Sen.* XVIII.1). Vergerio lists eighteen volumes of Petrarch's works, twelve in Latin prose, four in Latin meter, and two, the *RVF* and the *Triumphi*, in the vernacular. While the biography stands under the shadow of Salutati, it also indicates the manner in which other Humanists would define Petrarch's status more as a progenitor than as an exemplar of the Humanist movement: "He was of bright and powerful eloquence, as the style of his books indicate, and (to speak truthfully) the only one who called back to our own times the rhetorical skill [dicendi facultatem] that was in exile for so many centuries and nearly passed into obscurity [pene incognitam]."[9]

At the end of his *Dialogi* (c. 1405), dedicated to Vergerio, Leonardo Bruni (1370–1444) has his interlocutor Niccolò Niccoli echo this sentiment: Petrarch "restored humanistic studies, which had been extinguished, and opened the way for us to be able to learn."[10] Niccoli expresses this praise in the second part of the dialogues, after he has been led to recant an earlier indictment of Petrarch's worth. In effect, these dialogues capture the ambivalence the younger Humanists felt toward Petrarch, even inserting Salutati into the work as the one soliciting Niccoli's views. During the opening discussion, Niccoli had lamented the "great shipwreck of learning" since antiquity, which Petrarch had done little to remedy. The *Africa*, which was to ground Petrarch's fame, turned out to be, in the Horation phrase, a "ridiculous mouse." As for his other writings, "in his bucolics there is nothing that smacks of the pastoral or sylvan, and in his orations nothing that does not greatly desire the art of rhetoric." If Niccoli moves in the second part of the *Dialogi* from blaming to praising Petrarch, a good deal of the later eulogy is indirect, merely recounting what Petrarch's Paduan friends have told him. Niccoli's summation confirms, with a deep ambiguity noted by more than one critic, Salutati's assessment in the letter to Poggio: "I far prefer an oration of Petrarch to all the epistles of Virgil, and the poems of Petrarch to all the poems of Cicero."[11]

Some decades later, the appraisals became more nuanced. Ambrogio Traversari (1386–1439), undertaking monastic visitations in the Veneto, diverged from his route to visit Petrarch's tomb in Arquà and pronounced him "the illustrious and learned person of our time, to whom we generally owe the awakening [excitata] of humanistic studies."[12] Other Humanists still held Petrarch at a respectful distance, while using the same figure of speech. Sicco Polenton (1375–1447) included a biography of Petrarch in his *Eighteen Books of Famous Latin Authors*. Petrarch, he writes, was "initiator and author in arousing [excitandi] the studies both of poetry and all eloquence, so that these things, long neglected as if sound asleep [quasi sopita], returned at last to human knowledge and use."[13] If Petrarch was not the equal of Virgil and Cicero, this only confirms the adage of Cicero's *Brutus* (71) that nothing is both discovered and perfected at the same time. Poggio, in his 1440 dialogue *The Unhappiness of Princes*, has Niccoli commend Petrarch in words close to those of Traversari and Polenton: it was due to Petrarch's talent that "our humanistic studies, which had lain sound asleep [sopita] for many centuries, were now awakened [excitata], so that they might almost recover their earlier dignity and strength."[14] And to Flavio Biondo (1392–1463), composing his *Italy Illuminated* around 1450, Petrarch was "the first of all" who "truly taste[d] the flavor of Latin letters." Possessing "great talent and greater diligence, he began to arouse [excitare coepit] poetry and eloquence." His shortcomings in Ciceronean eloquence, Biondo adds, were due to the absence of Cicero's writings, which Biondo's contemporaries now possess.[15]

While these judgments largely tend to diminish Petrarch's importance, his legacy proved resilient. This was initially due to the Florentine Humanists, who felt charged with promoting the history and virtue of their city-state. In 1436, as Florentine chancellor, Bruni completed vernacular biographies of Dante and Petrarch, contrasting the two men's parallel lives in the vein of Plutarch. Dante, being more politically active, garners greater esteem than the contemplative Petrarch. But Petrarch was the first who "called back to the light of knowledge sublime studies long fallen and ignored" and "the classical grace of expression lost and extinguished."[16] To be sure, the progressive qualifications are in place: the knowledge has only increased since Petrarch's time, and his eloquence was imperfect. Yet the most telling aspect of the biography may be an omission: Bruni does not list Petrarch's works "because they are well-known."[17]

Around the same time as Bruni's work, Matteo Palmieri (1406–75) was composing his *On Civil Life*. These vernacular dialogues adapt Ciceronean moral philosophy to contemporary Florentine affairs. Explicitly praising Bruni's Latin eloquence, he sees his own Tuscan effort as a more modest expedient. In so doing, he rehabilitates the vernacular works of Petrarch. For Petrarch's poetry has moral suasion, if only in a more indirect way than prose precepts. Like Dante, Petrarch used "the veil of poetic language," which "gives more delight than benefit." While he "composed many things in the *volgare* that were moral . . . and expressed most fittingly," for Palmieri their figurative brevity does not help those who do not have the ability to understand their less obvious meaning.[18]

The most comprehensive biography of this period is that by Giannozzo Manetti (1396–1459) in his *Lives of Three Illustrious Florentine Poets* (1440), which sets Petrarch between Dante and Boccaccio. Manetti consciously builds upon the earlier efforts of Boccaccio, Villani, and Bruni, and relies also on Petrarch's epistolary collections. He cites Petrarch's efforts to revive Greek learning, as well as his Latin and vernacular compositions. To Manetti, Petrarch excelled in both Latin prose and verse, surpassing Dante in this regard. But if Petrarch "brought back to light . . . correctness and good taste in Latin diction," Dante's political engagement and deeper knowledge of mathematics, philosophy, and theology earn him pride of place.[19]

In assessing Petrarch's legacy, the Florentine civic Humanists therefore maintain the qualitative hierarchies of prose over poetry, Latin over the vernacular, and active political engagement over contemplative retirement. Other Quattrocento Humanists, however, challenged these hierarchies, locating Petrarch's merit in the vernacular verse that he composed in his *otium* at Vaucluse and elsewhere. Francesco Filelfo (1398–1481) wrote a series of remarks on the *RVF* for the Visconti around 1446. The vernacular commentary develops two contrasting points of emphasis. It rejects the idea of Laura as an allegorical figure, stressing instead – often scathingly – Petrarch's genuine erotic involvement with a real woman; and it notes at the same time the allusions and literary elegance of his verse. Filelfo reads the lyric sequence as a moral progression aided by grace, in which reason gains mastery over the emotions. The Sienese Pope Pius II (Aeneas Sylvius Piccolomini, 1405–64) declares in his *Commentaries* (c. 1460) that Petrarch might have been without equal "were his Latin works as fine as those he wrote in Tuscan."[20] Cristoforo Landino (1424–98), who held the chair in rhetoric and poetry at the Florentine *studio* after 1458, lectured on the *RVF*, most likely in the late 1460s. He praises Petrarch's *rime* for its invention, judiciousness, and ornament of speech. These verses became authorities for his commentary on Dante's *Commedia*, and his own Latin lyrics refer more often to Petrarch's vernacular meter than to his *Africa*. This influence of the *rime* also appears in the writings of Angelo Poliziano (1454–94): his *Stanze* allude a number of times to the *Rime sparse*, and both the Latin "Nutricia," from his *Sylvae*, and the bilingual exercises *Latini* cite the *Triumphi*.

The Italian Humanist readings of Petrarch would continue to be affected by the canon of Ciceronian Latinity well into the Cinquecento. Paolo Cortesi (1465–1510) critiques Petrarch's Latin accomplishments in the 1490–91 *Dialogue on Learned Men*: "His manner of speech is not Latin and sometimes worse [horridior]." Nonetheless, he was "the first to bring the study of eloquence back to light." And Cortesi too claims that Petrarch's vernacular verse demonstrates the potential of his talent, if only the "light and splendor of Latinity" had informed his expression.[21] The writings of Paolo Giovio (1483–1552) implicitly complete this turn: his 1546 *Elogia* praises Petrarch for bringing the Tuscan dialect "to the full maturity" of its eloquence; and in the second of the *Ischian* dialogues (c. 1530), he cites Petrarch, along with Dante and Boccaccio, for his "talent and hard work" in the vernacular, since shortly "writing in Tuscan will entirely take the place of Latin in everyday use."[22] He thus follows the influential *Writings on the Vernacular Language* (1525) of his colleague Pietro Bembo on the *questione della lingua*.

If, in Italy, Petrarch's Latin diction came under critical review, perhaps affecting the copying and publication of his work, editions and translations of his writings appeared in Spain, France, and throughout the Empire. Petrarch had befriended the imperial chancellor Johann von Neumarkt (Jan ze Středy, c. 1310–80, based in Prague), who fostered this diffusion; by the mid-fifteenth century, the *De remediis*, as well as the Griselda novella, had been translated into German. Sebastian Brandt (1457–1521) helped publish the *Opere latine* in Basel in 1496, which served as the basis for the 1501–03 Aldine edition. Rudolf Agricola (1444–85), while residing in Pavia, wrote an epideictic biography on the centennial of Petrarch's death. Critical for his legacy was the assessment of Erasmus (1466–1536), who, in his 1528 dialogue *Ciceronianus*, counters the Quattrocento canon by claiming that Petrarch not only brought eloquence again into flower, but also was superior to Biondo in his use of Latin. Members of Erasmus's circle promoted Petrarch's writings, including the Humanist publisher Aldo Manuzio (1449–1515), as well as Georg Spalatin (1484–1545), secretary to Frederick of Saxony and friend of Luther, who completed a translation of the *De remediis* in 1521.

The overt reception of Petrarch's writings shows us obvious impressions of his work. The Humanist response to Petrarch did not end there, however, gifted as Humanists were in textual imitation and emulation. Scholars have identified both thematic and formal categories for Petrarch's oeuvre, which produced notable affects upon later Humanism. Several categories – the revival of classical learning, the *studia humanitatis*, a renewed emphasis on rhetoric, compositions in both Latin and the vernacular – are evident in the foregoing discussion. Additional categories of influence bear mentioning:

> *Human dignity:* Petrarch wrote optimistically about human potential, a theme that was embellished or countered in the treatises of Manetti and Poggio, for example. According to this line of inquiry, typified by Charles Trinkaus,[23] Petrarch founded a new conception of the human capacity for achievement, whereby a person became an agent of his or her own destiny, and more greatly engaged in contemporary issues.
>
> *Secularism:* Petrarch's opposition to scholastic theology, as well as his independent search for moral verities, promoted a secular orientation, a turning toward assessing ethics, and in general human affairs, without resorting to theological conventions. According to Riccardo Fubini, this orientation of a "secret Petrarch," in conflict with his public portrait, paved the way for the cultural program of Poggio, Bruni, and Lorenzo Valla (1406–57).[24] Along with this secularism, as Paul Oskar Kristeller has argued, one could include Petrarch's promotion of Stoic

moral ideas, in which human reason was called on to master unruly emotions.[25]

Historical perspective: Petrarch heightened the Humanist sensibility to historical change and to one's immediate time and place. As Theodor E. Mommsen, Ronald Witt, and others have argued, this sensibility, fostered particularly by Petrarch's letters to the ancients (*Fam.* XXIV), bore fruit in the way later Humanists collected their own letters and composed their autobiographies and historical works.[26]

Defense of pagan literature: According to August Buck, David Robey, and others, Petrarch's validation of pagan literature, for example in his *Contra medicum*, was adapted by succeeding generations in the face of ecclesiastical criticism.[27] Humanist opinions differed over whether classical poets were divinely inspired, yet Petrarch's comments sanctioned their reading as morally edifying; a reading illustrated, for example, in Valla's *Apologia* to Eugenius IV.

Dialogue, rhetoric, and epistemology: Petrarch's writings have been analyzed, by Jerrold Seigel for example, for the way they distinguish between rhetoric and philosophy.[28] They have also been examined, by Nancy Struever and Christopher Celenza, for their use of dialogue as a medium for identifying the truth: a medium in which exchanging ideas and finding consensus are critical features.[29] In this respect, as various scholars have shown (including David Marsh, Francesco Tateo, and Timothy Kircher), Quattrocento dialogues and even polemics have roots in the Trecento as well as in the classical period.[30]

Moral philosophy: As the previous category indicates, Humanists were engaged in writing about philosophy and leading philosophical lives; in living well in an ethical sense. Humanist conceptions of the power of virtue and the contingencies of human existence (*casus, fortuna*) could look to Petrarch's *summa*, the *De remediis*, and the conflict between virtue and fortune was echoed in the writings of Leon Battista Alberti, Palmieri, Poggio, Lapo Castiglionchio the Younger, and Machiavelli. In another vein, Laura Cereta (1469–99) uses Petrarch's allegory in *Fam.* IV.1 as a matrix for the moral journeys she transcribes in her letters.[31]

Each of these categories draws upon disciplines promoted by Petrarch himself: classical philology, historical inquiry, moral philosophy, poetry, and rhetoric. Each can be based, therefore, on facets of Petrarch's expression, as these facets were burnished in the writings of succeeding Humanists.

These divergent approaches address the complexity of Petrarch's expression by prioritizing more salient features of his thinking according to theme, genre, or discipline. Yet a basic problem with this methodology becomes apparent. Each effort at ranking or categorization may be countered by an alternative. With regard to human dignity, for example, one could cite Petrarch's melancholic thoughts on human frailty and impotence; to secular orientation, one might consider his religious writings and devotion to St. Augustine; to historical perspective, his philosophical assessments of the human condition regardless of time or place. We may ask whether these disciplinary efforts fully or fundamentally capture Petrarch's importance for the Humanist movement, or whether they embrace only a partial aspect of his legacy. We come to a pause.

Rather than competing or conflicting categorical distinctions, we might therefore ponder how Petrarch's work thinks about the presence of conflict in itself. The oscillations among these alternatives may contain Petrarch's greatest influence for the Humanism that followed. His work moves between expressions of dignity and misery, secular and spiritual concerns, paganism and Christianity, past and present, doubt and certainty, movement and rest. He was fond of quoting the Heraclitean dicta, "everything exists by strife" and "in the same river we step and do not step."[32] These oscillations reveal Petrarch's feeling for time and change. He appreciated time not primarily as a concept or framework for historical study, but rather as a temporal, existential condition that underlay his observations.

This temporal sensibility inflects his poetry as well as his letters, and while escaping explicit comment by later Humanists, it informed their work. Bruni's *Dialogi* pivots on Niccoli's change of heart from one day to the next, and, in general, later Humanist dialogue offers the ability to shift focus and point of view, as exemplified by the three-day unfolding of perspectives in the *Secretum*. Alberti plumbs this potential most profoundly in his vernacular dialogues *On the Family*, *Theogenius*, and *Refuges from Hardships*. The timing and rhythm of these dialogues permit his various interlocutors – Lionardo, Teogenio, and Niccola de' Medici, for example – to revise their earlier conclusions. What an interlocutor posits as truth, therefore, is qualified by his human, and therefore temporal, status in the dialogue. And as the worth of his assertions depends on his character at a particular historical moment, so too do his listeners and readers filter their appreciation of his statements via their various, and variable, personalities.

Temporality underlays the movement not only of Petrarch's verses, but also of his epistolary collections. Petrarch himself would serve, in the letters of Poggio, as an index for the Quattrocento Humanist's changes in viewpoint. If Poggio had contested Petrarch's importance with Salutati in 1405, twenty years later he asked Niccoli to procure any books of Petrarch that might be for sale; he also commended Petrarch's prudent withdrawal from public life and his *De vita*. In 1455, a few years before his death, he wrote a letter cataloging the most eloquent writers of the time and ranked Petrarch in first position before Salutati, Bruni, and Niccoli, while modestly setting himself inferior to them all.

Due, therefore, in no small measure to Petrarch's innovations, Humanist expression reponds to the flux of human existence; it stands forth in an awareness of a given time and place. Petrarch's devotion to Laura led him to commemorate the anniversaries of their encounter, and thereby, through this commemoration, to observe the passing of time and emotion. A similar attitude toward time's flow marks later Humanist writings with a sense of finitude, mortality, and incompletion. This sense pervades not only the gloomy meditations of Poggio's late work, the *The Misery of the Human Condition*, but even the more playful treatments of the afterlife found in Alberti's *Dinner Pieces*.

Alluding directly to Petrarch's work, Alberti's *Theogenius* adapts an image from the *Secretum*, in which his Teogenio, echoing Petrarch's Augustinus, notices how insects above a river are born and die in a single day, and draws the analogy to human life. This observation, Augustinus notes, is found in Cicero's *Tusculans* (1.39.94), which in turn cites Aristotle's *History of Animals*. While Alberti's dialogue may seem to rely immediately on classical sources, two Petrarchan elements come to the fore, related to the quality of temporal awareness. The first is a sense of timing: in the *Tusculans*, the anecdote appears in the first part of the moral monologue pronounced by Cicero's unnamed speaker, but Augustinus and Teogenio cite it at a later moment, at an instant when they are most in need of persuading their respective interlocutors to reach an ethical decision. The second element is the way in which Teogenio, like Augustinus, emerges as a distinct personality, one not immune from one-sidedness or self-contradiction. Thus, the persona's authority is, as it were, human and transient, and dependent on the rhetorical moment, in which his interlocutor and reader take part. By means of these personae, Humanists challenged their readers to hold the various proclamations of their characters at arm's length, and to entertain the inherent theatricality of philosophical inquiry. A sense of drama did not undermine the pursuit of wisdom, but rather acknowledged that wisdom was more than intellectual knowledge: it entailed volition and emotional readiness for the moment of intellectual insight, as fleeting as it might be.

We may conclude, then, by bringing the Humanist heritage of Petrarch's vernacular and Latin writings into focus. These writings found disparate appreciations among Humanists, according to genre, discipline, and language – categories that Petrarch himself had applied to his own writing and that of the ancients. And the Humanist appraisals would have their own *fortuna*. Stendahl, worrying about his posthumous reputation, remarked that

Petrarch "counted on his Latin poem *Africa* to bring him fame, never dreaming that he would be known for his sonnets."[33] But Petrarch's compositions, no matter their genre or discipline, all bear the stamp of the poet's character, which he was quick to present as the mandatory mediator for his message. The Petrarchan notion that truth is mediated by personality, which changes with time, resonates not only in the dialogues of later Humanists, but also in their letters and dedications. It is also ironically validated by the faint disdain with which they sometimes held their fourteenth-century forerunner. This irony would not have been lost on Petrarch, nor on those Humanists, such as Alberti and Erasmus, who creatively entertained his legacy.

NOTES

1 Giovanni Boccaccio, *Vita di Petrarca*, ed. Gianni Villani (Florence: Salerno, 2004).
2 Angelo Solerti, ed., *Le vite di Dante, Petrarca e Boccaccio scritte fino al secolo decesimosesto* (Milan: Vallardi, 1904–1905), 275–281, quote 279 (unless otherwise noted, all translations from Latin are mine).
3 Boccaccio, *Vita*, 80.
4 Coluccio Salutati, *Epistolario*, ed. Francesco Novati (Rome: Istituto Storico Italiano, 1891–1911), 1:176–187, quote 176.
5 Salutati, *Epistolario*, 4:130–144.
6 Ibid., 4:165.
7 Ibid., 1:338–340.
8 Ibid., 1:183, 4:140.
9 Solerti, *Le vite*, 299.
10 Leonardo Bruni, "The Dialogues," in *The Humanism of Leonardo Bruni: Selected Texts*, eds. and trans. Gordon Griffiths, James Hankins, and David Thompson (Binghamton, NY: Medieval and Renaissance Texts and Studies, 1987), 63–84, quote 83.
11 Ibid., 68, 74, 83.
12 Ambrogio Traversari, *Hodeoporicon: Edizione critica e commento*, ed. S. Iaria, doctoral thesis, Universita' degli Studi di Firenze (2004), 75 (section 122).
13 Solerti, *Le vite*, 326. A vernacular biography attributed by Solerti to Antonio da Tempo (329–338) has now been shown to be that of the Milanese Humanist Pier Candido Decembrio, and most likely written for the Visconti court prior to 1426.
14 Poggio Bracciolini, *De infelicitate principum*, ed. Davide Canfora (Rome: Edizioni di Storia e Letteratura, 1998), 41.
15 Flavio Biondo, *Italia illustrata*, ed. and trans. Catherine J. Castner (Binghamton, NY: Global Academic Publishing, 2005), 1:45–47.
16 Solerti, *Le vite*, 289–290.
17 Ibid., 291.
18 Matteo Palmieri, *Vita civile*, ed. Gino Belloni (Florence: Sansoni, 1982), 6.
19 Giannozzo Manetti, *Biographical Writings*, eds. and trans. Stefano U. Baldassarri and Rolf Bagemihl (Cambridge, MA: Harvard University Press, 2003), 66.

20 Pius II, *Commentaries*, vol. 1, eds. and trans. Margaret Meserve and Marcello Simonetta (Cambridge, MA: Harvard University Press, 2004), 323 (translation slightly revised).

21 Paolo Cortesi, *De hominibus doctis dialogus* (Florence: Apud Bernardum Paperinium, 1734), 7–8.

22 Paolo Giovio, *Elogia virorum literis illustrium* (Basel: Petrus Perna, 1577), 8; *Notable Men and Women of Our Time*, ed. and trans. Kenneth Gouwens (Cambridge, MA: Harvard University Press, 2013), 251.

23 *In Our Image and Likeness. Humanity and Divinity in Italian Humanist Thought*, 2 vols. (Chicago, IL: University of Chicago Press, 1970).

24 Riccardo Fubini, *Humanism and Secularization: From Petrarch to Valla*, trans. Martha King (Durham, NC: Duke University Press, 2003).

25 Paul Oskar Kristeller, "The Moral Thought of Renaissance Humanism," in *Renaissance Thought II: Papers on Humanism and the Arts* (New York: Harper, 1965), 20–68.

26 Theodore E. Mommsen, "Petrarch's Conception of the Dark Ages," *Speculum* 2 (1942): 226–42; Ronald Witt, *"In the Footsteps of the Ancients"*.

27 Auguste Buck, *Italienische Dichtungslehren vom Mittelalter bis zum Ausgang der Renaissance*, vol. 94 in *Beihefte zur Zeitschrift für romanische Philologie* (Tübingen: Max Niemeyer, 1952); David Robey, "Humanist views on the study of poetry in the early Italian Renaissance," in *The Cambridge History of Literary Criticism*, eds. Alastair Minnis and Ian Johnson (Cambridge: Cambridge University Press, 2004), 2:626–647.

28 Jerrold Seigel, *Rhetoric and Philosophy in Renaissance Humanism: The Union of Eloquence and Wisdom: Petrarch to Valla* (Princeton, NJ: Princeton University Press, 1968).

29 Nancy Struever, *Theory as Practice*; Christopher S. Celenza, *The Lost Italian Renaissance: Humanists, Historians, and Latin's Legacy* (Baltimore, MD: Johns Hopkins University Press, 2004).

30 Marsh, *The Quattrocento Dialogue*; Francesco Tateo, "Note su Petrarca e l'umanesimo volgare," *Italianistica* 2 (2004): 179–184 and "L'Alberti fra il Petrarca e il Pontano: La metafora della fortuna," *Albertiana* 10 (2007): 45–67; Timothy Kircher, *Living Well in Renaissance Italy: The Virtues of Humanism and the Irony of Leon Battista Alberti* (Tempe, AZ: Medieval and Renaissance Texts and Studies, 2012).

31 Aileen A. Feng has recently shown how fifteenth-century Humanists also creatively adapted the *rime* in their Latin letters: "In Laura's Shadow: Casting Female Humanists as Petrarchan Beloveds in Quattrocento Letters" in *The Inner Life of Women in Medieval Romance Literature: Grief, Guilt, and Hypocrisy*, eds. Jeff Rider and Jamie Friedman (New York: Palgrave Macmillan, 2011), 223–247.

32 Timothy Kircher, *The Poet's Wisdom: The Humanists, the Church, and the Formation of Philosophy in the Early Renaissance* (Leiden: Brill, 2006), 216–221.

33 Stendahl, *Memoirs of Egotism*, trans. Hannah Josephson and Matthew Josephson (New York: Barnes & Noble, 2009), 64–65.

15

STEFANO JOSSA

Bembo and Italian Petrarchism

Community versus genius?

In his *History of Italian literature* (1871–72), the Italian critic Francesco De Sanctis (1817–83) pronounced a famous condemnation of Renaissance Petrarchism: "Rhymers were as thick as blackberries; from every corner of Italy were springing up sonnets and canzoni, while the ballads, the *rispetti*, the *stornelli*, and the other habitual forms of popular poetry were sinking little by little into [disuse]. It was all the fashion to Petrarchize – as much with women as with men."[1] De Sanctis recognized two main features in this historical and literary process: on the one hand, its diffusion: Petrarchism had spread all over Italy; on the other, its narrowing focus: Petrarchism eliminated all other poetical forms, such as ballads and so on. Diffusion and exclusivity worked together so as to construct an aristocratic community larger than a single city or region, but confined to well-educated and literate people. De Sanctis's condemnation, then, is based on the fact that Petrarchism is a collective phenomenon rather than an expression of individual creativity.

Following in De Sanctis's footsteps, Benedetto Croce, whose aesthetic judgments colored the first half of the twentieth century, wrote that "there were no great poets among the so-called Italian lyric poets of the fifteenth century, and Petrarch had no successor," concluding that "even the best of those lyric poets lacked something."[2]

These lamentations against Petrarchism are informed by the Romantic opposition between genius and technique, as between poetry and artifice. We now see things very differently. Petrarchism can no longer be studied as a list of names, as scholarly historiography has done in the past, but has to be regarded as a collective work, an enterprise of a group of people who were facing the birth of a new society in a transformed world.

Pietro Bembo and the foundation of the model

In a celebrated passage in the second book of his dialogue *Prose della volgar lingua* (*Writings on the Vernacular Language*, 1525), Pietro Bembo (1470–1547), a courtier, editor, poet, and, much later, cardinal, has his interlocutors discuss Dante's supposed primacy over Petrarch: while the argument of Dante's superiority rests on the greatness and vast scope of his subject, Bembo's speakers agree that what makes poetry good is style rather than content. How much better a poet Dante would have been, says his brother Carlo, Bembo's spokesman, had he not wished to appear something more than a poet in his poem; in his ambition to comprehend all things, he did not take sufficient care with his writing. His *Commedia*, therefore, appears like a field of grain full of weeds. In dismissing Dante in favor of Petrarch, Bembo was enunciating the aesthetic principles of classicism: purity, clarity, precision, and harmony. Politeness and friendliness had to prevail over gravity: in Bembo's view, the aim of poetry was to communicate and entertain, to build a community of people sharing the same values and devoted to the same practices. Being at the same time concrete and stylized, Petrarch's language could easily lead to the creation of productive stereotypes, favoring common views and shared habits.

Petrarchism cannot be understood without Bembo's rejection of Dante, the poet of knowledge, for Petrarch, the poet of artifice. Well aware of the potential of that recent invention, the printing press (c. 1439) – which was particularly present in his native Venice – Bembo aimed at enlarging literature's audience, as well as reinforcing its prestige among the arts. Well-defined rules, strictly observed, fostered the perception of literature as a highly cultivated field, and enabled all who mastered them to become poets. A new "democratic aristocracy" was born, where, within the restricted circles of the courtly elites, all were equals. Bembo's purpose was the foundation of a new, more united Italian society in response to the municipal aristocracies of the scattered Italian city-states and in the face of the pressures applied by the European nation-states, especially France and Spain. Petrarch was the means of a socio-political operation beginning with poetry and language and ending with ethics and politics. This process can be dated back to 1501, when Bembo edited *Le cose volgari di messer Francesco Petrarcha* (*The Vernacular Poetry of Francis Petrarch*) for the Venetian publisher Aldo Manuzio, which included both the *RVF* and the *Triumphi*. Reconstructing Petrarch's text based on the autograph manuscript in his possession, Bembo built a new classic within the panorama of contemporary culture. This was the first time that a vernacular text had been published with the same philological care as that given to Greek and Latin classics by the Quattrocento

Humanists (see Chapter 14). It was also the first time that such scrupulous attention had been paid to Petrarch's vernacular texts in and of themselves; throughout the fifteenth century, they had always been published with long commentaries, expositions, and notes. Moreover, promoting a division into a first part written during Laura's life and a second written after her death, Bembo endorsed the reading of Petrarch's masterpiece as an autobiographical narrative containing a spiritual journey from earthly to divine love. The *RVF* became a "mirror of life," in which anyone could see their own experiences reflected. This unconditional identification between poetry and life established a paradigm that was both "democratizing" and individualizing; that is, again, imitable by all individuals within well-educated courtly circles. A few years later, in his dialogue *Gli Asolani* (*The Wedding Feast at Asolo*, 1505), Bembo merged the Petrarchan lyric model with a Neo-Platonic theory of love mediated through the Humanist philosopher Marsilio Ficino (1433–99); this method would dominate courtly life throughout the sixteenth century. As a model of the good life transposed into poetry, Petrarch was to be emulated at the level of both aesthetics and morals. Indeed, in many cases, imitation of the poet became the basis not only for a code of behavior but also for a platonizing religious project: the object of earthly love became a vehicle for arriving at a mystic experience of the divine. At the same time, such imitation was a sign of social distinction in the courtly context.

Twenty years after the publication of his edition of the *RVF*, Bembo transposed his canonization of Petrarch from the literary to the linguistic level. In his *Prose*, he favored the birth of a normative grammar of the Italian language based on Petrarch's vocabulary as a model for poetry and on Boccaccio's for prose, in parallel with Humanist Latin grammars proposing Virgil for poetry and Cicero for prose. The superiority of the single model determined the prevalence of a more straightforward kind of imitation – based on strict rules and clear selective criteria for both vocabulary and syntax – over the imitation of a plurality of models: a much-debated issue in humanistic circles, with its peaks in the controversies between Politian and Cortesi and between Bembo himself and Giovan Francesco Pico della Mirandola. Moreover, the acknowledgment of repetition as a means of creating social cohesion and shared values within an otherwise rather dispersed community of individuals furthered the passage of Bembo's project from the linguistic and poetical to the political and social.

A decisive impetus toward the realization of Bembo's project came from the virtually simultaneous publication in 1530 of his *Rime* and the *Sonetti e canzoni* of Jacope Sannazaro (1457–1530). Sannazaro was the acknowledged master of contemporary poetry and another imitator of Petrarch. Bembo's Petrarchism was probably too strict and reductive to be taken as

the only model at the time; however, in conjunction with the example of
Sannazaro, who was much freer in his use of Petrarch's poetry and was
ready to combine it with other models, Bembo's authority was more easily accepted and followed by a large majority of poets. Having imitated
Petrarch, Bembo himself became imitable, to the extent that Bembism – the
model provided by Bembo's own petrarchizing poetry – often prevailed over
a direct imitation of Petrarch. Bembo's Petrarchism has therefore to be seen
in line with his theory of imitation: only by drawing on previous masters
could artists achieve excellence through means of imitation, variation, and
emulation. Originality was indeed a value; but it had to be achieved through
differentiation rather than invention *ex nihilo*. Petrarchism was not solely
Bembo's discovery, however: from Petrarch himself, who may rightly be considered the first Petrarchist, to Bembo's contemporaries Vincenzo Calmeta,
Ludovico Ariosto, and Trifon Gabriele, Petrarchist practices were already
in place in much Italian poetry. Yet Bembo's cultural hegemony, due to his
crucial role in the world of Venetian printing, his very close ties to the influential Medici family, and his eminent position in the central court of Italy –
that of the papacy – clearly established him as *the* point of reference for all
later Petrarchisms.

The spread of Petrarchism: *Petrarchini*, commentaries, and *centoni*

In a painting attributed to Andrea del Sarto, conventionally titled "The
Woman with the 'Petrarchino'" and dated to c. 1528, now at the Galleria
degli Uffizi in Florence, a woman, her head slightly tilted, points to Petrarch's
poems with an intimate glance at the beholder. The poems on the page
of the printed book she points to are clearly legible: *RVF* 103 and 104.
The book is a *Petrarchino*, a small-format book containing all Petrarch's
poems – usually both the *RVF* and the *Triumphi* – which was very popular
in sixteenth-century Italy. Being seen holding a *Petrarchino* was a fashion,
and became a visual form of courtly intellectual self-fashioning. As early as
December 1507, Bembo promised to send a *Petrarchino* to his friend, the
courtier, writer, and, later, cardinal, Bernardo Dovizi da Bibbiena.

Both in his comedy *La Cortigiana* (1526–34) and in his *Ragionamenti*
(1536), the anti-conformist writer Pietro Aretino mocked the courtiers' habit
of seeking to please women by "speaking Tuscan, and holding a 'Petrarchino' in their hand."[3] In Book III of Baldassar Castiglione's *The Book
of the Courtier* (1528), one of the interlocutors, Giuliano de' Medici, the
strenuous defender of women's worth, argues that a means by which men
woo women at court is the composing of love lyrics, the model for which is
Petrarch, "who wrote of his loves so divinely in this language of ours."[4] Such

advice could not but encourage the exponential growth of courtier-versifiers: more than a discourse on love, Petrarchism had become a social game.

Petrarchini, commentaries, *centoni* (see next paragraph), and anthologies immediately spread throughout the peninsula. In 1525, the same year in which Bembo's *Prose* appeared, Alessandro Vellutello published his commentary on Petrarch's vernacular works, which posited the equivalence between life and poetry in Petrarchan experience and enriched the interpretations of the poems with biographical and historical details, including a prefatory "Life of Petrarch" and a parallel "Life of Laura." Vellutello's commentary – reprinted twenty-three times between 1525 and 1584 – is another indication of the spread of the Petrarchan model. Petrarch and Laura appeared as the embodiments of the Neo-Platonic code of love typical of courtiers and ladies at the courts of Italy, defining, as we have seen, a social as well as a poetic system. Vellutello's commentary was followed by many others: four in the subsequent decade alone (by Sebastiano Fausto da Longiano, Silvano da Venafro, Giovanni Andrea Gesualdo, and Bernardino Daniello), all of which fostered the imitation of Petrarch not only as a poet, but particularly as a model for life. Rather than being moralized or allegorized, as in Quattrocento commentaries, Petrarch's poetry was regarded as a biographical source, guaranteeing both historical credibility and poetic imitability, to the extent that Gaspara Stampa began her *Rime* in 1554 with "Voi ch'ascoltate" ("You who hear") and Giovanni Della Casa included in his own in 1558 a canzone starting with "Errai gran tempo" ("Long I wandered"), both reproducing words of the opening sonnet of the *RVF*. The commentaries also helped Petrarch to reach beyond the court context to a wider and more varied readership, including landed nobility and an upper middle-class urban population.

Commentaries were not the only means of spreading the Petrarchan model. Sannazaro's collection featured a sonnet fashioned entirely out of verses taken from Petrarch, "L'alma mia fiamma oltra le belle bella" (*RVF* 289, 1: "The glorious flame . . . beautiful beyond the beautiful"). He was followed by Belisario da Cingoli, who added a similar poem at the end of the very rare 1536 Zoppino edition of the *RVF*, and Vittoria Colonna, whose 1539 *Rime* included two like sonnets, "Occhi miei, oscurato è il nostro sole" (*RVF* 275, 1: "My eyes, darkened is our sun") and "Amor mi sprona in un tempo et affrena" (*RVF* 178, 1: "Love at the same time spurs me and reins me in"). Similarly, the 1544 collection of poems by Giulio Bidelli, republished no less than ten times during the century, was entirely a collage of Petrarch's verses. These are some of the first examples of the "arte del centone" (art of *cento*, or patchwork) that became a crucial component of Renaissance Petrarchism. This method is codified by Girolamo Ruscelli in his 1558 anthology: "it is a rule that it is allowable to take only a verse, or two half verses from a single poem [of Petrarch]... or even one and a half... [but] taking two whole verses together from the same poem will never be allowed."[5] The practice of the *centone* became so widespread that lexicons, vocabularies, and collections of adjectives and words were published to enable it. Teachable technique alone suffices: no genius is required: the limited "democratization" promoted by Bembo had reached an extreme limit.

Petrarchism and anti-Petrarchism

At the beginning of the 1540s, Niccolò Franco lamented the fashion of Petrarch commentary: "I see Petrarch commented upon, soiled, all mixed-up, entirely ripped-off, secularized, spiritualized," he wrote in 1542.[6] Franco was echoing Pietro Aretino's criticism of Petrarch's commentators, "who make him say with their commentaries things that he would not confess even under the threat of hanging," in *La Cortigiana*.[7] Aretino and Franco's target was not so much Bembo's Petrarchism as it was ideological exploitations of Petrarch, such as Gesualdo's, or Malipiero's *Il Petrarca spirituale* (1536). They gave voice to a concern about Petrarchism already in place at the end of the 1530s. In 1537, Aretino had distinguished between two kinds of imitation in a letter to Lodovico Dolce, affirming that imitation of concepts and sentiments could be allowed, but not of words; further on, he proclaimed, with his usual provocativeness, that he imitated only himself, in the name of an absolute naturalism and against any claim to artifice and sophistication.

Aretino and Franco's claims are useful in distinguishing between imitators – still considered perfectly legitimate poets – and distorters, or deformers, or parasites, who were just abusing Petrarch's name. They were not against Bembo: in fact, at the latter's death (1547), Franco, in an imaginary letter to Dante, acknowledged Bembo's merit in having replaced the fourteenth-century tradition with a more modern approach to poetry, crediting him with rescuing the vernacular from the preciosity of a Tebaldeo.

Imitation had to show the way to originality: such was Petrarchism's paradox.[8] This led to the critical opposition between *res et verba*, things and words, as in the famous concluding line of the *capitolo* by Francesco Berni in praise of Michelangelo sent to Sebastiano del Piombo: "he [Michelangelo] says things, while you [orthodox Petrarchists] say words."[9] Two tendencies can thus be recognized: imitative Petrarchism and creative Petrarchism. The first belongs to those who use *Petrarchini*, tables, lists, *centos*, and so on; that is, Petrarch's own words. The second implies careful study and re-elaboration of Petrarch's works to reach an original synthesis. The extraordinary flourishing of parodies of Petrarch (so-called "anti-Petrarchism") should therefore be read in opposition to the mere collection and combination of Petrarch's words and style, rather than to the content of his poems. Indeed, anti-Petrarchism depends upon and in some sense is a form of Petrarchism.

In his dialogue *Il Petrarchista* (1539), Franco relates how pilgrims seeking relics belonging to the famous Laura discover secret letters that reveal a foolish Petrarch mooning over his shameless beloved. Parodies of Petrarchan verses flourish throughout the dialogue, to comical or scandalous effect, such as where the author claims that, according to a newly "discovered" (but obviously invented) manuscript, the original version of the famous opening of sonnet 61 of Petrarch's *RVF*, "Benedetto sia 'l giorno, e 'l mese et l'anno" ("Blessed be the day, the month and the year"), was "Maledetto sia 'l giorno" ("Cursed be the day"), or that the beginning of sonnet 240, "I' ò pregato Amor, e 'l ne riprego" ("I have begged Love, and I beg him again"), was originally "Io n'ho 'ncacato amore, e gliene incaco" ("I've beshat love, and beshit him still").[10] In so doing, Franco paved the way to Petrarchan parodies, countless numbers of which can be found in Cinquecento literature, such as *Cicalamenti del Grappa* and Andrea Calmo's *Commento di due sonetti del Petrarcha* (1553).

Annibal Caro, in his commentary on a *capitolo* by Francesco Maria Molza in praise of "figs," went so far in mocking Petrarchan language and values as to claim that the "fig" (Italian slang for "vagina") is much superior to the "laurel," and that lines 27–28 of canzone 135 ("a stone more greedy to draw flesh than iron") obviously refer to the "the hard flesh [ficotto] of lady Laura's sex, which was the real flesh-tormenting magnet of wretched Petrarch."[11] Not anti-Bembo, but anti-Bembism, then: Berni's famous parody of Bembo's sonnet "Curly hair of gold and amber pure and bright" in his sonnet "Hair of fine silver, shaggy and twisted," an inverted celebration of the lady as old and ugly rather than young and beautiful, can be traced back to another Bembo sonnet, "Oh, proud and cruel, oh, of beauty," where Berni had originally found the representation of the old lady with silver hair and lifeless eyes.[12] Parody was another way of demonstrating how rich and multi-faceted Petrarchism could be.

From the imitation of Petrarch to the Petrarchist community: the flourishing of anthologies

After the publication of Bembo's and Sannazaro's *Rime*, a long series of individual *canzonieri* (collections of poems following the model of the *RVF*) appeared, starting with Lodovico Martelli's (1533), Alvise Priuli's (1533), and Giovan Battista Schiafenato's (1534) *Rime*.[13] Petrarchists made, remade, and unmade Petrarch's concepts so as to simultaneously repeat them and differentiate them from their model: a key formulation like "et ardo, et son un ghiaccio" (*RVF* 134, 2: "[I] burn and am of ice"), expressing the contradictory sensations of love, becomes "alsi et arsi" in Bembo and Ariosto, "agghiacci e sudi" in Stampa, "arde e ghiaccia" in Michelangelo, "ardo e gelo" in Tansillo, and so on.[14] This can be seen as another of Petrarchism's axioms: if repetition is a force for community, difference is a force for identity. Speaking with Petrarch's voice, Petrarchists were both de-personalizing themselves and impersonating their model, but in so doing they were at the same time attempting to affirm their own distinctive personalities.

From the mid-1540s, however, a new tendency appeared: individual *canzonieri* were progressively replaced by anthologies of poems by different authors. In 1545, in Venice, Giolito printed the *Rime diverse di molti eccellentissimi autori*, edited by Lodovico Domenichi and including poems by Giovanni Guidiccioni, Giulio Camillo, Giovanni Muzzarelli, and Tommaso Castellani, among others, as well as by Bembo, Dolce, Molza, Caro, Gesualdo, Aretino, and Veronica Gambara. The book's purpose was clear from the first text of the collection: Bembo's sonnet "Se mai ti piacque, Apollo, non indegno" ("If you ever liked it, Apollo, not unworthy") guided the readers toward an institutional Petrarchism, promoting Bembo's own example and manner. As a consequence, a new poetical community was born: what counted was no longer the author's individual name but his or her belonging to that community, represented by the anthology, whose rules had to be respected. So successful was this initiative that the book was followed by a reprint with new additions in 1546, which was the beginning of a series of collections of "different verses of many excellent authors," from the second book, also published by Giolito in 1547, to the ninth, published in Cremona by Conti in 1560.

The Petrarchizing aim of these collections can be measured through a comparison with similar, previous collections. If the earlier *Sonetti e canzoni di diversi antichi auttori toscani in dieci libri raccolte* (1527) insisted on the necessity for contemporary poets to appreciate Petrarch but also to go back to earlier Tuscan poets, the Giolito collection of 1547 promoted Petrarch only, and specifically Bembo's Petrarch, as a model for contemporary and future poets. These later volumes became a sort of thesaurus for versifiers, books with a wide, exemplary range of variations on and combinations of Petrarch's lyrics, not dissimilar to the various *Petrarchini*.

Editors such as Dolce, Domenichi, and Ruscelli thus became the real protagonists of the new cultural policy in Italy. Another aim of these collections was to popularize Petrarch, in this sense countering Bembo's aristocratic approach. In his *Osservationi* (1550), Dolce had written that "Bembo spoke solely to well-educated people," but that "only he who starts from the bottom can reach the top."[15] Not only was Petrarch commented upon, imitated, published, and edited, but his vernacular works were printed so many times during the sixteenth century as to give them the status of the first classic of the printing era: more than 126 editions published between 1500 and 1599 can be listed, mostly in Venice, and including both the *RVF* and the *Triumphi*.

These anthologies or collections demonstrate that the Petrarchan idiom had reached the status of grammar or code; that is, a linguistic and poetic system transcending geographical, social, and gender boundaries. They were all-inclusive, because what now mattered above all was respect for the rules, rather than the poet's individuality. Superseding the individual narrative *canzonieri*, the anthologies worked as instruments allowing poets to place themselves within the aristocratic literary community to which they wished to belong, as well as to differentiate themselves from other imitators and from the model itself (since no two poems are quite the same). The various academies flourishing all over Italy during the sixteenth and seventeenth centuries played a key role in this direction.

The wide-ranging and ever more inclusive character of these anthologies facilitated and legitimized further groupings, for example in terms of gender and geography, as in collections such as *Rime di diversi illustri signori napoletani*, edited by Dolce for Giolito in 1552, and *Rime diverse d'alcune nobilissime, et virtuosissime donne*, edited by Domenichi in 1559. Petrarchism, as we have seen, had already become a social game, within which everything and everyone was allowed, provided that its fundamental rules were respected. Bembo's process of "democratizing" poetic language clearly helped all to be part of the community, as well as to build their own subcommunities. Dolce's Neapolitan collection inaugurated a series of anthologies devoted to specific regions of Italy, such as a collection of writers from Brescia edited by Ruscelli in 1553 and one of Tuscan poets by Dionigi Atanagi between 1565 and 1566. The spread of Petrarchism, prompted by the ever-increasing output of the press, provided a new space for new categories of authorship, with particularly important effects on the writing of women, such as Tullia d'Aragona (whose *Rime* appeared as early as 1547), Isabella di Morra (1552), Chiara Matraini (1555), Laura Battiferri (1560), and Veronica Franco (1576), as well as the previously mentioned Colonna, Stampa, and Gambara.

The spread of Petrarchism and its apparent anonymity also allowed for discourses other than those on Platonic love and the exploration of the inner self. At a time when religion was at the center of social life, Petrarchism provided space for both Reformed discourses, such as in Vittoria Colonna's

Rime and in Antonio Brucioli and Lodovico Castelvetro's commentaries on Petrarch, and for Catholic responses, such as the 1590 Cesare Della Rocca and Muzio Sforza collections of *Rime sacre*. No less than eighty-four titles in the Cinquecento are named *Rime spirituali*, among which are those of Vittoria Colonna, Luigi Tansillo, and Torquato Tasso. The route of Cinquecento Petrarchism can be measured by the words of Tasso himself, who, in his lesson on Della Casa's sonnet "Questa vita mortal" ("This mortal life"), c. 1568, inverted Bembo's argument in favor of Petrarch against Dante, stating that Dante's mistake was to privilege verse and rhyme over content, while Petrarch had happily combined them. Rather than a discourse divorced from social and historical realities, Petrarchism was clearly politically and religiously engaged, encompassing the full range of sixteenth-century culture in Italy.

NOTES

1 Francesco De Sanctis, *History of Italian Literature*, trans. Joan Redfern (London: Oxford University Press, 1930), 429.
2 Benedetto Croce, *Poesia popolare e poesia d'arte: studi sulla poesia italiana dal Tre al Cinquecento* [1930], ed. Piero Cudini (Naples: Bibliopolis, 1991), 312.
3 Pietro Aretino, *Tutte le commedie*, ed. Giovan Battista De Sanctis (Milan: Mursia, 1968), 136; Pietro Aretino, *Sei giornate*, ed. Giovanni Aquilecchia (Bari: Laterza, 1980), 95.
4 Baldassar Castiglione, *The Book of the Courtier*, III.52, trans. Charles Singleton, ed. Daniel Javitch (New York/London: W.W. Norton, 2002), 189.
5 Girolamo Ruscelli, *I fiori delle rime de' poeti illustri* (Venice: Sessa, 1558), 618.
6 Niccolò Franco, *Le pistole vulgari* [1542], ed. Francesca Romana de' Angelis (Sala Bolognese: Forni, 1986).
7 Pietro Aretino, *Tutte le commedie*, 118.
8 A paradox discussed by Petrarch himself in his letters on literary imitation (*Fam.* I.8, XXII.2, XXIII.19).
9 Francesco Berni, *Rime*, ed. Giorgio Barberi Squarotti (Turin: Einaudi, 1969), 179.
10 Niccolò Franco, *Il Petrarchista* [1539], ed. Roberto L. Bruni (Exeter: University of Exeter, 1979), 69–71.
11 Annibal Caro, *Gli Straccioni, commedia. La Ficheide, comento. La Nasea e La Statua della foia, dicerie* (Milan: Daelli, 1863), 148.
12 Pietro Bembo, *Prose e rime*, ed. Carlo Dionisotti (Turin: UTET, 1966), 510; Francesco Berni, *Rime burlesche*, ed. Giorgio Barberi Squarotti (Milan: Rizzoli, 1991), 103.
13 This title occurs no less than 974 times in the Italian Cinquecento.
14 See Roberto Gigliucci, *Contraposti. Petrarchismo e ossimoro d'amore nel Rinascimento* (Rome: Bulzoni, 2004), 163–174.
15 Lodovico Dolce, *Osservationi* (Venice: Giolito, 1554), 7–8 and 104.

16

ANN ROSALIND JONES

Female Petrarchists

Petrarch's *RVF* was the horizon for all love poets in Europe from the fifteenth through the seventeenth centuries. First printed from manuscript in 1470, by the year 1600 his collection had gone through over 170 editions (compared, for example, to only fifty-two of Dante's *Commedia*.) The speed-up of printing also enabled the publication from 1545 to 1590 of over 100 poetic anthologies presenting work by Italian poets writing in the Petrarchan style; these anthologies were the major medium for the importation of Petrarchism into other European countries. Female poets found another set of models in the anthologized lyrics of fifty-three women, *Rime diverse d'alcune nobilissime, et virtuosissime donne*, published by Ludovico Domenichi in 1559 and republished, in expanded versions, over many later years.

What was Petrarchism in women's poetry? Simply put, it was the gender-marked use and variation of the subject matter and style of the sonnets and other verse forms of the *RVF*. The 366 lyrics in Petrarch's collection are mostly the poet's meditations on the elusive figure of Laura, a name that combines "l'aura" ("a breeze"), "l'oro" ("gold"), and "lauro" ("laurel tree") and the poet's laurel, with which Petrarch had himself crowned in a ceremony in Rome in 1341). The speaker never wins Laura's love and rarely speaks to her, though he imagines conversations with her after her death, which turns him finally to God and to the Virgin Mary as his intercessor. Many of the poems focus closely on exemplary parts of Laura's body – her hair, her eyes, her smile – and items of her clothing – a veil, a glove – constructing a memory bank of disparate details to which the poet returns again and again as he laments her absence and voices his longing for her.[1] For women, there was an important advantage in adopting the position of Petrarch's persona in the *RVF*: it enabled them to write in ways that corresponded to contemporary gender decorum, especially the requirement of female chastity. Their themes, like Petrarch's, included love for a resistant, inaccessible, or absent beloved; the analysis of passion without its physical consummation; the turn from earthly love to love of God. Moreover, because women's sequences followed the genre of the *RVF*, they conformed to reigning ideologies of the proper genres of feminine writing: the short sonnet and the longer canzone, but not ambitious forms such as tragedy, epic, or poems written in Latin.

An extreme example of the sixteenth-century conviction that women poets were faithful followers of Petrarch is Rinaldo Corso's commentary on *Tutte le Rime di Vittoria Colonna*, first published in 1543, and frequently thereafter up to 1558. Throughout his "Esposizione," Corso cites short passages from Petrarch as the sources for almost all of Colonna's poems. But Corso was searching for isolated quotations, looking for the kind of piecemeal imitation that Thomas Greene defines as "eclectic or exploitative" because it "treats all traditions as stockpiles to be drawn on ostensibly at random."[2] An adequate analysis of women poets' use of Petrarch, rather, needs to be alert to the possibility that they are engaged in what Greene calls "dialectical imitation," in which the poet takes a critical distance toward her model but also acknowledges its power. This kind of imitation occurs in women Petrarchists from the beginning *because they speak as women*. Even when they repeat a line or a metaphor straight from Petrarch, the presentation of their work under a woman's name foregrounds the feminine gender of the speaker and shapes the reader's sense of what these echoes mean.

Such nuances are reinforced by the gendered grammar of the Romance languages. When Petrarch writes in his third sonnet that he was "preso, ... ché i be' vostr' occhi, Donna, mi legaro" (*RVF* 3, 3–4: "taken, ... for your lovely eyes, Lady, bound me") and "disarmato" by Love, the masculine form of the adjectives and the address to his "Lady" remind his readers that they are following the emotional vicissitudes of a male poet. The Venetian poet Gaspara Stampa (1523–54) opens her *Rime* (1554) with a direct echo of Petrarch's first line, matching his "Voi ch'ascoltate in rime sparse il suono" ("You who hear in scattered rhymes the sound") with her "Voi ch'ascoltate in queste meste rime" ("You who hear in these troubled rhymes").[3] But she ends the poem with a statement of her hope of being read by an audience of sympathetic and admiring women, in two lines that foreground both the speaker and her listener as feminine: "E spero ancor, che debba dir qualch'una / felicissima lei, da che sostenne / per si chiaro cagione danno sì chiaro" ("And I hope some woman will be moved to say / 'Most happy she who suffered famously/ for such a famous cause!'").

Another gender difference in the plots narrated by the poems in many women's sequences is their historical specificity. In her life, Petrarch's Laura is inaccessible because of her refusal of his attentions. Early commentators on the *RVF* explained this distance not only by her firm purity of soul but also by her married state, of which Petrarch himself makes no mention. The first women Petrarchists, however, wrote from a position of married love, though also of separation from their beloved husbands. For Vittoria Colonna (1490–1547) and Veronica Gambara (1485–1550), the principal separation was widowhood. Because they had been married to feudal aristocrats who died famously in battle, their mourning was literal: their longings for their men at war and in the tomb were understood by readers as reactions to public events. This self-positioning as wives and widows was radically reframed in the work of unmarried poets whose readers knew that their requited love was not for a husband. This, for example, was the case of Gaspara Stampa, whose liaison with the nobleman Collaltino di Collalto lasted only three years because of his absences, required by his military duties in foreign wars, and his much higher social rank relative to hers.

Many of Colonna and Gambara's poems show that they admired Petrarch but also re-oriented his poems for their own purposes. Colonna, in her *Rime* (1538), alternates, much as Petrarch does, between poems of praise for her beloved and intense grief at his death, while, in her *Rime spirituali* (so entitled in the fifth edition of her poems, published in 1539), she completes the turn to God that Petrarch began to dramatize toward the end of the *RVF*. It is clear in these poems that Colonna is inviting comparison to her model. However, she pinpoints a contrast between her holy sonnets and his worldly ones in the opening line of a sonnet (148) first published in her *Rime* of 1538 and again in her *Rime spirituali* of 1539. The first word, "L'AURA," with all its letters capitalized, recalls Petrarch's naming of Laura at the beginning of the *RVF*, with the striking difference that Colonna uses the word in the specifically Christian sense of divine life-giving breath, the inspiration that Jesus brought to the prophet Simeon (Luke, 2:25–29):

> L'AURA vital di Cristo in mezo 'l petto
> spirava à Simeon sì larga vita
> che con la propria sua da se sbandita
> stava in quella di Dio chiuso, e ristretto.[4]

(The life-giving breath of Christ deep into the breast/ of Simon, / blew such full life / that, with his own taken away, / he was enclosed and held in the breath of God.)

At the end of her *Rime* in the 1539 edition, in "Il Trionfo della Croce" ("The Triumph of the Cross"), a *capitolo* in *terza rima* narrating a vision of the Passion (echoing the verse form of Dante's *Commedia* and Petrarch's *Triumphi*), Colonna radically refocuses the Petrarchan blazon in lines that describe specific parts of Christ's body. As Janet Smarr points out, Colonna's is a "blazon of the [divine] body's various parts...It is Christ's body that is celebrated feature by feature,"⁵ transforming Petrarch's images of Laura into a celebration of the Incarnation:

> Io vedea l'honorata, e sacra testa...
> e piagata la man, che togli, e dona...
> sugli omer santi... a i santi piè.

(I saw his honored and sacred head.../ and his pierced hand, which takes and gives.../ Upon his sacred shoulders... at his sacred feet.)

At the end of her scene of the Crucifixion, Colonna describes the sorrowing Virgin Mary. She then singles out Mary Magdalene in a phrase that echoes Petrarch's polysemic "l'aura," but here points to the beauty of the penitent woman serving Christ:

> Ai santi piè colei, che simil nome
> onora, vidi ardendo d'Amor lieta
> risplender cinta *de l'aurate chiome.*
> (493–495, emphasis mine)

(At his sacred feet, I saw her whom a similar name/ honors, burning with joyful love, / shine forth, surrounded by her golden hair.)

A contemporary and admirer of Colonna, Veronica Gambara, also imitated Petrarch's *Rime* in her own. Like Petrarch, she focuses her first sequence of thirty poems on love as a struggle between longing and despair, and she remains close to the themes of the *RVF* by not specifying that her beloved is her husband away at war. But her sequence takes a sudden turn, earlier than Petrarch's two-thirds of the way through, when she declares the death of her beloved (poem 17):

> Quel nodo, in cui la mia beata sorte
> per ordine del Ciel legommi e strinse,
> con grave mio dolor sciolse e devinse
> quella crudel che 'l mondo chiama Morte.⁶

(That knot, in which my blessed fate / bound and fastened me by heaven's command / was untied and defeated to my deep dismay / by the cruelty known to the world as death.)

Like Petrarch toward the end of the *RVF*, for example in sonnets 345–349, she goes on to say she is confident that her beloved's beautiful face is now in heaven, a prospect that frees her from the fear of losing him forever. She is afraid of nothing now except whether she will be able to rise to his height there:

> [la tema] mitigato ha 'l dolor, che 'ngeno od arte
> far nol potea, sperando in Paradiso
> l'alma veder oltra le belle bella.

([this fear] has mitigated my pain, as intelligence and art / could not, for I hope
to see his soul in Paradise, / most beautiful among the beautiful.)

This hope links her final thirteen love lyrics together, but another turn
further differentiates her verse from Petrarch's. Some of her most intensely
affectionate poems are addressed to her family's feudal estate near Brescia,
from which they were exiled from 1512 to 1529 during the French-Italian
wars. Petrarch had celebrated Vaucluse, the valley west of Avignon where
he first saw Laura, but he described her more often in vaguer pastoral
settings, as in "Fresco ombroso fiorito et verde colle / ov' or pensando et
or cantando siede" (*RVF* 243, 1–2: "Fresh, shady, flowering green hill,
where, sometimes thoughtful, sometimes singing, she sits"). For Gambara,
however, her family fiefdom and her husband's city-state Correggio were
central to her aristocratic identity, and the joyful addresses she composed
to them when she returned from other courts and cities are among her most
intensely charged poems. She begins poem 34 with lines that could equally
well describe a lover:

> Con quel caldo desio che nascer sole
> in petto di chi torna, amando, assente,
> gli occhi vaghi a vedere e le parole
> dolci ascoltar del suo bel foco ardente;

(With that warm desire born only / in the breast of one who returns, loving
after absence, / to see the lovely eyes and hear / the sweet sounds [words] of
his beautiful burning fire.)

As the *ottava* unfolds, she clarifies the political object of her apostrophes:

> con quel proprio voi, piagge al mondo sole,
> fresch'acque, ombrosi colli, e te, possente
> più d'altra che 'l sol miri andando intorno,
> bella e lieta cittade, a veder torno.

(So I return to see you, peerless shores, unique in the world, / fresh waters,
shaded hills, / and you, beautiful joyful city, / more powerful than any under
the sun.)

The "possente" of line 6 opens into more explicitly political lines as Gambara imagines nature taking revenge against the enemies of Brescia for their
depredations. In a canzone listing a series of tragic metamorphoses (*RVF*
323), Petrarch had described himself as a poet in analogy to the mythical

phoenix, rising from its ashes to live again; in the canzone, he sees "a strange phoenix" appear, awe-inspiring in purple and gold, but it then attacks itself in grief at Laura's death and vanishes. Gambara omits this tragic ending. Instead, she attributes an organic power of revival to her city, rising triumphantly again after its capture by the French:

> Salve, mia bella patria, o tu, felice
> tanto amato dal Ciel ricco paese,
> ch'a guisa di leggiadra alma fenice
> mostri l'alto valor chiaro e palese;
> Natura, a te sol madre e pia nutrice,
> ha fatto agli altri mille gravi offese
> spogliandogli di quanto avean di buono
> per farne a te cortese e largo dono.

(Greetings, my beautiful homeland, and you, / rich country, blessed / and so beloved by the heavens / who, like a noble and graceful phoenix / show forth your eminence, clear and illustrious; / Nature, mother and kind provider for you alone / inflicted thousands of grave offenses on other lands, / divesting them of any bounty they had / to make gracious and abundant gifts to you.) (Translation mine.)

Colonna and Gambara's refocusing of the *RVF*'s themes in religious and political directions shows how seriously they took Petrarch's work. A more complex relationship to this model was elaborated by the later poet of Italy, Gaspara Stampa (*Rime*, Venice, 1554). A musical performer who circulated throughout the private homes and academies of Venice, she made her living by playing and singing. It was probably at one such performance that she met the man to whom she addressed poems of loss and longing similar to Petrarch's. But hers were grounded in an openly scandalous liaison.

In her 310 poems, she leaves no doubt as to the identity of the man she loves: the count Collaltino di Collalto, a nobleman of the Veneto whose family name was derived from their estate, built on a *colle* (hill) and *alto* (high). Half-way through her third sonnet, she addresses him with a metaphor repeated throughout her sequence: he is her high hill, so lofty a subject and muse that he has enabled her to surpass the Greek poet Hesiod:

> Se di rozo pastor di gregge, e folle
> il giogo Ascreo fe diventar Poeta
> lui, che poi salse à sì lodata meta,
> che quasi à tutti altri gli altri fama tolle;
> che meraviglia fia s'alza, e estolle
> me bassa e vile à scriver, tanta pietà,
> quel, che può più, che studio, e che pianeta,
> il mio verde, pregiato e alto Colle?

(If Ascrea's peak could turn an uncouth shepherd / of goats and sheep / into a poet – he who rose to such praiseworthy heights / that he stole renown from almost all others – / what marvel is it if that high and verdant hill / lifted up someone like me, base and lowly, / raised me up to write piteous verse, / doing far more than study or the stars?)

Stampa further links herself to Collalto by building on an element of his feudal landholding, like Gambara's geographically specific setting: she takes the pen name "Anassilla" from the river that flowed through the Collalto territory, the Anasso, the Latin-derived word for the Piave. From this wishfully invented union of the high hill and the lowly river, she derives poems at times despairing and at times exhilarated, including a startlingly frank one that celebrates a night of finally fulfilled passion with the count. Sonnet 104 begins:

> O' notte, a me più cara e più beata
> che i più beati giorni, e i più chiari...
> Tu de le gioie mie sola sei stata
> fida ministra, tu tutti gli amari
> de la mia vita hai fatto dolci e cari,
> resomi in braccia lui, che m'ha legato.

O night, to me more luminous and blessed / than the most blessed and luminous of days... / you alone have been the faithful minister of all my joys, / all that was bitter / in my life you've rendered sweet and dear, / and placed me in the arms of the man who bound me.

Such a poem is unimaginable in Petrarch's *RVF*. Stampa reworks many of Petrarch's tropes – the anniversary poem, the dialogue with the heartless god of Love – and his forms, as in the correlative sonnet (26) in which three or four nouns are brought together with matching verbs: "Arsi, piansi, cantai, piango, ardo, e canto... / A gli atti suoi, à i modi, à le parole / Splendor, dolcezza, e gratia ivi discerno" ("I burned, I wept, I sang, I weep, I burn, I sing... / in all his acts and words and ways, / I find such splendor, sweetness and grace.") But her insistence on the physical love she has shared, however briefly, with Collaltino radically recontextualizes the praises and laments she builds upon Petrarch's model.

Petrarchism in the mode of the *RVF* was taken up by many other women poets in Italy. Virginia Cox argues that courts and aristocratic clans encouraged women to write in this mode and others to bring distinction to the families and city-states to which they belonged.[7] This kind of elite social cadre also supported women writing in other parts of Europe. In the liberal city of Lyons, far from the royal court and the theological faculty of the Sorbonne, a young noblewoman, Pernette Du Guillet, wrote in the persona of a chaste disciple to a well-known poet also of Lyons, Maurice Scève. The virtuous, intellectually ambitious, and occasionally pedagogical mode of her *Rymes* (1545) had a good deal in common with the work of later women poets in Protestant England, where a less tolerant attitude toward female eroticism prevailed. Petrarchan lament was the central, even unrelenting theme of the courtly noblewoman Mary Wroth's *Pamphilia to Amphilanthus* (1621). Like Petrarch and the women poets who followed him, Pamphilia invokes her beloved as her Sun, longs to see his bright eyes, and laments their separation, though she accepts it as the condition of a chaste, life-long love, which she recommends to herself and to other lovers: "Be in [Love's] brave Court a glorious light / Shine in the eyes of Faith, and Constancy / Maintaine the fires of Love, still burning bright" (*Corona*, sonnet 4).[8]

On the other hand, in social ranks below the courtly elite – a situation, in fact, more like Petrarch's – women of the sixteenth century published a freer kind of love poetry. In Lyons, amid a circle of cosmopolitan men, including Humanist scholars, jurists, and publishers, Louise Labé, the daughter and wife of wealthy merchants supplying goods to ship-owners, wrote her *Rymes* (1555) in praise of a beautiful and learned blond man crowned with laurel (Petrarch is never far away!), often absent and indifferent, whose blazons of her eyes and blonde hair she quotes sarcastically back at him (sonnet 23), but with whom, in the mode of Stampa, she imagines a passionate exchange (sonnet 18): "Baise m'encore, rebaise-moi et baise" ("Kiss me again, rekiss me, and kiss").[9] In England, Isabella Whitney, working in London as a housemaid, wrote a boldly accusatory epistle to a beloved man not only absent but unfaithful: "The copy of a letter, lately written in meeter, by a yonge gentilwoman: to her vnconstant louer" (1567). She tells the stories of many women abandoned by their beloveds and warns young women against lovers' empty flattery. Thus, the two threads of Petrarchism I have been identifying, the chaste regendering and redirection of his sonnets of longing and the erotic and satirical challenge to his representation of disembodied love – perhaps better described as anti-Petrarchist – persisted in the work of women poets in France and England, as in his native Italy.

NOTES

1 On the fragmentary focus of the blazons detailing Laura's body, see Nancy J. Vickers, "Diana Described: Scattered Woman and Scattered Rhyme," in *Writing and Sexual Difference*, ed. Elizabeth Abel (Chicago, IL: University of Chicago Press, 1982), 95–109.

2 Thomas M. Greene, *The Light in Troy: Imitation and Discovery in Renaissance Poetry* (New Haven, CT: Yale University Press, 1982), 39.

3 Gaspara Stampa, *The Complete Poems: The 1554 Edition of the "Rime." A Bilingual Edition*, eds. Troy Tower and Jane Tylus, intr. and trans. Jane Tylus (Chicago, IL: University of Chicago Press, 2010), 59.

4 Vittoria Colonna, *Rime* (Venice: Marco Salvione, 1539), 411. All translations mine.

5 Janet Smarr, "Substituting for Laura: Objects of Desire for Renaissance Women Poets," *Comparative Literature Studies* 38.1 (2001): 1–30.

6 Veronica Gambara, *Complete Poems. A Bilingual Edition*, eds. and trans. Molly M. Martin and Paola Ugolino (Toronto, ON: Iter Inc. and The Centre for Renaissance and Reformation Studies, 2014). I have lightly revised the translations by Martin and Ugolino.

7 Virginia Cox, *Women's Writing in Italy, 1400–1650* (Baltimore, MD: Johns Hopkins University Press, 2008), Introduction and Chapter 1.

8 Mary Wroth, *Pamphilia to Amphilanthus*, in *The Poems of Lady Mary Wroth*, ed. Josephine A. Roberts (Baton Rouge, LA: Louisiana State University Press, 1983), 129.

9 My translation. See the excellent freer one by Annie Finch in Louise Labé, *Complete Poetry and Prose: A Bilingual Edition*, eds. and trans. Deborah Lesko Baker and Annie Finch (Chicago, IL: University of Chicago Press, 2006), 207.

17

WILLIAM J. KENNEDY

Iberian, French, and English Petrarchisms

If considered absolutely, one of the first Petrarchan imitations outside of Italy is Chaucer's adaptation of Petrarch's sonnet 132 in *Troilus and Criseyde* (1400–20). Another features forty-two sonnets by a Castilian court official, the Marqués de Santillana, composed in 1438–55. But a substantial Petrarchan poetics arrives in Europe only after the *RVF* and *Triumphi* enter into print (1470), reaching a high point after 1525. From the start, printed editions offer textual commentaries with various, usually competing views of the poet's achievement. The earliest ones, edited by Antonio da Tempo (pub. 1477), Francesco Filelfo (pub. 1476), and Hieronimo Squarzafico (1484), represent Petrarch as a poet-diplomat in service to northern Italian despots such as the Visconti of Milan. In the most widely reprinted edition (1525), Alessandro Vellutello rearranges the sequence to narrate a dramatically coherent account of the poet's life and his love for Laura. That same year, Pietro Bembo's *Prose della volgar lingua* (*Writings on the Vernacular*) authorizes Petrarch's archaic Tuscan style as the supreme model for Italian lyric. Later editors, such as Giovanni Andrea Gesualdo (1532), Sylvano da Venafro (1533), and Bernardino Daniello (1536), emphasize Petrarch's rhetorical skills in deploying literary allusion, classical myth, and poetic figuration. Still others, such as Fausto da Longiano (1532), Antonio Brucioli (1548), and Ludovico Castelvetro (pub. 1582) – all hospitable to religious reform – foreground Petrarch's Scriptural and doctrinal references and his criticism of the Avignon papacy. Taken together, these approaches to Petrarch mediate the *RVF*'s reception throughout Europe, offering multiple versions of Petrarch as a public figure, poet, lover, scholar, and Christian moralist. In Spain, Portugal, France, and England, these commentaries inflect imitations of Petrarch in different ways and at different times.

Iberian Petrarchism

A sustained cultivation of Petrarch's model in Spain begins in 1543 with the posthumous publication of *Las obras* of Juan Boscán (c. 1490–1542) and

Garcilaso de la Vega (c. 1501–36). The former, a Castilian-educated gentleman from Barcelona, and the latter, his aristocratic friend from Toledo, had served in Charles V's army (Garcilaso died fighting in southern France), and both exemplify Castiglione's ideal of the soldier-scholar. Their joint *obras* include *sonetos* in Italianate eleven-syllable meters and *canciones* (canzoni or odes) in stanzas of seven- and eleven-syllable meters, as well as elegies and epistolary poems in *terza rima*. Boscán's prologue defends his Castilian imitations of Italianate forms as augurs of a new literary standard for the rising Spanish Empire.

As it happens, Garcilaso's contributions to the volume proved more critically successful than Boscán's and exerted a greater impact upon later Spanish Petrarchism. The fluidity of his verse contrasts with Boscán's sometimes forced rhyme; the range of his allusions to Virgil, Horace, Ovid, Sannazaro, Bembo, and others exceeds that of Boscán; and the amplitude of his emotion as it wavers between certainty and uncertainty, melancholy and skepticism, contrasts with the easy resolution reached by his friend. Garcilaso's complaint in sonnet 25, "O fate, so active to promote my troubles," for example, leaves some doubt as to whether he is lamenting a failed love affair or bemoaning a deeper, more comprehensive loss: "With your destroying hands you felled the tree / and scattered on the ground the fruits and flowers."[1]

Within decades, Garcilaso's poetry came to be uncoupled from Boscán's and republished on its own. Soldier-poets such as Diego Hurtado de Mendoza at Granada (1503–75) and Gutierre de Cetina at Seville (1514–54) took inspiration from him, while detailed commentaries by Francisco Sánchez de las Brozas ("El Brocense") at Salamanca (1574) and Fernando de Herrera at Seville (1580) canonized his work as the Spanish equivalent of Petrarch's. Herrera's (c. 1534–97) commentary is important in two ways: first as a major contribution to vernacular literary criticism and poetics in Spain, and second as an articulation of principles that would animate his own substantial body of poetry (pub. 1582, 1619). Other poets would innovate in different ways. In his *Rimas humanas* (1602) and *Rimas sacras* (1614), for example, the immensely prolific and versatile Lope de Vega (1562–1635) offsets conventional Petrarchan poems with variously satiric, parodic, topical, and profane sonnets.

In the larger Iberian setting, Portuguese poets experimented early on with Petrarchism. Returning from study in Italy in 1526, Francisco de Sá de Miranda (1481–1558) composed sonnets, canzoni, sestinas, *terza rima* epistles, and *ottava rima* stanzas in eleven-syllable meters. His disciple António Ferreira (1528–69) adopted these forms for his *Poemas Lusitanos*, motivating a new generation of imitators. The greatest of them is Luís de Camões

(1524–80), author of the epic *Os Lusíadas* (1572) and of hundreds of posthumously published sonnets and other lyrics. While some of these poems date to the author's youth at the Lisbon court, most originate after his exile for public brawling in 1552 and his subsequent service in the Portuguese trading outposts of Goa and Macao. Sonnets such as "Here in this Babylon" recount the travails of his banishment.[2] Others, such as "Dear gentle soul, who has, too soon, departed" express his grief upon learning of his beloved's death in Lisbon. The biographical component of Camões's sonnets, like that of the sonnets of Garcilaso and other soldier-poets in Spain, suggests the influence of Italian commentaries concerned with Petrarch's lived experience.

At Cordova, in the last decades of the sixteenth century, Luis de Góngora y Argote (1561–1627) brought an eclecticism and heterogeneity to Spanish poetry with his virtuoso forays into disparate genres, extravagant experiments in diction and syntax, and profligate borrowings from authors as diverse as Pindar, Euripides, Seneca, Ariosto, Tasso, and Marino. Both early and late in his career, he wrote sonnets that toy with Petrarchism – some would say parody and distort it – inviting the opprobrium of other poets. Chief among them in Madrid was Francisco de Quevedo (1580–1645), whose intense dislike of pretension and hypocrisy motivated his incursions into many, often divergent literary forms. Alternately serious and funny, plangent and grotesque, he approached Petrarchan poetry with the aim of recovering its moral seriousness. The Stoic convictions, Neo-Platonic formulas, and Biblical resonances of his love poems alternate incongruously with a derision of vanity and illusion, promiscuity and self-blindness in his satiric verse. Some early poems simply parody Petrarchism, as in the sonnet to a cross-eyed lady, which assures her that if her vision focused straight ahead, it would scorch the earth.

At the opposite end of the spectrum, the publication at Madrid in 1692 of poetry by Sor Juana Inés de la Cruz, a nun at a Hieronymite convent in Mexico City, includes sixty-six sonnets on philosophical, mythological, religious, and amatory themes in the Petrarchan mode. As fictions conceived in solitude and enriched with philosophical and classical allusions, the best of her erotic poems turn familiar Petrarchan motifs about artifice and beauty into meditations upon human frailty and fragility. Sonnet 145, "This that you gaze on, colorful deceit," disparages a portrait that exaggerates the author's attractive features and "with its fallacious arguments of colors, is to the senses cunning counterfeit."[3] In the end, each of them "is but cadaver, ashes, shadow, void." Mirroring the split identity inscribed in Petrarch's imaginative consciousness, her poetry draws upon his figurations to soar across boundaries of ancestry and descent, territory and cultural behavior, marking European Petrarchism's incursion into and return from the New World.

French Petrarchism

The marriage of the future French king Henry II to Catherine de' Medici in 1533 stimulated interest in Petrarchan poetry as courtiers welcomed the Italian bride to France. The Humanist scholar-poet Maurice Scève (c. 1501–64) opined that he had discovered Laura's tomb in Avignon, and the court poet Mellin de Saint-Gelais (c. 1491–1558) used the sonnet form for occasional verse to honor royal favorites. To curry favor with Francis I in 1539, Clément Marot (1496–1544) published translations of six sonnets from Petrarch's *RVF*. But the first serious efforts to replicate Petrarchan motifs – though not in the sonnet or canzone forms – came in the urban culture of Lyon with Scève's deeply intellectualized sequence of 449 dizains, *Délie, object de plus haulte vertu* (1544), and with the varied *Rymes* (1545) of Pernette du Guillet (c. 1520–45), who is often considered the real-life prototype for Délie. A sense of Scève's powers can be gleaned from his reworking of Petrarch's celebrated sonnet 248, which begins: "Whoever wishes to see how much Nature and Heaven can do among us, let him come marvel at her." In the corresponding lines of Scève's dizain 278, a new emphasis on intellectual acuity ("scauoir") and listening competence ("ouyr") replaces Petrarch's emphasis upon visual experience ("veder," "mirar"): "Whoever wishes to know by evidence obvious to all how one can forget oneself, . . . come listen to her and unfold what she says."[4] Scève's influence upon succeeding efforts proved striking.

The publication of *Déffence et illustration de la langue francoyse* (1549) by Joachim Du Bellay (1522–60) bolstered French Petrarchism. Its author, a member of the provincial nobility, urged his peers to develop rhetorical skills that would vie with those of the educated gentry in service to the crown, and to this end he promoted an education in vernacular literacy based upon Humanist programs pioneered in Italy. To illustrate the possibilities for adapting Italian style to French poetry, Du Bellay published with the *Déffence* a collection of sonnets titled *Olive*. Sonnet 62 in this collection explicitly evokes Petrarch's sonnet 248: "Whoever would like to see the most precious tree that the orient or the south might offer, come to where my river frolics in the waves."[5] The poem's succeeding lines nominate a canon of modern authors by associating Petrarch with the Arno river and Marot, Saint-Gelais, Scève and the poet himself with corresponding French rivers. In later years, Du Bellay diversified his Petrarchan imitations in sonnet sequences that are both personal and philosophical in tone. *Les Regrets*

(1558) satirizes the depravity of sixteenth-century Rome, where Du Bellay spent four years at the papal court, while *Les Antiquitez de Rome* and *Songe* (1558) chart the demise of the ancient Roman Empire in contrastive sequences laden with classical allusion.

While Du Bellay considered himself the king's servant, his friend Pierre de Ronsard (1524–85) saw himself as a professional poet, and he wanted others to see him so as well. When his debut collection of *Odes* (1550) met with derision, he retreated from public life to prepare a sequence of Petrarchan poems, *Les Amours* (1552), whose sonnet 1 imitates Petrarch's sonnet 248. Instead of inviting readers to marvel at his beloved Cassandre, he urges them to look at him and read his poems: "Whoever wishes to see how a god overwhelms me... should come see me: he will see my suffering and the rigor of the archer who tames me."[6] In ensuing years, Ronsard sharpened his professional edge by revising *Les Amours*, first in an expanded edition (1553), and then in each successive edition of his *Oeuvres complètes* (seven between 1560 and 1587). He meanwhile augmented this sequence with others composed for different women, chiefly the rustic Marie, but also various mistresses (Sinope, Astrée) of high-ranking courtiers who paid him to celebrate their charms. These poems, too, received extensive revision and reorganization over the years.[7]

Other French poets followed Du Bellay and Ronsard. Six months after Du Bellay published *Olive*, Pontus de Tyard, in Lyon, issued his *Erreurs amoureuses* (1549), and then followed it with two more volumes of *Erreurs* (1551, 1555). In Poitiers, Ronsard's friend Jean-Antoine de Baïf assembled his *Amour de Francine* (1555). In 1555, at Lyon, Louise Labé (1522–66) included twenty-four Petrarchan sonnets in her *Evvres*. The volume's dedicatory preface sounds a ringing call for other women to join the ranks of men in scouting for "the honor that letters and learning bring to people who pursue them,"[8] and her poetry aims to inspire them with models. With these achievements, French Petrarchism temporarily ran its course by the end of the decade.

As France descended into its wars of religion during the 1560s and '70s, the Maréchale de Retz initiated a literary salon to counter the mounting rancor and violence by promoting an aesthetic ideal of virtuous and refined Petrarchism. Its rising star was the young Philippe Desportes (1546–1606). Writing on commission to fashionable courtiers, as Ronsard had done, Desportes assembled in *Premières oeuvres poétiques* (1573) various sonnet cycles, which display a notable lack of personality and fervor. Evidently, Ronsard thought he could do better than Desportes, and so he accepted Catherine de' Medici's challenge to address one of her maids in waiting, Hélène de Surgères. The result was his *Sonnets pour Hélène* (1578), an astonishing two-part sequence that records a battle of wits between the aging poet and a sophisticated, headstrong young woman, and brings Petrarchism in France to a rousing conclusion. Sonnet II.24, "When you are very old, in the evening by candlelight," cleverly turns the tables on the young beloved – and on Petrarch's premonitions of Laura's demise – by reimagining Hélène as an old lady full of regret for resisting the poet when she was young: "You will be an old woman hunched over the hearth, lamenting my love and your cruel disdain."

English Petrarchism

In England, an initial wave of Petrarchism broke during the early 1530s and then receded for several decades, surfacing at intervals before a tidal re-emergence in the 1590s. Its initiator was Sir Thomas Wyatt (1503–42), an adventurer and court-appointed diplomat whose mission to Italy in 1526–27 exposed him to Petrarch's *RVF*. His friend Henry Howard, Earl of Surrey (1517–47), the son of England's leading peer, joined him in translating, adapting, and imitating dozens of Petrarch's sonnets, with notable stylistic variations. Their respective treatments of Petrarch's sonnet 140, "Love, who lives and reigns in my thought," display the differences between them. Wyatt's "The longe love, that in my thought doeth harbar," with its jagged rhythms, abrupt turns of phrase, and use of colloquial dialect, conveys a dynamism that contrasts with the wit and polish of Howard's "Love that doth raine and live within my thought."[9] As aristocratic amateur poets who felt no need to publish, both reached print posthumously in Richard Tottel's multi-authored miscellany of *Songs and Sonnets* (1557), where their work caught the imagination of a middle-class readership curious about the passions and pastimes of the nobility. Tottel himself encouraged such curiosity by affixing to each poem a moralizing headnote, usually declaiming the folly of lust and the bitterness of repentance.

The popularity of this much-reprinted anthology spurred various efforts during the 1570s and '80s to engage with Petrarch and his continental imitators. George Gascoigne's prose narrative *The Adventures of Master FJ* (1573, revised 1575) – replete with eight Petrarchan sonnets – portrays its hero as a cad who seduces the wife of his benefactor, only to be replaced by her secret paramour. Two decades later, Thomas Nashe's novella *The Unfortunate Traveler* (1594) – with two Petrarchan sonnets and a ballad inserted – recounts how its narrator, Jack Wilton, takes sexual advantage of the mistress of his benefactor, a fictionalized Henry Howard. In the interval, poets with diverse agendas experimented with Petrarchan themes and verse forms, drawing upon the *RVF*, as well as Petrarch's Italian, French, and

Spanish epigones. Petrarchism was beginning to echo and repeat itself. Thomas Watson's *Hekatompathia* (1582) assembles paraphrases from Petrarch, Serafino, Ariosto, Ronsard, and others, with commentaries on their sources, analogues, and moral import. Thomas Lodge's *Phyllis* (mid-1580s, pub. 1593) delivers translations from Petrarch, Bembo, Ronsard, Desportes, and others. But the pivotal moment came in 1591, when Thomas Newman published a piratical edition of *Astrophil and Stella* by Philip Sidney (1554–86), igniting a Petrarchan sonnet craze six years after the English author's death.

Sidney composed his sequence of 108 sonnets and eleven songs around 1581–82 upon temporary banishment from court after decrying Elizabeth I's proposed marriage to the Duke of Anjou. A year or so earlier he had drafted *A Defence of Poesy* (pub. 1595), in which he argues that "passionate sonnets" such as Petrarch's run the risk of "abus[ing] men's wit" unless readers assess them constructively.[10] The poetry of *Astrophil and Stella* tests this theory, as Sidney ironizes his besotted persona with fleet, funny, and politically pungent insight into the lover's shortcomings. Sonnet 71, "Who will in fairest booke of Nature know, / How Vertue may best lodg'd in beautie be," is his imitation of Petrarch's sonnet 248, and it shows how Astrophil misreads the former's high moral sentiment through indolence and self-pity. Willfully distorting his verse with slant rhymes, mixed meters, and outrageous conceits – "As fast thy Vertue bends that love to good: / But ah, Desire still cries, give me some food" – Astrophil reveals himself sinking under the weight of his own incomprehension.

Sidney's reinvention of Petrarchism pervades the sonnets of Edmund Spenser (1551?–99), assembled in a sequence, *Amoretti* (1595), to commemorate the poet's marriage to Elizabeth Boyle. *Amoretti* offers a Reformed Protestant version of Petrarchan desire made conformable with married love: "Love is the lesson which the Lord us taught" (sonnet 68).[11] William Shakespeare (1564–1616) published his own *Sonnets* late in his career (1609, but begun in the early 1590s), cementing his claims as a professional poet and complementing his work as a successful dramatist. Laced with echoes from Horace and Ovid and with reminiscences from Sidney and Spenser, these sonnets recount a lover's tortuous relationship with a Young Man and a Dark Lady that appears quite remote from Petrarch's influence and that of continental Petrarchism. Still, a haunting recall of fleeting time and approaching death from the *RVF* punctuates sonnet 17, "Who will believe my verse in time to come," sonnet 64 "When I have seen by Time's fell hand defacèd," and sonnet 104, "To me, fair friend, you never can be old."[12] Other Petrarchan figurations float close to the surface throughout the collection.

Spenser and Shakespeare in turn furnished materials for their successors to transform. In *Idea* (1599), Michael Drayton revised his *Ideas Mirrour* (1594), where allusions to Petrarch and Ronsard jostle with echoes from Sidney and Daniel, adding references to Spenser and – in still later editions – Shakespeare. In 1621, Philip Sidney's niece, Mary Wroth (1586?–1651?) brought English Petrarchism to an end with her sonnet sequence, *Pamphilia to Amphilanthus*, appended as a supplement to her two-volume prose romance, *Urania*.[13] Its protagonists derive from her narrative (which itself incorporates other sonnets and poems): Pamphilia is Queen of Morea, a paragon of virginal chastity and communal obligation; Amphilanthus is King of Naples, Holy Roman Emperor, and a lout. Wroth uses witty echoes from her uncle's poetry to distinguish between their respective personae. Sonnet 14, "Am I thus conquer'd?," for example, rewrites Sidney's sonnet 47, "What, have I thus betrayed my libertie?" With Pamphilia's renunciation of servitude to Cupid, the trope of amatory enslavement takes its final turn.

Transmitted with commentaries in early printed editions of the *RVF*, Petrarch's figurations and motifs traveled outside of Italy. The commentators' multiple representations of Petrarch as a poet, lover, scholar, public servant, and religious moralist took flesh in myriad ways that would respond to turbulent cross-currents of new eras. The diplomat-poet in the earliest commentaries anticipates the poet-adventurer of Garcilaso, Camões, and Wyatt, while the scholar-poet of Bembo, Gesualdo, Daniello, and others nourishes the intellectual interests of Herrera, Scève, and Du Bellay. The lover beset with tribulation in Vellutello's re-ordered *RVF* subtends the sharply defined narratives of many sixteenth-century sequences, and with Ronsard and Sidney it bleeds into the figure of the scholar-poet. The proto-Reformation Petrarch of Brucioli and Castelvetro modulates the Protestant accents of Spenser, Wroth, and Sponde. Still later, the amatory Petrarch merges with the doctrinal and moralist poet in the sonnets of Quevedo and Sor Juana. Collectively, these poets rework Petrarch's fourteenth-century poetry as they respond to sixteenth- and seventeenth-century concerns. The plurivocity of the *RVF* invites such reactions, and the multiple voice of fifteenth- and sixteenth-century commentaries clears a capacious space for them. In diverse registers and tones, the voice of the *RVF*'s protagonist reverberates through the lyric poetry of Renaissance Europe.

NOTES

1 John Dent-Young, ed. and trans., *Selected Poems of Garcilaso de la Vega: A Bilingual Edition* (Chicago, IL: University of Chicago Press, 2007).
2 William Baer, ed. and trans., *Selected Poetry of Luís de Camões: A Bi-Lingual Edition* (Chicago, IL: University of Chicago Press, 2005).

3 Sor Juana Inés de la Cruz, *Poems, Protest, and a Dream*, ed. and trans. Margaret Sayers Peden (New York: Penguin Books, 1997).

4 Ian D. McFarlane, ed., *The Délie of Maurice Scève* (Cambridge: Cambridge University Press, 1966).

5 Joachim Du Bellay, *Oeuvres poétiques*, 2 vols., eds. Daniel Aris and Françoise Joukovsky (Paris: Bordas, 1993–96).

6 Pierre de Ronsard, *Oeuvres complètes*, 2 vols., eds. Jean Céard, Daniel Ménager, and Michel Simonin (Paris: Gallimard, 1993–94).

7 For English translations, see Pierre de Ronsard, *Selected Poems with a Prose Translation*, ed. and trans. Malcolm Quainton (London: Penguin Books, 2002).

8 Labé, *Complete Poetry and Prose*, 43.

9 Richard S. Sylvester, ed., *English Sixteenth-Century Verse: An Anthology* (New York: W.W. Norton, 1984).

10 Katherine Duncan-Jones, ed., *Sir Philip Sidney: The Major Works* (Oxford: Oxford University Press, 2002).

11 William A. Oram, Einar Bjorvand, Ronald Bond, Thomas H. Cain, Alexander Dunlop, and Richard Schell, eds., *The Yale Edition of the Shorter Poems of Edmund Spenser* (New Haven, CT: Yale University Press, 1989).

12 William Shakespeare, *The Complete Sonnets and Poems*, ed. Colin Burrow (Oxford: Oxford University Press, 2002).

13 Josephine A. Roberts, ed., *The Poems of Lady Mary Wroth* (Baton Rouge, LA: Louisiana State University Press, 1983).

Conclusion

PART VI

Conclusion

18

GIUSEPPE MAZZOTTA

Petrarch's confrontation
with modernity

It is not surprising that the question of Petrarch's "modernity" should have haunted the critical debates over where exactly he might belong in the canon of literary history. The terms of such a debate have long been firmly set: Is Petrarch the first "modern" man, who inaugurated and fashioned an individual-centered style of thought and who opened up a new way of looking at the world, a mode of consciousness and praxis destined to become dominant in European Humanism? Or is he an antiquarian, who was fundamentally disoriented by the new intellectual fashions, who ultimately succumbed to the "medieval" temptation of the theological "dark ages," and who rejected Arab medical science (*Sen.* XII.2), dialecticians (*Fam.* I.7), Averroists, and so on as inferior to the achievements of the Christian–Latin traditions?

Can these two sharply opposed judgments be correlated with each other? Raising this possibility is plainly a way of asking whether or not there is a unity to Petrarch's thought. Is his work divided between the lyrical and the philosophical, between modernity and anti-modernity, as it were? A first answer to these perplexities is that so self-contradictory is Petrarch's sense of "modernity" that it practically becomes a mirror for his own inner and well-known ambivalences: the love of and regrets about Laura, the uncertain relation to Augustine, the divided view of Rome, and so on. He reflects on these contradictions so ceaselessly that we are logically forced to speak of Petrarch's *confrontation* with modernity. The term "confrontation" evokes at least two altogether different worlds, both punctuated by an unbridled contradiction: the self, with its internalized, fragmentary sense of time (in the form of memory and future expectations), and the world outside, with its cultural (at once political and spiritual) conflicts. The way these two components of Petrarch's thought are related to each other lies at the center of the present discussion. I will argue for a third way of understanding his modernity: Petrarch is a modern who, paradoxically, disavows his modernity, and he does so mainly as a way of acknowledging his rootedness in the communal memories of tradition.

The arguments in favor of his active opposition to modernity have been well rehearsed. Francesco Bausi has recently cast Petrarch unequivocally as an "anti-modern." He bases his claim on Petrarch's fierce opposition to and polemics with the scientific rationalism and medical science articulated in one important work, the *Contra medicum*.[1] In a way, this reading is of a piece with Petrarch's own self-characterization in *De ignorantia*. This tract stems directly as a response to some opponents' perception of his apparent anachronism and to their charge that he should not be counted as one of the moderns (see Chapter 13). We recall the unfolding of the poet's argument. Four young men show up at his house and hurl accusations at him. They charge that he is out of touch with modern movements of thought such as the rigors of Aristotelian philosophizing and the complexities of scientific analyses and classifications. For them, he is just a man of the past who rehashes dated mythologies and a rhetorician without true knowledge. Not without condescension, Petrarch takes revenge by describing them, with elegant contempt, as conformists in the "modern philosophical fashion" (*Sen.* V.2).

They miss, he argues, the critical question of the deep bond linking knowledge and eloquence, which Socrates, Plato, Cicero, and Augustine had grasped but Aristotle had bypassed, and he levels against them the charge of not understanding what his own text proceeds to reveal: the knot tying together the disciplines of ethics, theology, and rhetoric. The solid foundations in moral philosophy were laid for Petrarch in classical antiquity, and his guiding light is Socrates, who admitted the limitations not just of his knowledge but of the pursuit of radical ignorance. By casting "ignorance" as the orienting center of his life-experience, Petrarch rejects the category of "modern" as the criterion of judgment and obliquely opposes to it the label of a "classic": he steadily suggests that he stands within the classical and Christian tradition and he displays his pleasure in being counted not a man for one season, but a genuinely classical thinker, one whose work transcends the vagaries of time. We know that he long entertained the grandiose project to write an epic poem, *Africa*. The collateral, persistent fascination for the poem's Roman hero, Scipio, a historic figure with an eternal existence on account of his world-shaping actions and his life as a literary character, defines, in spite of the total failure to finish the work, the contours of Petrarch's own trans-historical ambition.

Regardless of what Petrarch says he thinks of himself (for, no doubt, the penchant for circumspect self-definitions is constitutive of his character), it has also been argued that Petrarch's enthusiasm for new paths of the imagination – such as his valorization of modern painting, music, and poetry – grows out of his antiquarian interests. This third interpretive paradigm, which I am here putting forth, depends on one central insight: Petrarch's real intellectual passion is the project of a new culture that emanates from him and his work and that is meant to orient present (and future) moral and aesthetic values. An illustration of this claim is in order here. We know that his early involvement with Latin texts, Roman myth, and history (in the form of biographies) climaxes in his *Collatio laureationis*. In this oration, the past achievements of Rome are never considered with detached scientific objectivity, but as markers of a temporal trace across the movement of tradition flowing into the stream of the present and beyond. The past casts a beam of light on the devastations of the world inherited by the present, but the contemplation of the Roman ruins opens up possible new interpretations of the past and visions of future projects. Retrospection, thus, is haunted by the desire to have it lead to prospective plans.[2]

For all their respective limitations and differences, these three critical viewpoints share one perception: the heart of Petrarch's thought, whether it comes through as against or in favor of the new directions of philosophical thought, lies in history. More precisely, when taken together and in spite of their intentions, these three views show that Petrarch understands history as the decisive locus where the sense of one's existence is primarily grasped and played out. Understandably, therefore, the argument about Petrarch's modernity can only begin where he begins: by exploring his representation of "self." The biographies he had written – and the autobiography that he endlessly writes – show his conviction that the world of history can be understood only through the prism of particular lives and through the subjective lenses of the self. Indeed, general, abstract accounts of history are useless unless they are based on the particularities and concreteness of individual lives. By fathoming a life's deeper realities, ruptured and displaced though the self may be, Petrarch casts his own self as the model for how the search for new historical values can be carried out and for how human culture can be reinvented in the world of history.

How does he understand the "self"? And what does he think modernity is? Where does he stand in relation to Dante and Boccaccio's literary and linguistic sense of modernity? These are the main questions to be confronted at the outset, and I will deal with them by keeping in mind that much of Petrarch's work amounts to a quest for the self, in the sense that he wants to grasp its depths and possibilities, and he carves the way to the "self" through the only possible route, the region of language. I would further suggest that he provides a new language in which to talk about the self and to define the self's *place* and *time* in history. These questions stand at the forefront of his poetry. He makes *place*, in the sense of finding the ground and relocating oneself and human beings in history, a central concern of his subjective consciousness: "Where am I?" "When and how did I get here?" These are the radical questions articulated in one of his most extraordinary lyrics, "Chiare, fresche, e dolci acque" (*RVF* 126, esp. 62) (see Chapter 5). By coming to terms with this preliminary sense of displacement we can define the ultimate destination of his work: the project to rebuild a modern empire of culture by engaging with the debates and values going on in the world around him.

But what was the "modern" intellectual world like for Petrarch, above and beyond medical science or the dialecticians? What was the meaning of "modernity" within which he thought and wrote? He was certainly aware of the historical shifts a term such as "modern" had undergone over time: "moderni" and "antiqui," "via moderna" and "via antiqua," "uso moderno" or "new style" versus traditional style had long been bandied around as principles of evaluation, as the object of charges and countercharges in poetic and philosophical circles. And Petrarch knew that, etymologically, "modern," from "modo" ("just now") and modus ("measure" and "manner"), designates a temporal consciousness, namely that which occurs in the present time, such as Petrarch's sudden, beginning passion for Laura in the "now" of his experience.

He construes the horizon of time and the evanescence of the present as constitutive of his discourse on modernity. More than that, they condition his thinking about the phenomenon of Laura and of love throughout his *RVF*, side by side with the question of place. He commemorates this sense of a temporal *beginning* of his passion as the *source* of his subsequent efforts to probe the depths of his own self. As is known, his poetry seeks to define the multiple meanings of that enigmatic, fleeting moment of his vision of the beloved, while at the same time lamenting its irretrievably lost quality. Will that moment when he discovered his (ecstatic) subjection to love ever come back? He painfully realizes that, though the "now" of his original passion was a decisive event, it is also an unrepeatable occurrence. Because it can only recur in the poet's imagination, it follows that the language of poetry, its style and its originality, lies at the heart of any possible claim of Petrarch's modernity. As we saw earlier in the context of *De ignorantia*, "modern" at one point qualified for Petrarch the language of false knowledge and delusions; it entailed a newfangled but transient fashion, and it described the juvenile taste for a style that he viewed as a fad.

There is what can be called a tradition and a style of the new, however, within which Petrarch inscribes his own work and which he plans to alter and surpass. It is the modern manner of stilnovistic poetry and its rich complications concerning the mind of the lover, the nature of images, and the elevating, noble virtues of love. One thinks of Dante's reflections on modernity as a specifically poetic style, which can be summarized as the consciousness that modernity needs an appropriate language in order to express time's steady self-renewal; and, as a style, it contains within itself the twisted tangles of the past, present, and future dimensions of history. The *Vita nova* tells of the search for a new language, for a new consciousness of love, and for a new future work. More precisely, in the context of an elaborate debate over poetic schools, tastes of palate (and art), and oscillations of styles in Purgatory, he features Bonagiunta, who defines the "sweet new style" Dante has heralded (*Purgatorio* XXIV, 55–62.). In this moral region where gluttony is cleansed, we hear that a turn has occurred in poetic taste, a "sweetness" has taken hold that, ironically, has displaced the "goliardic," convivial poets of the old school, such as Bonagiunta.

Later in the narrative, Dante acknowledges the importance of modernity. He hails his own predecessor Guido Guinizelli's "modern usage" (*Purgatorio* XXVI, 113). The adjective, on the one hand, acknowledges the novelty of Guinizelli's rhetorical mode; on the other, it defines the "new" style as an inexorably time-bound and fleeting phenomenon. The "modern" modality comes through as a perpetual succession of repetitive and finite experiences that, like the flow of hours and days, will last a brief moment till it is inevitably superseded by the advent of future fashions (*Purgatorio* XI, 94–101). Modernity, in short, in its flight forward, re-enacts the contradictory nature of the present time itself: like the vanishing present, modernity both is and is not always with us.

For Petrarch, as for this lyrical tradition he systematically echoes, modernity comes through, though not exclusively, as a question of style. A fresh perception of the world can only be made possible by a new sense of language. Without a doubt, his awareness of the imaginative powers and limitations of the stilnovists is made manifest at the very start of his *RVF*. For instance, over and against their "sweet new style" of love, he announces a "varied" style ("vario stile") for the self and the love he experiences (*RVF* 1, 4). "Vario" suggests discrepancies, differences, and changes – the style of time in its constant permutations. In a way, through the inconstancies and oscillations of his individualized moods, elegantly articulated, Petrarch wants to escape time, to monumentalize himself and become a classic, which means making his past forever immediately available or relevant to the present. Nonetheless, this desire for everlasting fame cannot obscure his engagement with the concrete and real situations of history. He knows that, existentially, he cannot escape the spiral of time within which he must find his place: only in time can he start again, can he arrive again at the point where a new origin for his self and his purposes can be imagined. The *Bucolicum carmen* tells this story only in part.[3] The *RVF*, on the other hand, seeks at every point to start anew, and generally it falls back on previous experiences. Yet, this style of lyrical self-reflection, of folding back on oneself, constitutes the epochal mark of Petrarch's modernity: an inimitable and forever imitated "Petrarchan" style through which we glimpse the complexities of the poet's self.

But how "modern" is his understanding of the self? How does it differ from the figuration of the self in St. Augustine's *Confessions*, traditionally held to be Petrarch's model? There exist some essential differences between their two self-representations. The *Confessions*, a text that rethinks the tradition of the philosophical/spiritual autobiographies (beginning with David's confessional psalms), starts by grounding in the historical particularities of Augustine himself the conventional analysis of an individual provided by ancient variants of the genre. In asking who this particular man is, who concretely he is, Augustine recounts his life as a spiritual conversion, as the process of disclosure of a radical shift of orientation in the relation between God and the "I" of the narrator. Augustine entertains no illusions about the claims either of self-sufficiency of philosophical reason or of man's autonomy from God. This means that he seeks a Christian overcoming of the self, a self-transcendence that overlaps with the experience of freeing his very will by subjecting it to the sovereignty of God's law so that a new world may be born. A Christian form of modernity emerges with Augustine. It is characterized by the discovery that a man's quest does not just end merely with his encountering his own self. An authentic journey can only lead to God.

Petrarch, his hesitations in the confessional dialogue with Augustine in the *Secretum* notwithstanding, eventually will acknowledge and will endorse the power of the Augustinian spiritual standpoint. But there is a valuable intermediate stage in his own journey. As an illustration of his moving away from an involvement in a humanized world of self-discovery to a metaphysical and ideological perspective, I would like to recall the well-known episode of his Latin translation of Boccaccio's Italian-language novella of Griselda told by Dioneo (*Decameron* X, 10), which he calls *De obedientia* (*A Wife's Remarkable Obedience and Faithfulness*) (*Sen.* XVII.3). Because the friendship between the two writers originated and was sealed by Boccaccio's gift of St. Augustine's commentary on the Psalms, even a quick look at Petrarch's translation can help us situate where he stands in relation to Boccaccio (and, indirectly, Augustine).

In point of fact, the translation marks the distance between Boccaccio's form of "modernity" and Petrarch's own mature intellectual horizon, which edges toward an Augustinian frame of thought. Petrarch changes the novella's modern language into classical Latin, into a manner he calls a "stilo alio": it is as if he wants the Italian vernacular to surrender to the majesty and fixity of an ancient language, Latin, so that its enduring moral values can be appropriately restored. In rhetorical terms, furthermore, Petrarch adopts a medieval allegorical mode to "translate" Boccaccio's novella of absurd domestic (and political) sado-masochism into a moral fable:[4] an allegory of the soul's obedience to God's plans. Finally, we witness an overt thematic transformation of Boccaccio's narrative. By his translation, Petrarch, in reality, silences what I call Boccaccio's "ethics of play."

This ethics of play stands as the dominant and most significant mode of the poetics of the *Decameron*, and it constitutes the key to grasping the sense of the Griselda novella. Such an ethics can be defined as a modern, earth-bound humanistic perspective that entails the characters' freedom to play by subjective rules of which they themselves are the origin: of these, the free spirit of Dioneo, the story's teller, is the supreme emblem of misrule and capricious self-assertion. Play, understood as the principle from which human-centered values and freedom stem, is lost in Petrarch's translation. His choice is clear-cut: a letter to Boccaccio (*Sen.* V.2) juxtaposes "vernacular" writings, such as the *Decameron*, which Petrarch calls "still new and capable of development," with the "lofty Latin style" of Antiquity, his style of choice. The preference is shadowed by a double-edged awareness, as most of his preferences are, and this doubleness conveys a nuanced sense of Petrarch's problematical view of modernity: Boccaccio, like Petrarch, still operates within the parameters of Latin genealogies (which are literally family pedigrees of myths and values), and he embraces the "new" vernacular as both a break and a link in the chain of transmission of archaic depths; in Dante's understanding of modernity, the future is past and is forever transcended in the ongoing spiral of history; for Petrarch, as if he is backtracking from his own vernacular works, the future cannot escape the historical conditioning of the past: indeed, the past contains the seeds of the future. Yet, Petrarch's search for a continuity within the discontinuous movement of time leads him to share in and depart from St. Augustine in one crucial respect: Augustine's vision of the birth of a new Christian world is radicalized by Petrarch as the ground in which a new cultural world to be built is rooted.

The new cultural project he advances cannot be defined as an altogether secular undertaking that is opposed to the Augustinian two cities and is circumscribed within the dimension of immanence. An aura of ambiguity hangs on the *RVF*'s representation of the bond between the secular and the theological. The text worries explicitly about the relation between a new conception of worldly love for Laura and its place within a traditional Christian frame of reference. As is well known, the poet's love experience is mixed with a systematic recollection of religious events. His passion, for instance, is said to begin on Good Friday, the day of Christ's Passion and sacrifice on the Cross, which is referred to as the "comune dolor" (*RVF* 3, 8). Further, an analogy is drawn between the poet's pilgrimage of love in every place around him and the journey to Rome of an old man who wants to gaze at the image of the face of Christ imprinted on the veil of the Veronica (16). Finally, the prayer of repentance to the "Padre del ciel" (17) and the prayer to the Virgin, "Vergine bella" (366), to mention the most obvious occurrences of religious language in the collection, force us to consider the most likely rationale behind this rhetorical strategy above and beyond facile formulas concerning Petrarch's inescapable doubleness or contradictoriness.

One consequence of his mixing the secular and the sacred is that the representation of his private world of desire and regrets is placed within the intelligible context of universal and eternal history. Such a move implies his desire to show that his actual, present experience, which irreducibly engages his self and totally occupies his mind, makes sense and becomes intelligible only in relation to that eternal history. From this standpoint, Petrarch suggests that his own future resembles his past, and that his present might last forever. No doubt, the deployment of sacred language to communicate the sufferings of his erotic passion darkly expresses also the distance yawning between the two worlds: the private secular passion and the theological vision. Setting them apart from each other expresses the inner gap in the poet's mind. He will not bridge that gap as Dante has done. By not following Dante, Petrarch opens up a different poetic and moral space. He confronts the fact that he inhabits an ambiguous time-bound region, of which the sacred and the secular are the mutually implicating poles. The text acts as a public confession of the radical ambiguity of his state. By acknowledging it, he marks his moral ambiguity, the presence of simultaneously contradictory pulls in his mind, as a sign of his authenticity.

This strategy allows Petrarch to peek into the abyss of the self, to analyze its tangled structure, and, to use St. Augustine's metaphor for the self in the *Confessions*, to come to terms with the "riddle" he has become to himself. He gives a daily representation of a self governed by the despotic power of love, a man who has lost his grip, who experiences impotence of the will and knows despair. This poetic history of the self in love (though conducted by retrieving the language of the troubadours and of the Sweet New Style) aims at nothing less than a new confessional self-knowledge, which is at variance with St. Augustine's aims. In the *RVF*, Petrarch reaches for a knowledge of the self not in relation to God, whom he acknowledges and begs for mercy, but in relation to himself. He pursues a truth about himself under the gossamer veil of narcissistic fictions and evasions – and this self-knowledge, artfully contrived, entails the possible definition of the boundaries of the self and of the self's possible historical action.

To clarify the stakes in the originality and modernity of Petrarch's self-analysis within what I would call a topography of time, I would like to look briefly at two sonnets from the *RVF* (35 and 87) describing the passion into which he has been catapulted. First, let us look at sonnet 35:

> Solo e pensoso i più deserti campi
> vo mesurando a passi tardi e lenti,
> et gli occhi porto per fuggire intenti
> ove vestigio uman la rena stampi.
>   Altro schermo non trovo che mi scampi
> dal manifesto accorger de le genti,
> perché negli atti d'allegrezza spenti
> di fuor si legge com'io dentro avampi:
>   Sì ch' io mi credo omai che monti e piagge,
> et fiumi e selve sappian di che tempre
> sia la mia vita, ch' è celata altrui;
>   ma pur sì aspre vie, né sì selvagge
> cercar non so ch' Amor non venga sempre
> ragionando con meco; et io con lui.
>
> (*RVF* 35)

(Alone and filled with care, I go measuring the most deserted fields with steps delaying and slow, and I keep my eyes alert so as to flee from where any human footprint marks the sand. No other shield do I find to protect me from people's open knowing, for in my bearing, in which all happiness is extinguished, anyone can read from without how I am aflame within. So that I believe by now that mountains and shores and rivers and woods know the temper of my life, which is hidden from other persons; but still I cannot seek the paths so harsh or so savage that Love does not always come along discoursing with me and I with him.)

This sonnet locates the self in space, along solitary fields, wild forests, and deserted roads. Its primary purpose is to bring us back to the familiar theme of the poet's self-absorption: engulfed in his passion, the poet/lover seeks solitude in broad daylight over the grounds of the natural world as a way of concealing and sheltering his inwardness from the gaze of outsiders. When he is finally alone, Love, personified like an alien force, enters his mind, where "sempre" ("always"; that is, transgressing all limits of time) the two of them, Love and the lover, converse together, "ragionando." This word evokes the

GIUSEPPE MAZZOTTA

rigor of logical argument, dialogues between lovers in gardens, as well as what later will be known as "ragionamenti d'amore." Love makes the poet isolate himself, as if solitude were the condition for thinking: the alliterative two adjectives in the first line, in which the sibilant sound of "solo" glides into the syllables of "pensoso," subtly link solitude and thinking.

In *De vita* (first sketched in 1346), Petrarch reflects on the moral values of solitude and asks whether or not it offers the perspective from which to plumb the depths of reality (see Chapter 9). Set over and against the practical aims and entanglements of the busy life, solitude, which is distinguished from loneliness, is tied to knowledge and wisdom and becomes co-extensive with moral philosophy. The philosophy of solitude Petrarch sketches concerns those with a "noble soul" (I, 1): human beings who in the *Nicomachean Ethics* (1123b–1125a) are said to be gifted with "megalopsychia" ("greatness of soul") and thus avoid all "slavish" concerns. Solitude was the trait of Christians, such as Basil, Ambrose, Benedict, Romuald, and Abelard, but also of pagan philosophers, such as Democritus, Parmenides, Seneca, and Epicurus. Their penchant for solitude amounts to an ethics, in that it depends on the choice to clear a space for thinking and to devote oneself to one's tasks. For Petrarch, solitude appears as the essential condition for freedom.

In sonnet 35, the alliteration of "solo e pensoso" – and its implication of a thoughtful solitude – remove the poet from the constraints of the natural world into the space of his mind. There is nothing idyllic, however, in this solipsistic portrait of the mind-in-love: the fiction of the dialogue and of rational meditation only hides a straying divided self, who is shut within himself. By the end of the sonnet, the picture of the poet who seeks autonomy to indulge in solitary amorous reflections undergoes a reversal: he finds himself willfully searching wild routes and nearly gets lost in a labyrinth of love. He reaches a hellish, properly dantesque place, where Love joins him and holds him under the sway of the pleasures of the love-discourse. The conclusion seals the poet's self-consciousness of being near the loss of self-sovereignty in the sense that any other action is precluded from him.

This reversal is subtly dramatized by a number of textual and structural details that complicate the overt thematic burden of the sonnet. Its movement is plainly organized by a series of rhetorical polarities. An inside/outside dialectics is quickly established and is accompanied by the antithesis of "spenti" and "avampi," and the motif of a hostile distance between self and others is countered by the suggestion of an evident familiarity between self and the natural world, as well as between self and the thought of love. But this natural landscape is not the customary dwelling place for the poet. It is a strange terrain, which at the start he goes on "measuring" (v. 2). The metaphor of "measure" undercuts the implications conveyed by the temporal adverb "always." "Always" entails continuity, the erasure of the edges and differences of time. To measure, on the other hand, evokes the language of geometry and suggests the logical process of finding definite limits and limitable boundaries as a way of determining what is distant or near, the planning of a calculus to avoid being seen and appearing for what one is. The sonnet draws, thus, the geometry of both a willed and an aimless displacement, where fields, rivers, banks, and woods – connected by a polysyndeton (vv. 9–10) that heightens the multiple elements of the terrain – "read" and make visible the melancholy mood of the lover's hidden interiority.

The phrase "anyone can read" (v. 8) certainly expresses Petrarch's central concern: the perimeter of language that he neither wishes to nor can escape. Textually, "read" epitomizes how the self becomes a sonnet, as it were: an object whose secret glyphs are made public and can be deciphered by all, and in which, as through a transparent veil of allegory, the integument does not shelter the "inside" kernel. In short, the act of writing, as an action, counters the intended self-concealment of the lover. The topography of this drama of the mind is made unfamiliar and even terrifying by the subtle allusion to two of Dante's hellish landscapes: the first recalling the physical and spiritual loss of self in the opening scene of *Inferno* (I, 5), the second faintly alluding to the wood of the suicides (XIII, 7–8).

Seen through this elaborate rhetoric of natural and imaginary places, the sonnet dramatizes, by the sequence of shifts and unstable signifiers, Petrarch's exploration of boundaries. The passion of love, perceived here paradoxically in both its transgressive and wild nature and its constant ratiocinations, knows no boundaries. By contrast, Petrarch's search for boundaries he can control highlights his attempt to *locate* himself in a place which is neither the solid natural world nor the social world. It is, however, the place of the poetic tradition, which he thinks he can control. In reality, he seeks to define the ground where he stands and to try to answer the question, "Where, then, am I?" What the sonnet discloses is that he stands in the place of his mind and of his poetry, in a locus where his being is, so to speak, both rooted and displaced. He grasps the source of his thoughts and metaphors, which are variously experienced as imagination, passion, a discourse on love, a "measure" of boundaries or rational control, and the dangers of self-loss under the transgressive mastery of love. On this ground, then, Petrarch discovers his self adrift, which can be defined as the threat besetting his solitary subjectivism.

This representation of human subjectivity, in which love, far from bringing the transcendent experience sought by, say, the stilnovists, appears as an obsessive presence and a possible spiritual trap, leads Petrarch to explore whether there is anything that can lift him out of his condition of despair. I define "despair" as his consciousness of the temporal impasse suggested by the adverb "always" and its illusory stability. Does he have the possibility of a purposive action or of a possible way out that is not a repetitive, protracted, and solipsistic act of remembering and being stuck in the past? The writing of the sonnet, with its formal order and its implied conversation with the privileged poetic voice of an "ancient" (Dante), certainly counters the randomness of the mind's movement and opens a condition of detachment from that experience. But Petrarch strives to find the possibility of a genuine new beginning, a public role for himself, and he can only do so by steadily delving into the history of his love. To understand and transcend it, he must retrieve the *instant* that first changed his life and has since become the pivot of his enterprise, as in sonnet 87 ("As soon as he has released the string"):

> Sì tosto come aven che l'arco scocchi,
> buon sagittario di lontan discerne
> qual colpo è da sprezzar et qual d'averne
> fede ch' al destinato segno tocchi;
>   similmente il colpo de' vostr' occhi,
> Donna, sentiste a le mie parti interne
> dritto passare, onde conven ch' eterne
> lagrime per la piaga il cor trabocchi;
>   et certo sono che voi diceste allora:
> "Misero amante! a che vaghezza il mena?
> Ecco lo strale onde Amor vol ch' e' mora."
>   Ora, veggendo come 'l duol m'affrena,
> quel che mi fanno i miei nemici ancora
> non è per morte ma per più mia pena.
>
> (*RVF* 87)

(As soon as he has released the string, a good archer discerns from afar which shot is futile and which he can believe will strike the intended target; thus you, Lady, felt the shot from your eyes pass straight into my inward parts, wherefore my heart must overflow through the wound with eternal tears; and I am certain that you said then ("allora"): "Miserable lover! Where does his desire lead him? Here is the arrow by which Love wishes him to die." Now ("ora"), since they see how my pain checks me, what my two enemies [still ("ancora") keep doing] is not designed to kill me but to increase my suffering.)

The monotony of the temporal "always" in "Solo e pensoso" is replaced by the consciousness of time's passing, its movement from "allora" ("then") to "ora" ("now") and "ancora" ("still") (vv. 9, 12, 13), from the *then* of the beginning of his love-suffering, through the apparent persistence of its power, to the *now* of the present realization that it is not death but pain his enemies – Love and Laura – will to inflict on him. Their attack is not random, and the sonnet foregrounds the deliberate action and willful exercise of his two antagonists. In effect, sonnet 87 plays an important role in the economy of the *RVF*. It is correlated to sonnet 35, but it also rewrites sonnet 2. In sonnet 35, the poet moves in space as a way of orienting himself, and in the process he casts his mind as the place of an endless self-same private dialogue with Love. In sonnet 87, the attention shifts to time as if it were the genuine ground of the poet's self-consciousness. He tries to retrace the origin of his love back to the instant, to that original moment when the "colpo" of Laura's eyes, the blink-of-an-eye experience, hit him. The poet aims at catching and understanding the sense of that instant, which constitutes a fragment of time and which, radically distinct from everything that went on before, marked a beginning or a break, shaped his future, and threatened to bring him to a mournful end. It is by grasping the sense of the "instant" that he can resolutely anticipate what he most wills: a project that transcends the narrow, self-same focus of his private (and yet still made public) passion.

Sonnet 87 reverses key assumptions about Petrarch's powerful self-analysis. It begins by evoking the contours of his poetic world: his passion endures without a break from the moment when – like an archer shooting his arrows – Laura darted her ruthless glance and wounded him. By taking Laura's point of view, her will that his sufferings persist but keep him from death, Petrarch treads a new territory in the rhetoric of love discourse: the stilnovists' optics, whereby the eyes are the vehicle of love, come forth completely altered. He invests Laura's glance and the archer's arrow not just with the moment of "seeing" or revelatory vision, but with a direction of the will, and so he grasps an element that turns out to be crucial to his purposive action and project: the power of willing. In sonnet 2, love was seemingly a chance occurrence, or so *he* thought. Now, by taking the point of view of his antagonists, it appears as a willed act.

The subtle link Petrarch forges between willing (whereby one may take charge of one's choices) and the value of the instant, which constitutes a gap in the consciousness of the continuity of time, whereby the "new" is perceived as such, carries other implications. The first is the idea of freedom, which, from the standpoint of time and history, entails the possibility of starting anew. Originality or novelty presupposes and overlaps with the state of freedom. The freedom of the will amounts to the choice to reject or to submit to the yoke of the past and to the temptation of viewing one's history as an unalterable fatality. Such an understanding of freedom faintly recalls Boccaccio's ethics of play and its source in freedom. Plainly, Petrarch does not formulate a general truth in the way Boccaccio does: if he did, he would risk losing sight of the concreteness and specificity enveloping his idea of subjectivity.

The temporal discontinuity, the "instant" when he was wounded by love, introduced a novelty in the poet's life and ruptured any belief in the formula of *nihil novi sub sole*. In this sense, the "instant" coincides with the awareness of a freedom that, in terms of his cultural project, will present itself as dangerous for him and which, nonetheless, he decides to pursue prudently. What matters, however, is that Petrarch manages to locate the "instant" of the time when his passion began and his life changed because the thought of the first beginning of love allows him to conceive the possibility of a second beginning. In the light of the mechanism explored here, the desire to begin again appears, in fact, as the project of leaving behind concealments and speaking in one's own voice (however dissimulated that might be). This amounts to laying the foundation for a new public discourse and, thereby, rethinking the past and the present of culture. Such a project he has been carrying on all along, but we can now appreciate its full force. For him, such a fundamental project, at one and the same time profoundly conservative and profoundly revolutionary, is characterized by his will to become a historical agent, or what today, by straining language, we would call a public intellectual.

The language for the self as a historical agent can only be a language of action. Such a rhetoric is systematically deployed in the series of invectives, veritable *logomachies*, in which he wills to set the terms of the public debates, shape them, and counter public antagonists. Laura was the inner fantasy of an enemy. Now he faces objective figures of hostile power. An exemplary case of this polemical, public performance is the *Contra medicum*, to which I now turn. The text was written in 1352, on the heels of the Black Death (1348), and the memory of that tragic experience wrecking Europe (and of the failure of medical science to cope with it) resonates on every page (see Chapter 13). Indeed, the passion enflaming the four invectives that make up the text was inevitable at this critical time, when the fresh creation of values and meaning had become as difficult as it was necessary. There was, of course, Boccaccio, who did nothing but ponder the event of the plague in the *Decameron*. He made it the background of his novellas, the historical context within which problems such as medicine, bodies, nature, order, freedom, sexuality, hierarchy, tyranny, laws, and the ethics of virtues and vices could be radically rethought.

Petrarch takes a longer view of the crisis of his time than does Boccaccio, in the sense that his text does not deal with the plague as such, either the mortal catastrophe befalling the city of Florence or its attendant social anarchy. Petrarch thinks at a different level, which must be called the level of historical action in the light of a projected future. To gauge his commitment to his plan, it is well to recall the immediate occasion for his writing these invectives, namely the blundering and seemingly gratuitous attack against his public reputation as a man of letters and of knowledge by a physician. Petrarch never names this physician in his four invectives, but he identifies him as attending to the health of Pope Clement VI in Avignon from 1342 to 1352.

The counterattack is ostensibly directed against the physician's claims about the sovereign importance of medicine, which – as we infer from the statements Petrarch attributes to him – he considers not just a distinct science but a tectonic discipline that encompasses and heals cases of ethics (the art of living well), rhetoric, and the liberal arts more generally. Petrarch opposes to these claims a number of highly abstract arguments that emanate from his radically different conception of the limits of the various sciences and of medicine itself. He states at the start that he does not intend to attack medicine, the art of Hippocrates and Galen, but only to make manifest the inadequacies of this physician who is variously cast as a charlatan and a swindler, and who believes that life is reducible to the health of bodies and not the care of the soul. Petrarch should be taken here at his word: his aim cannot be reduced simply to the intellectual and moral destruction of an unreliable physician; rather, he wants to engage the nature and perversities of the culture which the physician expresses. Thus, the text's arguments are interspersed with lengthy digressions on a number of generalized subjects, ranging from the value of rhetoric to the classical theme of the link between philosophy and death, from Horace's *Ars Poetica* and the dignity of poetry (*Contra medicum* III.110) to St. Augustine's reflections on the relation between theology and philosophy (III.123 ff), and from the poet's ability to control the obscurities of style (III.130 ff) to the proper hierarchy of rhetoric over medicine, as well as the link between medicine and ethics. These themes, in turn, are punctuated, quite overtly, by many references to Petrarch's own biography. One infers that Petrarch's text transcends the contingencies of his designated antagonist and that he intends to display his own superior understanding, as well as his power to persuade about the superiority of his cultural vision.

An intricate net of tightly interwoven and correlated purposes can, thus, be discerned behind the invectives. One such purpose, as already stated, concerns the injury to Petrarch's reputation by the slander of the physician; another concerns his political–theological ideas, which will be accepted as credible if he himself appears publicly credible. The first evident purpose consists in cutting the physician down to size and debunking his impostures as a philosopher, because, by all appearances, he enjoys and exercises great political influence on Pope Clement VI. The implication is that the pope was ill advised. But a more sinister inference is borne out: the physician's wicked influence has had imponderable consequences for the Church. His corruption of the Avignonese court, an immoral condition Petrarch consistently denounces, is made to coincide with the wickedness of the physician's own values. To expose the physician's evil beliefs and practices, Petrarch hints at his secret atheism and aligns him with the doctrines of Averroes and the heresies of Islam (II.84–85), among other things. Fortunately, so Petrarch remarks, the present pontiff, Pope Innocent VI (1352–62), "values your nonsense no more than it deserves" (IV.184). The reference to the new pontiff gives a strong signal of the worthlessness of the physician, who did not have the skill to take care of Pope Clement's life. It also suggests the hope that Innocent VI, who unmasked the physician as a quack, may lend a favorable ear to Petrarch's own intellectual claims.

From this standpoint, the physician may, at least in part, be an afterthought and a necessary pretext for the invectives. The real target Petrarch aims at is Pope Innocent VI and the spiritual/philosophical direction he might impart to the Church. This suggestion is made plausible by a detail mentioned at the outset: the physician had insinuated that Petrarch had flattered the pope (I.6). Petrarch pleads innocent to the charge, but the accusation of flattery in the papal court leads us to the legitimate suspicion that the invectives, which Petrarch calls a "certamen" ("contest"), amount to a power play between these two figures, the physician and the poet, both of whom have access to the pope and each of whom wants to exclude the other from the halls of power. We are witnessing the clash between their two totally opposed visions of the world, and of the Avignonese Church within it.

To win his case, Petrarch needs to engage in a personal self-defense. He needs to restore the public credibility of his voice and fame over and against the defamatory schemes of his opponent, whom he cannot but defame and whose intellectual reputation he has to annihilate. The success of his cultural project depends on his heroic will and the benevolence of his eventual cohorts. In this sense, Petrarch stages a carefully orchestrated political theater of the self. He presents himself to his audience as the champion of faith fighting a skeptic, and his manner is poised between a show of modesty and intellectual pride; he displays brilliant polemical powers, cites with precision Biblical and classical texts, and shows intellectual dexterity in branching out into general questions of knowledge, rhetoric, and, above all, the political theology of his time. In reality, his desire is to tell the pope the necessity of pulling asunder the bond between theology and the belief in the false objectivity of science. The spiritual crisis of the present – and this is an argument that historically remains alive till the Council of Trent – consists in the rationalization of faith (making it co-extensive with science to invest it with the status of an objective reality) over and against a theology of interiority and contemplation, which Ambrose, Augustine, Benedict, Bernard of Clairvaux, Bonaventure, and the Franciscans, among others, had theorized and practiced. Retrospectively, this idea of a theology of interiority rescues the meditative self-reflections of the *RVF* from the charge that they amount to mere narcissistic self-indulgences.

To make his attack upon the Avignonese Church (that is, upon the afflictions of modern Christianity) and his spiritual vision acceptable – that is to say, in order to become a historical agent capable of entering the fray and changing the discourse of the Church – Petrarch had to develop a practical theory of a language of action. The rhetoric of the *Contra medicum* rediscovers and recaptures the *skandalon* voiced by classical and prophetic strains of the tradition. Such a rhetoric was notoriously deployed by Cicero and, in more recent times, by Dante, who echoed the prophetic seers of the Old Testament and of Apocalypse. Unlike Dante, Petrarch trusts the intellectual power of the word to bring about the new culture, which can literally be called the "empire of the word." To achieve his purpose, he first selects a practical focus and makes his invective display properties capable of creating a public space within which his views are heard and can resonate. To achieve this aim, he adopts a radical partisan standpoint in the persuasion that he must take sides, and he does so with such polemical force in order that the arguments be taken as objective statements. The unintended consequence of such a strategy is that the invectives do not aim at the representation of some objective reality, but at the creation of a reality by the sheer power of speech.

To be sure, this description of the *Contra medicum* in terms of a "language of action" would not have been possible without the insights gained concerning language and the self in the *RVF*. There, he had probed the power and the powerlessness of his language and his self; he had perceived the crisis of his wounded will; he had discovered through his poetic writing freedom as the state of possible and alternate actions, as well as the role of the consciousness of time and place in situating oneself in the spiral of history. Above all, in the *RVF* he had grasped and expressed the event of language. Now he builds on this insight: the rhetoric of the *Invectives* turns language into a praxis and into a historical agency.

Clearly, Petrarch had earlier treated practical and political themes in hopes of conditioning the historical realities of the present without necessarily engaging in invectives. Memorably, his interaction with Cola di Rienzo's dreams of restoring the Roman Republic (1347) uncovers his desire to advance the political dimension of his cultural project: his letters to Cola show him taking his distance from a number of stories about the "myth of Rome," such as the Roman tribune's revolutionary fantasy of restoring the Roman Republic over and against the pope's sense of the Church's mission. In his interactions with Cola, Petrarch also departed from the political framework of the Roman Empire put forth by Dante's *Monarchia*, and he redefined the myth of Rome for the present and the future. What mattered to him now more than ever before was not Rome as such but, as always, the discourse *of* Rome, the values of universality that emanated from it across the vast geography of the modern world.

NOTES

1 Francesco Bausi, *Petrarca antimoderno: Studi sulle invettive e sulle polemiche petrarchesche* (Florence: Franco Cesati Editore, 2008).
2 See Giuseppe Mazzotta, "Petrarca e il Discorso di Roma," in *Petrarca, canoni, esemplarità*, ed. Valeria Finucci (Rome: Bulzoni, 2006), 259–272.
3 For a discussion of this text in autobiographical terms, see Giuseppe Mazzotta, "The Road to Freedom," *Humanities Review* 6 (2008): 187–201.
4 See Susanna Barsella, "Tyranny and Obedience: A Political Reading of the Tale of Gualtieri (Dec.X,10)," *Italianistica* XLII, 2 (2013): 67–77.

Primary sources

Agricola, Rudolf. "Vita Petrarchae." Ed. Ludwig Bertalot. *La Bibliofilia* 20 (1928): 382–404.

Bembo, Pietro. *Prose e rime*. Ed. Carlo Dionisotti. Turin: UTET, 1966.

   Lettere. 4 vols. Ed. Ernesto Travi. Bologna: Commissione per i testi di lingua, 1987.

Bidelli, Giulio. *Centoni del Petrarca*. Venice: Leonardo Furlano, 1544.

Boccaccio, Giovanni. *Epistole e lettere*. Ed. Ginetta Auzzas. In *Tutte le opere di Giovanni Boccaccio*. Vol. 5, pt. 1. Ed. Vittore Branca. Verona: Mondadori, 1992. 493–878.

   Vita di Petrarca. Ed. Gianni Villani. Florence: Salerno, 2004.

Bruni, Leonardo. "The Dialogues." *The Humanism of Leonardo Bruni: Selected Texts*. Eds. and trans. Gordon Griffiths, James Hankins, and David Thompson. Binghamton, NY: Medieval and Renaissance Texts and Studies, 1987.

Colonna, Vittoria. *Rime*. Venice: Marco Salvione, 1539.

Contini, Gianfranco, ed. *Poeti del Duecento*. 2 vols. Milan: Ricciardi, 1960.

Dante Alighieri. *Rime*. Ed. Domenico De Robertis. Florence: Le Lettere, 2002.

   Vita Nova. Ed. Guglielmo Gorni. Turin: Einaudi, 1996.

Dotti, Ugo, ed. *Lettere a Petrarca*. Turin: Aragno, 2012.

Du Bellay, Joachim. *Joachim du Bellay: "The Regrets," with "The Antiquities of Rome," Three Latin Elegies, and "The Defense and Enrichment of the French Language." A Bilingual Edition*. Ed. and trans. Richard Helgerson. Philadelphia, PA: University of Pennsylvania Press, 2006.

Franco, Niccolò. *Il Petrarchista* [1539]. Ed. Roberto L. Bruni. Exeter: University of Exeter 1979.

Gambara, Veronica. *Complete Poems. A Bilingual Edition*. Ed. and trans. Molly M. Martin and Paola Ugolini; critical intro. Molly M. Martin. *The Other Voice in Early Modern Europe: The Toronto Series 34*. Toronto, ON: Iter Inc. and The Center for Reformation and Renaissance Studies, 2014.

Labé, Louise. *Complete Poetry and Prose: A Bilingual Edition*. Eds. and trans. Deborah Lesko Baker and Annie Finch. Chicago, IL: University of Chicago Press, 2006.

Malipiero. Girolamo. *Il Petrarcha spirituale*, Venice: Marcolini, 1536.

Manetti, Giannozzo. *Biographical Writings*. Eds. and trans. Stefano U. Baldassarri and Rolf Bagemihl. Cambridge, MA: Harvard University Press, 2003.

Petrarca, Francesco. *Rime, Trionfi e Poesie Latine*. Eds. Ferdinando Neri, Guido Martellotti, Enrico Bianchi, and Natalino Sapegno. Milan and Naples: Ricciardi, 1951.

Prose. Eds. Guido Martellotti, Pier Giorgio Ricci, Enrico Carrara, and Enrico Bianchi. Milan and Naples: Ricciardi, 1955.

Il Canzoniere e i Trionfi. Ed. Enrico Fenzi. Rome: Salerno, 1993.

De gestis Cesaris. Ed. Giuliana Crevatin. Pisa: Scuola Normale Superiore. 2003.

Le familiari = Familiarum rerum libri. Ed. and trans. Ugo Dotti, with Felicità Audisi and Elvira Nota. 5 vols. Racconigi: Aragno, 2004–09.

Scève, Maurice. *The Délie of Maurice Scève*. Ed. Ian D. McFarlane. Cambridge: Cambridge University Press, 1966.

Seneca. *Ad Lucilium epistulae morales*. 2 vols. Ed. Leighton Durham Reynolds. Oxford: Clarendon Press, 1965.

Stampa, Gaspara. *The Complete Poems: The 1554 Edition of the "Rime," A Bilingual Edition*. Eds. Troy Tower and Jane Tylus; intr. and trans. Jane Tylus. Chicago, IL: University of Chicago Press, 2010.

Secondary sources (English)

Ascoli, Albert Russell. "Petrarch's Middle Age: Memory, Imagination, History, and the 'Ascent of Mt. Ventoux.'" In *"A Local Habitation and a Name": Imagining Histories in the Italian Renaissance*. New York: Fordham University Press, 2011. 21–58. First published 1991.

"Blinding the Cyclops: Petrarch after Dante." In *Petrarch and Dante: Anti-Dantism, Metaphysics, Tradition*. Eds. Zygmunt Barański and Theodore J. Cachey, Jr. Notre Dame, IN: University of Notre Dame Press, 2009. 114–173.

"Favola fui: Petrarch Writes His Readers." In *Bernardo Lecture Series*, 17. Binghamton, NY: Center for Medieval and Renaissance Studies, State University of New York at Binghamton, 2010.

"Petrarch's Private Politics." In *"A Local Habitation and a Name": Imagining Histories in the Italian Renaissance*. New York: Fordham University Press, 2011. 118–158.

Barański, Zygmunt G. "Petrarch, Dante, Cavalcanti." In *Petrarch and Dante: Anti-Dantism, Metaphysics, Tradition*. Eds. Zygmunt G. Barański and Theodore J. Cachey, Jr. Notre Dame, IN: University of Notre Dame Press, 2009. 63–75.

Barański, Zygmunt G. and Theodore J. Cachey, Jr., eds. *Petrarch and Dante. Anti-Dantism, Metaphysics, Tradition*. Notre Dame, IN: University of Notre Dame Press, 2009.

Barolini, Teodolinda. "The Making of a Lyric Sequence. Time and Narrative in Petrarch's *Rerum vulgarium fragmenta*." *MLN* 104 (1989): 1–38. Now in *Dante and the Origins of Italian Literary Culture*. New York: Fordham University Press, 2006. 193–223.

"Petrarch at the Crossroads of Hermeneutics and Philology: Editorial Lapses, Narrative Impositions and Wilkins' Doctrine of the Nine Forms of the *Rerum vulgarium fragmenta*." *Petrarch and the Textuals Origins of Interpretation*. Eds. Teodolinda Barolini and Wayne Storey. Leiden: Brill, 2007. 21–44.

"Petrarch as the Metaphysical Poet Who Is Not Dante. Metaphysical Markers at the Beginning of the *Rerum vulgarium fragmenta*." *Petrarch and Dante*.

Anti-Dantism, Metaphysics, Tradition. Eds. Zygmunt G. Barański and Theodore J. Cachey, Jr. Notre Dame, IN: Notre Dame University Press, 2009. 195–225.

"The Self in the Labyrinth of Time: *Rerum vulgarium fragmenta.*" in *Petrarch: A Critical Guide to the Complete Works.* Eds. Victoria Kirkham and Armando Maggi. Chicago, IL: University of Chicago Press, 2009. 33–62.

Barolini, Teodolinda and Wayne Storey, eds. *Petrarch and the Textual Origins of Interpretation.* Leiden and Boston, MA: Brill, 2007.

Baron, Hans. *Petrarch's "Secretum": Its Making and Meaning.* Cambridge, MA: Medieval Academy of America, 1985.

In Search of Florentine Civic Humanism: Essays on the Transition from Medieval to Modern Political Thought. 2 vols. Vol. 2. Princeton, NJ: Princeton University Press, 1988.

Bernardo, Aldo S. "Petrarch's Attitude toward Dante." *PMLA* 70 (1955): 488–517.

"Letter Splitting in Petrarch's *Familiares.*" *Speculum* 33 (1958): 236–241.

"The Selection of Letters in Petrarch's *Familiares.*" *Speculum* 35 (1960): 280–288.

Petrarch, Scipio, and the Africa. Baltimore, MD: Johns Hopkins University Press, 1962.

Petrarch, Laura and the "Triumphs." Albany, NY: State University of New York Press, 1974.

"Introduction." In *Francesco Petrarca: Rerum Familiarum Libri, I–VIII.* Ed. and trans. Aldo S. Bernardo. Albany, NY: State University of New York Press, 1975. xvii–xxxiii.

"Introduction." In *Francesco Petrarca: Letters on Familiar Matters: Rerum Familiarum Libri IX–XVI.* Ed. and trans. Aldo S. Bernardo. Baltimore, MD: Johns Hopkins University Press, 1982. xvii–xxii.

"Introduction." In *Francesco Petrarca. Letters of Old Age: Rerum Senilium Libri I–XVIII.* Trans. Aldo S. Bernardo, Saul Levin, and Reta A. Benardo. 2 vols. Vol. 1. Baltimore, MD: Johns Hopkins University Press, 1992. xvii–xxi.

Bernardo, Aldo S., with Reta A. Bernardo. *A Concordance to the "Familiares" of Francesco Petrarca.* 2 vols. Padua: Antenore, 1994.

Blumenberg, Hans. *The Legitimacy of the Modern Age.* Trans. Robert M. Wallace. Cambridge, MA: MIT Press, 1983. First published in German, 1966.

Braden, Gordon. *Petrarchan Love and the Continental Renaissance.* New Haven, CT: Yale University Press, 1999.

Cachey, Theodore J., Jr. "Introduction." In *Petrarch's Guide to the Holy Land: Itinerary to the Sepulcher of Our Lord Jesus Christ.* Ed. and trans. Theodore J. Cachey, Jr. Notre Dame, IN: University of Notre Dame Press, 2002. 1–50.

"Between Petrarch and Dante: Prolegomenon to a Critical Discourse." In *Petrarch and Dante: Anti-Dantism, Metaphysics, Tradition.* Eds. Zygmunt G. Barański and Theodore J. Cachey, Jr. Notre Dame, IN: University of Notre Dame Press, 2009. 3–49.

Capodivacca, Angela. "'Di pensiero in pensiero, di monte in monte': Petrarch's 'Modern Curiosity' in *Familiares* I.4 and IV.1." *MLN* 127.1 (2012) (Italian Issue Supplement): S54–S63.

Celenza, Christopher S. *The Lost Italian Renaissance: Humanists, Historians, and Latin's Legacy.* Baltimore, MD: Johns Hopkins University Press, 2004.

"Petrarch, Latin, and Italian Renaissance Latinity." *Journal of Medieval and Early Modern Studies* 35 (2005): 509–536.

Cervigni, Dino, ed. "Petrarch and the European Lyric Tradition." *Annali d'Italianistica* 22 (2004): 321–336.

Constable, Giles. "Petrarch and Monasticism." In *Francesco Petrarca, Citizen of the World*. Ed. Aldo Bernardo. Albany, NY: State University of New York Press, 1980. 53–99.

Cox, Virginia. *Women's Writing in Italy, 1400–1650*. Baltimore, MD: Johns Hopkins University Press, 2008.

DellaNeva, JoAnn. *Unlikely Exemplars*. Newark, DE: University of Delaware Press, 2009.

De Nolhac, Pierre. *Petrarch and the Ancient World*. Norwood, Norwood Editions, 1976 [1907]. Originally published as *Pétrarque et l'humanisme*. 2 vols. Paris, E. Bouillon, 1892.

Durling, Robert M. "Petrarch's 'Giovane donna sotto un verde lauro.'" *MLN* 86 (1973): 1–20.

"The Ascent of Mt. Ventoux and the Crisis of Allegory." *Italian Quarterly* 18 (1974): 7–28.

"Introduction." In Francesco Petrarca. *Petrarch's Lyric Poems*. Ed. and trans. Robert M. Durling. Cambridge, MA: Harvard University Press, 1976.

Durling, Robert M. and Ronald L. Martinez. *Time and the Crystal: Studies in Dante's "Rime Petrose."* Berkeley, CA: University of California Press, 1990.

Dutschke, Dennis. "The Anniversary Poems in Petrarch's *Canzoniere*." *Italica* 58 (1981): 83–101.

Eisenbichler, Konrad and Amilcare A. Iannucci, eds. *Petrarch's "Triumphs." Allegory and Spectacle*. Ottawa, ON: Dovehouse, 1990.

Eisner, Martin. "Petrarch Reading Boccaccio: Revisiting the Genesis of the *Triumphi*." *Petrarch and the Textual Origins of Interpretation*. Eds. Teodolinda Barolini and Wayne Storey. Leiden and Boston: Brill, 2007. 131–146.

"In the Labyrinth of the Library: Petrarch's Cicero, Dante's Virgil, and the Historiography of the Renaissance." *Renaissance Quarterly* 67 (2014): 755–790.

Enenkel Karl A. E. and Jan Papy, eds. *Petrarch and His Readers in the Renaissance*. Leiden: Brill, 2006.

Falkeid, Unn. "Style, the Muscle of the Soul. Theories on Reading and Writing in Petrarch's Texts." *Quaderni d'Italianistica*, 29. 1 (2008): 21–38.

"Petrarch, Mont Ventoux and the Modern Self." *Forum Italicum*, 43.1 (2009): 5–29.

"Petrarch's Laura and the Critics." *MLN*, 127.1 (2012) (Italian Issue Supplement): S64–S71.

Farmer, Julia. "Return to Sender: Meta-Epistolary Reflections of Political Disillusionment in Petrarch's *Rerum Familiarum Libri*." *Forum Italicum* 40 (2006): 234–250.

Feng, Aileen A. "In Laura's Shadow: Casting Female Humanists as Petrarchan Beloveds in Quattrocento Letters." In *The Inner Life of Women in Medieval Romance Literature: Grief, Guilt, and Hypocrisy*. Eds. Jeff Rider and Jamie Friedman. New York: Palgrave Macmillan, 2011. 223–247.

Foster, Kenelm *Petrarch: Poet and Humanist*. Edinburgh: Edinburgh University Press, 1984.

Freccero, John. "The Fig Tree and the Laurel: Petrarch's Poetics." *Diacritics* 5.1 (Spring, 1975): 34–40.

Fubini, Riccardo. *Humanism and Secularization: From Petrarch to Valla.* Trans. Martha King. Durham, NC: Duke University Press, 2003.

Garin, Eugenio. *Italian Humanism: Philosophy and Civic Life in the Renaissance.* Trans. Peter Munz, Oxford, Blackwell, 1965 [1952].

Gaylard, Susan Louise. *Hollow Men: Writing, Objects, and Public Image in Renaissance Italy.* New York: Fordham University Press, 2013.

Gilson, Simon. *Dante and Renaissance Florence.* Cambridge: Cambridge University Press, 2006.

Greene, Roland. *Post-Petrarchism: Origins and Innovation of the Western Lyric Sequence.* Princeton, NJ: Princeton University Press, 1991.

Greene, Thomas M. *The Light in Troy: Imitation and Discovery in Renaissance Poetry.* New Haven, CT: Yale University Press, 1982.

"Petrarch Viator: The Displacements of Heroism." *Yearbook of English Studies* 12 (1982): 35–57. Later published in Thomas M. Greene. *The Vulnerable Text: Essays on Renaissance Literature.* New York: Columbia University Press, 1986. 18–45.

Hainsworth, Peter. *Petrarch the Poet.* London: Routledge, 1988.

Hampton, Timothy. *Literature and Nation in the Sixteenth Century.* Ithaca, NY: Cornell University Press, 2001.

Hankins, James. "Petrarch and the Canon of Neo-Latin Literature." *Quaderni petrarcheschi*, forthcoming.

Helgerson, Richard. *A Sonnet from Carthage.* Philadelphia, PA: University of Pennsylvania Press, 2007.

Holmes, George. *The Florentine Enlightenment, 1400–50.* New York: Pegasus, 1969.

Holmes, Olivia. *Assembling the Lyric Self: Authorship from Troubadour Song to Italian Poetry Book.* Minneapolis, MN: University of Minnesota Press, 2000.

Jones, Ann Rosalind. *The Currency of Eros: Women's Love Lyric in Europe, 1540–1620.* Bloomington, IN: Indiana University Press, 1990.

Jones, Frederic J. "Arguments in Favour of a Calendrical Structure for Petrarch's *Canzoniere.*" *Modern Language Review* 79 (1984): 579–588.

Kahn, Victoria. "The Figure of the Reader in Petrarch's *Secretum.*" *PMLA* 100 (1985): 154–66.

Kennedy, William J. *Authorizing Petrarch.* Ithaca, NY: Cornell University Press, 1994.

The Site of Petrarchism: Early Modern National Sentiment in Italy, France and England. Baltimore, MD: The Johns Hopkins University Press, 2003.

Kircher, Timothy. *The Poet's Wisdom: The Humanists, the Church, and the Formation of Philosophy in the Early Renaissance.* Leiden: Brill, 2006.

Kirkham, Victoria and Armando Maggi, eds. *Petrarch: A Critical Guide to the Complete Works.* Chicago, IL: University of Chicago Press, 2009.

Lerner, Robert. "Petrarch's Coolness toward Dante." In *Intellectuals and Writers in Fourteenth-Century Europe.* Eds. Pietro Boitani and Anna Torti. Tubingen: G. Narr, 1986. 204–225.

Lokaj, Rodney. *Petrarch's Ascent of Mount Ventoux: The Familiaris IV, 1.* Rome: Edizioni dell'Ateneo, 2006.

Mann, Nicholas. "The Making of Petrarch's *Bucolicum carmen*: A Contribution to the History of the Text," *Italia medioevale et umanistica* 20 (1977): 127–186. *Petrarch.* Oxford: Oxford University Press, 1984.

Marsh, David. *The Quattrocento Dialogue: Classical Tradition and Humanist Innovation.* Cambridge, MA: Harvard University Press, 1980.

"Petrarch and Alberti." In *Renaissance Studies in Honor of Craig Hugh Smyth.* Vol. 1. Ed. A. Morrogh, F. Superbi Gioffredi, P. Morselli, and E. Borsook. Florence: Giunti Barbèra, 1985. 363–375.

"Petrarch and Jerome." *Memoirs of the American Academy in Rome* 49 (2004): 85–98.

Martinez, Ronald L. "Places and Times of the Liturgy from Dante to Petrarch," in *Petrarch and Dante: Anti-Dantism, Metaphysics, Tradition.* Eds. Zygmunt G. Barański and Theodore J. Cachey, Jr. Notre Dame, IN: University of Notre Dame Press, 2009. 320–370.

"Petrarch's Lame Leg and the Corpus of Cicero: An Early Crisis of Humanism?" In *The Body in Early Modern Italy.* Eds. Julia Hairston and Walter Stephens. Baltimore, MD: Johns Hopkins University Press, 2010. 42–58.

Mazzotta, Giuseppe. "A Life in Progress (*De vita et moribus Francisci Petrarchi de Florentia*)." In *Boccaccio: A Critical Guide to the Complete Works.* Eds. Victoria Kirkham, Janet Smarr, and Michael Sherberg. Chicago, IL: University of Chicago Press, 2013. 207–212.

"Petrarch's Epistolary Epic." In *Petrarch: A Critical Guide to the Complete Works.* Eds. Victoria Kirkham and Armando Maggi. Chicago, IL: University of Chicago Press, 2009. 309–319.

The Worlds of Petrarch. Durham, NC: Duke University Press, 1993.

McGuire, Brian Patrick. "Peopling Solitude. Petrarch in Crisis Years 1346–50." In *A Literary Miscellany Presented to Eric Jacobsen.* Eds. Graham D. Caie and Holger Nørgaard. Copenhagen: University of Copenhagen, 1988. 17–31.

McLaughlin, Martin L. *Literary Imitation in the Italian Renaissance: The Theory and Practice of Literary Imitation in Italy from Dante to Bembo.* Oxford: Oxford University Press, 1995.

Mommsen, Theodor E. "Petrarch's Conception of the Dark Ages." In *Medieval and Renaissance Studies.* Ed. Eugene Rice. Ithaca, NY: Cornell University Press, 1959. 106–129. First printed in *Speculum* 2 (1942): 226–242.

Najemy, John. *Between Friends: Discourses of Power and Desire in the Machiavelli-Vettori Correspondence of 1513–1515.* Princeton, NJ: Princeton University Press, 1993.

Navarrete, Ignacio. *Orphans of Petrarch: Poetry and Theory in the Spanish Renaissance.* Berkeley, CA: University of California Press, 1994.

Paden, William D. "Petrarch as a Poet of Provence." *Annali d'Italianistica* 22 (2004): 19–44.

Papy, Jan. "Creating an 'Italian' Friendship: From Petrarch's Ideal Literary Critic 'Socrates' to the Historical Reader Ludovicus Sanctus of Beringen." In *Petrarch and His Readers in the Renaissance.* Eds. Karl A. E. Enenkel and Jan Papy. Leiden: Brill, 2006. 13–30.

Perry, Kathleen Anne. *Another Reality: Metamorphosis and the Imagination in the Poetry of Ovid, Petrarch, and Ronsard.* New York: Peter Lang, 1990.

Petrucci, Armando. *Writers and Readers in Medieval Italy: Studies in the History of Written Culture*. Trans. Charles Radding. New Haven, CT: Yale University Press, 1995.

Prescott, Anne Lake. *French Poets and the English Renaissance*. New Haven, CT: Yale University Press, 1978.

Quillen, Carol Everhart. *Rereading the Renaissance: Petrarch, Augustine, and the Language of Humanism*. Ann Arbor, MI: University of Michigan Press, 1998.

Quint, David. "Humanism and Modernity: A Reconsideration of Bruni's *Dialogues*." *Renaissance Quarterly* 38 (1985): 423–445.

Rivers, Elias L., ed. and trans. *Renaissance and Baroque Poetry of Spain*. Long Grove, IL: Waveland Press, 1988.

Robbins, Jill. *Prodigal Son/Elder Brother: Interpretation and Alterity in Augustine, Petrarch, Kafka, Levinas*. Chicago, IL: University of Chicago Press, 1991.

Roche, Thomas P. "The Calendrical Structure of Petrarch's *Canzoniere*." *Studies in Philology* 71 (1974): 152–171.

Petrarch and the English Sonnet Sequences. New York: AMS Press, 1995.

Shapiro, Marianne. *Hieroglyph of Time: The Petrarchan Sestina*. Minneapolis, MN: University of Minnesota Press, 1980.

Seigel, Jerrold. *Rhetoric and Philosophy in Renaissance Humanism: The Union of Eloquence and Wisdom, Petrarch to Valla*. Princeton, NJ: Princeton University Press, 1968.

Smarr, Janet. "Petrarch: A Vergil without a Rome." In *Rome in the Renaissance: The City and the Myth*. Ed. Paul A. Ramsey. Binghamton, NY: Medieval and Renaissance Texts and Studies, Center for Medieval & Early Renaissance Studies, 1992. 133–140.

"Substituting for Laura: Objects of Desire for Renaissance Women Poets." *Comparative Literature Studies* 38.1 (2001): 1–30.

Steinberg, Justin. "Dante Estravagante, Petrarca Disperso, and the Spectre of the Other Woman." In *Petrarch and Dante: Anti-Dantism, Metaphysics, Tradition*. Eds. Zygmunt G. Barański and Theodore J. Cachey, Jr. Notre Dame, IN: University of Notre Dame Press, 2009. 263–290.

"Petrarch's Damned Poetry and the Poetics of Exclusion." In *Petrarch: A Critical Guide to the Complete Works*. Eds. Victoria Kirkham and Armando Maggi. Chicago, IL: University of Chicago Press, 2009. 85–100.

Stock, Brian. "Reading, Writing, and the Self: Petrarch and His Forerunners." *New Literary History* 26 (1995): 717–730.

After Augustine: The Meditative Reader and the Text. Philadelphia, PA: University of Pennsylvania Press, 2001.

Ethics through Literature: Ascetic and Aesthetic Reading in Western Culture. Lebanon, NH: University Press of New England, 2007.

Storey, H. Wayne. *Transcription and Visual Poetics in the Early Italian Lyric*. New York: Garland, 1993.

"Doubting Petrarca's Last Words. Erasure in MS Vaticano Latino 3195." In *Petrarch and the Textual Origins of Interpretation*. Eds. Teodolinda Barolini and H. Wayne Storey. Leiden and Boston: Brill, 2007. 67–91.

"A Note on the Application of Petrarchan Textual Cultures." In *Petrarch and the Textual Origins of Interpretation*. Eds. Teodolinda Barolini and H. Wayne Storey. Leiden and Boston: Brill, 2007. 13–19.

Struever, Nancy S. *Theory as Practice: Ethical Inquiry in the Renaissance.* Chicago, IL: University of Chicago Press, 1992.

"Petrarch's *Invective Contra Medicum*: An Early Confrontation of Rhetoric and Medicine." *MLN* 108 (1993): 659–679.

Sturm-Maddox, Sarah. *Ronsard, Petrarch, and the "Amours."* Gainesville, FL: University Press of Florida, 1999.

Trinkaus, Charles. *In Our Image and Likeness. Humanity and Divinity in Italian Humanist Thought.* 2 vols. Chicago, IL: University of Chicago Press, 1970.

The Poet as Philosopher: Petrarch and the Formation of Renaissance Consciousness. New Haven, CT: Yale University Press, 1979.

Vickers, Nancy J. "Remembering Dante: Petrarch's 'Chiare, fresche et dolci acque.'" *MLN* 96 (1981): 1–11.

"Diana Described: Scattered Woman and Scattered Rhyme." In *Writing and Sexual Difference,* ed. Elizabeth Abel. Chicago, IL: University of Chicago Press, 1982. 95–109.

Wallace, David. *Chaucerian Polity: Absolutist Lineages and Associational Forms in England and Italy.* Stanford, CA: Stanford University Press, 1997.

Waller, Marguerite R. *Petrarch's Poetics and Literary History.* Amherst, MA: University of Massachusetts Press, 1980.

Warley, Christopher. *Sonnet Sequences and Social Distinction.* Cambridge: Cambridge University Press, 2005.

Warner, J. Cristopher. *The Augustinian Epic, Petrarch to Milton.* Ann Arbor, MI: University of Michigan Press, 2005.

Watkins, Renee Neu. "Petrarch and the Black Death: From Fear to Monuments." In *Studies in the Renaissance.* Vol. XIX. New York: Renaissance Society of America, 1972. 196–223.

Wilkins, Ernest Hatch. *The Making of the "Canzoniere" and Other Petrarchan Studies.* Rome: Edizioni di Storia e Letteratura, 1951.

"*Peregrinus Ubique.*" In *The Making of the "Canzoniere" and Other Petrarchan Studies.* Rome: Edizioni di Storia e Letteratura, 1951. 1–8.

The Prose Letters of Petrarch: A Manual. New York: S. F. Vanni, 1951.

Studies in the Life and Works of Petrarch. Cambridge, MA: Medieval Academy of America, 1955.

Petrarch's Eight Years in Milan. Cambridge, MA: Medieval Academy of America, 1958.

Petrarch's Correspondence. Padua: Antenore, 1960.

Life of Petrarch. Chicago, IL: University of Chicago Press, 1961.

Witt, Ronald G. "Medieval *Ars Dictaminis* and the Beginnings of Humanism: A New Construction." *Renaissance Quarterly* 35 (1982): 1–35.

"*In the Footsteps of the Ancients*": The Origins of Humanism from Lovato to Bruni. Leiden: Brill, 2000.

Wojciehowski, D. A. [Hannah]. *Old Masters, New Subjects: Early Modern and Poststructuralist Theories of Will.* Stanford, CA: Stanford University Press 1995.

"Francis Petrarch: First Modern Friend." In *Texas Studies in Language and Literature* 47 (2005): 269–298.

Zak, Gur. *Petrarch's Humanism and the Care of the Self.* Cambridge: Cambridge University Press, 2010.

Secondary sources (Italian and languages other than English)

Afribo, Andrea. *Petrarca e petrarchismo: capitoli di lingua, stile e metrica.* Rome: Carocci, 2009.

Anselmi, Gian Mario, Luigi Tassoni, and Beáta Tombi, eds. *Petrarca europeo.* Bologna: Gedit, 2009.

Antognini, Roberta. *Il progetto autobiografico delle "Familiares" di Petrarca.* Milan: LED, 2008.

Antonelli, Roberto. "Petrarca, *Rerum vulgarium fragmenta.*" In *Letteratura italiana. Le opere, I. Dalle origini al Cinquecento.* General editor, Alberto Asor Rosa. Turin: Einaudi, 1992. 379–471.

Aurnhammer, Achim, ed. *Francesco Petrarca in Deutschland: Seine Wirkung in Literatur, Kunst und Musik.* Tübingen: Max Niemeyer, 2006.

Avena, Antonio. *Il "Bucolicum carmen" e i suoi commenti inediti.* Padua: Società cooperativa tipografica, 1906.

Baldacci, Luigi. *Il Petrarchismo italiano del Cinquecento.* 2nd edn. Padua: Liviana, 1974.

Baldassari, Gabriele. *"Unum in locum": Strategie macrotestuali nel Petrarca politico.* Milan: LED, 2006.

Bartuschat, Johannes. *Les "vies" de Dante, Pétrarque et Boccacce en Italie XIVe–XVe siècles.* Ravenna: Longo, 2007.

Bausi, Francesco. *Petrarca antimoderno. Studi sulle invettive e sulle polemiche petrarchesche.* Florence: Franco Cesati, 2008.

Belloni, Gino, Furio Brugnolo, H. Wayne Storey, and Stefano Zampi, eds. *"Rerum vulgarium fragmenta": Facsimile del codice autografo Vaticano Latino 3195.* 2 vols. Padua and Rome: Antenore, 2003–04.

Berra, Claudia, ed. *I "Triumphi" di Francesco Petrarca.* Bologna: Cisalpino, 1999.
Motivi e forme delle "Familiari" di Francesco Petrarca: Gargnano del Garda, 2–5 ottobre 2002. Milan: Cisalpino, 2003.

Berra, Claudia and Paola Vecchi Galli, eds. *Estravaganti, disperse, apocrifi petrarcheschi. Gargnano del Garda, 25–27 settembre 2006.* Milan: Cisalpino, 2007.

Berté, Monica, Vincenzo Fera, and Tiziana Presenti, eds. *Petrarca e la medicina. Atti del convegno di Capo d'Orlando, 27–28 giugno 2003.* Messina: Centro Interdipartimentale di Studi Umanistici, 2006.

Bertolani, Maria Cecilia. *Il corpo glorioso. Studi sui "Trionfi" del Petrarca.* Rome: Carocci, 2001.
Petrarca e la visione dell'eterno. Bologna: Il Mulino, 2005.

Biancardi, Giovanni. "L'ipotesi di un ordinamento calendariale del *Canzoniere* petrarchesco." *Giornale storico della letteratura italiana* 172 (1995): 1–55.
Petrarca e la visione dell'eterno. Bologna: Il Mulino, 2005.

Bianco, Monica and Elena Strada, eds. *I piu vaghi e i piu soavi fiori. Studi sulle antologie di lirica del Cinquecento.* Alessandria: Edizioni dell'Orso, 2001.

Billanovich, Giuseppe. "Petrarca e Cicerone." In *Miscellanea Giovanni Mercati.* Vol. 4. Vatican City: Biblioteca Apostolica Vaticana, 1946. 90–102.
Petrarca letterato. I. Lo scrittoio del Petrarca. Rome: Edizioni di Storia e Letteratura, 1947.

"Petrarch and the Textual Tradition of Livy." *Journal of the Warburg and Courtauld Institutes* 14 (1951): 137–208.

"Nella biblioteca del Petrarca: Il Petrarca, il Boccaccio, e le *Enarrationes in psalmos* di S. Agostino." *Italia medioevale e umanistica* 3 (1960): 1–58.

"Petrarca e il Ventoso." *Italia medioevale e umanistica* 9 (1966): 389–401.

Petrarca e il primo umanesimo. Padua: Edizioni Antenore, 1996.

Blanc, Pierre, ed. *Dynamique d'une expansion culturelle: Pétrarque en Europe, XIVe–XXe siècle: actes du XXVIe Congrès international du CEFI, Turin et Chambéry, 11–15 décembre 1995: à la mémoire de Franco Simone*. Paris, Honoré Champion, 2001.

Boriaud, Jean-Yves and Henri Lamarque, eds. *Pétrarque épistolier: actes des journées d'études, Université de Toulouse-Le Mirail, Toulouse, 26–27 mars 1999*. Paris: Les Belles Lettres, 2004.

Bosco, Umberto. "Particolari petrarcheshi. Precisazioni sulle *Invettive contra medicum*." *Studi petrarcheschi* 1 (1948): 97–109.

Brugnolo, Furio. "Libro d'autore e forma-canzoniere: implicazioni petrarchesche." *Atti e memorie dell'Accademia patavina di scienze lettere ed arti* 103.3 (1990–1991): 259–290.

Cachey, Theodore J. Jr., "'Peregrinus quasi ubique': Petrarca e la storia del viaggio." *Intersezioni: Rivista di storia delle idee* 17.3 (1997): 369–385.

Calcaterra, Carlo. "La leggenda di Laura." In idem., *Nella selva del Petrarca*. Bologna: Cappelli, 1942. 77–111.

Caputo, Rino. *Cogitans fingo: Petrarca fra "Secretum" e "Canzoniere."* Rome: Bulzoni, 1987.

Carrai, Stefano. "Petrarca e la tradizione delle rime per anniversario." *Italianistica* 33.2 (May/August 2004): 47–53.

Carrara, Enrico. "Feria sexta aprilis." In *Studi petrarcheschi e altri scritti*. Turin: Bottega d'Erasmo, 1959. 209–246.

Caruso, Carlo and Annalisa Cipollone, eds. *Petrarca e Boccaccio: Modelli letterari fra Medioevo e Umanesimo*. Alessandria: Edizioni dell'Orso, 2005.

Cherchi, Paolo. *Verso la chiusura. Saggio sul "Canzoniere" di Petrarca*. Bologna: Mulino, 2008.

Chines, Loredana, Floriana Calitti, and Roberto Gigliucci, eds. *Il petrarchismo: un modello di poesia per l'Europa*. 2 vols. Rome: Bulzoni, 2006.

Contini, Gianfranco. "Préhistoire de l'aura de Pétrarque." In *Varianti e altra linguistica*. Turin: Einaudi, 1970. 193–199.

"Preliminari sulla lingua del Petrarca." In *Il "Canzoniere" di Francesco Petrarca: La critica contemporanea*. Eds. Gennaro Barbarisi and Claudia Berra. Milan: Edizioni Universitarie di Lettere Economia Diritto, 1992. 57–85.

Collarile, Luigi and Daniele Maira, eds. *Nel libro di Laura*. Basel: Schwabe Verlag, 2004.

David, Michel. "La canzone 126 dei 'Rerum vulgarium fragmenta.'" *Lectura Petrarce* 8 (1988): 111–161.

De Venuto, Domenico. "Lacrime d'amante." *Linguistica e letteratura* 12 (1987): 67–74.

Dionisotti, Carlo. "Fortuna del Petrarca nel Quattrocento." *Italia medioevale e umanistica* 17 (1974): 61–113.

Dotti, Ugo. *Petrarca e la scoperta della coscienza moderna*. Milan: Feltrinelli, 1978.

Vita di Petrarca. Rome-Bari: Laterza, 1987.

Petrarca civile: alle origini dell'intellettuale moderno. Rome: Donzelli, 2001.

Petrarca a Parma. Reggio Emilia: Diabasis, 2006.

Fasani, Remo. "Legami lessicali." *Studi e problemi di critica testuale* 21 (1980): 165–179.

Fedi, Roberto. *La memoria della poesia. Canzonieri, lirici e libri di rime nel Rinascimento*. Rome: Salerno, 1990.

Fenzi, Enrico. "Petrarca e la scrittura dell'amicizia (con un'ipotesi sul libro VIII)." In *Motivi e formi delle "Familiari" di Francesco Petrarca*. Ed. Claudia Berra. Università degli Studi di Milano, Facoltà di Lettere e Filosofia, Quaderni di Acme 57. Milan: Cisalpino, 2003. 549–590.

Saggi petrarcheschi. Fiesole: Cadmo, 2003.

Petrarca. Bologna: Il Mulino, 2008.

Feo, Michele. "Fili petrarcheschi." *Rinascimento* n.s. 19 (1979): 3–89.

"La prima corrispondenza poetica fra Rinaldo da Villafranca e Francesco Petrarca." *Quaderni petrarcheschi* 4 (1987): 13–33.

"Il poema epico latino nell'Italia medievale." In *Il linguaggio della propaganda, studi di casi*. Ed. Istituto storico della resistenza in Piemonte. Milan: Bruno Mondadori, 1991. 30–73.

Fera, Vincenzo. *La revisione petrarchesca dell' "Africa."* Messina: Centro di Studi Umanistici, 1984.

Ferraro, Domenico. *In limine temporis. Memoria e scrittura in Petrarca*. Rome: Edizioni di Storia e Letteratura, 2008.

Finucci, Valeria, ed. *Petrarca, canoni, esemplarità*. Rome: Bulzoni, 2006.

Forni, Giorgio. *La pluralità del Petrarchismo*. Ospedaletto (Pi): Pacini, 2011.

Frasso, Giuseppe, Giuseppe Velli, and Maurizio Vitali, eds. *Petrarca e la Lombardia, Atti del Convegno di Studi, Milano, 22–23 maggio 2003*. Rome and Padua: Antenore, 2005.

Geri, Lorenzo, *Ferrea voluptas: Il tema della scrittura nell'opera di Francesco Petrarca*. Rome: Edizioni Nuova Cultura, 2007.

Gigliucci, Roberto. *Contraposti. Petrarchismo e ossimoro d'amore nel Rinascimento*. Rome: Bulzoni, 2004.

"Alcune cose sull'antipetrarchismo." *Critica letteraria* 38.2 (2010): 211–225.

Giuliani, Oscar. *Allegoria, retorica, e poetica nel "Secretum" del Petrarca*. Bologna: Patron, 1977.

Giunta, Claudio. "Memoria di Dante nei *Trionfi*." *Rivista di letteratura italiana* 11 (1993): 411–452.

Lafleur, Claude. *Pétrarque et l'amitié: doctrine et pratique de l'amitié chez Pétrarque à partir de ses textes latins*. Paris: Vrin, 2001.

Lanza, Antonio, ed. *Polemiche e berte litterarie nella Firenze del primo Rinascimento (1375–1449)*. Rome: Bulzoni, 1989.

L'Io lirico: Francesco Petrarca. Critica del Testo 6.1: 2003.

Luciani, Evelyn. *Les "Confessions" de saint Augustin dans les lettres de Pètrarque*. Paris: Études augustiniennes, 1982.

Marcozzi, Luca. *Bibliografia petrarchesca, 1989–2003*. Florence: Olschki, 2005.

Petrarca Platonico: Studi sull'imaginario filosofico del "Canzoniere." Rome: Aracne, 2011.

Martellotti, Guido. "Sulla composizione del *De viris* e dell'*Africa* del Petrarca." In *Scritti petrarcheschi.* Eds. Michele Feo and Silvia Rizzo. Padua: Antenore, 1983. 3–26.

Martinelli, Bortolo. *Petrarca e il Ventoso.* Bergamo: Minerva Italica, 1977.

"Il Petrarca e la medicina." In Francesco Petrarca. *Invective contra medicum.* Ed. Pier Giorgio Ricci. Rome: Edizioni di Storia e Letteratura, 1978. 205–249.

Mazzotta, Giuseppe. "Petrarca e il discorso di Roma." In Valeria Finucci, ed. *Petrarca, canoni, esemplarità*, Rome: Bulzoni, 2006. 259–272.

Mezzanotte, Gabriella. "Pier Candido Decembrio e la 'Vita' del Petrarca attribuita a Antonio da Tempo." *Studi petrarcheschi* n.s. 1 (1984): 211–224.

Niederer, Christoph. "La bipartizione in vita/in morte del *Canzoniere* di Petrarca." In *Petrarca e i suoi lettori.* Eds. Vittorio Caratozzolo and Georges Güntert. Ravenna: Longo, 2000. 19–41.

Noferi, Adelia. *Frammenti per i "Fragmenta" di Petrarca.* Ed. Luigi Tassoni. Rome: Bulzoni, 2001.

Pasquini, Emilio. "Preliminari all'edizione dei *Trionfi.*" In *Il Petrarca ad Arquà. Atti del Convegno di Studi nel VI Centenario (1370–1374).* Eds. Giuseppe Billanovich and Giuseppe Frasso. Padua: Antenore, 1975. 199–240.

Perugi, Maurizio. *Trovatori a Valchiusa: Un frammento della cultura provenzale del Petrarca.* Padua: Antenore, 1985.

Petrarca e Roma. Atti del convegno di studi (Roma, 2–4 dicembre 2004). Rome: Roma nel Rinascimento, 2005.

Petrarca politico. Atti del convegno (Roma-Arezzo, 19–20 marzo 2004). Rome: Istituto Storico Italiano per il Medio Evo, 2006.

Petrucci, Armando. *La scrittura di Francesco Petrarca.* Vatican City: Biblioteca Apostolica Vaticana, 1967.

"Minuta, autografo, libro d'autore." *Il libro e il testo.* Eds. Cesare Questa and Renato Raffaelli. Urbino: Università degli Studi di Urbino, 1984. 399–414.

Picone, Michelangelo. "Petrarca e il libro non finito." *Italianistica* 33.2 (May/August 2004): 83–93.

Porcelli, Bruno, ed. *Petrarca volgare e la sua fortuna sino al Cinquecento.* Pisa/Rome: Istituti Editoriali e Poligrafici Internazionali, 2004.

Quondam, Amadeo. *Il naso di Laura. Lingua e poesia lirica nella tradizione del Classicismo.* Modena: Panini, 1991.

Riccucci, Marina. "L'esordio dei *Triumphi*: tra *Eneide* e *Commedia.*" *Rivista di letteratura italiana* 12 (1994): 313–349.

Rico, Francisco. *Vida u obra de Petrarca. Studi sul Petrarca.* Vol. 4. Padua: Editrice Antenore, 1974.

Rizzo, Silvia. "Il latino del Petrarca nelle *Familiari.*" In *The Uses of Greek and Latin.* Eds. A. Carlotta Dionisotti, Anthony Grafton, and Jill Kraye. London: The Warburg Institute, 1988. 41–56.

"Introduzione." In Francesco Petrarca. *Res Seniles, Libri I-IV.* Ed. Silvia Rizzo with Monica Berté. Florence: Le Lettere, 2006.

Rossi, Vittorio. "Sulla formazione delle raccolte epistolari petrarchesche." *Annali della cattedra petrarchesca* 3 (1932): 53–73.

Santagata, Marco. *Dal sonetto al canzoniere: Ricerche sulla preistoria e la costituzione di un genere.* Padua: Liviana, 1979.

Per moderne carte: la biblioteca volgare di Petrarca, Bologna: Il Mulino, 1990.

I frammenti dell'anima. Storia e racconto nel "Canzoniere" di Petrarca. Bologna: Il Mulino, 1993.

Solerti, Angelo, ed. *Le vite di Dante, Petrarca e Boccaccio scritte fino al secolo decesimosesto.* Milan: Vallardi, 1904–1905.

Stierle, Karlheinz. *Francesco Petrarca: ein Intellektueller im Europa des 14. Jahrhunderts.* München: Hanser, 2003. Italian translation: *La vita e i tempi di Petrarca alle origini della moderna coscienza europea.* Venice: Marsilio, 2007.

Storey, H. Wayne. "Canzoniere e Petrarchismo: un paradigma di orientamento formale e materiale." In *Il Petrarchismo. Un modello di poesia per l'Europa.* Vol. 1. Ed. Loredana Chines. Rome: Bulzoni, 2007. 291–310.

Tarugi, Luisa Secchi, ed. *Francesco Petrarca. L'opera latina: Tradizione e fortuna. Atti del xvi convegno internazionale (Chianciano-Pienza 19–22 luglio 2004).* Florence: Franco Cesati, 2006.

Tateo, Francesco. *L'ozio segreto di Petrarca.* Bari: Palomari, 2005.

Tradizione e realtà nell'Umanesimo italiano. Bari: Dedalo, 1967.

Tonelli, Natascia. *Varietà sintattica e costanti retoriche nei sonetti dei "Rerum Vulgarium Fragmenta."* Florence: Olschki, 1999.

Trovato, Paolo. *Dante in Petrarca.* Florence: Olschki, 1979.

Velli, Giuseppe. "Il proemio dell'*Africa.*" *Italia Medioevale e umanistica* 8 (1965): 323–332.

"La memoria poetica del Petrarca." *Italia medioevale e umanistica* 19 (1976): 171–207.

"Il Dante di Francesco Petrarca." *Studi petrarcheschi N.S,* 2 (1985): 185–199.

"Petrarca e la grande poesia latina del XII secolo." *Italia medioevale e umanistica* 28 (1985): 295–310.

Voce, Stefania. *Bibliografia sull' "Africa" di Petrarca, dal 1900 al 2002.* Cesena: Stilgraf, 2004.

Zamponi, Stefano. "Il libro del *Canzoniere*: modelli, strutture, funzioni." In *Rerum vulgarium fragmenta, Codice Vat. Lat. 3195. Commentario all'edizione in facsimile.* Eds. Gino Belloni, H. Wayne Storey, and Stefano Zamponi. Rome and Padua: Editrice Antenore, 2004. 13–72.

Zanzotto, Andrea. "Petrarca fra il palazzo e la cameretta." In *Scritti sulla letteratura.* Vol. I. Ed. Gian Mario Villalta. Milan: Mondadori, 2001. 261–271.

Zingarelli, Nicola. "Petrarca e i trovatori." In *Provenza e Italia.* Ed. Vincenzo Crescini. Florence: Bemporad, 1930. 97–139.

INDEX

Abizzi, Franceschino degli, 161
Accursio, Mainardo, 27, 30
adynaton, 157, 158
Africa, xvi, 2–3, 7, 14, 17, 18–21, 25, 56,
    75, 85–86, 87–98 *passim*, 104, 108,
    123, 125, 132, 134–135, 145,
    147–148, 150, 180, 182, 184, 189,
    222 (*see also* Scipio Africanus)
  Book III, 93
  Book IV, 94
  Book V, 94
  Book VI, 94
    885–918, 93
  Book VII, 94
  Book VIII, 95
  Book IX, 95
    60–64, 97
    98–103, 145
    101, 145
    217–19, 98
    235–36, 93
    275–6, 98
    279–80, 85, 98
  Bucolicum carmen and, 87, 89, 91, 125
  Christian style in, 150
  De viris and, xvi, 14, 17–20
  Ennius' prophetic vision in, 98
  epic tradition in, 17, 21, 93–94, 96, 125
  Epystole and, 87, 93, 125
  fictional veil in, 94
  historical basis of, 93–94
  Humanist views on, 182
  incompletion of, 19, 56, 86, 88, 123, 125,
    134
  influence of, 2, 180, 182, 184, 189
  inspiration for, 87
  Massinissa episode in, 97
  praise of Rome and Scipio in, 95

  premature consecration of, 88
  Rome's war with Carthage in, 95–96
  Secretum and, 104, 108, 123, 148
  Triumphi and, 21, 25, 29, 84
  work begun on, xvi, 87–88, 93
Agricola, Rudolf, 185
Albanzani, Donato, 172
Alberti, Leon Battista, 186, 188
  On the Family, 187
  Refuges from Hardships, 187
  Theogenius, 187, 188
allegory
  allegorical canzoni of Dante, 165, 183
  in *Bucolicum carmen*, 91–92
  fictional veil, 93–94
  of laurel, 91–92
  Petrarch's allegorization of Griselda tale,
    226–227, 231 (*see also Seniles,*
    Book XVII)
  in *Secretum*, 100–101, 107
  in *Triumphi*, 77–78, 83, 161–162
"Ambrosian Virgil" (Petrarch's copy of
    Virgil), 50, 85, 87, 93, 98, 142–143
amicitia vera, 31 (*see also* friendship)
Amor triumphans (topos), 80
anti-Petrarchism, 196–197 (*see also*
    Petrarchism)
Apollo, 41–42, 55, 160, 198 (*see also*
    Daphne; Laura; laurel, myth of;
    laurel crown/laureation)
Appenninigena, Donato, 130
Aretino, Pietro
  La Cortigiana, 194, 196
  Ragionamenti, 194
Ariosto, Ludovico, 194
Aristotle, 144, 146, 150, 172–173, 222
  History of Animals, 188
  Nicomachean Ethics, 230

Aristotelianism (*see* Aristotle, *De ignorantia*, Scholasticism)
Atanagi, Dionigi, 199
Augustine, Saint, 20, 56, 143 (*see also* *Secretum*; will)
   City of God, 169
   Commentaries on the Psalms, 149
   Confessions, 20, 41, 56, 101, 103, 106, 109, 226, 228
   De vera religione, 101, 103–104, 106, 109, 115–116
   Soliloquia, 103, 112
Augustinus (character in *Secretum*) (*see* *Secretum*)
author's book, 51, 161, 165
Avignon
   as cultural and political center, 4, 27–28
   Papacy and the (*see* Papacy, in Avignon; Petrarch, Francesco, and the Avignonese Papacy)
   Petrarch's residence in, xv–xvii, 3–6, 14–15, 17, 94, 112, 127, 132, 135, 141–142, 154 (*see also* Petrarca, Francesco, residence in Vaucluse)

Babylonian captivity of the Church (*see* Church, Babylonian Captivity of; Papacy, in Avignon; Petrarch, Francesco, and the Avignonese Papacy)
Barański, Zygmunt, 38
Barbato da Sulmona, xvi, 28, 88, 90, 93 (*see also* Petrarch, friends of)
Barolini, Teodolinda, 72, 163
Baron, Hans, 5
Barrili, Giovanni, 28, 89
Battiferri, Laura, 199
Belisario da Cingoli, 195
Bembo, Pietro, 184, 192
   De Imitatione, 62
   Gli Asolani, 193
   Le cose volgari di messer Francesco Petrarcha, 192
   and Petrarchism, 192–200 *passim*, 211, 216–217
   Prose della volgar lingua, 52–53, 184, 192, 193, 210
   Rime, 193
   role in editing *RVF*, 52–53
Bembo, Torquato, 53
Bernard of Clairvaux
   On Consideration, 175
Berni, Francesco, 196–197

Bersuire, Pierre, 93
Bidelli, Giulio, 195
Biondo, Flavio, 183
Black Death, xvii, xviii, 29–31, 34, 38, 56–67, 90, 121, 124, 127, 133, 146, 151, 170, 234
Blumenberg, Hans, 1
   Legitimacy of the Modern Age, 102
Boccaccio, Giovanni, 22, 23, 30–31, 130–131 (*see also* *Familiaries*, Boccaccio in; Petrarch, friends of; *Seniles*, Boccaccio in)
   Amorosa visione, 80
   De casibus virorum illustrorum, 2
   De claris mulieribus, 2
   Decameron, xviii, 30, 51, 133, 227
      book 10, story 10 (Griselda), xviii, 122, 132–134, 152, 185, 226
   Exposition on Dante's Comedy, 180
   Genealogy of the Pagan Gods, 180
   in *Familiares*, 124, 127, 129, 130, 162
   in *Seniles*, xviii, 5, 126, 128, 130–131, 132–134, 141–142, 181, 227–228
   Life of Petrarch, 132, 134, 180
   modernity and, 226–227
   visit to Padua, xvii
Boscán, Juan, 210–211
Bracciolini, Poggio, 175, 181, 186
   Misery of the Human Condition, The, 188
   Unhappiness of Princes, The, 182
Brandt, Sebastian, 185
Brucioli, Antonio, 199, 210
Bruni, Leonardo, 100, 182–183, 186
   Dialogi, 182–186, 187
   Brutus (Cicero), 182
Buck, August, 186
Bucolicum carmen, xvii–xviii, 2, 7, 17, 21, 22, 25, 85, 87–88, 89–92, 123, 125, 226
   Apicius (character), 91
   composition of
      final manuscript copying of, 17
      work begun on, xvii
      years written, 90–91
   conclusion of, xviii
   continuous narrative in, 92
   Dane (character), 91
   individual eclogues
      I *Parthenias*, 90–92, 148, 149
      II, 90–92
      III *Amor pastorious*, 90–92
      IV, 90–91, 92
      V *Pieta pastoralis*, 90–92

Bucolicum carmen (*cont.*)
  VI, 90–92
  VII, 90–91
  IX, 90–91, 92
  X, 90–92
  XI, 90–91, 92
  XII, 90–92
  influence of, 2
  inspiration for, 87
  Martius (character), 91
  number of eclogues in, 21
  Silvius in, 148–149
  structure of, 91–92
  Stupeus (character), 91
  summaries of three individual eclogues, 91
  Triumphi and, 22
  Virgilian pastoral in, 92
  Volucer (character), 91
Burckhardt, Jacob, 1

Cabassoles, Philippe de, xvi, 20, 28, 111,
  112, 116 (*see also* Petrarch, friends
  of)
Calmeta, Vincenzo, 194
Camillo, Giulio, 198
Camões, Luís de
  Os Lusíadas, 211–212
canson, 156, 157, 158
cansos, 154–155
Canzoniere (*see Rerum vulgarium
  fragmenta*)
capfinidas, 163–164
Caraman, Jean de, 170–171
care, philosophy of, 142–151 *passim* (*see
  also* ethics)
Caro, Annibal, 197
Carrara family, 3, 5 (*see also* Patrons)
  Francesco da Carrara, 19, 122, 126
  Jacopo da Carrara, 132
Casini, Francesco, 168
Castellani, Tommaso, 198
Castelvetro, Lodovico, 199, 210
Castiglione, Baldassare
  Book of the Courtier, The, 194
Cathedral Library of Verona, 29, 121
Cavalcanti, Guido, 56, 161
Celenza, Christopher, 186
Celestine V, Pope, 114–115
centone, 195–196
Cetina, Gutierre de, 211
Charles IV, Emperor, xvii, xviii, 4, 33, 115,
  122, 126–127 (*see also* Patrons)
Charles V, Emperor, 211

Charles V, King of France, 173
Chaucer, Geoffrey
  Troilus and Criseyde, 210
Church, 115–116, 146–148, 175 (*see also*
  Avignon, Popes and Papacy)
  Babylonian captivity of, 86, 173
Cicero, 3, 5, 28, 29, 31, 32, 56, 79, 85, 100,
  109, 113, 125–129 *passim*, 142–152
  passim, 170–175 *passim*, 180–181,
  183–184, 193, 222, 237
  Ad Quintus, 146–147
  Brutus, 182
  De amicitia, 27, 31–34
  De officiis, 31
  De oratore, 144
  De re publica (lost dialogue), 99 (*see also*
    Macrobius)
  dialogues, as model for Petrarch, 100,
    112, 180, 183
  discovery of letters, by Petrarch, 3, 7, 29,
    121, 141
  discovery of orations by Petrarch, xvii
  Hortensius, 172
  letters of, as model for Petrarch, 7, 29, 85,
    121, 125, 129, 141, 152
  Letters to Atticus, 7, 141
  On the Nature of the Gods, 172
  Petrarch's letter to, 29, 121, 141, 152
  Pro Archia, xvi, 96
  Pro Plancio, 112
  Tusculan Disputations, 104, 142, 188
Cielo d'Alcamo, 163
Cino da Pistoia, 161
Cinquecento (16th century), 52–53
Clement V, Pope, 4
Clement VI, Pope, 168, 170, 221, 222, 235,
  236
coblas singulars (poetic form), 155
Collalto, Collaltino di, 206
Collatio laureationis (Coronation Oration),
  xvi, 86, 96, 179, 180, 223 (*see also*
  laurel crown/laureation)
Colonna, Giacomo, xv, xvii, 27
Colonna, Giovanni, xvi, 4–5, 27–29, 44,
  122, 124, 167, 195 (*see also* patrons;
  Petrarch, friends of)
  death of, xvii, 29
  Petrarch's appointment as chaplain to,
    4
Colonna, Vittoria, 199, 200, 202–204, 206
  Il trionfo della Croce, 203–204
  Rime, 199, 203
  Rime spirituali, 200, 203

Colonna family, 3, 15, 27, 29–30, 91
  Petrarch's conflict with, 29
commentaries on Petrarch's works, 184,
    193–197 passim, 200, 202, 210,
    212, 217
congedo (poetic device), 156, 157, 159,
    160–161
Contarini, Zaccaria, 171
contempus mundi ("contempt of worldly
    things"; topos), 117
Contini, Gianfranco, 44
Contra eum (see Invectives)
Contra medicum (see Invectives)
Contra quendam (see Invectives)
"Corona of Love Casuistry" (poem), 164
Correggio (city), 15
Correggio, Azzo da, xvi, 21, 22, 28, 57 (see
    also patrons)
Correggio form of RVF, 21, 22, 48–49,
    57–58 (see also RVF)
Corso, Rinaldo
  Tutte le Rime di Vittoria Colonna, 202
Cortesi, Paolo
  Dialogue on Learned Men, 184
Council of Trent, 237
Cox, Virginia, 207
Cristiani, Luca, 27
Croce, Benedetto, 191
cursus (Latin prose meter), 145

d'Abano, Pietro
  Conciliator of Differences between
    Philosophers and Physicians, 169
d'Alife, Niccolò, 28
Dandolo, Andrea, 171
Dandolo, Leonardo, 171
Daniel, Arnaut, 156, 157, 159, 162
  "Lo ferm voler," 159
Daniello, Bernardino, 195, 210
Dante Alighieri, 56
  Commedia, 38, 55, 72–74, 81, 82–83, 88,
    161, 192, 201
    Inferno, 81, 97, 115, 231
    Paradiso, 46, 97
    Purgatorio, 80, 88, 225
  Convivio, 135
  De vulgari eloquentia, 157
  influence in Petrarch's vernacular poetry,
    8, 22–23, 41, 44–47, 56, 72–73,
    154–155, 157–159, 162, 165,
    230–232
    on Africa, 88, 92, 99
    on Bucolicum Carmen, 92

  on RVF, 41, 44–45, 47, 55, 56, 72–73,
    155, 161
  on Triumphi, 23, 38, 74–76, 80–84,
    159, 161–162, 203
  Monarchia, 4, 238
  Petrarch's attitude toward, 3, 4, 22–23,
    122, 127, 130, 145, 159, 162, 223,
    225, 227–228, 232, 238
  Petrarch's letters about, 22, 82, 122,
    162
  rime petrose, 159–161, 166
    "Al poco giorno," 156, 158, 159
    "Così nel mio parlar," 159
  Vita nova, 41, 44–45, 47, 155, 225
Daphne, 41–42, 55–56, 136, 160 (see also
    Apollo; Laura; laurel, myth of; RVF,
    myth of Apollo and Daphne in)
d'Aragona, Tullia
  Rime, 199
Davanzati, Chiaro, 161
de Baïf, Jean-Antoine
  Amour de Francine, 214
De ignorantia (On His Own Ignorance and
    That of Many Others) (see
    Invectives)
de la Cruz, Sor Juan Inés, 212–213
De otio religioso, 85, 111–119
  chain between material and spiritual
    world in, 117–118
  Christian Humanism in, 116
  as critique of European politics, 111
  discerning Christ in, 116, 117
  eternal Spectator in, 111, 118
  ideological orientation for, 19–20
  illusions of the world in, 118
  opening scene, 20
  sermon-like discourses in, 20
  soliloquies, 112
  St. Francis in, 118
  vertical movement in, 115–116
  work begun on, xvii
  writing during Lent, 111–112
De regimine principium tradition, 125
De remediis utriusque fortunae, 2, 22, 49
  completion of, 17–18
  dialogue form in, 17, 86
  work begun on, xvii
de Retz, Maréchale, 214
de' Rossi, Nicolò, 161
De Sanctis, Francesco
  History of Italian Literature, 191
de Tyard, Pontus
  Erreurs amoureuses, 214

De viris illustribus (*On the Lives of Illustrious Men*), xvi, xviii, 2, 20, 21, 56, 86, 94, 123, 145, 147–148, 150
  Africa and, 14, 17–20, 94, 145, 147, 148, 150
  Christian style in, 150
  Griselda (character), 152
  influence of, 2
  last version of, xviii, 133–134
  Petrarch's departure/arrival in, 18
  RVF and, 21, 49
  structure of, 49
  work begun on, xvi, 145
De vita solitaria, 111–119, 229–231
  authors quoted in, 113
  contemplative life, 113–114
  counter-power in, 115–116
  as critique of European politics, 111
  first written during Lent, xvii, 111–112
  ideological orientation of, 19–20
  leisure and business in, 112
  opening scene, 20, 112–113
  Pope Celestine V in, 114–115
  popes and monarchs in, 115
  soliloquies, 112
  solitary life, 114
  two books, 114
Del Sarto, Andrea, 194–195
Della Casa, Giovanni, 195
Della Rocca, Cesare, 200
Derrida, Jacques, 32
Desportes, Philippe
  Premieres oeuvres poétiques, 214
dialogue form, 112, 186
  in *De remediis*, 17, 86
  influence of Petrarchan dialogue on Humanism, 186–189
  in *Secretum*, 2, 100, 180, 226
  in *Tusculans*, 188
Disperse, 91, 121, 122–123
Dolce, Lodovico, 196
  Observationi, 198
  Rime, 199
Domenichi, Lodovico
  Rime diverse d'alcune nobilissime, et virtuosissime donne, 199, 201
  Rime diverse di molti eccellentissimi autori, 198
Dondi, Giovanni, 169
Dotti, Ugo, 121
Dovizi da Bibbiena, Bernardo, 194
Drayton, Michael

Idea, 217
Ideas Mirrour, 217
Du Bellay, Joachim
  Défense et illustration de la langue francoyse, 213–214
  Les Antiquitez de Rome, 213
  Les Regrets, 213
  Olive, 213
  Songe, 213
Du Guillet, Pernette, 208
  Rymes, 213

endecasillabo (*see* hendecasyllable)
English Petrarchism, 215–217 (*see also* Petrarchism)
Ennius, 98 (*see also Africa*)
Epystole (*Verse Letters*), xvii, xviii, 16–17, 20, 25, 88–90, 120, 121, 123, 125, 136, 121, 123
  arrangement and publication of, 88
  Book I
    1, 90
    2–3, 89
    4, 89
    7, 89
    12, 89
    13, 89
    14, 89
  Book II, 89–90
    8, 90
    10, 90, 93
    17, 90
    18, 18, 89
  Book III, 90
    8, 89
    19, 13
    21–3, 89
    24 ("Ad Italiam"), 16, 89
    29, 89
  completion of, 17
  early Capitoline triumph in, 90
  early versions of individual poems, 89
  hexameter in, 87
  named recipients in, 88
  Petrarch's achievement in Latin language and, 120
  Petrarch's career as poet laureate and, 89–90
  publication of, xviii
  Seneca in, 113
  temporal range in, 89
Erasmus
  Ciceronianus, 185

ethics
  aim of, 144
  medicine and, 233
  moral philosophy and, 186
  of play, 226–227, 233
  Roman, vs. Greek philosophy, 175
  secularism and, 185–186
  styles and, 142

Faidit, Gaucelm, 162
Familiares, 85, 121
  Book I, 125
    1, 13, 16, 20, 51, 57, 125, 146, 152
    3, 16
    4, 16
    5, 16, 40
    8, 122
    9, 142, 144
  Book IV, 126
    1 ("Letter from Mt. Ventoux"), xvi, 102–103, 106–107, 122, 126
  Book V
    19, 168
  Book VI
    2, 122
  Book VII, 126
  Book VIII, 126, 127–128
    3–5, 30
    7, 146, 147–148
    10, 30
  Book IX, 126, 127
  Book X, 126
    3, 149
    4, 77, 87, 91, 109, 125, 126–127, 132, 148, 149
  Book XI
    1, 129
    2, 129
    5, 127, 130
    6, 129
    15, 130
  Book XII, 126
  Book XIII
    19, 79, 130
  Book XIV, 126
    1, 145
  Book XV
    3, 32
  Book XVI
    11–12, 127
  Book XVII, 126
  Book XVIII, 127–130
    2–5, 128

    4, 129
    5, 128
    7, 121, 128, 129
    8, 128, 129
    11–12, 128
    12, 128
    14, 128
    15, 127, 129–130
  Book XIX, 126, 127, 130
  Book XX
    13, 32–33
  Book XXI
    10, 126
    15, 22, 122, 162
  Book XXII
    2, 122
    10, 149
  Book XXIII
    19, 122
  Book XXIV, 186
    3, 29 (*see also* "Cicero, letter to")
    3–13, 122
    5, 141
  Boccaccio in, 124, 127, 129, 130, 162
  coherence with Petrarch's works, 124–125
  composition of
    completion of, 17
    work begun on, xvii
  death and, 124
  inspiration for, 29
  "Letter from Mt. Ventoux" (*Fam.* IV.1), 102–103, 106–107, 122, 126
  as macro-epistle to Socrates, 123–124
  as mega-macrotext, 123
  opening letter of, 152
  Petrarch's achievement in Latin language and, 120
  Petrarch's departure/arrival in, 16, 18
  post-plague years in, 30
  relationship to *Seniles*, 123–124, 125, 126–127, 129–131, 132–133
  writing style in, 146
fantasmata (illusions), 101, 103, 106–107
female Petrarchists, 201–208 (*see also* Petrarchism)
Fenzi, Enrico, 150
Ferreira, António
  Poemas Lusitanos, 211
Ficino, Marsilio, 193
Filelfo, Francesco, 184
Folgore de San Gimignano, 164
Folquet de Marseille, 162
Francis, Saint, 118

Franco, Niccolò, 196
  Il Petrarchista, 197
Franco, Veronica, 199
Frederick II, Emperor, 154
French Petrarchism, 213–215 (*see also*
  Petrarchism)
friendship, 26–34, 120–133 *passim*, 136,
  167, 180 (*see also* Petrarch, friends
  of)
  absence and, 32, 123–124, 127–128, 133
  Ciceronian, 31, 33
  classical ideals of, 31
  as deepest of all relationships, 33
  as a masculine virtue, 31
  Petrarchan, 34
  social mobility and, 27–28
  solitude and, 112
  through letters, 33, 133
Fubini, Riccardo, 185

Gabriele, Trifon, 194
Gambara, Veronica, 198, 204
Garcilaso de la Vega, 211
Gascoigne, George
  Adventures of Master FJ, The, 215
Gaul (France), 175
Gerolamo (copyist), 57
Gesualdo, Giovanni Andrea, 195, 210
Gherardo (brother of Petrarch), xv, xvi,
  19–20, 33, 85, 91, 111, 116, 126,
  127, 128, 149
Giolito, Gabriele de' Ferrari (printer),
  198
Giovio, Paolo
  Elogia, 184
  Ischian dialogues, 184
Góngora y Argote, Luis de, 212
grand climacteric, 131
Greene, Thomas, 123, 202
Guidiccioni, Giovanni, 198
Guido da Bagnolo, 171
Guilhelm de Saint Gregori, 160
Guinizelli, Guido, 225
Guittone d'Arezzo, 155, 161, 163, 164

Hankins, James, 2
Hannibal, 95–96
hendecasyllable (poetic line), 74, 159
Herrera, Fernando de, 211
Hesdin, Jean de, 173–174, 175
Hesiod, 206
hexameter, Latin (poetic meter), 87–99
  passim, 145, 147

Horace, 39, 142
  Ars Poetica, 88, 93, 221, 236
  Epistulae, 87, 93
  Odes, 39
Howard, Henry (Earl of Surrey), 215
Hugh of St. Victor
  Didascalicon, 168–173
human dignity, 185
Humanism, 1, 85, 98
  Christian, 116, 172
  Italian, 100, 175
  Petrarch and, 23, 77, 84, 172, 179,
    181
  Petrarch as father of, 141, 179
  and Renaissance, 172, 179
Humanists, 3, 113, 117, 167, 174–176,
  177–189, 192–193
  in Cinquecento (sixteenth century), 3
  Florentine, 183
  historical perspective, 186
  intellectual freedom and, 113
  moral philosophy and, 186
  pagan literature and, 187
  Quattrocento (fifteenth century), 3, 173,
    184, 187, 192
  and Renaissance, 117, 179
Hurtado de Mendoza, Diego, 211

imitative Petrarchism (*see* Petrarchism)
Innocent VI, Pope, 170, 236
Invectives, 8, 17, 127, 167–176,
  234–236
  Contra eum, xviii, 17, 18, 167, 173–176
  Contra medicum, xvii, 17, 18, 167,
    168–169, 170, 186, 222, 232, 233,
    234, 235–237
    Book 1, 169
    Book 2, 169
    Book 4, 170
    confrontation with modernity in, 222,
      232, 233
    first draft, xvii
    pagan literature in, 186
  Contra quendam, xvii, 17, 18, 167,
    170–171
  De ignorantia, xviii, 17, 18, 144,
    150–151, 167, 171, 172, 222, 224
    Aristotle's authority in, 172
    confrontation with modernity in, 222,
      224
    devotional statement in, 150
    strong style in, 150–151
    against Trecento culture, 167

Itinerarium ad sepulchrum Domini, xviii, 86
 (*see also* Petrarch, travel)

John of Garland
 Poetria, 87
John XXII, Pope, 170

Kempen, Ludwig van (*see* Socrates)
Kircher, Timothy, 186
Kristeller, Paul Oskar, 1, 185

Labé, Louise
 Evvres (Works), 214
 Rymes, 208
Lactantius, *Divine Institutes*, 80
Laelius (Lello Stefano de' Tosetti) (*see*
 Petrarch, friends of, Laelius)
Landino, Cristoforo, 184
Lanfranchi, Paolo, 157
Lapo Castiglionchio the Younger,
 186
Laura, 38, 40
 in *Bucolicum carmen*, 91–92
 death of, xvii, 29, 38, 40, 43, 44, 124
 after death of, 58
 in *Familiares*, 124–125
 first meeting with, xv, 40, 48, 63, 64–66
 imagining new Laura after death, 45
 and laurel, 39–40, 41–42, 47, 49, 91,
  124–125, 135, 156, 201–202
 reorientation by female poets, 203,
  205–206
 representations of Petrarch's love for, 33,
  38, 42, 57–58, 224–227, 233
 reunification with, 24
 in *RVF*, 46
  in Chigi form of, 23
  in Corregio form of, 22, 23
  final appearance in, 46
 in *Testamentum*, 15
 tomb of, 213
 in *Triumphi*, 76, 77–78, 82
laureation, 3, 87, 89, 90, 93, 126
laurel
 generals (or rulers) and, 96
 and Laura, 39–40, 41–42, 47, 49, 91–92,
  124–125, 135, 156, 197, 201–202
 myth of, 47, 55, 87
 status and responsibilities conferred on
  Petrarch, 89–90
laurel crown/laureation, xvi, 3, 15, 28, 55,
 80–81, 86, 87, 89–90, 93, 95, 96, 98,
 126, 135, 179, 180, 201–202, 223

"Letters on Familiar Matters" (*see*
 Familiares)
"Letter to Posterity" (*see Seniles*,
 Book XVIII)
Livy, 56
 History of Rome (*Ab urbe condita*), 3, 56,
  94, 142
Lodge, Thomas
 Phyllis, 216
Longhi, Matteo, 27
Longiano, Sebastiano Fausto da, 195
lyrics, vernacular, 154–165
 beloved-as-wind motif, 156
 fin' amors and, 155
 origins of, 154–165
 wordplay and, 155–156

Machiavelli, Niccolò, 186
macrotexts, 120, 122–123
 Familiares as, 123, 132
 microtexts and, 122–123, 162–163
 RVF as, 162–163, 165
 Seniles as, 123, 131, 132
Malatesta, Pandolfo, xviii, 51, 59–60
Malipiero, Girolamo
 Il Petrarca spirituale, 196
Malpaghini, Giovanni (scribe), 17, 18, 23,
 51, 59, 61
Manetti, Giannozzo
 *Lives of Three Illustrious Florentine
  Poets*, 183, 184
Manuzio, Aldo (printer), 185, 192
Marcabru, 155
 Cercamon *canson*, 156, 157
Marcozzi, Luca, 38
Marot, Clément, 213
Marqués de Santillana, 210
Marsh, David, 101, 186
Martelli, Lodovico, 197
Martini, Simone, 4, 40, 87
Maternus, 131
 Astrology, 131
Matraini, Chiara, 199
Mazzeo di Ricco da Messina, 163
Mazzotta, Giuseppe, 6, 8, 38, 112, 122–123,
 132
Medici, Giuliano de', 194
Mellin de Saint-Gelais, 213
Miraval, Raimon de, 163
modernity, 221–238
 Boccaccio's form of, 226–227
 meanings of, 224
 Petrarch and, 1–2, 6, 8, 120

modernity (*cont.*)
 of *Secretum*, 100
 secularism and, 102
 self and, 223–224
Molza, Francisco Maria, 197
Mommsen, Theodor E., 1, 186
Monte Andrea, 161
Morra, Isabella di, 199
mourning, weak style and, 147 (*see also* style*)
Muzzarelli, Giovanni, 198

Nashe, Thomas
 Unfortunate Traveler, The, 215
negotium, 112 (*see also otium*)
Nelli, Francesco (Simonides), 32, 93, 121, 124, 130, 149 (*see also* Petrarch, friends of)
Neumarkt, Johann von, 185
Newman, Thomas, 216
Nolhac, Pierre de, 53

Occitan poetry, 58, 76, 82, 154–157, 159, 160, 162, 163, 165
Onesto da Bologna, 161
Orsini, Fulvio, 53
otium, 113, 116
 negotium and, 112
Ovid, 56, 143, 147
 Amores, 80, 147
 Ex Ponto, 148
 Tristia, 147
 influence in Petrarch's poetry, 49, 54–55, 56

paganism
 afterlife and, 103
 ancients and, 181
 existence of God and, 101
 literature, 186
 philosophers, 230
 styles, 148–150
Palmieri, Matteo, 186
 On Civil Life, 183
patrons (*see* Petrarch, patrons)
Peter I, King, 171
Petracco, Ser (father of Petrarch), 15, 27
Petrarch, Francesco, 15, 180
 Filostrato's Philology (lost Latin play), 180
 adversaries, 167–176 *passim*
 ancients and, 139–153

Christian vs. pagan styles, 148–150
 ethics and styles in, 142
 Petrarch's library of, 141–142
 strong vs. weak styles, 146–148
 artistic development, 18
 Avignon papacy and, 235–237 (*see* Popes and Papacy, in Avignon)
 birth of, xv
 chronology of life and works, xv–xviii
 as cleric, xvi
 contradictions in life and works of, 3
 coronation as poet laureate, xvi, 3, 15, 28, 80–81, 86, 89–90, 93, 96, 98, 126, 179, 180, 201–202, 223 (*see also* laurel crown/laureation)
 death of, xvii, xviii, 51, 52, 61, 122, 180, 181, 185
 education of, xv
 family, xv, xvii, 4, 26, 33, 127 (*see also* Gherardo (brother of Petrarch))
 friends of, 26–34 (*see also Familiares*, Boccaccio in; *Seniles,* Boccaccio in; Barbato da Sulmona; Boccaccio, Giovanni; Cabassoles, Philippe de; Colonna, Giacomo; Colonna, Giovanni; Correggio, Azzo da; Laelius (Lello Stefano de' Tosetti); Rienzo, Cola di; Sette, Guido; Simonides (Francesco Nelli); Socrates (Ludwig van Kempen); Zanobi da Strada)
 conflicts between, 32–33
 post-plague letters for, 31
 Humanists and, 177–189 (*see also* Humanism; Humanists)
 influence of (*see also* Petrarchism)
  in 16th century (Cinquecento), 52–53
  on English poets, 215–217
  on female poets, 201–208
  on French poets, 213–215
  on Italian Humanists, 191–200
  on Renaissance Humanists, 177–189
  on Spanish poets, 210–213
 letters (*see also Disperse*; *Epystole*; *Familiares*; *Seniles*; *Sine Nomine*)
  Christian vs. pagan styles, 148–150
  four collections, 120–121
  friendship through, 33, 133
  as Humanist project for reproducing classical past, 144–146
  macrotexts, 123
  post-plague, 31
  strong vs. weak styles, 146–148

as living *auctor*, 14
patrons, 4, 5, 14, 15, 19–20, 27, 30, 124,
    167 (*see also* Carrara family;
    Colonna, Giovanni; Correggio, Azzo
    da; Robert of Anjou; Visconti family)
as "peregrinus ubique" (a wanderer
    everywhere), 13–16, 89
places as inspirations for, 13–14
pre-arrangement of own burial site, 15
residence in Vaucluse, xvi, xvii, 5, 13–14,
    16, 26, 28, 29, 31, 87, 89, 93, 111,
    127, 184, 205
between *RVF* and *Triumphus Eternitatus*,
    21–24
shift in ideology, 5
travels, xvi, xvii, xviii, 7, 13–24 *passim*,
    106
and Visconti family, xvii, 3, 5, 15, 22, 30,
    127, 170–171, 210
works of Virgil, Petrarch's copy of (*see*
    "Ambrosian Virgil")
Petrarchism, 2, 191–200
    anthologies, 197–200
    anti-Petrarchism and, 191, 196–197
    centoni, 195–196
    condemnation of, 191
    creative, 196–197
    English, 215–217
    female Petrarchists and, 201–208
    French, 213–215
    imitative, 196–197
    Petrarchino and, 194–196
    Pietro Bembo and, 52–53, 191–200
        passim
    Spanish, 210–213
    spread of, 194–196
philosophy, moral (*see* ethics)
Piccolomini, Aeneas Sylvius
    Commentaries, 184
Pistoia, Cino da, 55
Pius II, Pope, 184
plague (*see* Black Death)
Pliny, 169
    Natural History, 169
Plotinus, 113
    Enneads, 113
Polenton, Sicco
    Eighteen Books of Famous Latin Authors,
        182
Poliziano, Angelo
    Stanze, 184
Popes and Papacy, 115–116
    Celestine V, 114–115

Clement V, 4
Clement VI, 168, 170, 221, 222, 235, 236
Innocent VI, 170, 236
John XXII, 170
Pius II, 184
Urban V, xviii, 31, 121, 125, 173
    in Avignon, 4, 14–15, 26–27, 86, 89,
        91–92, 111, 115, 118, 121, 122,
        168, 170, 173–174, 210, 235–237
printing press, 37, 52–53, 61–62, 192, 194,
    195, 198, 199, 201, 210, 217 (*see*
    also RVF, printed editions of)
Priuli, Alvise, 197
Prosper of Aquitaine, 111
Proust, Marcel
    Recherche de Temps Perdus, 41
Psalmi penitentiales, xvii, 86
Psalms (book of the Bible)
    54.7, 149

Queriniana Library, 60
Quevedo, Francisco de, 212
Quillen, Carol, 102

Rerum memorandarum, 19, 21, 56, 86,
    123
Rerum vulgarium fragmenta (*Canzoniere*), 2,
    5, 21–24, 37
    arrivals in, 21–22
    confrontation with modernity in,
        224–226, 227–230
    division into parts
        Part One, 46–48
        Part Two, 46, 47
    imitation of earlier poetry (*see also* Virgil)
        imitation of Dante, 159, 161, 162
        influence of Ovid, 49, 54–55, 56
        medieval lyric poetry and, 154–155
        Occitan lyrics in, 156, 157 (*see also*
            Occitan poetry)
    individual poems in, 38
        1, 37, 39, 55, 66, 68, 97, 108, 162,
            202, 225
        1–8, 41
        1–21, 46–47
        3, 202, 227–228
        6, 43
        17, 204
        22, 46–47, 158–159
        23, 46–47, 49, 54, 147–148, 160
        28, 47
        30, 47, 160
        33, 44

Rerum vulgarium fragmenta (cont.)
  34, 54, 55
  35, 55, 63, 228–230
  41–43, 40
  44, 55
  53, 47
  55, 40
  61, 42
  62, 42–43, 44
  66, 157
  70, 159, 160–161, 162
  72, 63, 64–66, 71
  73, 155
  80, 40, 159
  81, 44
  87, 231
  90, 42, 155
  118, 63, 64–66
  125, 49
  125–9, 47
  126, 70–71, 224
  127, 42
  128 (My Italy), 47
  134, 158, 198
  136–8, 48
  142, 44, 48, 57–58
  166, 48
  181, 69
  189, 16, 23, 44
  196, 42
  205, 47
  207, 67–68, 69–70
  211, 42, 49
  214, 159
  229, 47
  230, 47
  237, 46–47, 48
  239, 46–47, 48
  240–53, 46–47
  243, 205
  263, 43, 44
  264, 43, 44, 46, 48–49, 57–58
  266, 43, 44–45
  267, 43, 44–45
  268, 46, 47, 58
  270, 45, 46
  271, 45
  287, 162
  323, 205–206
  331, 14
  344, 47, 205
  345–9, 204–205
  359, 43, 46
    360, 43, 46
    361–6, 40
    366, 46, 59
  key images, myths and topics
    Laura/laurel, 39–40, 47, 49, 91,
      124–125, 156, 201–202 (see also
      laurel; laurel crown/laureation)
    myth of Daphne and Apollo in, 41–42,
      55–56, 160, 198 (see also Apollo;
      Daphne)
    seasonal motifs, 157–158
    singularity and selfhood, 63–72
    winter topoi in, 157
  literary forms in
    ballate, 46–47
    canzoni, 46–48
    sestina, 47, 48, 57–58, 156, 164
    sonnets, 46–47
  making of, 51–61
    Chigi form of, xviii, 22–23, 58–59
    codice degli abbozzi (see RVF,
      manuscript versions of, Vat. Lat.
      3196)
    Correggio form of, xviii, 21, 22, 48–49,
      57–58
    early reference collection, 54–55
    first reference collection, 55
    first version, xvi
    Giovanni form of, 17, 18, 23, 51, 59,
      61 (see also Malpaghini, Giovanni)
    last version of, xviii, 38
    Malatesta manuscript, xviii, 51, 59–60
    Queriniana form of, xviii, 60
    renumbering of last thirty-poems of,
      23
    resolution of, 23
  manuscript versions of
    Vat. Lat. 3195 codex, 17, 23, 51–54,
      59–62, 166
    Vat. Lat. 3196 codex, 25, 52, 53,
      54–55, 57, 58
    Vat. Lat. 3197 codex, 52
  "Passa la nave mia" (see RVF 189)
  poems excluded from
    "Donna mi vene spesso ne la mente,"
      60
  poems in 189, 23
  printed editions of, 37, 52, 53, 61–62,
    192, 194, 195, 198, 199
    Aldine edition, 52–53
  reception of, in late 14th to 15th century,
    52, 181–182, 184, 194–196,
    201–202

structure and narrative, 39–50
  key narrative events, 40
  numerological patterns, 48
  titles of, 39–40
  truthfulness of, 41
  sub-groups of poems
    anniversary poems, 38, 40
    Avignonese sonnets, 46–47, 48
    political poems, 89
    stony poems, 159 (see also Dante, rime
      petrose)
  title(s) of, xvi, 2, 5, 37, 39–40, 51
  Triumphi and, 21
  women poets' interpretation of, 201–208
rhetoric, 186
Rico, Francisco, 5, 100
Rienzo, Cola di, xvi, xvii, 4, 29, 34, 86, 91,
    92, 122, 142, 174, 237 (see also
    Petrarch, friends of)
Rime sacre, 200
Riquier, Guiraut, 161, 163, 164
Robert of Anjou, King of Naples, xvi, xvii, 3,
    15, 19–20, 28, 90, 92–94, 126, 167
    (see also patrons; Petrarch, patrons
    of)
Robey, David, 186
Roman de la Rose, 82
Roman Senate, Petrarch invited by, 28
Rome, myth of, 3, 4, 79, 86, 91, 94, 95, 123,
    126, 174, 175, 221, 223, 238 (see
    also Africa, Cola di Rienzo,
    laureation
Ronsard, Pierre de, 214
  Les Amours, 214
  Odes, 214
  Oeuvres complètes, 214
  Sonnets pour Hélène, 214
Rossi, Nicolò de', 163
rota Virgilii, 87
Ruscelli, Girolamo, 195, 199

Sá de Miranda, Francisco de, 211
Salutati, Coluccio, 100, 180, 181
Samuel (book of the Bible), 150
Sánchez de las Brozas, Francisco, 211
Sannazaro, Jacopo, 195–196
  Sonetti e canzoni, 193
Santagata, Marco, 51, 163–164
sapientia (wisdom), 181
Scève, Maurice, 213
  Délie, object de plus haulte vertu,
    213
  Rymes, 208

Schiafenato, Giovan Battista
  Rime, 197
Scipio Africanus, 5, 27, 79, 84, 93, 104, 145
    (see also Africa, De Viris, Triumphi)
Secretum, 7, 16–17, 20, 22, 56, 75, 85, 92,
    100–110, 120, 123, 150, 180, 226
    (see also allegory, Augustine,
    dialogue form, fantasmata)
  aesthetic pleasure in, 108–109
  afterlife in, 103
  allegory in, 107
  ancients in, 104–105
  Augustine's conflicted role in, 150
  Augustinian problem of interpreting
    images in, 104
  Book I, 14, 104–106
  Book II, 16, 106–107, 143
  Book III, 16, 20, 56, 107–109, 148, 150
  Christian spirituality in, 100–101,
    105–106, 108
  confrontation with modernity in, 226
  curiosity in, 102
  defense of poetry in, 100–109
  departure-arrivals and, 16
  dialogue between Franciscus and
    Augustinus in, 100
  ending of, 20–22, 56, 84
  Franciscus' statement at end of, 20
  Humanists and, 180, 187, 188
  illusions/fantasmata/truth in, 102,
    103–104, 105, 106–107
  images of death in, 106
  incompletion of, 17
  influence of, 2
  Latin dialogue in, 100–109
  literary fame and, 108
  love for Laura in, 107
  opening sentence, 14
  Petrarch as intended audience for,
    120
  Prologue, 104
  revision of Augustine in, 101–102
  secularization thesis and, 102
  will, problem of, in, 66, 101
secularism, 2, 77, 92, 102, 116, 185–186,
    227–228
Seigel, Jerrold, 186
Seneca, 3, 85, 113, 121, 125, 141, 144
  Ad Lucilium (Letters to Lucilius),
    142–144
  in Epistles 82, 113
  Petrarch's letter to (Familiares XXIV.5),
    141

Seniles, xviii, 2, 13, 18, 32, 120–126, 127,
129, 130–135, 151–153, 168–169,
173
Book I
1–3, 121, 151
3, 32
5, 131, 151
7, 131
Book III, 130
1, 32, 121, 130, 131, 151
1–2, 130
5, 130
6, 128
Book V, 130
2, 122, 227–228
3, 130
Book VI
1–2, 128
2, 130
Book VII, 126, 130
1, 131, 173
Book VIII, 126, 131–132, 136
1, 167, 172
2, 33, 180
3, 131
4, 131
5, 131
Book IX, 126
1, 173
Book X
2, 26
Book XIII
11, 51, 59
Book XV
8, 130
Book XVI
3, 168
Book XVII, 126, 130–135
1, 133, 134
2, 5, 133, 134, 181
2–4, 133
3 (Griselda story), xviii, 122, 132–134,
151–153, 185, 226–227, 226
4, 133, 134, 152
Book XVIII
1 ("Letter to Posterity"), 13, 16, 19, 25,
77, 93, 122, 124, 126, 132, 134,
152, 167, 172, 179, 181
Boccaccio in, xviii, 5, 126, 128, 130–131,
132–134, 141–142, 180, 227–228
books, 125–126
death and, 124
editio princeps of, 134

introductory letter, 151
as macro-epistle to Simonides, 123–124
as mega-macrotext, 123
pagan eloquence in, 151
Petrarch's achievement in Latin language
and, 120
relationship to *Familiares*, 123–124, 125,
126–127, 129–131, 132–133
Sennuccio del Bene, 161
sermo humilis, 143, 150 (*see also* styles)
Servius, *Commentary on the Aeneid of
Virgil*, 87, 88, 91
Sette, Guido, xv, 26 (*see also* Petrarch,
friends of)
Sforza, Muzio, 200
Shakespeare, William
Sonnets, 216
Sicilian School, 154, 164
Sidney, Philip
Astrophil and Stella, 216
Silvestri, Domenico, 175
Simmel, Georg, 27–28
Simonides (Francesco Nelli), 32, 93, 121,
124, 130, 149 (*see also* Petrarch,
friends of)
Sine nomine, xvii, 16, 86, 121
denunciation of Avignon papacy in, 173
as form of invective, 123
preface to, 91
sirventes (poetic form), 154–155
social mobility, 27–28
social network theory, 27–28
Socrates (Greek philosopher), 222
Socrates (Ludwig van Kempen), xvi, xviii,
27, 32–33, 56, 121, 124, 130, 146
(*see also* Petrarch, friends of)
death of, xviii, 124
dedicatee of *Fam.*, 121, 124
falling out with Laelius, 32–33
Soldani, Arnaldo, 51, 61
soliloquies, 112
*Sonetti e canzoni di diversi antichi auttori
toscani in dieci libri raccolte*, 198
Spalatin, Georg, 185
Spanish Petrarchism, 210–213 (*see also*
Petrarchism)
Spenser, Edmund
Amoretti, 216
Stampa, Gaspara, 206–207
Rime, 195, 202
Statius, 142
Achilleid, 93, 96
Thebaid, 93

stilnovisti (poetic movement), 55, 161
Storey, H. Wayne, 51, 60
stornelli (poetic form), 191
Struever, Nancy, 122–123, 186
studia humanitatis, 185 (*see also* Humanism)
styles
  Christian, 148–150
  pagan, 148–150
  Petrarch's style in later years, 150
  strong, 146–148, 150–151
  weak, 146–148

Talenti, Tommaso, 171, 172
Talleyrand, Cardinal, 145
Tansillo, Luigi, 200
Tasso, Torquato, 200
Tateo, Francesco, 186
Tempo, Antonio da, 210
tensos (poetic form), 154–155
terza rima (poetic metre), 38, 74, 161–162
Testamentum, xviii, 23, 86
  bequest to Boccaccio in, 30–31
  possible burial sites named in, 15
  work begun on, xviii
Tosetti, Lello di Pietro dei (Laelius) (*see*
  Petrarch, friends of, Laelius)
Tottel, Richard, 215
  Songs and Sonnets, 215
Traversari, Ambrogio, 182
Triumphi, 17, 74–84
  chapter divisions in, 74–75
  compositional history of, 6, 21, 38
    completion of, 17, 21, 24, 75
    conclusion of, 24
    first version, xvii, 21, 38, 75
    unfinished state of, 75
  criticisms of, 83–84
  dream-vision of poet-protagonist in,
    76
  influence of, 2, 83
  narrative in, 77–78
  prologue, 80
  and *Rerum vulgarium fragmenta*, 21
  Roman triumph as model for, 79–80
  sources, 77
    Boccaccio, 38, 84
    Dante, 23, 38, 74, 76, 81–84, 159,
      161
    Scriptural and Christian, 75
  synthesis in, 80–81
  terza rima in, use of, 38, 74, 161–162
  Triumphus Cupidinis (Triumph of Love),
    xvii, 74, 76, 80–81, 82, 161–162

Love's victims in, 76
  opening chapter of, 78–79
Triumphus Eternitatis (Triumph of
  Eternity), xviii, 14, 17, 21–24, 74,
  79, 80–81, 83
Triumphus Fame (Triumph of Fame),
  xvii, 75, 76, 79–80
Triumphus Mortis (Triumph of Death),
  75, 77–78, 82
  vernacular lyrics recalled in, 161–162
  vernacular used in, 82–83
  vertical askesis of, 17
troubadours, 154–157, 158, 159, 160, 161,
  162, 163–164 (*see also* Occitan
  poetry)

Ubaldini, Federigo, 53
Ubertino da Casale, 4
Uguccione da Thiene, 173
University of Paris, xvi, 28
Urban V, Pope, xviii, 4, 31, 121, 125, 173

Valdezocco, Bartolomeo di, 52
Valla, Lorenzo, 100, 173, 175, 186
  Apologia, 186
van Kempen, Ludwig (*see* Petrarch, friends
  of, Socrates; Socrates)
Vatican Library, 53
Vaucluse (*see* Avignon, Petrarch's residence
  in; Petrarch, Francesco, residence in
  Vaucluse)
Vega, Lope de
  Rimas humanas, 211
  Rimas sacras, 211
Vellutello, Alessandro, 210
  "Life of Laura," 195
  "Life of Petrarch," 195
Venafro, Silvano da, 195, 210
Vergerio, Pier Paolo, 181–182
vetustas (old age), 181 (*see also* Seniles)
Villani, Giovanni
  *Origins of the City of Florence and its
    Famous Citizens, The*, 180
Virgil, 56
  Aeneid, 55, 74, 87, 104, 105, 107
  Eclogues, 87, 91
  Georgics, 87
  Petrarch's copy of Virgil's works (*see*
    "Ambrosian Virgil")
  Petrarch's imitation of Virgil, 21, 56,
    87–88, 90–93, 95, 97–98, 104–105,
    107–108, 143, 145, 147–148,
    150–151, 180–182

Virgilio, Giovanni del, 92
virtues, ladder of, 113 (*see also* ethics)
Visconti, Brizio, 90, 171 (*see also* patrons)
Visconti family, xvii, 3, 5, 15, 22, 30, 127,
    170–171, 210 (*see also* patrons)

Walter of Châtillon
    Alexandreis, 96
Watson, Thomas
    Hekatompathia, 216
Whitney, Isabella, 208
Wilkins, Ernest Hatch, 14, 33, 60, 121
    Life of Petrarch, 14, 134, 180
    The Making of the "Canzoniere," 22, 33,
        51, 54, 58
    on Petrarch's desire to love and to be
        loved, 33
    use of the letters for biography, 121
William of Ockham, 4
will (faculty of), 66, 101, 105, 108, 120,
    144, 152, 226, 228, 233, 237
Will (*see Testamentum*)
Witt, Ronald G., 2, 179, 186
Wojciehowski, Hannah, 5

Woman with the Petrarchino, The
    (painting), 194
women poets, 201–208
    Colonna, Vittoria, 203–204
    Du Guillet, Pernette, 208
    Gambara, Veronica, 203–204, 205,
        206–207
    Labé, Louise, 208
    scholarship on, 201–208
        Cox, Virginia, 207
    Stampa, Gaspara, 206–207
    Whitney, Isabella, 208
    Wroth, Mary, 208
    Rerum vulgarium fragmenta and,
        201–202, 203, 204–207
Wordsworth, William
    The Prelude, 41
Wroth, Mary
    Pamphilia to Amphilanthus, 208, 217
    Urania, 217
Wyatt, Thomas, 215

Zanobi da Strada, 31 (*see also* Petrarch,
    friends of)

Cambridge Companions to . . .

AUTHORS

Edward Albee edited by Stephen J. Bottoms

Margaret Atwood edited by
Coral Ann Howells

W. H. Auden edited by Stan Smith

Jane Austen edited by Edward Copeland and
Juliet McMaster (second edition)

Beckett edited by John Pilling

Bede edited by Scott DeGregorio

Aphra Behn edited by Derek Hughes and
Janet Todd

Walter Benjamin edited by David S. Ferris

William Blake edited by Morris Eaves

Jorge Luis Borges edited by Edwin Williamson

Brecht edited by Peter Thomson and
Glendyr Sacks (second edition)

The Brontës edited by Heather Glen

Bunyan edited by Anne Dunan-Page

Frances Burney edited by Peter Sabor

Byron edited by Drummond Bone

Albert Camus edited by Edward J. Hughes

Willa Cather edited by Marilee Lindemann

Cervantes edited by Anthony J. Cascardi

Chaucer edited by Piero Boitani and Jill Mann
(second edition)

Chekhov edited by Vera Gottlieb and
Paul Allain

Kate Chopin edited by Janet Beer

Caryl Churchill edited by Elaine Aston and
Elin Diamond

Cicero edited by Catherine Steel

Coleridge edited by Lucy Newlyn

Wilkie Collins edited by Jenny Bourne Taylor

Joseph Conrad edited by J. H. Stape

H. D. edited by Nephie J. Christodoulides and
Polina Mackay

Dante edited by Rachel Jacoff (second edition)

Daniel Defoe edited by John Richetti

Don DeLillo edited by John N. Duvall

Charles Dickens edited by John O. Jordan

Emily Dickinson edited by Wendy Martin

John Donne edited by Achsah Guibbory

Dostoevskii edited by W. J. Leatherbarrow

Theodore Dreiser edited by Leonard Cassuto
and Claire Virginia Eby

John Dryden edited by Steven N. Zwicker

W. E. B. Du Bois edited by Shamoon Zamir

George Eliot edited by George Levine

T. S. Eliot edited by A. David Moody

Ralph Ellison edited by Ross Posnock

Ralph Waldo Emerson edited by Joel Porte and
Saundra Morris

William Faulkner edited by
Philip M. Weinstein

Henry Fielding edited by Claude Rawson

F. Scott Fitzgerald edited by Ruth Prigozy

Flaubert edited by Timothy Unwin

E. M. Forster edited by David Bradshaw

Benjamin Franklin edited by Carla Mulford

Brian Friel edited by Anthony Roche

Robert Frost edited by Robert Faggen

Gabriel García Márquez edited by
Philip Swanson

Elizabeth Gaskell edited by Jill L. Matus

Goethe edited by Lesley Sharpe

Günter Grass edited by Stuart Taberner

Thomas Hardy edited by Dale Kramer

David Hare edited by Richard Boon

Nathaniel Hawthorne edited by
Richard Millington

Seamus Heaney edited by
Bernard O'Donoghue

Ernest Hemingway edited by Scott Donaldson

Homer edited by Robert Fowler

Horace edited by Stephen Harrison

Ted Hughes edited by Terry Gifford

Ibsen edited by James McFarlane

Henry James edited by Jonathan Freedman

Samuel Johnson edited by Greg Clingham

Ben Jonson edited by Richard Harp and
Stanley Stewart

James Joyce edited by Derek Attridge
(second edition)

Kafka edited by Julian Preece

Keats edited by Susan J. Wolfson

Rudyard Kipling edited by Howard J. Booth

Lacan edited by Jean-Michel Rabaté

D. H. Lawrence edited by Anne Fernihough

Primo Levi edited by Robert Gordon

Lucretius edited by Stuart Gillespie and
Philip Hardie

Machiavelli edited by John M. Najemy

David Mamet edited by Christopher Bigsby

Thomas Mann edited by Ritchie Robertson

Christopher Marlowe edited by Patrick Cheney

Andrew Marvell edited by Derek Hirst and
Steven N. Zwicker

Herman Melville edited by Robert S. Levine
Arthur Miller edited by Christopher Bigsby
(second edition)
Milton edited by Dennis Danielson
(second edition)
Molière edited by David Bradby and
Andrew Calder
Toni Morrison edited by Justine Tally
Nabokov edited by Julian W. Connolly
Eugene O'Neill edited by Michael Manheim
George Orwell edited by John Rodden
Ovid edited by Philip Hardie
Petrarch edited by Albert Russell Ascoli and
Unn Falkeid
Harold Pinter edited by Peter Raby
(second edition)
Sylvia Plath edited by Jo Gill
Edgar Allan Poe edited by Kevin J. Hayes
Alexander Pope edited by Pat Rogers
Ezra Pound edited by Ira B. Nadel
Proust edited by Richard Bales
Pushkin edited by Andrew Kahn
Rabelais edited by John O'Brien
Rilke edited by Karen Leeder and Robert Vilain
Philip Roth edited by Timothy Parrish
Salman Rushdie edited by Abdulrazak Gurnah
Shakespeare edited by Margareta de Grazia
and Stanley Wells (second edition)
Shakespearean Comedy edited by
Alexander Leggatt
Shakespeare and Contemporary Dramatists
edited by Ton Hoenselaars
Shakespeare and Popular Culture edited by
Robert Shaughnessy
Shakespearean Tragedy edited by
Claire McEachern (second edition)
Shakespeare on Film edited by Russell Jackson
(second edition)
Shakespeare on Stage edited by Stanley Wells
and Sarah Stanton
Shakespeare's History Plays edited by
Michael Hattaway

Shakespeare's Last Plays edited by
Catherine M. S. Alexander
Shakespeare's Poetry edited by Patrick Cheney
George Bernard Shaw edited by
Christopher Innes
Shelley edited by Timothy Morton
Mary Shelley edited by Esther Schor
Sam Shepard edited by Matthew C. Roudané
Spenser edited by Andrew Hadfield
Laurence Sterne edited by Thomas Keymer
Wallace Stevens edited by John N. Serio
Tom Stoppard edited by Katherine E. Kelly
Harriet Beecher Stowe edited by
Cindy Weinstein
August Strindberg edited by Michael Robinson
Jonathan Swift edited by Christopher Fox
J. M. Synge edited by P. J. Mathews
Tacitus edited by A. J. Woodman
Henry David Thoreau edited by Joel Myerson
Tolstoy edited by Donna Tussing Orwin
Anthony Trollope edited by Carolyn Dever
and Lisa Niles
Mark Twain edited by Forrest G. Robinson
John Updike edited by Stacey Olster
Mario Vargas Llosa edited by Efrain Kristal
and John King
Virgil edited by Charles Martindale
Voltaire edited by Nicholas Cronk
Edith Wharton edited by Millicent Bell
Walt Whitman edited by Ezra Greenspan
Oscar Wilde edited by Peter Raby
Tennessee Williams edited by
Matthew C. Roudané
August Wilson edited by Christopher Bigsby
Mary Wollstonecraft edited by
Claudia L. Johnson
Virginia Woolf edited by Susan Sellers
(second edition)
Wordsworth edited by Stephen Gill
W. B. Yeats edited by Marjorie Howes and
John Kelly
Zola edited by Brian Nelson

TOPICS

The Actress edited by Maggie B. Gale and
John Stokes
The African American Novel edited by
Maryemma Graham
The African American Slave Narrative edited
by Audrey A. Fisch

Theatre History by David Wiles and
Christine Dymkowski
African American Theatre by Harvey Young
Allegory edited by Rita Copeland and
Peter Struck
American Crime Fiction edited by
Catherine Ross Nickerson

American Modernism edited by
Walter Kalaidjian
American Poetry Since 1945 edited by
Jennifer Ashton
American Realism and Naturalism edited by
Donald Pizer
American Travel Writing edited by
Alfred Bendixen and Judith Hamera
American Women Playwrights edited by
Brenda Murphy
Ancient Rhetoric edited by Erik Gunderson
Arthurian Legend edited by
Elizabeth Archibald and Ad Putter
Australian Literature edited by
Elizabeth Webby
British Literature of the French Revolution
edited by Pamela Clemit
British Romanticism edited by Stuart Curran
(second edition)
British Romantic Poetry edited by
James Chandler and Maureen N. McLane
British Theatre, 1730–1830, edited by
Jane Moody and Daniel O'Quinn
Canadian Literature edited by
Eva-Marie Kröller
Children's Literature edited by M. O. Grenby
and Andrea Immel
The Classic Russian Novel edited by
Malcolm V. Jones and Robin Feuer Miller
Contemporary Irish Poetry edited by
Matthew Campbell
Creative Writing edited by David Morley and
Philip Neilsen
Crime Fiction edited by Martin Priestman
Early Modern Women's Writing edited by
Laura Lunger Knoppers
The Eighteenth-Century Novel edited by
John Richetti
Eighteenth-Century Poetry edited by
John Sitter
Emma edited by Peter Sabor
English Literature, 1500–1600 edited by
Arthur F. Kinney
English Literature, 1650–1740 edited by
Steven N. Zwicker
English Literature, 1740–1830 edited by
Thomas Keymer and Jon Mee
English Literature, 1830–1914 edited by
Joanne Shattock
English Novelists edited by Adrian Poole
English Poetry, Donne to Marvell edited by
Thomas N. Corns
English Poets edited by Claude Rawson

English Renaissance Drama, second edition
edited by A. R. Braunmuller and
Michael Hattaway
English Renaissance Tragedy edited by
Emma Smith and Garrett A. Sullivan Jr.
English Restoration Theatre edited by
Deborah C. Payne Fisk
The Epic edited by Catherine Bates
European Modernism edited by Pericles Lewis
European Novelists edited by Michael Bell
Fairy Tales edited by Maria Tatar
Fantasy Literature edited by Edward James
and Farah Mendlesohn
Feminist Literary Theory edited by
Ellen Rooney
Fiction in the Romantic Period edited by
Richard Maxwell and Katie Trumpener
The Fin de Siècle edited by Gail Marshall
The French Enlightenment edited by
Daniel Brewer
The French Novel: from 1800 to the Present
edited by Timothy Unwin
Gay and Lesbian Writing edited by
Hugh Stevens
German Romanticism edited by Nicholas Saul
Gothic Fiction edited by Jerrold E. Hogle
The Greek and Roman Novel edited by
Tim Whitmarsh
Greek and Roman Theatre edited by
Marianne McDonald and J. Michael Walton
Greek Comedy edited by Martin Revermann
Greek Lyric edited by Felix Budelmann
Greek Mythology edited by Roger D. Woodard
Greek Tragedy edited by P. E. Easterling
The Harlem Renaissance edited by
George Hutchinson
The History of the Book edited by
Leslie Howsam
The Irish Novel edited by John Wilson Foster
The Italian Novel edited by Peter Bondanella
and Andrea Ciccarelli
The Italian Renaissance edited by
Michael Wyatt
Jewish American Literature edited by
Hana Wirth-Nesher and Michael P. Kramer
The Latin American Novel edited by
Efraín Kristal
The Literature of the First World War edited
by Vincent Sherry
The Literature of London edited by
Lawrence Manley
The Literature of Los Angeles edited by
Kevin R. McNamara

The Literature of New York edited by
Cyrus Patell and Bryan Waterman
The Literature of Paris edited by
Anna-Louise Milne
The Literature of World War II edited by
Marina MacKay
Literature on Screen edited by
Deborah Cartmell and Imelda Whelehan
Medieval English Culture edited by
Andrew Galloway
Medieval English Literature edited by
Larry Scanlon
Medieval English Mysticism edited by
Samuel Fanous and Vincent Gillespie
Medieval English Theatre edited by
Richard Beadle and Alan J. Fletcher
(second edition)
Medieval French Literature edited by
Simon Gaunt and Sarah Kay
Medieval Romance edited by
Roberta L. Krueger
Medieval Women's Writing edited by
Carolyn Dinshaw and David Wallace
Modern American Culture edited by
Christopher Bigsby
Modern British Women Playwrights edited by
Elaine Aston and Janelle Reinelt
Modern French Culture edited by
Nicholas Hewitt
Modern German Culture edited by
Eva Kolinsky and Wilfried van der Will
The Modern German Novel edited by
Graham Bartram
The Modern Gothic edited by Jerrold E. Hogle
Modern Irish Culture edited by Joe Cleary and
Claire Connolly
Modern Italian Culture edited by
Zygmunt G. Barański and Rebecca J. West
Modern Latin American Culture edited by
John King
Modern Russian Culture edited by
Nicholas Rzhevsky
Modern Spanish Culture edited by
David T. Gies
Modernism edited by Michael Levenson
(second edition)
The Modernist Novel edited by
Morag Shiach
Modernist Poetry edited by Alex Davis and
Lee M. Jenkins
Modernist Women Writers edited by
Maren Tova Linett
Narrative edited by David Herman

Native American Literature edited by
Joy Porter and Kenneth M. Roemer
*Nineteenth-Century American Women's
Writing* edited by Dale M. Bauer and
Philip Gould
Old English Literature edited by
Malcolm Godden and Michael Lapidge
(second edition)
Performance Studies edited by Tracy C. Davis
Piers Plowman by Andrew Cole and
Andrew Galloway
Popular Fiction edited by David Glover and
Scott McCracken
Postcolonial Literary Studies edited by
Neil Lazarus
Postmodernism edited by Steven Connor
The Pre-Raphaelites edited by
Elizabeth Prettejohn
Pride and Prejudice edited by Janet Todd
Renaissance Humanism edited by Jill Kraye
The Roman Historians edited by
Andrew Feldherr
Roman Satire edited by Kirk Freudenburg
Science Fiction edited by Edward James and
Farah Mendlesohn
Scottish Literature edited by Gerald Carruthers
and Liam McIlvanney
Sensation Fiction edited by Andrew Mangham
The Sonnet edited by A. D. Cousins and
Peter Howarth
The Spanish Novel: from 1600 to the Present
edited by Harriet Turner and
Adelaida López de Martínez
Textual Scholarship edited by Neil Fraistat and
Julia Flanders
Travel Writing edited by Peter Hulme and
Tim Youngs
*Twentieth-Century British and Irish Women's
Poetry* edited by Jane Dowson
The Twentieth-Century English Novel edited
by Robert L. Caserio
Twentieth-Century English Poetry edited by
Neil Corcoran
Twentieth-Century Irish Drama edited by
Shaun Richards
Twentieth-Century Russian Literature edited
by Marina Balina and Evgeny Dobrenko
Utopian Literature edited by Gregory Claeys
Victorian and Edwardian Theatre edited by
Kerry Powell
The Victorian Novel edited by Deirdre David
(second edition)
Victorian Poetry edited by Joseph Bristow

Victorian Women's Writing edited by
Linda H. Peterson
War Writing edited by Kate McLoughlin
Women's Writing in Britain, 1660–1789 edited
by Catherine Ingrassia

Women's Writing in the Romantic Period
edited by Devoney Looser
Writing of the English Revolution edited by
N. H. Keeble